I0447069

Survival Communications
in Alaska

John E. Parnell, KK4HWX

10 ISBN 1478172908
13 ISBN 978-1478172901

© 2012 by John E. Parnell
All rights reserved. No part of the material protected by this copyright notice may be reproduced or utilized in any form or by any means, electronic or mechanical, including photocopying and recording, or by any information storage and retrieval system without written permission from the copyright owner.

Cover design by:
Lynda Colón
FREELANCE GRAPHIC DESIGN &
MARKETING COMMUNICATIONS
www.hirelynda.webs.com

I do wish to acknowledge the hard work of **Angie Shirley** in putting together the database required for this book. Without her efforts, this book could not have been done.

Titles available in this series:

Survival Communications in Alabama
Survival Communications in Alaska
Survival Communications in Arizona
Survival Communications in Arkansas
Survival Communications in California
Survival Communications in Colorado
Survival Communications in Connecticut
Survival Communications in Delaware
Survival Communications in Florida
Survival Communications in Georgia
Survival Communications in Hawaii
Survival Communications in Idaho
Survival Communications in Illinois
Survival Communications in Indiana
Survival Communications in Iowa
Survival Communications in Kansas
Survival Communications in Kentucky
Survival Communications in Louisiana
Survival Communications in Maine
Survival Communications in Maryland
Survival Communications in Massachusetts
Survival Communications in Michigan
Survival Communications in Minnesota
Survival Communications in Mississippi
Survival Communications in Missouri

Survival Communications in Montana
Survival Communications in Nebraska
Survival Communications in Nevada
Survival Communications in New Hampshire
Survival Communications in New Jersey
Survival Communications in New Mexico
Survival Communications in New York
Survival Communications in North Carolina
Survival Communications in North Dakota
Survival Communications in Ohio
Survival Communications in Oklahoma
Survival Communications in Oregon
Survival Communications in Pennsylvania
Survival Communications in Rhode Island
Survival Communications in South Carolina
Survival Communications in South Dakota
Survival Communications in Tennessee
Survival Communications in Texas
Survival Communications in Utah
Survival Communications in Vermont
Survival Communications in Virginia
Survival Communications in Washington
Survival Communications in West Virginia
Survival Communications in Wisconsin
Survival Communications in Wyoming

The above titles are available from your favorite online or brick-and-mortar bookstore or directly from the publisher at Tutor Turtle Press LLC, 1027 S. Pendleton St. – Suite B-10, Easley, SC 29642.

TABLE OF CONTENTS

Appendix A – Alaska Ham Radio Clubs

ARRL Affiliated Amateur and Ham Radio Clubs – By City

Appendix B – Alaska Ham Licensees by City

Survival Communications in Alaska

Perhaps you have prepared for WTSHTF or TEOTWAWKI with respect to food, water, self-defense and shelter. But what about communication?

Whenever there is a disaster (hurricane, earthquake, economic collapse, nuclear war, EMF, solar eruption, etc.), the normal means of communication that we're all reliant upon (cell phone, land line phone, the Internet, etc.) will probably be, at best, sporadic and at worst, non-existent.

As this author sees it, short of smoke signals and mirrors, there are three options for communication in "trying times": (1) GMRS or FRS radios; (2) CB radios; and (3) ham or amateur radio. Let's consider each of these options to come up with the most acceptable one.

GMRS (General Mobile Radio Service) / FRS (Family Radio Service)

GMRS (General Mobile Radio Service) / FRS (Family Radio Service) radios work optimally over short distances where there is minimal interference. Originally designed to be used as pagers, particularly inside a building or other such confined area, these radios are low-cost and convenient to carry. Unfortunately their small size and light weight comes with a trade-off – short range and short battery life. These radios are supposed to be able to communicate for up to 25-30 miles. Right. That's on level terrain, without buildings or trees getting in the way. While battery life technology is constantly improving, you will need spare batteries to keep communicating or someway of recharging the ones in the radio. In this author's opinion, GMRS/FRS radios are not first choice when concerned with medium or long range communication.

CB (Citizens Band)

CB (Citizens Band) radios operate in a frequency range originally reserved for ham or amateur radio operation. Because of the overwhelming number of people wishing quick, low-cost, regulation-free communication, the FCC (Federal Communication Commission) split off a portion of the frequency spectrum and allowed anyone to purchase a CB radio and start communicating. No test. No license. Just personal/business communication. Today, CB radios are readily available in such outlets as eBay and Craigslist. This author has seen them at yard/garage/tag sales and at flea markets.

CB radios come in a variety of "flavors." Fixed units, sometimes referred to as base units are intended for home use. For the most part, they derive their power from the utility company. In the event of loss of electricity, most base units can also be connected to a 12-volt battery, like that in your car/truck. If you choose to obtain a fixed unit, make sure you know how to connect the unit to the battery – ahead of time. Trying to figure this out when you're under extra stress is not a good situation.

A second type of CB radio is designed to be mobile, that is, installed in your car/truck. It gets its power from the vehicle's battery. You can either attach an antenna permanently to the vehicle or have a removable, magnetic type antenna.

The third type of CB radio is designed for handheld use. They are small and light. Most weigh less than a pound and operate on batteries. Yes, using batteries in a CB poses the same limitations as those by the GMRS/FRS radios, but have the added advantage that most handheld units come with a cigarette lighter adapter. Comes in handy when you are on the move and wish to be able to communicate both from a vehicle and also when you have to abandon it.

While they have a greater range than GMRS/FRS radios, CB radios are, legally, limited to operate on 40 channels, with a power rating of four (4) watts or less. Yes, it is possible to alter CB radios to get around these limitations, but not legally,

Ham/Amateur Radio

Ham/Amateur radio is very appealing. With a ham radio, you are not limited to less than 50 miles, but can communicate with anyone in the world (who also has access to a ham radio, of course).

Standardized Amateur Radio Prepper Communications Plan

In the event of a nationwide catastrophic disaster, the nationwide network of Amateur Radio licensed preppers will need a set of standardized meeting frequencies to share information and coordinate activities between various prepper groups. This Standardized Amateur Radio Communications Plan establishes a set of frequencies on the 80 meter, 40 meter, 20 meter, and 2 meter Amateur Radio bands for use during these types of catastrophic disasters.

Routine nets will not be held on all of these frequencies, but preppers are encouraged to use them when coordinating with other preppers on a routine basis. Routine nets may be conducted by The American Preparedness Radio Net (TAPRN) on these or other frequencies as they see fit. However, TAPRN will promote the use of these standardized frequencies by all Amateur Radio licensed preppers during times of catastrophic disaster. The promotion of this Standardized Amateur Radio Communications Plan is encouraged by all means within the prepper community, including via Amateur Radio, Twitter, Facebook, and various blogs.

Standardized Frequencies and Modes
80 Meters – 3.818 MHz LSB (TAPRN Net: Sundays at 9 PM ET)
40 Meters – 7.242 MHz LSB
40 Meters Morse Code / Digital – 7.073 MHz USB (TAPRN: Sundays at 7:30 PM ET on CONTESTIA 4/250)
20 Meters – 14.242 MHz USB
2 Meters – 146.420 MHz FM

Nets and Network Etiquette

In times of nationwide catastrophic disaster, the ability of any one prepper to initiate and sustain themselves as a net control may be limited by the availability of power and other resource shortages. However, all licensed preppers are encouraged to maintain a listening watch on these frequencies as often as possible during a catastrophic disaster. Preppers may routinely announce themselves in the following manner:

• This is [Your Callsign Phonetically] in [Your State], maintaining a listening watch on [Standard Frequency] for any preppers on frequency seeking information or looking to provide information. Please call [Your Callsign Phonetically]. Preppers exchanging information that may require follow up should agree upon a designated time to return to the frequency and provide further information. If other stations are utilizing the frequency at the designated time you return, maintain watch and proceed with your communications when those stations are finished. If your communications are urgent and the stations on frequency are not passing information of a critical nature, interrupt with the word "Break" and request use of the frequency.

For More Information

Catastrophe Network: http://www.catastrophenetwork.org or @CatastropheNet on Twitter The American Preparedness Radio Network: http://www.taprn.com or @TAPRN on Twitter

© 2011 Catastrophe Network, Please Distribute Freely

In order to use a ham radio, legally, one must be licensed to do so by the FCC (other countries have analogous governmental bodies to regulate ham radio). To obtain a license is quite easy – take a test and pay your license fee. There are currently three classes of license – Technician, General, and Amateur Extra. With each of these licenses come specific abilities.

Technician class is the beginning level. The exam consists of 35 multiple choice questions randomly drawn from a pool of 395 questions. The question pool is readily available online for free downloading (http://www.ncvec.org/downloads/Revised%20Element%202.Pdf) or in such publications at *Ham Radio License Manual Revised 2nd Edition* (ISBN 978-0-87259-097-7). The current Technician pool of questions is to be used from July 1, 2010 to June 30, 2014. Be sure the question pool you are studying from is current. You will need to score at least 26 correct to pass. (Do not worry, Morse Code is no longer on the test, although many ham operators use it anyway.) You do not need to take a formal class in order to qualify to take the exam. You can learn the material on your own. Most people spend 10-15 hours studying and then successfully take the exam. The cost of taking the exam is under $20. The exam is given in MANY locations throughout the US. Usually the exam is given by area ham clubs. You do not have to belong to the club to take the exam. Check Appendix A for a listing of clubs in South Carolina.

Topics for the Technician License in Amateur Radio

The Technician license exam covers such topics as basic regulations, operating practices, and electronic theory, with a focus on VHF and UHF applications. Below is the syllabus for the Technician Class.

Subelement T1 – FCC Rules, descriptions and definitions for the amateur radio service, operator and station license responsibilities

[6 Exam Questions – 6 Groups]

T1A – Amateur Radio services; purpose of the amateur service, amateur-satellite service, operator/primary station license grant, where FCC rules are codified, basis and purpose of FCC rules, meanings of basic terms used in FCC rules

T1B – Authorized frequencies; frequency allocations, ITU regions, emission type, restricted sub-bands, spectrum sharing, transmissions near band edges

T1C – Operator classes and station call signs; operator classes, sequential, special event, and vanity call sign systems, international communications, reciprocal operation, station license licensee, places where the amateur service is regulated by the FCC, name and address on ULS, license term, renewal, grace period

T1D – Authorized and prohibited transmissions

T1E – Control operator and control types; control operator required, eligibility, designation of control operator, privileges and duties, control point, local, automatic and remote control, location of control operator

T1F – Station identification and operation standards; special operations for repeaters and auxiliary stations, third party communications, club stations, station security, FCC inspection

Subelement T2 – Operating Procedures

[3 Exam Questions – 3 Groups]

T2A – Station operation; choosing an operating frequency, calling another station, test transmissions, use of minimum power, frequency use, band plans

T2B – VHF/UHF operating practices; SSB phone, FM repeater, simplex, frequency offsets, splits and shifts, CTCSS, DTMF, tone squelch, carrier squelch, phonetics

T2C – Public service; emergency and non-emergency operations, message traffic handling

Subelement T3 – Radio wave characteristics, radio and electromagnetic properties, propagation modes

[3 Exam Questions – 3 Groups]

T3A – Radio wave characteristics; how a radio signal travels; distinctions of HF, VHF and UHF; fading, multipath; wavelength vs. penetration; antenna orientation

T3B – Radio and electromagnetic wave properties; the electromagnetic spectrum, wavelength vs. frequency, velocity of electromagnetic waves

T3C – Propagation modes; line of sight, sporadic E, meteor, aurora scatter, tropospheric ducting, F layer skip, radio horizon

Subelement T4 - Amateur radio practices and station setup

[2 Exam Questions – 2 Groups]

T4A – Station setup; microphone, speaker, headphones, filters, power source, connecting a computer, RF grounding

T4B – Operating controls; tuning, use of filters, squelch, AGC, repeater offset, memory channels

Subelement T5 – Electrical principles, math for electronics, electronic principles, Ohm's Law

[4 Exam Questions – 4 Groups]

T5A – Electrical principles; current and voltage, conductors and insulators, alternating and direct current

T5B – Math for electronics; decibels, electronic units and the metric system

T5C – Electronic principles; capacitance, inductance, current flow in circuits, alternating current, definition of RF, power calculations

T5D – Ohm's Law

Subelement T6 – Electrical components, semiconductors, circuit diagrams, component functions

[4 Exam Groups – 4 Questions]

T6A – Electrical components; fixed and variable resistors, capacitors, and inductors; fuses, switches, batteries

T6B – Semiconductors; basic principles of diodes and transistors

T6C – Circuit diagrams; schematic symbols

T6D – Component functions

Subelement T7 – Station equipment, common transmitter and receiver problems, antenna measurements and troubleshooting, basic repair and testing

[4 Exam Questions – 4 Groups]

T7A – Station radios; receivers, transmitters, transceivers

T7B – Common transmitter and receiver problems; symptoms of overload and overdrive, distortion, interference, over and under modulation, RF feedback, off frequency signals; fading and noise; problems with digital communications interfaces

T7C – Antenna measurements and troubleshooting; measuring SWR, dummy loads, feedline failure modes

T7D – Basic repair and testing; soldering, use of a voltmeter, ammeter, and ohmmeter

Subelement T8 – Modulation modes, amateur satellite operation, operating activities, non-voice communications

[4 Exam Questions – 4 Groups]

T8A – Modulation modes; bandwidth of various signals

T8B – Amateur satellite operation; Doppler shift, basic orbits, operating protocols

T8C – Operating activities; radio direction finding, radio control, contests, special event stations, basic linking over Internet

T8D – Non-voice communications; image data, digital modes, CW, packet, PSK31

Subelement T9 – Antennas, feedlines

[2 Exam Groups – 2 Questions]

T9A – Antennas; vertical and horizontal, concept of gain, common portable and mobile antennas, relationships between antenna length and frequency

T9B – Feedlines; types, losses vs. frequency, SWR concepts, matching, weather protection, connectors

Subelement T0 – AC power circuits, antenna installation, RF hazards

[3 Exam Questions – 3 Groups]

T0A – AC power circuits; hazardous voltages, fuses and circuit breakers, grounding, lightning protection, battery safety, electrical code compliance

T0B – Antenna installation; tower safety, overhead power lines

T0C – RF hazards; radiation exposure, proximity to antennas, recognized safe power levels, exposure to others

Once your name and call sign are available in the FCC database, you have the privilege of operating on all VHF (2 m) and UHF (70 cm) frequencies above 30 megahertz (MHz) and HF frequencies 80, 40, and 15 meter, and on the 10 meter band using Morse code (CW), voice, and digital mode. For a Technician license in Alaska, your call sign will consist of a two-letter prefix beginning with AL, KL, NL or WL, then any of the numbers zero (0) through seven (7), and a three-letter suffix. The single digit number in the call sign is determined according to which area of the US you obtain your first license. Even though you may move to another state, you keep this number in your call sign. This is also true should you upgrade to a higher license and get a new call sign. The numeral portion of your call sign stays the same.

Call Sign Numbers

Below is a chart showing the various numbers and the state(s) in which you would obtain the number.

Call Sign Number	State(s)
0	CO, IA, KS, MN, MO, NE, ND, SD
1	CT, ME, MA, NH, RI, VT
2	NJ, NY
3	DE, DC, MD, PA
4	AL, FL, GA, KY, NC, SC, TN, VA
5	AR, LA, MS, NM, OK, TX
6	CA
7	AZ, ID, MT, NV, OR, WA, UT, WY
8	MI, OH, WV
9	IL, IN, WI

Residents of Alaska may have any of the following call sign prefixes assigned to them: AL0-7, KL0-7, NL0-7, or WL0-7. Likewise, residents of Hawaii may have the prefix AH6-7, KH6-7, NH6-7, or WH6-7 assigned.

Once you obtain your Technician license, do not stop there. Go and get your General license.

General is the second of three ham license classes. Like the Technician license, to get a General license, you merely have to take a 35-question multiple choice exam and pay your license fee. Passing is still at least 26 correct answers and the fee is the same (less than $20). Again the question pool is available for free online (http://www.ncvec.org/page.php?id=358). It is also available in such print publications as *The ARRL General Class License Manual 7ᵗʰ Edition* (ISBN 978-0-87259-811-9). The current General pool of questions is to be used from July 1, 2011 to June 30, 2015. Be sure the question pool you are using is current. Being a bit more comprehensive than the Technician license, the General license usually requires 15-20 hours of study to learn the material. Check Appendix A for a listing of clubs in Alaska where you might take your exam. Once your name and NEW call sign is listed in the FCC database, you're good to go. For a General license in Alaska, your call sign will consist of a two-letter prefix beginning with AL, KL, NL or WL, the any of the numbers zero (0) through (7), and a three-letter suffix.

Topics for the General License in Amateur Radio

The General license exam covers regulations, operating practices and electronic theory. Below is the syllabus for the General Class.

Subelement G1 – Commission's Rules
(5 Exam Questions – 5 Groups) G1A – General Class control operator frequency privileges; primary and secondary allocations G1B – Antenna structure limitations; good engineering and good amateur practice, beacon operation; restricted operation; retransmitting radio signals G1C – Transmitter power regulations; data emission standards G1D – Volunteer Examiners and Volunteer Examiner Coordinators; temporary identification G1E – Control categories; repeater regulations; harmful interference; third party rules; ITU regions

Subelement G2 – Operating procedures
(5 Exam Questions – 5 Groups) G2A – Phone operating procedures; USB/LSB utilization conventions; procedural signals; breaking into a OSO in progress; VOX operation G2B – Operating courtesy; band plans, emergencies, including drills and emergency communications

G2C – CW operating procedures and procedural signals; Q signals and common abbreviations; full break in

G2D – Amateur Auxiliary; minimizing interference; HF operations

G2E – Digital operating; procedures, procedural signals and common abbreviations

Subelement G3 – Radio wave propagation

(3 Exam Questions – 3 Groups)

G3A – Sunspots and solar radiation; ionospheric disturbances; propagation forecasting and indices

G3B – Maximum Usable Frequency; Lowest Usable Frequency; propagation

G3C – Ionospheric layers; critical angle and frequency; HF scatter; Near Vertical Incidence Sky waves

Subelement G4 – Amateur radio practices

(5 Exam Questions – 5 Groups)

G4A – Station Operation and setup

G4B – Test and monitoring equipment; two-tone test

G4C – Interference with consumer electronics; grounding; DSP

G4D – Speech processors; S meters; sideband operation near band edges

G4E – HF mobile radio installations; emergency and battery powered operation

Subelement G5 – Electrical principles

(3 Exam Questions – 3 Groups)

G5A – Reactance; inductance; capacitance; impedance; impedance matching

G5B – The Decibel; current and voltage dividers; electrical power calculations; sine wave root-mean-square (RMS) values; PEP calculations

G5C – Resistors; capacitors and inductors in series and parallel; transformers

Subelement G6 – Circuit components

(3 Exam Questions – 3 Groups)

G6A – Resistors; capacitors; inductors

G6B – Rectifiers; solid state diodes and transistors; vacuum tubes; batteries

G6C – Analog and digital integrated circuits (ICs); microprocessors; memory; I/O devices; microwave ICs (MMICs); display devices

Subelement G7 – Practical circuits

(3 Exam Questions – 3 Groups)

G7A – Power supplies; schematic symbols

G7B – Digital circuits; amplifiers and oscillators

G7C – Receivers and transmitters; filters, oscillators

Subelement G8 – Signals and emissions

(2 Exam Questions – 2 Groups)
G8A – Carriers and modulation; AM; FM; single and double sideband; modulation envelope; overmodulation
G8B – Frequency mixing; multiplication; HF data communications; bandwidths of various modes; deviation

Subelement G9 – Antennas and feed lines

(4 Exam Questions – 4 Groups)
G9A – Antenna feed lines; characteristic impedance and attenuation; SWR calculation, measurement and effects; matching networks
G9B – Basic antennas
G9C – Directional antennas
G9D – Specialized antennas

Subelement G0 – Electrical and RF safety

(2 Exam Questions – 2 Groups)
G0A – RF safety principles, rules and guidelines; routine station elevation
G0B – Safety in the ham shack; electrical shock and treatment, safety grounding, fusing, interlocks, wiring, antenna and tower safety

With a General license, you can use all VHF and UHF frequencies and most of the HF frequencies. You would have access to the 160, 30, 17, 12, and 10 meter bands and access to major parts of the 80, 40, 20, and 15 meter bands. Of course, this is in addition to all bands available to Technician license holders.

Amateur Extra is the third of three ham license classes. Like the Technician and General classes, you merely have to pass a test and pay your fee to get your Amateur Extra license. This class of license is more comprehensive than the lower license classes. The exam is longer – 50 questions – and the minimum passing score is higher – 37. However, once you get your Amateur Extra license, all ham frequencies, VHF, UHF and HF are available for your enjoyment. The Extra exam covers regulations, specialized operating practices, advanced electronics theory, and radio equipment design.

Like for the other license classes, the question pool for the Amateur Extra license is available online for downloading (http://www.ncvec.org/downloads/Final%202008%20Extra.pdf or http://www.ncvec.org/downloads/REVISED%202012-2016%20Extra%20Class%20Pool.doc). It is also available in print form in such publications as *The ARRL Extra Class License Manual Revised 9th Edition* (ISBN 978-0-87259-887-4).

Topics for the Extra License in Amateur Radio

Subelement E1 – Commission's Rules

[6 Exam Questions – 6 Groups]

E1A – Operating Standards: frequency privileges; emission standards; automatic message forwarding; frequency sharing; stations aboard ships or aircraft

E1B – Station restrictions and special operations: restrictions on station location; general operating restrictions, spurious emissions, control operator reimbursement; antenna structure restrictions; RACES operations

E1C – Station control: definitions and restrictions pertaining to local, automatic and remote control operation; control operator responsibilities for remote and automatically controlled stations

E1D – Amateur Satellite service: definitions and purpose; license requirements for space stations; available frequencies and bands; telecommand and telemetry operations; restrictions, and special provisions; notification requirements

E1E – Volunteer examiner program: definitions, qualifications, preparation and administration of exams; accreditation; question pools; documentation requirements

E1F – Miscellaneous rules: external RF power amplifiers; national quiet zone; business communications; compensated communications; spread spectrum; auxiliary stations; reciprocal operating privileges; IARP and CEPT licenses; third party communications with foreign countries; special temporary authority

Subelement E2 – Operating procedures

[5 Exam Questions – 5 Groups]

E2A – Amateur radio in space: amateur satellites; orbital mechanics; frequencies and modes; satellite hardware; satellite operations

E2B – Television practices: fast scan television standards and techniques; slow scan television standards and techniques

E2C – Operating methods: contest and DX operating; spread-spectrum transmissions; selecting an operating frequency

E2D – Operating methods: VHF and UHF digital modes; APRS

E2E – Operating methods: operating HF digital modes; error correction

Subelement E3 – Radio wave propagation

[3 Exam Questions – 3 Groups]

E3A – Propagation and technique, Earth-Moon-Earth communications; meteor scatter

E3B – Propagation and technique, trans-equatorial; long path; gray-line; multi-path propagation

E3C – Propagation and technique, Aurora propagation; selective fading; radio-path horizon; take-off angle over flat or sloping terrain; effects of ground on propagation; less common propagation modes

Subelement E4 – Amateur practices

[5 Exam Questions – 5 Groups]

E4A – Test equipment: analog and digital instruments; spectrum and network analyzers, antenna analyzers; oscilloscopes; testing transistors; RF measurements

E4B – Measurement technique and limitations: instrument accuracy and performance limitations; probes; techniques to minimize errors; measurement of "Q"; instrument calibration

E4C – Receiver performance characteristics, phase noise, capture effect, noise floor, image rejection, MDS, signal-to-noise-ratio; selectivity

E4D – Receiver performance characteristics, blocking dynamic range, intermodulation and cross-modulation interference; 3rd order intercept; desensitization; preselection

E4E – Noise suppression: system noise; electrical appliance noise; line noise; locating noise sources; DSP noise reduction; noise blankers

Subelement E5 – Electrical principles

[4 Exam Questions – 4 Groups]

E5A – Resonance and Q: characteristics of resonant circuits: series and parallel resonance; Q; half-power bandwidth; phase relationships in reactive circuits

E5B – Time constants and phase relationships: RLC time constants: definition; time constants in RL and RC circuits; phase angle between voltage and current; phase angles of series and parallel circuits

E5C – Impedance plots and coordinate systems: plotting impedances in polar coordinates; rectangular coordinates

E5D – AC and RF energy in real circuits: skin effect; electrostatic and electromagnetic fields; reactive power; power factor; coordinate systems

Subelement E6 – Circuit components

[6 Exam Questions – 6 Groups]

E6A – Semiconductor materials and devices: semiconductor materials germanium, silicon, P-type, N-type; transistor types: NPN, PNP, junction, field-effect transistors: enhancement mode; depletion mode; MOS; CMOS; N-channel; P-channel

E6B – Semiconductor diodes

E6C – Integrated circuits: TTL digital integrated circuits; CMOS digital integrated circuits; gates

E6D – Optical devices and toroids: cathode-ray tube devices; charge-coupled devices (CCDs); liquid crystal displays (LCDs); toroids: permeability, core material, selecting, winding

E6E – Piezoelectric crystals and MMICs: quartz crystals; crystal oscillators and filters; monolithic amplifiers

E6F – Optical components and power systems: photoconductive principles and effects, photovoltaic systems, optical couplers, optical sensors, and optoisolators

Subelement E7 – Practical circuits

[8 Exam Questions – 8 Groups]

E7A – Digital circuits: digital circuit principles and logic circuits: classes of logic elements; positive and negative logic; frequency dividers; truth tables

E7B – Amplifiers: Class of operation; vacuum tube and solid-state circuits; distortion and intermodulation; spurious and parasitic suppression; microwave amplifiers

E7C – Filters and matching networks: filters and impedance matching networks: types of networks; types of filters; filter applications; filter characteristics; impedance matching; DSP filtering

E7D – Power supplies and voltage regulators

E7E – Modulation and demodulation: reactance, phase and balanced modulators; detectors; mixer stages; DSP modulation and demodulation; software defined radio systems

E7F – Frequency markers and counters: frequency divider circuits; frequency marker generators; frequency counters

E7G – Active filters and op-amps: active audio filters; characteristics; basic circuit design; operational amplifiers

E7H – Oscillators and signal sources: types of oscillators; synthesizers and phase-locked loops; direct digital synthesizers

Subelement E8 – Signals and emissions

[4 Exam Questions – 4 Groups]

E8A – AC waveforms: sine, square, sawtooth and irregular waveforms; AC measurements; average and PEP of RF signals; pulse and digital signal waveforms

E8B – Modulation and demodulation: modulation methods; modulation index and deviation ratio; pulse modulation; frequency and time division multiplexing

E8C – Digital signals: digital communications modes; CW; information rate vs. bandwidth; spread-spectrum communications; modulation methods

E8D – Waves, measurements, and RF grounding: peak-to-peak values, polarization; RF grounding

Subelement E9 – Antennas and transmission lines

[8 Exam Questions – 8 Groups]

E9A – Isotropic and gain antennas: definition; used as a standard for comparison; radiation pattern; basic antenna parameters: radiation resistance and reactance, gain, beamwidth, efficiency

E9B – Antenna patterns: E and H plane patterns; gain as a function of pattern; antenna design; Yagi antennas

E9C – Wire and phased vertical antennas: beverage antennas; terminated and resonant rhombic antennas; elevation above real ground; ground effects as related to polarization; take-off angles

E9D – Directional antennas: gain; satellite antennas; antenna beamwidth; losses; SWR bandwidth; antenna efficiency; shortened and mobile antennas; grounding

E9E – Matching: matching antennas to feed lines; power dividers

E9F – Transmission lines: characteristics of open and shorted feed lines: 1/8 wavelength; 1/4 wavelength; 1/2 wavelength; feed lines: coax versus open-wire; velocity factor; electrical length; transformation characteristics of line terminated in impedance not equal to characteristic impedance

E9G – The Smith chart

E9H – Effective radiated power; system gains and losses; radio direction finding antennas

[1 exam question – 1 group]
E0A – Safety: amateur radio safety practices; RF radiation hazards; hazardous materials

Once your new call sign is listed in the FCC database, you are good to go. For a Amateur Extra license in Alaska, your call sign will consist of a single letter prefix beginning with A, K, N or W, then any of the numbers zero (0) through seven (7), and a two-letter suffix, or a single letter prefix beginning with A, N, K or W, then any of the numbers zero (0) through seven (7), and a one-letter suffix, or a single letter prefix beginning with A, then any of the numbers zero (0) through seven (7), and a two-letter suffix.

Ham radio equipment can be expensive or you can do it "on the cheap." The cost will run from a couple hundred dollars to well in the thousands, depending on what you have available. eBay, and Craigslist are good places to start looking. Most ham clubs do some sort of hamfest annually wherein club members or others are willing to part with older equipment. See Appendix A for a list of clubs in Alaska.

Another excellent source of equipment, as well as advice on setting the equipment up and how to use it properly, is current ham operators. In Appendix B, the author has listed all the FCC licensed ham operators in Alaska, listed by city, and then sorted by street and house number on the street. Who knows, maybe someone who lives close to you is a ham operator. Be a good neighbor, stop by and have a chat with him/her.

Like CB radios, ham radios come in three formats – base, mobile, and handheld. They can use the electric company for power, or operate off a car battery. In the opinion of this author, in spite of the slightly higher cost of the equipment and having to take a test to legally use the equipment, ham radio is the way to go when concerned about communication during times of crisis.

Canadian Call Sign Prefixes

Because of our proximity to Canada, many times ham contact is made with our northern neighbors. Below is a chart showing the origin of Canadian call sign prefixes.

Call Sign Prefix	Provence or Territory
CY0	Sable Island
CY9	St. Paul Island
VA1, VE1	New Brunswick, Nova Scotia
VA2, VE2	Quebec
VA3, VE3	Ontario
VA4, VE4	Manitoba
VA5, VE5	Saskatchewan
VA6, VE6	Alberta
VA7, VE7	British Columbia
VE8	North West Territories
VE9	New Brunswick

VO1	Newfoundland
VO2	Labrador
VY0	Nunavut
VY1	Yukon
VY2	Prince Edward Island

Common Radio Bands in the United States

Certain radio bands are more popular with ham radio enthusiasts than others. Below is a chart showing these bands and when they are most popular.

	Band (meter)	Frequency (MHz)	Use
HF	160	1.8 – 2.0	Night
	80	3.5 – 4.0	Night and Local Day
	40	7.0 – 7.3	Night and Local Day
	30	10.1 – 10.15	CW and Digital
	20	14.0 – 14.350	World Wide Day and Night
	17	18.068 – 18.168	World Wide Day and Night
	15	21.0 – 21.450	Primarily Daytime
	12	24.890 – 24.990	Primarily Daytime
	10	28.0 – 29.70	Daytime during Sunspot highs
VHF	6	50 – 54	Local to World Wide
	2	144 – 148	Local to Medium Distance
UHF	70 cm	430 – 440	Local

Common Amateur Radio Bands in Canada

160 Meter Band - Maximum bandwidth 6 kHz

1.800 - 1.820 MHz - CW
1.820 - 1.830 MHz - Digital Modes
1 830 - 1.840 MHz - DX Window
1.840 - 2.000 MHz - SSB and other wide band modes

80 Meter Band - Maximum bandwidth 6 kHz

3.500 - 3.580 MHz - CW
3.580 - 3.620 MHz - Digital Modes
3.620 - 3.635 MHz - Packet/Digital Secondary
3.635 - 3.725 MHz - CW
3.725 - 3.790 MHz - SSB and other side band modes*
3.790 - 3.800 MHz - SSB DX Window
3.800 - 4.000 MHz - SSB and other wide band modes

40 Meter Band - Maximum bandwidth 6 kHz

7.000 - 7.035 MHz - CW
7.035 - 7.050 MHz - Digital Modes

7.040 - 7.050 MHz - International packet
7.050 - 7.100 MHz - SSB
7.100 - 7.120 MHz - Packet within Region 2
7.120 - 7.150 MHz - CW
7.150 - 7.300 MHz - SSB and other wide band modes

30 Meter Band - Maximum bandwidth 1 kHz

10.100 - 10.130 MHz - CW only
10.130 - 10.140 MHz - Digital Modes
10.140 - 10.150 MHz - Packet

20 Meter Band - Maximum bandwidth 6 kHz

14.000 - 14.070 MHz - CW only
14.070 - 14.095 MHz - Digital Mode
14.095 - 14.099 MHz - Packet
14.100 MHz - Beacons
14.101 - 14.112 MHz - CW, SSB, packet shared
14.112 - 14.350 MHz - SSB
14.225 - 14.235 MHz - SSTV

17 Meter Band - Maximum bandwidth 6 kHz

18.068 - 18.100 MHz - CW
18.100 - 18.105 MHz - Digital Modes
18.105 - 18.110 MHz - Packet
18.110 - 18.168 MHz - SSB and other wide band modes

15 Meter Band - maximum bandwidth 6 kHz

21.000 - 21.070 MHz - CW
21.070 - 21.090 MHz - Digital Modes
21.090 - 21.125 MHz - Packet
21.100 - 21.150 MHz - CW and SSB
21.150 - 21.335 MHz - SSB and other wide band modes
21.335 - 21.345 MHz - SSTV
21.345 - 21.450 MHz - SSB and other wide band modes

12 Meter Band - Maximum bandwidth 6 kHz

24.890 - 24.930 MHz - CW
24.920 - 24.925 MHz - Digital Modes
24.925 - 24.930 MHz - Packet
24.930 - 24.990 MHz - SSB and other wide band modes

10 Meter Band - Maximum band width 20 kHz

28.000 - 28.200 MHz - CW
28.070 - 28.120 MHz - Digital Modes

28.120 - 28.190 MHz - Packet
28.190 - 28.200 MHz - Beacons
28.200 - 29.300 MHz - SSB and other wide band modes
29.300 - 29.510 MHz - Satellite
29.510 - 29.700 MHz - SSB, FM and repeaters

160 Meters (1.8-2.0 MHz)

1.800 - 2.000 CW
1.800 - 1.810 Digital Modes
1.810 CW QRP
1.843-2.000 SSB, SSTV and other wideband modes
1.910 SSB QRP
1.995 - 2.000 Experimental
1.999 - 2.000 Beacons

80 Meters (3.5-4.0 MHz)

3.590 RTTY/Data DX
3.570-3.600 RTTY/Data
3.790-3.800 DX window
3.845 SSTV
3.885 AM calling frequency

40 Meters (7.0-7.3 MHz)

7.040 RTTY/Data DX
7.080-7.125 RTTY/Data
7.171 SSTV
7.290 AM calling frequency

30 Meters (10.1-10.15 MHz)

10.130-10.140 RTTY
10.140-10.150 Packet

20 Meters (14.0-14.35 MHz)

14.070-14.095 RTTY
14.095-14.0995 Packet
14.100 NCDXF Beacons
14.1005-14.112 Packet
14.230 SSTV
14.286 AM calling frequency

17 Meters (18.068-18.168 MHz)

18.100-18.105 RTTY
18.105-18.110 Packet

15 Meters (21.0-21.45 MHz)

21.070-21.110 RTTY/Data
21.340 SSTV

12 Meters (24.89-24.99 MHz)

24.920-24.925 RTTY
24.925-24.930 Packet

10 Meters (28-29.7 MHz)

28.000-28.070 CW
28.070-28.150 RTTY
28.150-28.190 CW
28.200-28.300 Beacons
28.300-29.300 Phone
28.680 SSTV
29.000-29.200 AM
29.300-29.510 Satellite Downlinks
29.520-29.590 Repeater Inputs
29.600 FM Simplex
29.610-29.700 Repeater Outputs

6 Meters (50-54 MHz)

50.0-50.1 CW, beacons
50.060-50.080 beacon subband
50.1-50.3 SSB, CW
50.10-50.125 DX window
50.125 SSB calling
50.3-50.6 All modes
50.6-50.8 Nonvoice communications
50.62 Digital (packet) calling
50.8-51.0 Radio remote control (20-kHz channels)
51.0-51.1 Pacific DX window
51.12-51.48 Repeater inputs (19 channels)
51.12-51.18 Digital repeater inputs
51.5-51.6 Simplex (six channels)
51.62-51.98 Repeater outputs (19 channels)
51.62-51.68 Digital repeater outputs
52.0-52.48 Repeater inputs (except as noted; 23 channels)
52.02, 52.04 FM simplex
52.2 TEST PAIR (input)
52.5-52.98 Repeater output (except as noted; 23 channels)
52.525 Primary FM simplex
52.54 Secondary FM simplex
52.7 TEST PAIR (output)
53.0-53.48 Repeater inputs (except as noted; 19 channels)
53.0 Remote base FM simplex

53.02 Simplex
53.1, 53.2, 53.3, 53.4 Radio remote control
53.5-53.98 Repeater outputs (except as noted; 19 channels)
53.5, 53.6, 53.7, 53.8 Radio remote control
53.52, 53.9 Simplex

2 Meters (144-148 MHz)

144.00-144.05 EME (CW)
144.05-144.10 General CW and weak signals
144.10-144.20 EME and weak-signal SSB
144.200 National calling frequency
144.200-144.275 General SSB operation
144.275-144.300 Propagation beacons
144.30-144.50 New OSCAR subband
144.50-144.60 Linear translator inputs
144.60-144.90 FM repeater inputs
144.90-145.10 Weak signal and FM simplex (145.01,03,05,07,09 are widely used for
    packet)
145.10-145.20 Linear translator outputs
145.20-145.50 FM repeater outputs
145.50-145.80 Miscellaneous and experimental modes
145.80-146.00 OSCAR subband
146.01-146.37 Repeater inputs
146.40-146.58 Simplex
146.52 National Simplex Calling Frequency
146.61-146.97 Repeater outputs
147.00-147.39 Repeater outputs
147.42-147.57 Simplex
147.60-147.99 Repeater inputs

1.25 Meters (222-225 MHz)

222.0-222.150 Weak-signal modes
222.0-222.025 EME
222.05-222.06 Propagation beacons
222.1 SSB & CW calling frequency
222.10-222.15 Weak-signal CW & SSB
222.15-222.25 Local coordinator's option; weak signal, ACSB, repeater inputs, control
222.25-223.38 FM repeater inputs only
223.40-223.52 FM simplex
223.52-223.64 Digital, packet
223.64-223.70 Links, control
223.71-223.85 Local coordinator's option; FM simplex, packet, repeater outputs
223.85-224.98 Repeater outputs only

70 Centimeters (420-450 MHz)

420.00-426.00 ATV repeater or simplex with 421.25 MHz video carrier control links and
    experimental

426.00-432.00 ATV simplex with 427.250-MHz video carrier frequency
432.00-432.07 EME (Earth-Moon-Earth)
432.07-432.10 Weak-signal CW
432.10 70-cm calling frequency
432.10-432.30 Mixed-mode and weak-signal work
432.30-432.40 Propagation beacons
432.40-433.00 Mixed-mode and weak-signal work
433.00-435.00 Auxiliary/repeater links
435.00-438.00 Satellite only (internationally)
438.00-444.00 ATV repeater input with 439.250-MHz video carrier frequency and repeater links
442.00-445.00 Repeater inputs and outputs (local option)
445.00-447.00 Shared by auxiliary and control links, repeaters and simplex (local option)
446.00 National simplex frequency
447.00-450.00 Repeater inputs and outputs (local option)

33 Centimeters (902-928 MHz)

902.0-903.0 Narrow-bandwidth, weak-signal communications
902.0-902.8 SSTV, FAX, ACSSB, experimental
902.1 Weak-signal calling frequency
902.8-903.0 Reserved for EME, CW expansion
903.1 Alternate calling frequency
903.0-906.0 Digital communications
906-909 FM repeater inputs
909-915 ATV
915-918 Digital communications
918-921 FM repeater outputs
921-927 ATV
927-928 FM simplex and links

23 Centimeters (1240-1300 MHz)

1240-1246 ATV #1
1246-1248 Narrow-bandwidth FM point-to-point links and digital, duplex with 1258-1260.
1248-1258 Digital Communications
1252-1258 ATV #2
1258-1260 Narrow-bandwidth FM point-to-point links digital, duplexed with 1246-1252
1260-1270 Satellite uplinks, reference WARC '79
1260-1270 Wide-bandwidth experimental, simplex ATV
1270-1276 Repeater inputs, FM and linear, paired with 1282-1288, 239 pairs every 25 kHz, e.g. 1270.025, .050, etc.
1271-1283 Non-coordinated test pair
1276-1282 ATV #3
1282-1288 Repeater outputs, paired with 1270-1276
1288-1294 Wide-bandwidth experimental, simplex ATV
1294-1295 Narrow-bandwidth FM simplex services, 25-kHz channels

1294.5 National FM simplex calling frequency
1295-1297 Narrow bandwidth weak-signal communications (no FM)
1295.0-1295.8 SSTV, FAX, ACSSB, experimental
1295.8-1296.0 Reserved for EME, CW expansion
1296.00-1296.05 EME-exclusive
1296.07-1296.08 CW beacons
1296.1 CW, SSB calling frequency
1296.4-1296.6 Crossband linear translator input
1296.6-1296.8 Crossband linear translator output
1296.8-1297.0 Experimental beacons (exclusive)
1297-1300 Digital Communications

2300-2310 and 2390-2450 MHz

2300.0-2303.0 High-rate data
2303.0-2303.5 Packet
2303.5-2303.8 TTY packet
2303.9-2303.9 Packet, TTY, CW, EME
2303.9-2304.1 CW, EME
2304.1 Calling frequency
2304.1-2304.2 CW, EME, SSB
2304.2-2304.3 SSB, SSTV, FAX, Packet AM, Amtor
2304.30-2304.32 Propagation beacon network
2304.32-2304.40 General propagation beacons
2304.4-2304.5 SSB, SSTV, ACSSB, FAX, Packet AM, Amtor experimental
2304.5-2304.7 Crossband linear translator input
2304.7-2304.9 Crossband linear translator output
2304.9-2305.0 Experimental beacons
2305.0-2305.2 FM simplex (25 kHz spacing)
2305.20 FM simplex calling frequency
2305.2-2306.0 FM simplex (25 kHz spacing)
2306.0-2309.0 FM Repeaters (25 kHz) input
2309.0-2310.0 Control and auxiliary links
2390.0-2396.0 Fast-scan TV
2396.0-2399.0 High-rate data
2399.0-2399.5 Packet
2399.5-2400.0 Control and auxiliary links
2400.0-2403.0 Satellite
2403.0-2408.0 Satellite high-rate data
2408.0-2410.0 Satellite
2410.0-2413.0 FM repeaters (25 kHz) output
2413.0-2418.0 High-rate data
2418.0-2430.0 Fast-scan TV
2430.0-2433.0 Satellite
2433.0-2438.0 Satellite high-rate data
2438.0-2450.0 WB FM, FSTV, FMTV, SS experimental

3300-3500 MHz

3456.3-3456.4 Propagation beacons

5650-5925 MHz

5760.3-5760.4 Propagation beacons

10.00-10.50 GHz

10.368 Narrow band calling frequency 10.3683-10.3684 Propagation beacons
10.3640 Calling frequency

Now that you have your license (you do, don't you?), and your equipment, you are ready to go live. Below is a suggested start.

1) Assuming you have the HT set up to the appropriate frequency, and offset, press the mic button on the HT and say, "KK4HWX listening." Replace the KK4HWX with your own call sign, the one assigned to you by the FCC (it's the law). If no one responds to your call, you may wish to try again. Hopefully someone will respond to your call.

2) Once you get a response, it will be in the form of something like, "KK4HWX this is ??1??? in Eastport returning. My name is Florence. Back to you. ??1???" then a tone. Let us examine the response more closely. She first acknowledged your call sign (KK4HWX), then identified hers (??1???). From the 1 in her call sign, you know that she first got her license in Region 1, meaning she got it while a resident of CT, ME, MA, NH, RI, or VT. She then told you where she's transmitting from (Eastport). The term "returning" means that she is returning your call. Her name is Florence. The phrase, "Back to you" indicates that she is turning over the conversation to you. She then repeats her call sign. The tone indicates to you that it is okay to proceed with your response. BTW if she had used the term "Over" instead of "Back to you," it would mean the same thing, just fewer words.

3) At this point, press the mic button and continue with the conversation. You should restate your call sign often during the conversation (perhaps every 10 minutes or less and whenever you begin transmitting). Don't forget to say, "Over" or "Back to you" whenever you are giving Florence control of the conversation again.

4) When you are ready to stop the conversation, you should say goodbye or use the phrase "73", meaning "best wishes." Your conversation would end something like, "??1??? 73, this is KK4HWX clear and monitoring." The "clear and monitoring" indicates that you are going to continue to monitor the frequency. If you are not going to continue monitoring, you may wish to end the conversation with Florence with, "clear and QRT" instead. The QRT means that you are stopping transmissions.

Call Sign Phonics

Because of different accents of various people, sometimes it is difficult to understand call sign letters when spoken. For this reason, most ham operators verbalize their call sign using phonics. Below is a table listing the accepted phonics for letters and numbers.

A = ALFA	S = SIERRA
B = BRAVO	T = TANGO
C = CHARLIE	U = UNIFORM
D = DELTA	V = VICTOR
E = ECHO	W = WHISKEY
F = FOXTROT	X = X-RAY
G = GOLF	Y = YANKEE
H = HOTEL	Z = ZULU (ZED)
I = INDIA	1 = ONE
J = JULIETT	2 = TWO
K = KILO	3 = THREE (TREE)
L = LIMA	4 = FOUR
M = MIKE	5 = FIVE (FIFE)
N = NOVEMBER	6 = SIX
O = OSCAR	7 = SEVEN
P = PAPA (PA-PA')	8 = EIGHT
Q = QUEBEC (KAY-BEK')	9 = NINE (NINER)
R = ROMEO	0 = ZERO

The words in parentheses are the pronunciation or the alternate pronunciations for the words or numbers, but you will hear both used. With the letter Z, (ZED) is by far the most commonly used. With the number 9, NINER is the most common and easiest to understand ON THE AIR.

If you wish to use Morse code (CW) instead of voice communication, the "conversation" would follow the same steps, with a few modifications. To type out each word would require a lot of typing and translating. If you are like this author, more means more, i.e., more typing means more typos are likely. To help with this situation, CW enthusiasts have developed a language all their own – they use abbreviations for common phrases. Below is a chart showing some of these abbreviations.

Abbreviation	Use
AR	Over
de	From or "this is"
ES	And
GM	Good Morning
K	Go
KN	Go only
NM	Name

QTH	Location
RPT	Report
R	Roger
SK	Clear
tnx	Thanks
UR	Your, you are
73	Best Wishes

Morse Code and Amateur Radio

If you wish to use CW, but are concerned about accuracy, you might consider purchasing a Morse code translator. This is an electronic device that you place in front of your speakers. It takes the CW sounds and translates them into English and displays the transmission on an LCD display. For the reverse, you can pick up a CW keyboard. With the keyboard, you type in your message and it converts the text to Morse code. The translator does not need to be attached to your ham equipment, whereas the keyboard would.

For your convenience, below is a table showing the Morse code signals and their meaning.

Character	Code
A	· —
B	— · · ·
C	— · — ·
D	— · ·
E	·
F	· · — ·
G	— — ·
H	· · · ·
I	· ·
J	· — — —
K	— · —
L	· — · ·
M	— —
N	— ·
O	— — —
P	· — — ·
Q	— — · —
R	· — ·
S	· · ·
T	—
U	· · —
V	· · · —
W	· — —
X	— · · —

Y	— · — —
Z	— — · ·
0	— — — — —
1	· — — — —
2	· · — — —
3	· · · — —
4	· · · · —
5	· · · · ·
6	— · · · ·
7	— — · · ·
8	— — — · ·
9	— — — — ·
Ampersand [&], Wait	· — · · ·
Apostrophe [']	· — — — — ·
At sign [@]	· — — · — ·
Colon [:]	— — — · · ·
Comma [,]	— — · · — —
Dollar sign [$]	· · · — · · —
Double dash [=]	— · · · —
Exclamation mark [!]	— · — · — —
Hyphen, Minus [-]	— · · · · —
Parenthesis closed [)]	— · — — · —
Parenthesis open [(]	— · — — ·
Period [.]	· — · — · —
Plus [+]	· — · — ·
Question mark [?]	· · — — · ·
Quotation mark ["]	· — · · — ·
Semicolon [;]	— · — · — ·
Slash [/], Fraction bar	— · · — ·
Underscore [_]	· · — — · —

An advantage of using Morse Code is that when broadcasting CW, you are using reduced power, thereby saving your battery. Your battery is used only while actually transmitting or receiving.

International Call Sign Prefixes

As was stated earlier, all ham radio call signs begin with letters (or numbers) taken from blocks assigned to each country of the world by the *ITU - International Telecommunications Union,* a body controlled by the United Nations. The following chart indicates which call sign series are allocated to which countries.

Call Sign Series	Allocated to
AAA-ALZ	**United States of America**
AMA-AOZ	Spain

APA-ASZ	Pakistan (Islamic Republic of)
ATA-AWZ	India (Republic of)
AXA-AXZ	Australia
AYA-AZZ	Argentine Republic
A2A-A2Z	Botswana (Republic of)
A3A-A3Z	Tonga (Kingdom of)
A4A-A4Z	Oman (Sultanate of)
A5A-A5Z	Bhutan (Kingdom of)
A6A-A6Z	United Arab Emirates
A7A-A7Z	Qatar (State of)
A8A-A8Z	Liberia (Republic of)
A9A-A9Z	Bahrain (State of)
BAA-BZZ	China (People's Republic of)
CAA-CEZ	Chile
CFA-CKZ	Canada
CLA-CMZ	Cuba
CNA-CNZ	Morocco (Kingdom of)
COA-COZ	Cuba
CPA-CPZ	Bolivia (Republic of)
CQA-CUZ	Portugal
CVA-CXZ	Uruguay (Eastern Republic of)
CYA-CZZ	Canada
C2A-C2Z	Nauru (Republic of)
C3A-C3Z	Andorra (Principality of)
C4A-C4Z	Cyprus (Republic of)
C5A-C5Z	Gambia (Republic of the)
C6A-C6Z	Bahamas (Commonwealth of the)
C7A-C7Z	World Meteorological Organization
C8A-C9Z	Mozambique (Republic of)
DAA-DRZ	Germany (Federal Republic of)
DSA-DTZ	Korea (Republic of)
DUA-DZZ	Philippines (Republic of the)
D2A-D3Z	Angola (Republic of)
D4A-D4Z	Cape Verde (Republic of)
D5A-D5Z	Liberia (Republic of)
D6A-D6Z	Comoros (Islamic Federal Republic of the)
D7A-D9Z	Korea (Republic of)
EAA-EHZ	Spain
EIA-EJZ	Ireland
EKA-EKZ	Armenia (Republic of)
ELA-ELZ	Liberia (Republic of)
EMA-EOZ	Ukraine
EPA-EQZ	Iran (Islamic Republic of)
ERA-ERZ	Moldova (Republic of)
ESA-ESZ	Estonia (Republic of)

ETA-ETZ	Ethiopia (Federal Democratic Republic of)
EUA-EWZ	Belarus (Republic of)
EXA-EXZ	Kyrgyz Republic
EYA-EYZ	Tajikistan (Republic of)
EZA-EZZ	Turkmenistan
E2A-E2Z	Thailand
E3A-E3Z	Eritrea
E4A-E4Z	Palestinian Authority
E5A-E5Z	New Zealand - Cook Islands (WRC-07)
E7A-E7Z	Bosnia and Herzegovina (Republic of) (WRC-07)
FAA-FZZ	France
GAA-GZZ	United Kingdom of Great Britain and Northern Ireland
HAA-HAZ	Hungary (Republic of)
HBA-HBZ	Switzerland (Confederation of)
HCA-HDZ	Ecuador
HEA-HEZ	Switzerland (Confederation of)
HFA-HFZ	Poland (Republic of)
HGA-HGZ	Hungary (Republic of)
HHA-HHZ	Haiti (Republic of)
HIA-HIZ	Dominican Republic
HJA-HKZ	Colombia (Republic of)
HLA-HLZ	Korea (Republic of)
HMA-HMZ	Democratic People's Republic of Korea
HNA-HNZ	Iraq (Republic of)
HOA-HPZ	Panama (Republic of)
HQA-HRZ	Honduras (Republic of)
HSA-HSZ	Thailand
HTA-HTZ	Nicaragua
HUA-HUZ	El Salvador (Republic of)
HVA-HVZ	Vatican City State
HWA-HYZ	France
HZA-HZZ	Saudi Arabia (Kingdom of)
H2A-H2Z	Cyprus (Republic of)
H3A-H3Z	Panama (Republic of)
H4A-H4Z	Solomon Islands
H6A-H7Z	Nicaragua
H8A-H9Z	Panama (Republic of)
IAA-IZZ	Italy
JAA-JSZ	Japan
JTA-JVZ	Mongolia
JWA-JXZ	Norway
JYA-JYZ	Jordan (Hashemite Kingdom of)
JZA-JZZ	Indonesia (Republic of)
J2A-J2Z	Djibouti (Republic of)
J3A-J3Z	Grenada

J4A-J4Z	Greece
J5A-J5Z	Guinea-Bissau (Republic of)
J6A-J6Z	Saint Lucia
J7A-J7Z	Dominica (Commonwealth of)
J8A-J8Z	Saint Vincent and the Grenadines
KAA-KZZ	**United States of America**
LAA-LNZ	Norway
LOA-LWZ	Argentine Republic
LXA-LXZ	Luxembourg
LYA-LYZ	Lithuania (Republic of)
LZA-LZZ	Bulgaria (Republic of)
L2A-L9Z	Argentine Republic
MAA-MZZ	United Kingdom of Great Britain and Northern Ireland
NAA-NZZ	**United States of America**
OAA-OCZ	Peru
ODA-ODZ	Lebanon
OEA-OEZ	Austria
OFA-OJZ	Finland
OKA-OLZ	Czech Republic
OMA-OMZ	Slovak Republic
ONA-OTZ	Belgium
OUA-OZZ	Denmark
PAA-PIZ	Netherlands (Kingdom of the)
PJA-PJZ	Netherlands (Kingdom of the) - Netherlands Antilles
PKA-POZ	Indonesia (Republic of)
PPA-PYZ	Brazil (Federative Republic of)
PZA-PZZ	Suriname (Republic of)
P2A-P2Z	Papua New Guinea
P3A-P3Z	Cyprus (Republic of)
P4A-P4Z	Netherlands (Kingdom of the) - Aruba
P5A-P9Z	Democratic People's Republic of Korea
RAA-RZZ	Russian Federation
SAA-SMZ	Sweden
SNA-SRZ	Poland (Republic of)
SSA-SSM	Egypt (Arab Republic of)
SSN-STZ	Sudan (Republic of the)
SUA-SUZ	Egypt (Arab Republic of)
SVA-SZZ	Greece
S2A-S3Z	Bangladesh (People's Republic of)
S5A-S5Z	Slovenia (Republic of)
S6A-S6Z	Singapore (Republic of)
S7A-S7Z	Seychelles (Republic of)
S8A-S8Z	South Africa (Republic of)
S9A-S9Z	Sao Tome and Principe (Democratic Republic of)
TAA-TCZ	Turkey

TDA-TDZ	Guatemala (Republic of)
TEA-TEZ	Costa Rica
TFA-TFZ	Iceland
TGA-TGZ	Guatemala (Republic of)
THA-THZ	France
TIA-TIZ	Costa Rica
TJA-TJZ	Cameroon (Republic of)
TKA-TKZ	France
TLA-TLZ	Central African Republic
TMA-TMZ	France
TNA-TNZ	Congo (Republic of the)
TOA-TQZ	France
TRA-TRZ	Gabonese Republic
TSA-TSZ	Tunisia
TTA-TTZ	Chad (Republic of)
TUA-TUZ	Côte d'Ivoire (Republic of)
TVA-TXZ	France
TYA-TYZ	Benin (Republic of)
TZA-TZZ	Mali (Republic of)
T2A-T2Z	Tuvalu
T3A-T3Z	Kiribati (Republic of)
T4A-T4Z	Cuba
T5A-T5Z	Somali Democratic Republic
T6A-T6Z	Afghanistan (Islamic State of)
T7A-T7Z	San Marino (Republic of)
T8A-T8Z	Palau (Republic of)
UAA-UIZ	Russian Federation
UJA-UMZ	Uzbekistan (Republic of)
UNA-UQZ	Kazakhstan (Republic of)
URA-UZZ	Ukraine
VAA-VGZ	Canada
VHA-VNZ	Australia
VOA-VOZ	Canada
VPA-VQZ	United Kingdom of Great Britain and Northern Ireland
VRA-VRZ	China (People's Republic of) - Hong Kong
VSA-VSZ	United Kingdom of Great Britain and Northern Ireland
VTA-VWZ	India (Republic of)
VXA-VYZ	Canada
VZA-VZZ	Australia
V2A-V2Z	Antigua and Barbuda
V3A-V3Z	Belize
V4A-V4Z	Saint Kitts and Nevis
V5A-V5Z	Namibia (Republic of)
V6A-V6Z	Micronesia (Federated States of)
V7A-V7Z	Marshall Islands (Republic of the)

V8A-V8Z	Brunei Darussalam
WAA-WZZ	**United States of America**
XAA-XIZ	Mexico
XJA-XOZ	Canada
XPA-XPZ	Denmark
XQA-XRZ	Chile
XSA-XSZ	China (People's Republic of)
XTA-XTZ	Burkina Faso
XUA-XUZ	Cambodia (Kingdom of)
XVA-XVZ	Viet Nam (Socialist Republic of)
XWA-XWZ	Lao People's Democratic Republic
XXA-XXZ	China (People's Republic of) - Macao (WRC-07)
XYA-XZZ	Myanmar (Union of)
YAA-YAZ	Afghanistan (Islamic State of)
YBA-YHZ	Indonesia (Republic of)
YIA-YIZ	Iraq (Republic of)
YJA-YJZ	Vanuatu (Republic of)
YKA-YKZ	Syrian Arab Republic
YLA-YLZ	Latvia (Republic of)
YMA-YMZ	Turkey
YNA-YNZ	Nicaragua
YOA-YRZ	Romania
YSA-YSZ	El Salvador (Republic of)
YTA-YUZ	Serbia (Republic of) (WRC-07)
YVA-YYZ	Venezuela (Republic of)
Y2A-Y9Z	Germany (Federal Republic of)
ZAA-ZAZ	Albania (Republic of)
ZBA-ZJZ	United Kingdom of Great Britain and Northern Ireland
ZKA-ZMZ	New Zealand
ZNA-ZOZ	United Kingdom of Great Britain and Northern Ireland
ZPA-ZPZ	Paraguay (Republic of)
ZQA-ZQZ	United Kingdom of Great Britain and Northern Ireland
ZRA-ZUZ	South Africa (Republic of)
ZVA-ZZZ	Brazil (Federative Republic of)
Z2A-Z2Z	Zimbabwe (Republic of)
Z3A-Z3Z	The Former Yugoslav Republic of Macedonia
2AA-2ZZ	United Kingdom of Great Britain and Northern Ireland
3AA-3AZ	Monaco (Principality of)
3BA-3BZ	Mauritius (Republic of)
3CA-3CZ	Equatorial Guinea (Republic of)
3DA-3DM	Swaziland (Kingdom of)
3DN-3DZ	Fiji (Republic of)
3EA-3FZ	Panama (Republic of)
3GA-3GZ	Chile
3HA-3UZ	China (People's Republic of)

3VA-3VZ	Tunisia
3WA-3WZ	Viet Nam (Socialist Republic of)
3XA-3XZ	Guinea (Republic of)
3YA-3YZ	Norway
3ZA-3ZZ	Poland (Republic of)
4AA-4CZ	Mexico
4DA-4IZ	Philippines (Republic of the)
4JA-4KZ	Azerbaijani Republic
4LA-4LZ	Georgia (Republic of)
4MA-4MZ	Venezuela (Republic of)
4OA-4OZ	Montenegro (Republic of) (WRC-07)
4PA-4SZ	Sri Lanka (Democratic Socialist Republic of)
4TA-4TZ	Peru
4UA-4UZ	United Nations
4VA-4VZ	Haiti (Republic of)
4WA-4WZ	Democratic Republic of Timor-Leste (WRC-03)
4XA-4XZ	Israel (State of)
4YA-4YZ	International Civil Aviation Organization
4ZA-4ZZ	Israel (State of)
5AA-5AZ	Libya (Socialist People's Libyan Arab Jamahiriya)
5BA-5BZ	Cyprus (Republic of)
5CA-5GZ	Morocco (Kingdom of)
5HA-5IZ	Tanzania (United Republic of)
5JA-5KZ	Colombia (Republic of)
5LA-5MZ	Liberia (Republic of)
5NA-5OZ	Nigeria (Federal Republic of)
5PA-5QZ	Denmark
5RA-5SZ	Madagascar (Republic of)
5TA-5TZ	Mauritania (Islamic Republic of)
5UA-5UZ	Niger (Republic of the)
5VA-5VZ	Togolese Republic
5WA-5WZ	Samoa (Independent State of)
5XA-5XZ	Uganda (Republic of)
5YA-5ZZ	Kenya (Republic of)
6AA-6BZ	Egypt (Arab Republic of)
6CA-6CZ	Syrian Arab Republic
6DA-6JZ	Mexico
6KA-6NZ	Korea (Republic of)
6OA-6OZ	Somali Democratic Republic
6PA-6SZ	Pakistan (Islamic Republic of)
6TA-6UZ	Sudan (Republic of the)
6VA-6WZ	Senegal (Republic of)
6XA-6XZ	Madagascar (Republic of)
6YA-6YZ	Jamaica
6ZA-6ZZ	Liberia (Republic of)

7AA-7IZ	Indonesia (Republic of)
7JA-7NZ	Japan
7OA-7OZ	Yemen (Republic of)
7PA-7PZ	Lesotho (Kingdom of)
7QA-7QZ	Malawi
7RA-7RZ	Algeria (People's Democratic Republic of)
7SA-7SZ	Sweden
7TA-7YZ	Algeria (People's Democratic Republic of)
7ZA-7ZZ	Saudi Arabia (Kingdom of)
8AA-8IZ	Indonesia (Republic of)
8JA-8NZ	Japan
8OA-8OZ	Botswana (Republic of)
8PA-8PZ	Barbados
8QA-8QZ	Maldives (Republic of)
8RA-8RZ	Guyana
8SA-8SZ	Sweden
8TA-8YZ	India (Republic of)
8ZA-8ZZ	Saudi Arabia (Kingdom of)
9AA-9AZ	Croatia (Republic of)
9BA-9DZ	Iran (Islamic Republic of)
9EA-9FZ	Ethiopia (Federal Democratic Republic of)
9GA-9GZ	Ghana
9HA-9HZ	Malta
9IA-9JZ	Zambia (Republic of)
9KA-9KZ	Kuwait (State of)
9LA-9LZ	Sierra Leone
9MA-9MZ	Malaysia
9NA-9NZ	Nepal
9OA-9TZ	Democratic Republic of the Congo
9UA-9UZ	Burundi (Republic of)
9VA-9VZ	Singapore (Republic of)
9WA-9WZ	Malaysia
9XA-9XZ	Rwandese Republic
9YA-9ZZ	Trinidad and Tobago

Third-Party Communications and Amateur Radio

If all of this information about ham radios is somewhat intimidating, do not despair. "You" can still use ham radios for communications without being a licensed operator. Yes, you do have to have a ham license in order to legally transmit by ham equipment (or be under the direct supervision of someone else who is licensed), but there is an alternative – third-party communication.

Third-party communications occur when a licensed operator sends either written or verbal messages on behalf of unlicensed persons or organizations. There are two "controls" on third-party communication.

First, the communication must be noncommercial and of a personal nature. Asking a ham operator to contact another ham operator located in an area just hit by tornados and, because of being without power, phones do not work in Grandma Sally's city so you can check up on her, is okay. Asking a ham to send a message out that you have an old Chevy for sale would not be okay.

Second, the message must be going to a permitted area. Transmitting from a US location to another US location is okay, but transmitting from the US to another country may not. Because third-party communications bypass a country's normal telephone and postal systems, many foreign governments forbid such communications. In order to transmit from one country to another, the other country must have signed a third-party agreement with the US. What follows is a list of those countries that do have third-party a communications agreement with the US.

V2	Antigua / Barbuda
LU	Argentina
VK	Australia
V3	Belize
CP	Bolivia
T9	Bosnia-Herzegovina
PY	Brazil
VE	Canada
CE	Chile
HK	Colombia
D6	Comoros (Federal Islamic Republic of)
TI	Costa Rica
CO	Cuba
HI	Dominican Republic
J7	Dominica
HC	Ecuador
YS	El Salvador
C5	Gambia, The
9G	Ghana
J3	Grenada
TG	Guatemala
8R	Guyana
HH	Haiti
HR	Honduras
4X	Israel
6Y	Jamaica
JY	Jordan

EL	Liberia
V7	Marshall Islands
XE	Mexico
V6	Micronesia, Federated States of
YN	Nicaragua
HP	Panama
ZP	Paraguay
OA	Peru
DU	Philippines
VR6	Pitcairn Island
V4	St. Christopher / Nevis
J6	St. Lucia
J8	St. Vincent and the Grenadines
9L	Sierra Leone
ZS	South Africa
3DA	Swaziland
9Y	Trinidad / Tobago
TA	Turkey
GB	United Kingdom
CX	Uruguay
YV	Venezuela
4U1ITUITU	Geneva
4U1VICVIC	Vienna

Remember, before TSHTF, keep your pantry well stocked, your powder dry, and your batteries fully charged. 73

APPENDIX A

American Radio Relay League

Affiliated Amateur Radio Clubs in

Alaska

ARRL Affiliated Club: **Borealis Amateur Radio Club Prudhoe Bay**
City: Anchorage, AK
Call Sign: WL7CXA

ARRL Affiliated Club: **Anchorage ARC Inc**
City: Anchorage, AK
Call Sign: KL7AA
Links: www.KL7AA.net

ARRL Affiliated Club: **Elmendorf ARS**
City: Elmendorf AFB, AK
Call Sign: KL7AIR
Links: http://www.kl7air,us, http://www.kl7air.us

ARRL Affiliated Club: **Arctic Amateur Radio Club (AARC)**
City: Fairbanks, AK
Call Sign: KL7KC
Links: www.kl7kc.com

ARRL Affiliated Club: **Alaska VHF-UP Group**
City: Nikiski, AK
Call Sign: KL7UW
Links: http://www.kl7uw.com/avg.htm

ARRL Affiliated Club: **Moose Horn ARC**
City: Sterling, AK
Call Sign: AL7LE
Links: http://www.moosehornarc.com

ARRL Affiliated Club: **Matanuska Amateur Radio Association**
City: Wasilla, AK
Call Sign: KL7JFU
Links: www.kl7jfu.com

APPENDIX B

Amateur Radio License Holders

in

Alaska
(by City)

FCC Amateur Radio Licenses in Adak

Call Sign: W6KZT
Charles W Luck Jr
112D Beverly Cove
Adak AK 995462032

Call Sign: WL7BUU
Mary J Garigen
Box 29 Nsga
Adak AK 98777

Call Sign: NL7SJ
Michael J Donovan
Box 557 Nsga
Adak AK 98777

Call Sign: KL0SR
Mary E Flavell
Mile 1 Main St
Akiachak AK 99955

Call Sign: WL7CCY
Mark A Anaruk
Akiak AK 99552

FCC Amateur Radio Licenses in Akue Bay

Call Sign: WL7CVL
Juneau Amateur Radio Club
Akue Bay AK 998210123

Call Sign: KL7JRC
Juneau Amateur Radio Club
Akue Bay AK 998210123

FCC Amateur Radio Licenses in Akutan

Call Sign: KL1RB
John H Pelkey
Akutan AK 99553

FCC Amateur Radio Licenses in Aleknagik

Call Sign: KL1RA
Debbie M Reiswig
106 Suravak Rd
Aleknagik AK 99555

Call Sign: KB7LON
Debbie M Reiswig
106 Suravak Rd
Aleknagik AK 99555

Call Sign: KB7KSQ
Kenneth N Reiswig
106 Suravak Rd
Aleknagik AK 995550106

Call Sign: KC7DQI
Brooke C Reiswig
106 Suravak Rd
Aleknagik AK 995550106

Call Sign: AL2G
Bethany R Reiswig
Aleknagik AK 99555

Call Sign: KL0UU
Bethany R Reiswig
Aleknagik AK 99555

FCC Amateur Radio Licenses in Anaktuvuk Pass

Call Sign: KL0JC
Riley R Sikvayugak
Gen Del
Anaktuvuk Pass AK 99721

Call Sign: KL0JM
Charles A Ahgook
Anaktuvuk Pass AK 99721

FCC Amateur Radio Licenses in Anchor Point

Call Sign: NL7AE
Victor R Smart
Box 354
Anchor Point AK 99556

Call Sign: NL7XP
Michael G Prouty
69440 Chris Ct
Anchor Point AK 99556

Call Sign: NL7YN
Connie L Prouty
69440 Chris Ct
Anchor Point AK 99556

Call Sign: NL7QS

James W Schopp
HC 67 Box 669
Anchor Point AK 99556

Call Sign: KL7JL
John R Stannard
65190 Nordvik Ave
Anchor Point AK 995569214

Call Sign: WL7CNQ
Billy L Sturgis
PO Box 1029
Anchor Point AK 99556

Call Sign: AL2U
Steven J Friend
PO Box 1455
Anchor Point AK 99556

Call Sign: AC6CL
Steven J Friend
PO Box 1455
Anchor Point AK 99556

Call Sign: N7GLP
Robert D Phillips
28755 Sterling Hwy
Anchor Point AK 99556

Call Sign: KD7NNF
Wayne W Flint
35410 Sterling Hwy
Anchor Point AK 99556

Call Sign: KL7CR
Robert D Phillips
38755 Sterling Hwy
Anchor Point AK 99556

Call Sign: AL2F
Kristoffer P Kerce
Anchor Point AK 99556

Call Sign: KL1QY
Sandra E Nelson
Anchor Point AK 99556

Call Sign: AL7JX
Glen A Fuller
Anchor Point AK 99556

Call Sign: KL0OA
Alfred C Erion
Anchor Point AK 99556

Call Sign: KL7HBK
John D O Larey
Anchor Point AK 99556

Call Sign: KL7HD
Mark A Hadley
Anchor Point AK 99556

Call Sign: WL7MA
Cheri L Worley
Anchor Point AK 99556

Call Sign: WL7CGA
Thomas M Bell III
Anchor Point AK 99556

FCC Amateur Radio Licenses in Anchorage

Call Sign: WL7OR
Brian A Niswander
7921A Little Dipper Ave
Anchorage AK 99504

Call Sign: NL7ZZ
Connie L Hardwick
8330 Northwind Ave
Anchorage AK 99504

Call Sign: WL7IW
Thomas B J Schoenbergera
826B West 19th Ave
Anchorage AK 99503

Call Sign: KC0RJA
Richard C Burrell
1712 A St
Anchorage AK 99501

Call Sign: W7NUT
Stephen H Bloom
1430 A St 11
Anchorage AK 99501

Call Sign: NB4U
George O Sharrock
317 A St 512
Anchorage AK 99501

Call Sign: KL2JH
James M Scherr
3140 Admiralty Bay Dr
Anchorage AK 99515

Call Sign: KL0IL
Thomas J Bunger
1648 Alder Dr
Anchorage AK 99508

Call Sign: KL7NK
Joseph C Talbott
2143 Alder Dr
Anchorage AK 99508

Call Sign: WD6BMJ
Mark E Sabel
1737 Aleutian St
Anchorage AK 99508

Call Sign: WL7ED
Michael A Mellor
901 Allison Cir
Anchorage AK 99515

Call Sign: KL7VC
Frederick F Erickson
12531 Alpine Dr
Anchorage AK 99516

Call Sign: WL7IB
Joan B Erickson
12531 Alpine Dr
Anchorage AK 99516

Call Sign: KL7JE
Joan B Erickson
12531 Alpine Dr
Anchorage AK 99516

Call Sign: KL7FE
Frederick F Erickson
12531 Alpine Dr
Anchorage AK 99516

Call Sign: WL7CPG
Richard M O Connor
3080 Amber Bay Loop
Anchorage AK 99515

Call Sign: WL7ZT
Kristina M O Connor
3080 Amber Bay Loop
Anchorage AK 99515

Call Sign: WL7ZU
Frank R O Connor
3080 Amber Bay Loop

Anchorage AK 99515

Call Sign: KL2GV
Roy L Sursa
3291 Amber Bay Loop
Anchorage AK 99515

Call Sign: KL2NG
Michael R Sweet
3291 Amber Bay Loop
Anchorage AK 99515

Call Sign: KL2XA
Tobyann Sursa
3291 Amber Bay Loop
Anchorage AK 99515

Call Sign: NL7TF
Dennis J Martin I
3130 Amberbay Loop
Anchorage AK 99515

Call Sign: KL3LM
Scott Masten
7110 Ambler Ln 16
Anchorage AK 99504

Call Sign: KL2NW
Eric H Reimer
1246 Annapolis Dr 1
Anchorage AK 99508

Call Sign: KL2OH
Lisa M Reimer
1246 Annapolis Dr 1
Anchorage AK 99508

Call Sign: NL7LD
Stephen B Bowhey
3809 Apollo Dr
Anchorage AK 99504

Call Sign: KL3JG
Eric C Anderson
3849 Apollo Dr
Anchorage AK 99504

Call Sign: WL7AYY
Bruce A La Londe
2215 Arbor Cir
Anchorage AK 995171342

Call Sign: W1ZKA
Robert W Raymond

2226 Arbor Cir
Anchorage AK 995171342

Call Sign: WL7DV
Douglas B Baily
3705 Arctic 1444
Anchorage AK 995035774

Call Sign: KL4X
Lance C Lobo
3705 Arctic 1487
Anchorage AK 99503

Call Sign: KB1IMU
Lance C Lobo
3705 Arctic 1487
Anchorage AK 99503

Call Sign: KL7PT
Carol A Boyt
2457 Arctic Blvd
Anchorage AK 99503

Call Sign: WL7CWL
North County Dx Association -
Alaska Chapter
3705 Arctic Blvd - 1830
Anchorage AK 99507

Call Sign: KL7RST
North County Dx Association -
Alaska Chapter
3705 Arctic Blvd - 1830
Anchorage AK 99507

Call Sign: KL3FT
John J Garteiz
3705 Arctic Blvd 903
Anchorage AK 99503

Call Sign: WL7MY
Claire A Hadfield
3705 Arctic Blvd - Unit 1830
Anchorage AK 99503

Call Sign: W7VZY
Stanley M Barge
3705 Arctic Blvd 1149
Anchorage AK 995035774

Call Sign: KL7HQY
Frank G Chalifour Jr
3705 Arctic Blvd 1323
Anchorage AK 995035774

Call Sign: KL7PA
Lone E Janson
3705 Arctic Blvd 1431
Anchorage AK 99503

Call Sign: KL7BUR
Bayard M Bird
3705 Arctic Blvd 1545
Anchorage AK 99503

Call Sign: KL7JES
Karin E Preston
3705 Arctic Blvd 217
Anchorage AK 99503

Call Sign: KL7OA
Charles M Preston
3705 Arctic Blvd 217
Anchorage AK 99503

Call Sign: WL7FL
David B Goss
3705 Arctic Blvd 241
Anchorage AK 99503

Call Sign: W9WLN
William L Newman Jr
3705 Arctic Blvd 354
Anchorage AK 995035774

Call Sign: WL7PS
Kristine A Benson
3605 Arctic Blvd 699
Anchorage AK 99503

Call Sign: WL7KI
Cameale C Johnson
3705 Arctic Blvd 887
Anchorage AK 99503

Call Sign: AL7EY
Andrew J Hilowitz
3605 Arctic Blvd 976
Anchorage AK 99503

Call Sign: AL7KM
Anne M Darrow
3705 Arctic Blvd Pmb 1352
Anchorage AK 99503

Call Sign: WL7ON
Nelson W Gibson Sr
3705 Arctic Blvd Pmb 1352

Anchorage AK 99503

Call Sign: KL0KM
Peter Argetsinger
3705 Arctic Blvd Ste 2328
Anchorage AK 99503

Call Sign: AL4S
Richard G Gillin
5313 Arctic Boulevard Ste 206
Anchorage AK 995181111

Call Sign: KL0KN
Judith M Argetsinger
3705 Arctic Ste 2328
Anchorage AK 99503

Call Sign: KL2HX
John David E Thacker
3903 Arkansas Dr
Anchorage AK 99517

Call Sign: KL3EQ
Scott M Reed
3700 B Arkansas Dr
Anchorage AK 99517

Call Sign: KL1UJ
Geffrey P Travis
9400 Arlene Dr
Anchorage AK 99502

Call Sign: KL1SN
Michael A Cuilla
7001 Arlene St
Anchorage AK 99502

Call Sign: WL7AME
Gerald Ganopole
2536 Arlington Dr
Anchorage AK 995171303

Call Sign: KL2OC
Kirk A Foster
9138 Arlon St Ste A3-206
Anchorage AK 99507

Call Sign: KB9WYV
Michael A Zhang
9138 Arlon St Ste A3-253
Anchorage AK 99507

Call Sign: KB9WKC
Anna T Baumgartner

9138 Arlon St Ste A3-253
Anchorage AK 99507

Call Sign: KA3PSY
Charles E Schmitt
9138 Arlon St Ste A3-502
Anchorage AK 99507

Call Sign: KL1OG
Christie L Brown
3705 Artic 2520
Anchorage AK 99503

Call Sign: KL2PV
Christie L Brown
3705 Artic 2520
Anchorage AK 99503

Call Sign: KL3IC
Richard E Peterson Jr
3705 Artic 2914
Anchorage AK 99503

Call Sign: WL7CWK
Aurora Dx Club-Northern
Canada Chapter
3705 Artic Blvd - 1830
Anchorage AK 99503

Call Sign: KL7MN
Aurora Dx Club-Northern
Canada Chapter
3705 Artic Blvd - 1830
Anchorage AK 99503

Call Sign: WP2JR
North Country Dx Association
3705 Artic Blvd 1830
Anchorage AK 99503

Call Sign: KL2DE
James M Call
3705 Artic Blvd -476
Anchorage AK 99503

Call Sign: AL3B
James M Call
3705 Artic Blvd -476
Anchorage AK 99503

Call Sign: KL2IG
Kristine A Conquergood
3705 Artic Blvd -476
Anchorage AK 99503

Call Sign: WL7ND
David D Ochoa
2819 Aspen Ct
Anchorage AK 99508

Call Sign: KL0NG
Michael E Johnston
2405 Aspen Dr
Anchorage AK 995173642

Call Sign: KL7HFD
John S O Brien
2615 Aspen Dr
Anchorage AK 99517

Call Sign: NL7MJ
Michael A Tucker
2807 Aspen Dr
Anchorage AK 99517

Call Sign: KL7JHQ
Robert S Flint
2902 Aspen Dr
Anchorage AK 99517

Call Sign: NL7XC
Catherine Flint
2902 Aspen Dr
Anchorage AK 99517

Call Sign: KL2HW
Robert F Valentz
9216 Atelier Dr
Anchorage AK 99507

Call Sign: KL0XY
Maxwell D Thomas
1416 Atkinson Dr
Anchorage AK 99504

Call Sign: W1JM
William J Missal
12000 Audubon Dr
Anchorage AK 99516

Call Sign: KL0PO
Ira L Kessler
8672 Augusta Cir
Anchorage AK 99504

Call Sign: KL2BX
Ian R Murphy
402 Aurora Dr

Anchorage AK 99503

Call Sign: KL2RZ
Mark V Ward
6021 Austria Dr
Anchorage AK 99516

Call Sign: NL7EB
Jeffrey L Edmundson
6130 Austria Dr
Anchorage AK 99516

Call Sign: KC4PTI
Dow S Buzzell
1310 Autumn Ln
Anchorage AK 99504

Call Sign: KL3CC
Steven J Flippen
1320 Autumn Ln
Anchorage AK 99504

Call Sign: KL3HF
James P Werner Jr
11309 Avion St
Anchorage AK 99516

Call Sign: KL2GJ
Sean M Riordan
6100 Azalea Dr
Anchorage AK 99516

Call Sign: AL2X
Donald J Bassler
13100 Badger Ln
Anchorage AK 99516

Call Sign: WL7BZM
Donald J Bassler
13100 Badger Ln
Anchorage AK 99516

Call Sign: KL1FU
Travis L Gray
1230 Balfour Ct Apt 2
Anchorage AK 99515

Call Sign: KL3FB
Tisha M Zeutzius
1300 Balfour Ct Apt 2
Anchorage AK 99515

Call Sign: KA7ETQ
Eric S Geisler

2301 Banbury Dr
Anchorage AK 99504

Call Sign: NL7K
Lyle B Easterly
1526 Bannister Dr
Anchorage AK 99508

Call Sign: N5CSO
Jeff Hittson
1737 Bannister Rd
Anchorage AK 99508

Call Sign: KL0HO
Richard R Karr
3810 Barbara Dr
Anchorage AK 99517

Call Sign: NL7UV
Clifford C Tice
2813 Bass
Anchorage AK 99507

Call Sign: KL0WV
Brian D Metras Mr
2906 Bass St
Anchorage AK 99507

Call Sign: KL3GZ
Keith M Hall
6820 Baxter Terrace Cir
Anchorage AK 99504

Call Sign: KL7JC
Peter C Willis
12421 Beachcomber Dr
Anchorage AK 99515

Call Sign: AL7QN
William E Chord Jr
12501 Beachcomber Dr
Anchorage AK 99515

Call Sign: NL7YP
Harold J Steffen
7110 Beaumont Cir
Anchorage AK 99502

Call Sign: KE7UY
David A Eilertsen
7110 Beaumont Cir
Anchorage AK 995022280

Call Sign: WL7IZ

Leo J Valdrow Sr
4201 Beechcraft Dr
Anchorage AK 995172724

Call Sign: KL0UN
Michael T Grueber
8740 Bell Place
Anchorage AK 99507

Call Sign: KL7QO
Christopher Q Conway
1722 Bellevue Loop
Anchorage AK 99515

Call Sign: NL7PO
Maurice J Cruickshank Jr
12840 Ben Ct
Anchorage AK 99515

Call Sign: KL1UO
Von D Christley
1031 Bentree Cir
Anchorage AK 99504

Call Sign: WL7MM
Von D Christley
1031 Bentree Cir
Anchorage AK 99504

Call Sign: NL7MM
Dwight D Christley
1031 Bentree Cir
Anchorage AK 995041780

Call Sign: KL2EN
David A Howe
2421 Bentzen Cir
Anchorage AK 99517

Call Sign: KL2QK
Christie J Love
2451 Bentzen Cir F34
Anchorage AK 99517

Call Sign: KI6YXZ
Gregory E Pfeifer
2411 Bentzen Cir Apt B15
Anchorage AK 99517

Call Sign: AL7AR
Larry D Sliger
8321 Berry Patch Dr
Anchorage AK 99502

Call Sign: KA7ZRI
Cara J Wright
2440 Berryman Ln
Anchorage AK 99502

Call Sign: K1TF
Thomas R Farrington
17330 Bettijean St
Anchorage AK 99516

Call Sign: AL7JA
Robert W Scoggin Jr
3154 Bettles Bay Loop
Anchorage AK 99515

Call Sign: KL7ISP
Stephen T Schneider
1650 Betula Cir
Anchorage AK 99507

Call Sign: KL2NZ
Gregory D Wilkie
10311 Betula Dr
Anchorage AK 99507

Call Sign: KF6KAG
Preston L Schanbeck
9300 Bietinger Dr
Anchorage AK 99515

Call Sign: KL0AK
Steven R Kaleta Pe
5913 Big Bend Loop Dr
Anchorage AK 99502

Call Sign: WL7BKG
Jack B Karterman
675 Birch St
Anchorage AK 99501

Call Sign: WL7HG
Robert A French
685 Birch St
Anchorage AK 99501

Call Sign: KL1OF
Charles C Bader
1341 Birchwood St
Anchorage AK 99508

Call Sign: NL7IM
Richard A Williams
1530 Birchwood St
Anchorage AK 99508

Call Sign: WL7CMZ
Kevin M Kelly
13121 Biscayne Cir
Anchorage AK 99516

Call Sign: KL7EN
Robert K Kelly Jr
13121 Biscayne Cir
Anchorage AK 99516

Call Sign: NL7II
Tommy G Heinrich Sr
6339 Blackberry
Anchorage AK 99502

Call Sign: NL7YW
Matthew T Griffin
7727 Blackberry
Anchorage AK 99502

Call Sign: NL7ZP
Robert L Griffin
7727 Blackberry
Anchorage AK 99502

Call Sign: KL2BA
Pamela A Trodden
1940 Bluegrass Cir
Anchorage AK 99502

Call Sign: KL1HD
Gerald A Trodden
1940 Bluegrass Cir
Anchorage AK 99502

Call Sign: WL7JH
Andy T Suess
2900 Boniface 116
Anchorage AK 99504

Call Sign: KL0JO
John H Burkle III
2900 Boniface 160
Anchorage AK 995043195

Call Sign: WL7CTN
Mike A Willoughby
2205 Boniface 80
Anchorage AK 99504

Call Sign: KL2EU
Darrell B Wayman
3205 Boniface Pkwy

Anchorage AK 99504

Call Sign: WL7BSJ
Larry C Volz Jr
3307 Boniface Pkwy 152
Anchorage AK 995043763

Call Sign: KI4WOI
Edward B Standefer
3325 Boniface Pkwy 6
Anchorage AK 99504

Call Sign: KL7CH
Clarence W Hammer
1001 Boniface Pkwy Spc 7
BlkO
Anchorage AK 99504

Call Sign: WL7KJ
Thomas K Spence
1001 Boniface Pky 15B
Anchorage AK 99504

Call Sign: NL7KN
Dianne Hammer
1001 Boniface Pky Sp 7 Blk 0
Anchorage AK 995041672

Call Sign: KL7GHG
John Skurla
3945 Borland Dr
Anchorage AK 99517

Call Sign: AL7OR
Vincent M Withington
1020 Botanical Heights Cir
Anchorage AK 99515

Call Sign: KF6TGR
Melkart F Hawi
7784 Boundary Ave
Anchorage AK 99504

Call Sign: WL7BF
Paul M Spatzek
5800 Boundary Ave 44
Anchorage AK 99504

Call Sign: WA3HDS
Robert A Rodgers
5800 Boundary Ave Apt 5
Anchorage AK 99504

Call Sign: KL2FM

Eric K Mcintosh
921 Bounty Dr
Anchorage AK 99515

Call Sign: KL7ZC
Harold D Nixon
Box 112314
Anchorage AK 99511

Call Sign: KL7GH
William D Mc Kinney
Box 190331
Anchorage AK 99519

Call Sign: NL7MG
John D Mc Clellan
Box 92314
Anchorage AK 99509

Call Sign: WL7CXA
Borealis Amateur Radio Club
Prudhoe Bay
Bp Exploration H 6 Attn Allen
Koenig
Anchorage AK 99519

Call Sign: WL7EJ
Jean Pierre J Legault
2016 Brandilyn St
Anchorage AK 99516

Call Sign: KL1LT
Eric J Straker
2900 Brandywine
Anchorage AK 99502

Call Sign: KL0AN
Paul D Jordan
13316 Brant Way
Anchorage AK 99515

Call Sign: KL0DD
Anita L Jordan
13316 Brant Way
Anchorage AK 99515

Call Sign: WB7QQU
Donald F Ridlon
12101 Brayton Dr
Anchorage AK 99516

Call Sign: KL7IPU
Frederick C Hudson
9499 Brayton Dr 201

Anchorage AK 99507

Call Sign: KL0UV
David W Boynton
9499 Brayton Dr Sp 71
Anchorage AK 99507

Call Sign: NL7UH
Robert O Baker
840 Breakwater Cir
Anchorage AK 99515

Call Sign: NL7UQ
Robert O Baker Jr
840 Breakwater Cir
Anchorage AK 99515

Call Sign: KL1OL
Joseph R Quickel Jr
3917 Brentwood Cir
Anchorage AK 99502

Call Sign: KL0CX
Brian J Mcclaskey
3931 Brentwood Cir
Anchorage AK 995024218

Call Sign: KL1ZC
Kevin C Cordell
7708 Brentwood Dr
Anchorage AK 99502

Call Sign: KL2GC
Jill A Fredston
9140 Brewsters Dr
Anchorage AK 99516

Call Sign: KL0ZS
Larry L Heuer
3241 Briarcliff Dr
Anchorage AK 99508

Call Sign: WL7CMX
William F Batsell Jr
3305 Briarcliff Dr
Anchorage AK 99508

Call Sign: WL7CMY
Sarah A Batsell
3305 Briarcliff Dr
Anchorage AK 99508

Call Sign: KL0QX
Haydn Widtfeldt

3405 Briarcliff Dr
Anchorage AK 99508

Call Sign: KL0UDS
Haydn Widtfeldt
3405 Briarcliff Dr
Anchorage AK 99508

Call Sign: KC8NOY
Michell B Ammann
715 Bridgestone Ct
Anchorage AK 99518

Call Sign: KL3FV
Christopher M Bryant
4201 Bridle Cir
Anchorage AK 99517

Call Sign: KL2YZ
Rhonda M Anderson
4221 Bridle Cir
Anchorage AK 99517

Call Sign: KL7HDY
Robert J Zarkovich
9501 Brien St
Anchorage AK 99516

Call Sign: WL7AP
Andy B Fyodorov
2041 Brigadier Dr
Anchorage AK 99507

Call Sign: KL3GJ
Barney L Baty
10653 Brigantine Cir
Anchorage AK 99515

Call Sign: KL0IW
Louis-Philippe L Hammond
6001 Bristol Dr
Anchorage AK 99516

Call Sign: KL7IKV
Lynn R Hammond III
6001 Bristol Dr
Anchorage AK 99516

Call Sign: KL3LP
Matthew L Peltier
2806 Brittany Dr
Anchorage AK 99504

Call Sign: AL3M

Andrew T Driggers
1102 Broaddus St Apt 1
Anchorage AK 995153064

Call Sign: N4HZU
Andrew T Driggers
1102 Broaddus St Apt 1
Anchorage AK 995153064

Call Sign: KL1UT
Joshua R Stroud
8691 Brookridge Dr
Anchorage AK 99504

Call Sign: NL7BL
Craig B Leuthe
3921 Bryant Ridge Place
Anchorage AK 99504

Call Sign: KC0LLL
Eric C Cannon
7350 Bulen Dr
Anchorage AK 99507

Call Sign: NL7AD
Guy H Rossini
100 Bunnell St 1B
Anchorage AK 99508

Call Sign: WL7BQL
Cameron J Stewart
1700 Burlington St
Anchorage AK 99508

Call Sign: WL7BYL
Kenneth D Steward
6820 Burlwood
Anchorage AK 99507

Call Sign: WL7HZ
James B Steward
6820 Burlwood Dr
Anchorage AK 99507

Call Sign: KL1RT
Eric M Godden
1209 C St
Anchorage AK 99501

Call Sign: KL3AD
Robin M Barber
6441 C St
Anchorage AK 99518

Call Sign: KL7RLB
Richard L Block
2120 C St Ste 100
Anchorage AK 99503

Call Sign: W3JPN
Akihiro Aoki
3601 C St Ste 1300
Anchorage AK 995035921

Call Sign: KL3JB
James A Jones
5007 Cambridge Way
Anchorage AK 99503

Call Sign: KL7ZM
Richard A Whitney
2925 Campbell Airstrip Rd
Anchorage AK 99504

Call Sign: KL2SC
Cameron D Hokenson
3043 Campbell Airstrip Rd
Anchorage AK 99504

Call Sign: AL7BK
Lance W Dunbar
3153 Campbell Airstrip Rd
Anchorage AK 99504

Call Sign: WL7VH
Ned W Lewis
9300 Campbell Ter
Anchorage AK 99515

Call Sign: KL1NL
Bradley D Smith
7811 Canal St
Anchorage AK 99502

Call Sign: NL7YA
William A Weeks
7811 Canal St
Anchorage AK 99502

Call Sign: NL7NP
Robert L Schwebel
4801 Canterbury Way
Anchorage AK 99503

Call Sign: KL4C
James C Brown
5273 Cape Seville Dr
Anchorage AK 99516

Call Sign: KL3KF
Glynn S Jones
5424 Cape Seville Dr
Anchorage AK 99516

Call Sign: KL3AH
Timothy A Kyle
2911 Capstan Dr
Anchorage AK 99516

Call Sign: KL2RL
Joel F Breiner
2932 Captain Cook Estate Cir
Anchorage AK 99517

Call Sign: WL7GR
Roy W Snyder Jr
2909 Carnaby Way
Anchorage AK 99504

Call Sign: KL1RY
Luke H Smith
4811 Carousel Cir
Anchorage AK 99502

Call Sign: N5WE
William C Edmonds Sr
2010 Casey Cusack Loop
Anchorage AK 99515

Call Sign: NH7AQ
John David Kerley
2011 Casey Cusack Loop
Anchorage AK 99515

Call Sign: KL0OQ
Dennis W Whittenburg
4962 Castle Ct
Anchorage AK 99508

Call Sign: KL0CB
Wanda L Pearce
4965 Castle Ct
Anchorage AK 99504

Call Sign: NL7OO
Gerard F Johnson
601 Cedar Park Cir
Anchorage AK 99515

Call Sign: KL0LI
Alan B Caruth
7908 Chaimi Loop

Anchorage AK 99504

Call Sign: KL7FRO
Robert M Holt
12844 Chapel Cir
Anchorage AK 99516

Call Sign: KL2HI
Hugh A Mclaughlin
7820 Charlotte Cir
Anchorage AK 99502

Call Sign: KL2NU
Vicky L Mclaughlin
7820 Charlotte Cir
Anchorage AK 99502

Call Sign: K5RD
Ralph Dahlstrom
7841 Charlotte Place
Anchorage AK 995024294

Call Sign: KD7TOJ
Tim Wainscott
1532 Charter Cir
Anchorage AK 99508

Call Sign: NL7WQ
Mickey W Bettis
4206 Checkmate
Anchorage AK 99508

Call Sign: NL7DK
Harvey E Rookus
3310 Checkmate Dr
Anchorage AK 99508

Call Sign: WL7CSN
Charles T Osborn
3241 Cherry
Anchorage AK 99504

Call Sign: AL7GA
Kenneth J Perry
3420 Cherry St
Anchorage AK 995044121

Call Sign: KL7IHV
David H Barrett
4122 Chess Dr
Anchorage AK 99504

Call Sign: KL3HU
James A Medaris

5643 Chilkoot Ct
Anchorage AK 99504

Call Sign: N7IA
Gary N Dixon
8060 Chipper Tree Cir
Anchorage AK 99507

Call Sign: KL7FHX
Fielder G Dowding
909 Chugach Way Spc 35
Anchorage AK 995035667

Call Sign: KL2TH
David G Summerfeldt II
2050 Churchill Dr
Anchorage AK 99517

Call Sign: AL7GP
Horace N Maxwell Jr
7061 Clairmont Cir
Anchorage AK 99507

Call Sign: WL7CFA
Marium L Clare
10901 Clare Cir
Anchorage AK 99516

Call Sign: KL1QI
David J Coleman
650 Clipper Ship Ct
Anchorage AK 99515

Call Sign: KL1HV
Scott Dahlbeck
6421 Cobblecreek Cir
Anchorage AK 99507

Call Sign: KL1VK
Roger R Saft
6359 Colgate Dr
Anchorage AK 995043305

Call Sign: NL7RW
Jimmy D Platt
5810 College Dr
Anchorage AK 99504

Call Sign: KL7IUJ
Curtis M Harris
6242 Collins Way
Anchorage AK 99502

Call Sign: KU6Z

Bixler P Mcclure
6800 Colonial Ct 4
Anchorage AK 99502

Call Sign: KL3BC
Joey A Alexander
1811 Colony Place
Anchorage AK 99507

Call Sign: KL2FO
Sharon Kay
1413 Columbine St
Anchorage AK 99508

Call Sign: AL7PU
Ronald G Hallmark
9740 Conifer St
Anchorage AK 99516

Call Sign: NL7G
Michael J Baker
6310 Connors Trail
Anchorage AK 99502

Call Sign: WL7CVX
N S Kuparuk Amateur Radio
Club
Conoco Phillips Alaska Inc
Anchorage AK 995196105

Call Sign: KL7NSK
N S Kuparuk Amateur Radio
Club
Conoco Phillips Alaska Inc
Anchorage AK 995196105

Call Sign: AL7CW
N S Kuparuk Amateur Radio
Club
Conoco Phillips Alaska Inc
Anchorage AK 995196105

Call Sign: KL7JJQ
Robert L Hunt
4355 Constellation Ave
Anchorage AK 99517

Call Sign: NL7LN
James L Brenner
10521 Constitution St
Anchorage AK 99515

Call Sign: NL7TC
Susan R Brenner

10521 Constitution St
Anchorage AK 99515

Call Sign: KL7CU
Sheila R Berticevich
3306 Cope St
Anchorage AK 99503

Call Sign: NL7FM
Thomas G Berticevich
3306 Cope St
Anchorage AK 99503

Call Sign: KL1GX
Kanoe A Barlow
4206 Cope St
Anchorage AK 99503

Call Sign: KL1GY
Noa M Barlow
4206 Cope St
Anchorage AK 99603

Call Sign: KL0AS
Clyde N Mc Curdy II
3938 Cope St 6
Anchorage AK 99509

Call Sign: WL7DF
Larry T Coleman
2451 Copperwood Dr
Anchorage AK 99516

Call Sign: KL2LL
Jaime P Mencias
2510 Copperwood Dr
Anchorage AK 99516

Call Sign: KL3IK
Mark E Richey
960 Coral Ln
Anchorage AK 99515

Call Sign: KL3MR
Mark E Richey
960 Coral Ln
Anchorage AK 99515

Call Sign: KL3FU
Jacob P Stepanoff
3530 Corona Cir
Anchorage AK 99517

Call Sign: KL1XW

Philip M Mieczynski
6121 Country Ln Cir
Anchorage AK 99504

Call Sign: KE5DQV
Eric M Bressler
3840 Coventry Dr
Anchorage AK 99507

Call Sign: KE5FOC
Amanda L Bressler
3840 Coventry Dr
Anchorage AK 99507

Call Sign: KL3KH
Eric M Bressler
3840 Coventry Dr
Anchorage AK 99507

Call Sign: KL3KI
Amanda L Bressler
3840 Coventry Dr
Anchorage AK 99507

Call Sign: KL3IS
Peter C Pritchard
1112 Covington Ct
Anchorage AK 99503

Call Sign: KL7EWR
June E Fowler
2022 Crataegus Cir
Anchorage AK 99508

Call Sign: KL2TT
Kenneth H Holmes
7880 Creekside Center Dr 2
Anchorage AK 99504

Call Sign: KL7CCI
Ted R Cadman
3212 Creekside Dr
Anchorage AK 99504

Call Sign: KL1DK
Leon J Smith
3300 Creekside Dr
Anchorage AK 99504

Call Sign: AL7TA
Leon J Smith
3300 Creekside Dr
Anchorage AK 99504

Call Sign: WL7SQ
Matthew D Kerr
6520 Crooked Tree
Anchorage AK 995077001

Call Sign: K9ETM
Gregory S Maatta
8700 Cross Pointe Loop
Anchorage AK 99504

Call Sign: KL3DW
Michele D Hurst
2512 Curlew Cir
Anchorage AK 99502

Call Sign: AL7AS
David B Hingst
10610 Cutter Cir
Anchorage AK 995152725

Call Sign: KL7YA
Gerald J Rapp
6885 Cutty Sark St
Anchorage AK 995022808

Call Sign: KL0AI
Charlie D Starner
429 D St Apt 219
Anchorage AK 99501

Call Sign: WL7GZ
Ty W Hardt
473 Dailey 13
Anchorage AK 99515

Call Sign: KL2HP
Martin E Tirador
256 Dailey Ave
Anchorage AK 99515

Call Sign: N4ERF
Joel W Spivey
433 Dailey Ave Nr 11
Anchorage AK 99515

Call Sign: N7HHH
Glenn A Ferris
4001 Dale St 216
Anchorage AK 99508

Call Sign: K7DOA
David D Mc Neil
1800 Dare Ave
Anchorage AK 99515

Call Sign: WL7CNM
Hal R Horton
3010 Dartmouth St
Anchorage AK 99508

Call Sign: W6DDP
Richard F Barnes
936 David Place
Anchorage AK 99501

Call Sign: KL1IU
Richard F Barnes
936 David Place
Anchorage AK 99501

Call Sign: NL7PF
Jeanne L Hitchings
4915 De Armoun Rd
Anchorage AK 995163625

Call Sign: WL7WY
Jack K Vandelaar
6311 Debarr Rd 411
Anchorage AK 99504

Call Sign: KL1PM
Pablo N Perez
4110 Debarr Rd Ep E15
Anchorage AK 99508

Call Sign: WL7ARV
George W Maguire
4110 Debarr Rd Space D3
Anchorage AK 99508

Call Sign: WL7PT
Terry T Albert
7800 Debarr Sp 64
Anchorage AK 99504

Call Sign: WL7CRN
Stuart C Memering
4030 Defiance St
Anchorage AK 99504

Call Sign: KL3HT
Grant S Perry
1563 Demeure Place
Anchorage AK 99508

Call Sign: KL7ION
Polar Amateur Rad Klub Of Ak
1030 Denali

Anchorage AK 99501

Call Sign: KL7YF
Frederick L Marvin
1030 Denali
Anchorage AK 99501

Call Sign: NL7DL
Lillian Marvin
1030 Denali
Anchorage AK 99501

Call Sign: KL7HDJ
Richard W Nehls
1201 Denali St 307
Anchorage AK 99501

Call Sign: N4CZB
Paul M Barzler
2841 Devin Cir
Anchorage AK 99516

Call Sign: WL7BYJ
Randy W Brooks
13411 Diggins Dr
Anchorage AK 99515

Call Sign: KL0XH
Michael K Lamagdeleine
1816 Dimond Dr
Anchorage AK 995071308

Call Sign: WL7CSA
Brant D Pierce
2535 Discovery Ct
Anchorage AK 995171238

Call Sign: KL1MO
Mark J Bly
11400 Doggie Ave
Anchorage AK 99507

Call Sign: KL1M
Mark J Bly
11400 Doggie Ave
Anchorage AK 99507

Call Sign: WL7DR
Richard A Willard
6131 Doil Cir
Anchorage AK 99507

Call Sign: KL0LO
Loren H Stickley

2005 Dolly Varden Ave
Anchorage AK 99516

Call Sign: KL1QW
Walter A Glooschenko
6017 Doncaster Dr
Anchorage AK 995043233

Call Sign: AL2H
Walter A Glooschenko
6017 Doncaster Dr
Anchorage AK 995043233

Call Sign: AD5CM
Lola C Nolan
355 Donna Dr 9
Anchorage AK 99504

Call Sign: KL2A
Jonathan R Kimball
2915 Donnington Dr
Anchorage AK 99504

Call Sign: KL2X
Bernd Langer
2915 Donnington Dr
Anchorage AK 99504

Call Sign: AL7KQ
Bernd Langer
2915 Donnington Dr
Anchorage AK 99504

Call Sign: KL7PU
Jerome R George III
3640 Dora
Anchorage AK 99516

Call Sign: KL0KO
Myron K Meinhardt
3601 Doroshin Ave Box 110336
Anchorage AK 99516

Call Sign: WL7BYN
John M Sandiford
5819 Dow Place A
Anchorage AK 99507

Call Sign: WL7AA
James R Ely
140 Dowling Rd
Anchorage AK 99518

Call Sign: WL7CUW

Emily A Brooking
6101 Downey Finch Dr
Anchorage AK 99516

Call Sign: WL7CCS
Lawrence M Whiting
7300 Durenda Cir
Anchorage AK 99507

Call Sign: KL0NC
Arnie G Link II
2220 Duvoy Ct
Anchorage AK 99502

Call Sign: KL1ZG
Paul H Kvernplassen
4220 East 104th Ave
Anchorage AK 99507

Call Sign: KG4OXD
Kenneth M Schulz
4721 East 104th Ave
Anchorage AK 99507

Call Sign: KL0UP
Marion C Daniel
926 East 10th Ave
Anchorage AK 99501

Call Sign: KL2PY
Britt M Mccarthy
6941 East 10th Ave 2
Anchorage AK 99504

Call Sign: KC0TQF
Mark B West Jr
3131 East 112th Ave
Anchorage AK 99516

Call Sign: AH0AH
Raj D Choudhury
6200 East 112th Ave
Anchorage AK 99516

Call Sign: KL0RE
Dan Thomson
6300 East 112th Ave
Anchorage AK 995161893

Call Sign: KL7ZQ
Richard J Evans
6511 East 11th
Anchorage AK 99504

Call Sign: KL2FP
James A Short
110 East 11th Ave Apt 21
Anchorage AK 99501

Call Sign: KL7TL
Patsy J Evans
6511 East 11th St
Anchorage AK 99504

Call Sign: N8KYW
Timothy P Nixon
308 East 12th Ave
Anchorage AK 99501

Call Sign: AL7PA
Charles R Skow
843 East 12th Ave 4
Anchorage AK 99501

Call Sign: KL3BN
Rachel A Gwizdak
6008 East 12th Ave 6
Anchorage AK 99504

Call Sign: KE7RVE
George Jarvi
403 East 12th Ave Apt 1
Anchorage AK 99501

Call Sign: KL2TJ
Wayne A Carter
305 East 13th Ave
Anchorage AK 99501

Call Sign: KL1LG
Joseph M Mactavish
805 East 13th Ave
Anchorage AK 99501

Call Sign: KL0DU
Foster E Leng
805 East 13th Ave
Anchorage AK 99501

Call Sign: WL7SO
John F Blasko
3501 East 144th
Anchorage AK 99516

Call Sign: WL7HF
Christian O Wilkins
6025 East 144th Ave
Anchorage AK 995164355

Call Sign: KL2HJ
Adam F Grove
4701 East 145th Ave
Anchorage AK 99516

Call Sign: KL7WS
Robert C Pelz
2800 East 15th Ave
Anchorage AK 99508

Call Sign: KL2VI
Michael W Demolina
6101 East 162nd Ave
Anchorage AK 99516

Call Sign: KL3BJ
Chantz M Gaither
201 East 16th Ave 312
Anchorage AK 99501

Call Sign: KL7SB
Stephen H Bloom
1023 East 17th Ave
Anchorage AK 99501

Call Sign: KL7AMY
Amy Whinston
1023 East 17th Ave
Anchorage AK 99501

Call Sign: KB2JWV
Amy Whinston
1023 East 17th Ave
Anchorage AK 99501

Call Sign: WL7HN
Eddie C Beasley Jr
1441 East 17th Ave 10
Anchorage AK 99501

Call Sign: WL7KP
Maria M Beasley
1441 East 17th Ave 10
Anchorage AK 99501

Call Sign: KL2QO
Dustin D Rider
3434 East 18th Ave
Anchorage AK 99508

Call Sign: WL7BO
James R Lane
8310 East 20th

Anchorage AK 99504

Call Sign: KL2OA
Garry J Wallan
7215 East 20th Ave
Anchorage AK 99504

Call Sign: KL7RX
Frank G Pratt Jr
7446 East 20th Ave
Anchorage AK 99504

Call Sign: KL7FSE
Frank G Pratt Jr
7446 East 20th Ave
Anchorage AK 99504

Call Sign: NL7A
John J Jones
8260 East 20th Ave
Anchorage AK 99504

Call Sign: KL1JG
Fidel O Castellanos
919 East 20th Ave C
Anchorage AK 99501

Call Sign: KL2JZ
Robert E Richie
7240 East 21st Ave
Anchorage AK 99504

Call Sign: KL7GM
William J Barber
5201 East 22nd Ave
Anchorage AK 995083705

Call Sign: KC7COW
Justin G Bennett
5311 East 22nd Ave Apt A
Anchorage AK 99508

Call Sign: KC7HPF
Chelly D Bennett
5311 East 22nd Ave Apt A
Anchorage AK 99508

Call Sign: KL3FE
Taylor P Aikens
5223 East 24th 15
Anchorage AK 99508

Call Sign: NL7J
Michael A Baker

5223 East 24th 15
Anchorage AK 99508

Call Sign: KL0AR
Michael A Baker
5223 East 24th 15
Anchorage AK 99508

Call Sign: KL3FK
Ivan W Wilkison
5223 East 24th Ave 19
Anchorage AK 99508

Call Sign: WL7CPD
Michael R Willoya
5205 East 26th Apt 1
Anchorage AK 99508

Call Sign: WL7CDC
Douglas T Stowers
1051 East 26th Ave
Anchorage AK 99508

Call Sign: KI4VAK
Philip E Martin
5440 East 26th Ave 19
Anchorage AK 99508

Call Sign: KL7GBC
Benjamin O Walters Jr
1034 East 27th Ave
Anchorage AK 99508

Call Sign: KL7BDG
Richard M Zook
1710 East 27th Ave
Anchorage AK 995084017

Call Sign: KL2KA
Haris Velic
6406 East 31st Ave
Anchorage AK 99504

Call Sign: WL7COA
Sean M Gould
7121 East 34th
Anchorage AK 99504

Call Sign: KL7AID
Elbert C Scott
1925 East 37th Ave
Anchorage AK 99508

Call Sign: NL7VU

Adam J Spater
2020 East 39th Ave
Anchorage AK 99508

Call Sign: WL7CTE
Ralph G Hartke Jr
4618 East 3rd Ave
Anchorage AK 995082212

Call Sign: KL0UQ
Kyle L Maze
3230 East 41st Ave A
Anchorage AK 99508

Call Sign: WL7CCI
Kathleen A Thomas
6200 East 41st Ct Apt 4
Anchorage AK 99504

Call Sign: WL7ZS
Mark L Schellhorn
810 East 42nd 20
Anchorage AK 99503

Call Sign: NL7SQ
Rip W Curtis
2501 East 42nd Ave
Anchorage AK 99508

Call Sign: WL7BTE
Richard W Curtis
2501 East 42nd Ave
Anchorage AK 99508

Call Sign: N3GQV
Michael P Zeglen
4938 East 43rd Ave A6
Anchorage AK 99508

Call Sign: KL3GT
Michael R Ford
3130 East 46th 1
Anchorage AK 99507

Call Sign: KL3GX
Jennifer L Sherwin
3130 East 46th 1
Anchorage AK 99507

Call Sign: KL3BM
Paul D Grimsley
3318 East 46th Ave
Anchorage AK 99507

Call Sign: KL2JD
Alfred H Andre
917 East 46th Ct C
Anchorage AK 99503

Call Sign: AL2L
Joseph S Koford
2360 East 48th St Unit B
Anchorage AK 99507

Call Sign: KL3GR
Holly M De Land
2303 East 49th Ct
Anchorage AK 99507

Call Sign: KL2XF
James A Bush
337 East 4th Ave
Anchorage AK 99501

Call Sign: WL7COR
Charles R Berry
1020 East 4th Ave
Anchorage AK 99501

Call Sign: KL2UY
Matt A Schroepfer
337 East 4th Ave 107
Anchorage AK 99501

Call Sign: KL2VU
Gregory S Maatta
5300 East 4th Ave 211
Anchorage AK 99508

Call Sign: KL3LS
Michelle A Semerad
337 East 4th Ave 69
Anchorage AK 99501

Call Sign: AL7IF
Louis M Tozzi Jr
330 East 4th Ave Ste 206
Anchorage AK 99501

Call Sign: KL3LU
Christopher R Ferguson
2140 East 56th Ave 111
Anchorage AK 99507

Call Sign: KB2ZME
Matthew C Krueger
2241 East 56th Ave 7
Anchorage AK 99507

Call Sign: KG6VCU
Michael S Marshall
2160 East 56th Ave Apt A106
Anchorage AK 99507

Call Sign: K4JCB
James C Brown
2176 East 56th Ave N102
Anchorage AK 99507

Call Sign: KL2VQ
Dennis J Stankewich
1736 East 58th Cir
Anchorage AK 99507

Call Sign: KL2PI
Melissa B Bodarte
4426 East 5th Ave
Anchorage AK 99508

Call Sign: KL2BH
Andrew W Demos
2110 East 5th Ave   G102
Anchorage AK 99507

Call Sign: KL3AF
Jodi A Gongora
3610 East 66th
Anchorage AK 99502

Call Sign: KL3FG
James O Wilkinson
2341 East 66th Ave
Anchorage AK 99507

Call Sign: KL3KP
Adam C Fredericksen
3921 East 66th Ave
Anchorage AK 99507

Call Sign: KL2BD
Kenneth R Baptiste
3924 East 66th Ave
Anchorage AK 99507

Call Sign: KL2TO
Joey A Edades
4000 East 66th Ave
Anchorage AK 99507

Call Sign: KL3GL
Susan J Corinth
3847 East 67th Ave

Anchorage AK 99507

Call Sign: N0XKY
Jesse W Glosser
4021 East 67th Ave
Anchorage AK 99507

Call Sign: KL0XK
Donald E Koehler
4819 East 6th Ave
Anchorage AK 99508

Call Sign: KL7EC
Pete B Aiman
7309 East 6th Ave
Anchorage AK 99504

Call Sign: WL7BPE
James F Strang
5901 East 6th Space 274
Anchorage AK 99504

Call Sign: WL7DZ
Alan C Frensley
646 East 72nd
Anchorage AK 99518

Call Sign: KL7FFY
Kenneth R Baptiste
621 East 73rd
Anchorage AK 99518

Call Sign: KL0HM
Howard W Wright Jr
835 East 74th Ave
Anchorage AK 99518

Call Sign: KL2NX
Leanna D Rein
647 East 74th Ave 2
Anchorage AK 99518

Call Sign: KC6RJW
Ulla M Rasilainen
734 East 76th Ave 2
Anchorage AK 99518

Call Sign: KL7AMH
John B Griffin
4530 East 7th Ave
Anchorage AK 99508

Call Sign: KL2QM
Lisa M Howe

221 East 7th Ave 115
Anchorage AK 99501

Call Sign: WB7NCV
Chester C Bostek
221 East 7th Ave 115
Anchorage AK 99501

Call Sign: NL7JQ
John W Platt
2621 East 84th Ave
Anchorage AK 995073601

Call Sign: KL3FI
Rick D Pruett
3821 East 86th Ave
Anchorage AK 99507

Call Sign: WL7CVW
American Red Cross Of Alaska
Amateur Radio Club
235 East 8th Ave - Ste 200
Anchorage AK 99501

Call Sign: KL7ARC
American Red Cross Of Alaska
Amateur Radio Club
235 East 8th Ave - Ste 200
Anchorage AK 99501

Call Sign: WL7CVH
Alaska Repeater Linking
Association
1250 East 8th Ave 1046
Anchorage AK 99501

Call Sign: KL3K
Alaska Repeater Linking
Association
1250 East 8th Ave 1046
Anchorage AK 99501

Call Sign: KL2OS
David A Koch
5702 East 97th Ave
Anchorage AK 99507

Call Sign: KL2TX
Dwayne D Jones
5720 East 97th Ave
Anchorage AK 99507

Call Sign: WL7CNP
Susan A Rostin

5540 East 99th Ave
Anchorage AK 99516

Call Sign: KL3AE
David A Elliott
5541 East 99th Ave
Anchorage AK 99507

Call Sign: KL1LO
Ryan M Sandel
900 East Benson Mb 12-4
Anchorage AK 99508

Call Sign: AL7J
Kyle W Sandel
900 East Benson Mb 12-4
Anchorage AK 99508

Call Sign: WL7CVE
D John Mckay
117 East Cook Ave
Anchorage AK 99501

Call Sign: KL7AVX
John W Mc Queen
1928 East Dimond Blvd
Anchorage AK 995073426

Call Sign: KL2IH
William A Moore
205 East Dimond Blvd 223
Anchorage AK 99515

Call Sign: KL7WAM
William A Moore
205 East Dimond Blvd 223
Anchorage AK 99515

Call Sign: WL7S
Tom J Sockolosky
1013 East Dimond Blvd 257
Anchorage AK 99515

Call Sign: WL7AUS
Billie B Wilson
1013 East Dimond Ste 530
Anchorage AK 99515

Call Sign: KD7GFG
Pere L Davison
8035 East Frostline Ct
Anchorage AK 99507

Call Sign: WL7YC

David L Erickson
421 East Harvard Ave 1
Anchorage AK 99501

Call Sign: KL7JJH
David L Byrd
2900 East Huffman Rd
Anchorage AK 995162017

Call Sign: KL0YP
Brady W Turner
1120 East Huffman Rd 307
Anchorage AK 99515

Call Sign: WL7LY
Carl A Peterson
1330 East Huffman Rd 408
Anchorage AK 99515

Call Sign: KL1WU
Robert E Mcfarlane
13201 East Mccabe Cir
Anchorage AK 99516

Call Sign: WL7CWC
Cortaro Contest Club
5432 East Northern Lights 130
Anchorage AK 995084713

Call Sign: KL0ON
Joseph J Tracanna
5432 East Northern Lights Blvd
132
Anchorage AK 99508

Call Sign: AL1J
Joseph J Tracanna
5432 East Northern Lights Blvd
132
Anchorage AK 99508

Call Sign: KL7CL
Clare Lattimore
5432 East Northern Lights Blvd
431
Anchorage AK 995084713

Call Sign: NL7ME
Clare Lattimore
5432 East Northern Lights Blvd
431
Anchorage AK 995084713

Call Sign: KL1CR

Michael W Singsaas
5201 East Northern Lights Blvd
5E
Anchorage AK 99508

Call Sign: KL1RF
George M Ramos
2440 East Tudor 1149
Anchorage AK 99507

Call Sign: KL7DG
John P Trent
1700 East Tudor Rd
Anchorage AK 99507

Call Sign: WL7ABU
William D Stafford
2440 East Tudor Rd   Pmb 100
Anchorage AK 99507

Call Sign: WL7GKM
Gregory K Martin
2440 East Tudor Rd 302
Anchorage AK 99507

Call Sign: WL7CF
Timothy L Lightner
1805 East Tudor Rd A102
Anchorage AK 995071051

Call Sign: KL2YG
Kevin G Passa
2440 East Tudor Rd 176
Anchorage AK 99507

Call Sign: KL7FR
Sandra L Gagnon
2440 East Tudor Rd 367
Anchorage AK 99507

Call Sign: KE5WHT
Jonathan J Givens
2440 East Tudor Rd 861
Anchorage AK 99507

Call Sign: KE5WHU
Austin A Givens
2440 East Tudor Rd 861
Anchorage AK 99507

Call Sign: KC5YOB
Lora Ann Givens
2440 East Tudor Rd 861
Anchorage AK 99507

Call Sign: N5HPW
James A Givens IV
2440 East Tudor Rd 861
Anchorage AK 99507

Call Sign: KL7HOU
Joel V R Gaines
2440 East Tudor Rd Ste 325
Anchorage AK 99507

Call Sign: KC7BUL
Lynda D Clark
7524 Eastbrook Cir
Anchorage AK 99521

Call Sign: KL7SS
Michael E Stichick
2067 Eastridge Dr
Anchorage AK 995015719

Call Sign: KL1TZ
Karen M Walker
1640 Eastridge Dr 301
Anchorage AK 99501

Call Sign: KL7UU
Karen M Walker
1640 Eastridge Dr 301
Anchorage AK 99501

Call Sign: KL7KK
Karen M Walker
1640 Eastridge Dr 301
Anchorage AK 99501

Call Sign: KL7KW
Karen M Walker
1640 Eastridge Dr 301
Anchorage AK 99501

Call Sign: WL7EN
Robert K Kelly Jr
13530 Ebbtide Cir
Anchorage AK 99516

Call Sign: WL7BPZ
Joseph Stubbins
4020 Edinburg
Anchorage AK 99515

Call Sign: KL0BW
Chris A Richardson
4220 Edinburgh Dr

Anchorage AK 99502

Call Sign: KL7EH
Michael E Westley
4621 Edinburgh Dr
Anchorage AK 99515

Call Sign: KL3BU
Michael T Williams
351 Egavik Dr
Anchorage AK 99503

Call Sign: KL1JY
William H Bayless
420 Egavik Dr
Anchorage AK 99503

Call Sign: KC7MPY
Olen R Northern Jr
404 Eklutna Unit A
Anchorage AK 995042141

Call Sign: KL2PL
Sherry F Worthy
807 Elaine Dr
Anchorage AK 99504

Call Sign: KA7TMU
Laurie A Gangi
914 Elaine Dr
Anchorage AK 99504

Call Sign: NL7PB
Anthony P Gangi
914 Elaine Dr
Anchorage AK 99504

Call Sign: KL0KG
Oliver B Coolidge
1761 Elcadore Dr A 3
Anchorage AK 99507

Call Sign: WL7BZA
Linda H Plumb
1254 Elegante Ln
Anchorage AK 99501

Call Sign: KL3HA
Stephanie L Smith
1407 Elmendorf Dr
Anchorage AK 99504

Call Sign: WD6BRK
Peter P Rodriguez Jr

1409 Elmendorf Dr
Anchorage AK 99504

Call Sign: KL3AS
Siaosi Soane
1410 Elmendorf Dr
Anchorage AK 99504

Call Sign: NL7WJ
Kenneth F Lower
1419 Elmendorf Dr
Anchorage AK 99504

Call Sign: KL2NY
Jonathan P Walker
13100 Elmhurst Cir
Anchorage AK 99515

Call Sign: WL7CWX
Anchorage Police Department
Amateur Radio Club
4501 Elmore Rd
Anchorage AK 99507

Call Sign: KL7APD
Anchorage Police Department
Amateur Radio Club
4501 Elmore Rd
Anchorage AK 99507

Call Sign: KL0MQ
Jayson D Knutson
13741 Elmore Rd
Anchorage AK 99516

Call Sign: KC2HRV
Dustin D Rider
10613 Elmore Rd Apt 3
Anchorage AK 99507

Call Sign: KL2PF
Michael A Busey
8222 Endicott St
Anchorage AK 99502

Call Sign: KL1ER
Robert A Doehl
2024 Esquire Dr
Anchorage AK 99517

Call Sign: AL2Y
Pedro Del Compare
2024 Esquire Dr
Anchorage AK 995171345

Call Sign: N5XLI
Carl J London Sr
2048 Esquire Dr
Anchorage AK 99517

Call Sign: N2CXH
Pedro Del Compare
2024 Esquire Dri
Anchorage AK 995171345

Call Sign: KL0VX
Dinah M Burk
2205 Euerka St 246
Anchorage AK 99503

Call Sign: KL1WF
Charles A Baker
3421 Evergreen
Anchorage AK 99504

Call Sign: KB0APK
Charles A Baker
3421 Evergreen
Anchorage AK 99504

Call Sign: N7JLR
Scott A Edson
10300 Evergreen
Anchorage AK 99516

Call Sign: KL2SO
Mathew M Olson
1417 F St
Anchorage AK 99501

Call Sign: KL2WZ
Laurence Blakely
1308 F St 3
Anchorage AK 99501

Call Sign: KL7MW
Mark L Wenig
2222 Fairbanks St
Anchorage AK 99503

Call Sign: KL7Z
William R Vallee
7009 Fairweather Dr
Anchorage AK 99518

Call Sign: KL2SD
Lee A Wells
7009 Fairweather Dr

Anchorage AK 99518

Call Sign: KL7LW
Lee A Wells
7009 Fairweather Dr
Anchorage AK 99518

Call Sign: KL7G
South Central Radio Club
7009 Fairweather Dr
Anchorage AK 99518

Call Sign: WL7CWD
Deadhorse Amateur Radio
Association
7009 Fairweather Dr
Anchorage AK 99518

Call Sign: WL7YN
Fredrick D Byron
1210 Farrow Cir
Anchorage AK 995042238

Call Sign: NL7UO
Gary L De Haven
219 Fawn Ct
Anchorage AK 99515

Call Sign: KL0PQ
Richard E Jonsson
223 Fawn Ct
Anchorage AK 995153471

Call Sign: KD7FUL
Catherine S Roso
320 Fischer Ave B
Anchorage AK 99518

Call Sign: KL0QJ
Richard J Harkness
10753 Flagship Cir
Anchorage AK 99515

Call Sign: WL7MX
Arthur T Kohler
8660 Flamingo Dr
Anchorage AK 99502

Call Sign: KL7CP
Clyde D Plunkett
4901 Folker St
Anchorage AK 99507

Call Sign: AL7ER

Bret F Haering
2100 Forest Park Dr
Anchorage AK 995171320

Call Sign: KL7JHV
John H Bowerman
2141 Forest Park Dr
Anchorage AK 99517

Call Sign: KL2AZ
Richard P Tweet
2442 Forest Park Dr
Anchorage AK 99517

Call Sign: KL2PG
Eric C Dale
2310 Forest Park Dr 3
Anchorage AK 99517

Call Sign: KL3KZ
John K Harju
4401 Forest Rd 1
Anchorage AK 99517

Call Sign: KL0YG
Robert P Wagner
8920 Forest Village Dr
Anchorage AK 99502

Call Sign: NL7XT
Lowell A Krise
4301 Forrest Rd 3
Anchorage AK 99517

Call Sign: KL7HAB
David E Lawrence
13040 Foster Rd
Anchorage AK 99516

Call Sign: WL7NQ
Thea L Dowling
5550 Four Winds Dr
Anchorage AK 99518

Call Sign: KL9PC
Paul W Carter
7422 Foxridge Way 12C
Anchorage AK 99518

Call Sign: WA4NJE
Richard K Miller
410 Fredricks Dr
Anchorage AK 995041162

Call Sign: KL2DJ
Nolan J Willis
444 Fredricks Dr
Anchorage AK 99504

Call Sign: WL7FU
Robert S Gunson
6730 Freebird Cir
Anchorage AK 99507

Call Sign: KL0TM
Joel L Collins
1030 Friendly Ln
Anchorage AK 99504

Call Sign: KL0SK
William H Ross
1010 Friendly Ln Apt 3
Anchorage AK 995042022

Call Sign: KL7TG
Blaine G Berg
4210 Frontier Ln
Anchorage AK 995162219

Call Sign: NL7RE
Linda S Berg
4210 Frontier Ln
Anchorage AK 995162219

Call Sign: AL7GS
Howard P Hornsby Jr
1568 G St
Anchorage AK 99501

Call Sign: WL7CHE
Paul J Cossman
645 G St 892
Anchorage AK 99501

Call Sign: KL2MY
Diane L Dughman
4140 Galactica Dr
Anchorage AK 99517

Call Sign: KL0QK
William R Theuer
4321 Gannett Cir
Anchorage AK 99504

Call Sign: KC5LKF
Maximilian D Gruner
4208 Garfield St
Anchorage AK 99503

Call Sign: KC5LKG
Amy L Loyd
4208 Garfield St
Anchorage AK 99503

Call Sign: KL7GNP
John C A Bierman
4304 Garfield St
Anchorage AK 995036438

Call Sign: KB1QCD
Janis A Abbott
3720 Gary Cooper Cir
Anchorage AK 99507

Call Sign: KB1QCE
Allen L Abbott
3720 Gary Cooper Cir
Anchorage AK 99507

Call Sign: KL1XU
John P Jones
5615 Gatekeeper Ave
Anchorage AK 99504

Call Sign: KL1YG
Margaret A Jones
5615 Gatekeeper Ave
Anchorage AK 99504

Call Sign: KL1HA
Hannah V Beckett
7010 Gibbs Hill Cir
Anchorage AK 99504

Call Sign: KL1HC
Alan S Beckett
7010 Gibbs Hill Cir
Anchorage AK 99504

Call Sign: NL7XQ
Michael S Purcella
3430 Gibstay Cir
Anchorage AK 99516

Call Sign: KL1PB
John W Macclarence
10840 Glazanof Dr
Anchorage AK 99507

Call Sign: KL2YH
Terry L Walters
6821 Gold Kings Cir D8

Anchorage AK 99504

Call Sign: KL1TT
Ross A Henikman
1100 Golden Berry Ave
Anchorage AK 99515

Call Sign: NK5G
Joseph S Koford
8540 Golden St 2
Anchorage AK 99502

Call Sign: WL7CUK
Joseph D Anderson
14250 Golden View Dr
Anchorage AK 99516

Call Sign: KL1LP
Harold D Townsend
14641 Golden View Dr
Anchorage AK 99516

Call Sign: KL2UW
Andrew W Taylor
1130 Goldenberry Ave
Anchorage AK 99515

Call Sign: WL7DQ
Robert L Walker
10132 Gooseberry Place
Anchorage AK 99515

Call Sign: WL7WH
Robert G Prescott
12041 Graiff St
Anchorage AK 99507

Call Sign: KL2KN
Takahiro Kosaka
6242 Green Tree Cir
Anchorage AK 99507

Call Sign: NL7RY
Roger L Sheley
8830 Greenbelt Dr
Anchorage AK 99502

Call Sign: KA9GYQ
John F Knue Jr
1811 Greendale Dr
Anchorage AK 995042921

Call Sign: AL7B
Richard M Mobley

1830 Greendale Dr
Anchorage AK 99504

Call Sign: KL2FC
Michael E Westley
8500 Greenhill Way
Anchorage AK 99502

Call Sign: KL0YH
Peter A Westley
8500 Greenhill Way
Anchorage AK 99502

Call Sign: KL1DV
Benjamin P Westley
8500 Greenhill Way
Anchorage AK 99502

Call Sign: WL7IL
George R Mc Cament Jr
7666 Griffith St
Anchorage AK 99516

Call Sign: KL1KK
Suzan L Hartlieb
3419 Grissom Cir
Anchorage AK 99517

Call Sign: KL0ZC
Gordon W Hartlieb
3419 Grissom Cir
Anchorage AK 99517

Call Sign: KL2SG
Miranda J Johnson
3518 Grissom Cir
Anchorage AK 99517

Call Sign: KL7EQX
Earl R Plumb
1212 H St
Anchorage AK 99501

Call Sign: WL7CQ
Frieda Plumb
1212 H St
Anchorage AK 99501

Call Sign: KL0IU
Susan L Adkison
12420 Hace St
Anchorage AK 99515

Call Sign: WL7NJ

James D Adkison Sr
12420 Hace St
Anchorage AK 99515

Call Sign: WL7YO
Patrick J Worcester
12610 Hace St
Anchorage AK 99515

Call Sign: WL7DS
George R Featherly IV
8121 Harvest Cir
Anchorage AK 99502

Call Sign: KL2IJ
James B Regg
2440 Hastings Ln
Anchorage AK 99504

Call Sign: KL7IBY
Clyde L Bloker
2500 Hastings Ln
Anchorage AK 99504

Call Sign: NL7WF
Pamela K Jennings
3541 Hazen Cir
Anchorage AK 99515

Call Sign: NL7YH
Gerald P Hallgrimson
3520 Heartwood Place
Anchorage AK 99504

Call Sign: N0TPM
Thomas R Renz Jr
1414 Helen Dr
Anchorage AK 99515

Call Sign: KL0VP
Richard L Block
2347 Hialeah Dr
Anchorage AK 99517

Call Sign: KL3LG
Paul Newman
10801 Hideaway Lake Dr
Anchorage AK 995076139

Call Sign: KL1FT
Denise R Haviland
605 Highlander Cir
Anchorage AK 99518

Call Sign: KL0DJ
Arthur S Morton
660 Highlander Cir
Anchorage AK 99518

Call Sign: AL1P
Brian D Sarka
3501 Hiland Dr
Anchorage AK 99504

Call Sign: KL2LM
John M Main
4936 Hillandale Ave
Anchorage AK 99516

Call Sign: KL3HC
Barbara J Pepek
1331 Hillcrest Dr
Anchorage AK 99503

Call Sign: NL7AF
Charles M Bertholf Jr
1361 Hillcrest Dr 205
Anchorage AK 99503

Call Sign: KL7FBS
William C Dibb
10980 Hillside Dr
Anchorage AK 99516

Call Sign: KL7CWM
George B Woodbury Jr
11201 Hillside Dr
Anchorage AK 99516

Call Sign: KL3BE
Juliann A Applegate
3440 Hines Cir
Anchorage AK 99516

Call Sign: KL3GM
Tim D Breidinger
6635 Holly Ln
Anchorage AK 99502

Call Sign: KL3AR
Bruce L Scott
3510 Hollywood Cir
Anchorage AK 99507

Call Sign: KL1HU
James P Hubbard II
701 Hollywood Dr
Anchorage AK 995011222

Call Sign: KL2PX
Ross F Arter
3151 Horizon St
Anchorage AK 99517

Call Sign: AL7OK
John E Hendricks
12840 Huffman Cir
Anchorage AK 99516

Call Sign: KL2YR
Raquel Y Fucci
7381 Huntsmen Cir H
Anchorage AK 99518

Call Sign: KL0DA
David A Bauer
1569 I St
Anchorage AK 995015035

Call Sign: KL2OI
Clarence Davis
1200 I St 809
Anchorage AK 99501

Call Sign: KL0NX
Dennis M Snider
3644 Image Dr
Anchorage AK 99504

Call Sign: KL7S
Michael S Wood
9645 Independence Dr D305
Anchorage AK 99507

Call Sign: K6MW
Michael S Wood
9645 Independence Dr D305
Anchorage AK 99507

Call Sign: KL2UN
Nolan S Oliver
9725 Independence Dr A309
Anchorage AK 99507

Call Sign: KL0LD
Daniel S Jordi
12350 Industry Way 218
Anchorage AK 99515

Call Sign: KL1PA
Patrick W Morrow
4011 Iona Cir

Anchorage AK 99507

Call Sign: KL2ID
Gale M Haller
3908 Iowa Dr
Anchorage AK 99517

Call Sign: KL3LL
John V Long
4002 Iowa Dr 1
Anchorage AK 99517

Call Sign: KL0WY
James V Tatum
1920 Ivan Dr
Anchorage AK 99507

Call Sign: WL7VN
Pamela D Engle
720 Jack St
Anchorage AK 99515

Call Sign: KL0TB
Andrew D Shears
8620 Jade St
Anchorage AK 995025025

Call Sign: KL1UR
Kori E Myers
4306 James Dr
Anchorage AK 99504

Call Sign: KL2US
Destiny M Hacker
4306 James Dr
Anchorage AK 99504

Call Sign: KL1DY
Christopher R Myers
4306 James Dr
Anchorage AK 99504

Call Sign: KL1DJ
Douglas J Myers
4306 James Dr
Anchorage AK 995044647

Call Sign: KL1CS
Kay A Bartlett
13700 Jarvi Dr
Anchorage AK 99515

Call Sign: KL1CT
Lynn P Bartlett

13700 Jarvi Dri
Anchorage AK 99515

Call Sign: KL1KZ
Melvin G Sheppard
2203 Jefferson Ave
Anchorage AK 99517

Call Sign: KL7TO
Alfred W Giebel
8110 Jewel Lake Rd
Anchorage AK 995024255

Call Sign: KD7DUQ
John R Larson Jr
9307 Jewel Lake Rd Number
202
Anchorage AK 99502

Call Sign: NL7RB
Ralph D Montgomery
4800 Jewel Terrace Cir
Anchorage AK 99502

Call Sign: KL3JI
Shannon M Methe
12301 Johns Rd 29
Anchorage AK 99515

Call Sign: KL7HF
Delano U Seay
8425 Jupiter
Anchorage AK 99507

Call Sign: KL7KM
Kenneth M Morton
10830 Kamishak Bay Cir
Anchorage AK 99515

Call Sign: KL3GF
Andrea K Morton
10830 Kamishak Bay Cir
Anchorage AK 99515

Call Sign: KL3GG
Bradley M Morton
10830 Kamishak Bay Cir
Anchorage AK 99515

Call Sign: KL3GH
Scott C Morton
10830 Kamishak Bay Cir
Anchorage AK 99515

Call Sign: KL1HW
Kenneth M Morton
10830 Kamishak Bay Cir
Anchorage AK 99515

Call Sign: KL2XK
Amy E Zaremba
6547 Kara Sue Loop
Anchorage AK 99504

Call Sign: WL7BSH
Kevin L Borgan
13516 Karen St
Anchorage AK 99515

Call Sign: KC7ENM
Damian V Livengood
1308 Karluk St 4
Anchorage AK 99501

Call Sign: KA3ZOI
Katy S Chandler
10920 Kasilof Blvd
Anchorage AK 99507

Call Sign: N3MNF
Jared D Chandler
10920 Kasilof Blvd
Anchorage AK 99507

Call Sign: KL7QN
Bruce P Chandler
10920 Kasilov Blvd
Anchorage AK 99507

Call Sign: WL7NI
Mark A Huelskoetter
5908 Katahdin
Anchorage AK 99502

Call Sign: KL3IF
Duane L Risse
5954 Kathadin Dr
Anchorage AK 99502

Call Sign: KL2ZE
Daehoon Y Chang
9430 Kavik St
Anchorage AK 99502

Call Sign: KL3GN
Charles F Becker
2621 Kelsan Cir
Anchorage AK 99508

Call Sign: AL7JT
William P Barker
5640 Kenai Fjords Loop
Anchorage AK 995024048

Call Sign: KL7MJ
Michael A Mellor
5693 Kenai Fjords Loop
Anchorage AK 99502

Call Sign: AL7MM
Michael A Mellor
5693 Kenai Fjords Loop
Anchorage AK 99502

Call Sign: KL7MJ
Michael A Mellor
5693 Kenai Fjords Loop
Anchorage AK 99502

Call Sign: KL7SI
John Pash
5553 Kennyhill Dr
Anchorage AK 99504

Call Sign: KL0GC
Thomas K Raboin
2409 Kensington Dr
Anchorage AK 995043249

Call Sign: KL7JA
Thomas S Choate
3130 Kenwood Cir
Anchorage AK 99504

Call Sign: KB0TSU
Nathan P Skinner
1515 Kepner Dr
Anchorage AK 99504

Call Sign: WL7VW
Sharon A Carrick
5951 Key Ann Cir
Anchorage AK 99504

Call Sign: NL7DI
Gilbert F Blue
5910 Keyann Cir
Anchorage AK 99504

Call Sign: NL7LW
Lorna M Blue
5910 Keyann Cir

Anchorage AK 99504

Call Sign: NL7PP
Kim Y Evans
7805 Kiana Cir
Anchorage AK 99507

Call Sign: AL1V
Laurence J Howell
6981 Kincaid Rd
Anchorage AK 99502

Call Sign: KL2TS
Patrick M Thornton
601 King Arthur Cir
Anchorage AK 99518

Call Sign: KL2UE
Dale R Brabec
3003 Kingfisher Dr
Anchorage AK 99502

Call Sign: KL1ND
Jacqueline A Holzman
3023 Kingfisher Dr
Anchorage AK 99502

Call Sign: KL7ICE
Jacqueline A Holzman
3023 Kingfisher Dr
Anchorage AK 99502

Call Sign: KL2BC
Francis L Jeffries
3023 Kingfisher Dr
Anchorage AK 99502

Call Sign: KL7JH
Jacqueline A Holzman
3023 Kingfisher Dr
Anchorage AK 99502

Call Sign: KL2BB
Jordan L Jeffries
3023 Kingfisher Dr
Anchorage AK 99502

Call Sign: NL7DD
Scott A Banks
4234 Kingston Dr
Anchorage AK 99504

Call Sign: KL2VN
Edward H Hoffman Jr

4244 Kingston Dr
Anchorage AK 99504

Call Sign: KL3EK
Scott R Wheaton
1327 Kinnikinnick St
Anchorage AK 99508

Call Sign: WL7FX
Ronald A Gehres
9214 Kirkwall Cir
Anchorage AK 99502

Call Sign: KL7GEG
Myron E Elliott
4930 Knights Way
Anchorage AK 995084808

Call Sign: KL7IJ
George L Stewart
4949 Knights Way
Anchorage AK 99508

Call Sign: KL7IYX
Stephen A Norrell
5018 Knights Way
Anchorage AK 99504

Call Sign: AL7LO
David H Heimke
2927 Knik Ave
Anchorage AK 99517

Call Sign: WL7BTT
Jill T Heimke
2927 Knik Ave
Anchorage AK 99517

Call Sign: AL7JR
Ronald S Klein
3316 Knik Ave
Anchorage AK 99517

Call Sign: KL1XF
Jonathan T Klein
3316 Knik Ave
Anchorage AK 99517

Call Sign: NL7NX
William W Barnwell
3629 Knik Ave
Anchorage AK 99517

Call Sign: NL7BX

Charles M Kopp
3701 Knik Ave
Anchorage AK 99517

Call Sign: WL7CMW
Michael M Dasilva
315 Krane Dr 20
Anchorage AK 99504

Call Sign: K7CEZ
Benjamin M Ewing
11905 Kristie Cir
Anchorage AK 99516

Call Sign: KL2WX
Tyson O Wetzel
8080 Kronos Dr 1
Anchorage AK 99502

Call Sign: KL7ZJ
Steven A Morrison
2100 Lake George Dr
Anchorage AK 99504

Call Sign: KL7FU
Robert J Burek
5700 Lake Otis D95
Anchorage AK 99507

Call Sign: KL7SH
Richard L Day
4200 Lake Otis 204
Anchorage AK 99508

Call Sign: KF6QOJ
Philip A Bock
8406 Lake Otis Pkwy
Anchorage AK 99507

Call Sign: AL7MB
Barney K Kay
14501 Lake Otis Pkwy
Anchorage AK 99516

Call Sign: N8DDY
Robert J Burek
5700 Lake Otis Pkwy D95
Anchorage AK 99507

Call Sign: KD7OUL
Michael W Swartz
3105 Lakeshore Dr Unit B532
Anchorage AK 995172885

Call Sign: KL1EL
Thomas D Simes
6981 Laser Dr
Anchorage AK 99504

Call Sign: AB7VU
Joshua T Gates
2687 Lauren Creek Loop
Anchorage AK 99507

Call Sign: KL2PE
Richard L Baum
2311 Leary Bay Cir
Anchorage AK 99515

Call Sign: KL2BW
Claude D Barker
521 Ledora Cir
Anchorage AK 99515

Call Sign: KL0FK
Cornelius J Eastman
3751 Leyden Rd
Anchorage AK 995162814

Call Sign: KL7HO
Arlene B Steward
12102 Lilac Cir
Anchorage AK 99516

Call Sign: KL7IZZ
Harley F Steward
12102 Lilac Cir
Anchorage AK 99516

Call Sign: KL1YZ
Paul J Welp
3711 Lincoln Ellsworth Ct B
Anchorage AK 99517

Call Sign: KL7DZ
Paul J Welp
3711 Lincoln Ellsworth Ct B
Anchorage AK 99517

Call Sign: KL1PL
Ronald R Keech Sr
7702 Linda Ln
Anchorage AK 99518

Call Sign: KL7YK
Ronald R Keech Sr
7702 Linda Ln
Anchorage AK 99518

Call Sign: KL7AIR
Elmendorf Amateur Radio
Society
7702 Linda Ln
Anchorage AK 99518

Call Sign: KL7JX
Janis M Monroe
3134 Linden Dr
Anchorage AK 99502

Call Sign: KL2UR
Warren M Weber
7112 Linden Dr
Anchorage AK 99502

Call Sign: WL7BHN
Harry H Post Jr
7343 Linden Dr
Anchorage AK 99502

Call Sign: WL7BKV
Michel R Sitbon
1702 Link Ct
Anchorage AK 99504

Call Sign: WL7PF
Tina M Twiggs
5212 Lionheart Dr
Anchorage AK 99508

Call Sign: KL2PJ
Gary A Taylor
7600 Little Bend Cir
Anchorage AK 99507

Call Sign: KL3EE
Keith A Williams
8741 Little Brook Cir
Anchorage AK 99507

Call Sign: KL2ZG
Jay K Kim
9126 Little Brook St
Anchorage AK 99507

Call Sign: WL7AMK
Charles W Floyd
5240 Little Tree
Anchorage AK 99507

Call Sign: WL7BW
Peter G Bailey

3630 Loc Sault Ave
Anchorage AK 99516

Call Sign: NL7PQ
Ian R George
3916 Locarno Dr
Anchorage AK 99508

Call Sign: KL7PJ
Charles H Sappah
1711 Logan St
Anchorage AK 99508

Call Sign: KL7YG
Marjorie C Sappah
1711 Logan St
Anchorage AK 99508

Call Sign: KL2FH
Dwain M Whitley
4307 Lois Dr
Anchorage AK 99517

Call Sign: KL1JJ
George D Wilkinson II
3061 Lois Dr   611
Anchorage AK 99517

Call Sign: KL1US
Phillip D Schobert
3081 Lois Dr 805
Anchorage AK 99517

Call Sign: KB0JJY
Lisa A Schobert
3081 Lois Dr 805
Anchorage AK 99517

Call Sign: KL0QW
Phillip D Mannie
3602 Lois Dr Nr 6
Anchorage AK 99517

Call Sign: WL7XD
Barbara A Starr List
9825 Lone Tree Dr
Anchorage AK 99516

Call Sign: WL7VI
Jerome O List
9825 Lone Tree Dr
Anchorage AK 99516

Call Sign: KL7QY

Sherman G Reynolds
2848 Lore Rd
Anchorage AK 99507

Call Sign: KL7SLM
Scott L Mc Cormick
611 Lori Dr
Anchorage AK 99504

Call Sign: KL2UV
Pamela S Mccormick
611 Lori Dr
Anchorage AK 99504

Call Sign: WL7CJM
Scott L Mc Cormick
611 Lori Dr
Anchorage AK 99504

Call Sign: WL7YR
Bruce W Mc Cormick
611 Lori Dr
Anchorage AK 99504

Call Sign: KL7BM
Bruce W Mc Cormick
611 Lori Dr
Anchorage AK 995042113

Call Sign: AL7IY
Douglas R Green
701 Lori Dr
Anchorage AK 99504

Call Sign: WL7RZ
Veronica Allmaras
6320 Lost Cir
Anchorage AK 99502

Call Sign: NL7PJ
Paul Jendryk
6320 Lost Cir
Anchorage AK 99502

Call Sign: KL7IXV
Robert V Wells
7831 Lotus Dr
Anchorage AK 99502

Call Sign: KL7JLJ
Shirley J Wells
7831 Lotus Dr
Anchorage AK 99502

Call Sign: WL7KL
Gunnar Flygenring
2300 Loussac Dr
Anchorage AK 99517

Call Sign: KL0HG
Jeanette A Morton
7800 Lucy St
Anchorage AK 99502

Call Sign: AL0U
Arthur S Morton
7800 Lucy St
Anchorage AK 99502

Call Sign: KL2BL
Ventis Plume
6601 Lunar Dr
Anchorage AK 99504

Call Sign: WL7RI
Marc D Hendrickson
3623 Lynn Dr
Anchorage AK 99508

Call Sign: KL0HN
Donald G Wilcox Mr
433 M St
Anchorage AK 99501

Call Sign: KL2VK
Timothy M Crowley
836 M St 305
Anchorage AK 99501

Call Sign: KL2VL
Dorothy R Besch
836 M St 313
Anchorage AK 99501

Call Sign: KL7JFM
Buddy J Orand
4101 Mac Innes
Anchorage AK 99508

Call Sign: AL7HX
Eugene D Eaton Jr
2952 Madison Way
Anchorage AK 995084477

Call Sign: NL7UX
Carol B Eaton
2952 Madison Way
Anchorage AK 995084477

Call Sign: KL0SN
Donald G Fall
11361 Mael St
Anchorage AK 99516

Call Sign: WD5GEW
Lubbie A Jenkins
13320 Mainsail Dr
Anchorage AK 99516

Call Sign: KE7GOE
James B Branch Md
13447 Mainsail Dr
Anchorage AK 99516

Call Sign: KL7JBB
James B Branch
13447 Mainsail Dr
Anchorage AK 99516

Call Sign: KL7HOJ
Thomas R Bender MD
8111 Majestic Ct
Anchorage AK 995044750

Call Sign: AL1D
Michael G Willmon
10121 Mamrot Ct
Anchorage AK 99515

Call Sign: KL2TB
Brett J Wilbanks
4701 Mantytell Ave
Anchorage AK 99516

Call Sign: WL7ASH
David D Daly
2502 Maplewood
Anchorage AK 99508

Call Sign: KL7DJ
David M Johnson
2334 Marian Bay Cir
Anchorage AK 99515

Call Sign: KL7ISN
Linda A Johnson
2334 Marian Bay Cir
Anchorage AK 99515

Call Sign: KL3LA
Justin T Doll
17250 Marijane St

Anchorage AK 99516

Call Sign: KL2D
Justin T Doll
17250 Marijane St
Anchorage AK 99516

Call Sign: KL3AV
David J Tobin
310 Mariner Dr
Anchorage AK 99515

Call Sign: KL2OF
Mitchell K Wyatt
311 Mariner Dr
Anchorage AK 99515

Call Sign: KL3IJ
Thomas L Ireland
12650 Mariner Dr
Anchorage AK 99515

Call Sign: KE7AOI
Ross W Emerson
2719 Marston
Anchorage AK 99517

Call Sign: KL1WT
Ross W Emerson
2719 Marston
Anchorage AK 99517

Call Sign: KB8JUT
Gary L Poorman
8900 Mast Cir
Anchorage AK 995025589

Call Sign: WL7CHI
Alden S Cramer
8941 Mast Cir
Anchorage AK 99502

Call Sign: KL1SI
Deborah C Luper
3751 Matthews Dr
Anchorage AK 99516

Call Sign: KL2HO
Jerimiah J Grantham
7641 Mayfair Dr Apt D
Anchorage AK 99502

Call Sign: WL7EI
Michael R Richardson Sr

3801 Mc Cain Loop
Anchorage AK 99503

Call Sign: K0AZZ
Howard D Okland
2702 Mc Kenzie Dr
Anchorage AK 99517

Call Sign: KL7ON
Linda E Okland
2702 Mc Kenzie Dr
Anchorage AK 99517

Call Sign: KL1KN
David L Popken
3802 Mccain Loop
Anchorage AK 99503

Call Sign: NL7I
James A Rogers
12450 Mclain Rd
Anchorage AK 99516

Call Sign: KL1VL
Laddie Shaw
2029 Meander Dr
Anchorage AK 99516

Call Sign: KA0SIM
Paul D Anderson
1321 Medfra St
Anchorage AK 99501

Call Sign: WL7TD
James P Duffy
311 Melody Place Unit B
Anchorage AK 99504

Call Sign: KL2BN
Karen L Jasper
2631 Melvin
Anchorage AK 99517

Call Sign: N3JUG
Alexia L Gordon
8450 Mentra Ct 2
Anchorage AK 955182909

Call Sign: KL7VV
Carman H Smith
3201 Merganser Ave
Anchorage AK 99516

Call Sign: AL7MF

Robert F Leach
4010 Merrill Dr
Anchorage AK 99503

Call Sign: KJ4NPK
Jarrard L Breeding
6530 Michigan Blvd
Anchorage AK 99516

Call Sign: AL3X
Jarrard L Breeding
6530 Michigan Blvd
Anchorage AK 99516

Call Sign: KL1JT
Adrian W Beebee
9571 Midden Way
Anchorage AK 99507

Call Sign: KL0ZX
Robert J Nielsen
4938 Mills Dr
Anchorage AK 995084737

Call Sign: KL7M
David E Cloyd
2155 Minerva St
Anchorage AK 99515

Call Sign: KL0GA
Joseph J Lynn
2064 Minerva Way
Anchorage AK 99515

Call Sign: KB7SIQ
Brian C Vandervort
4003 Minnesota Dr 23
Anchorage AK 99503

Call Sign: WL7LL
Jay S Freeman
3664 Mirage Cir
Anchorage AK 99504

Call Sign: KL7WE
Timothy N Pettis
12950 Mission Cir
Anchorage AK 99516

Call Sign: WB7SZJ
Donald M Irving
2005 Misty Medows Dr
Anchorage AK 99502

Call Sign: KD6YKS
John C Ramsey
5410 Mockingbird Ave 118
Anchorage AK 99507

Call Sign: KL3EF
Jessie S Deuell
5411 Mockingbird Dr 218
Anchorage AK 99507

Call Sign: AL7RB
John W Pendrey IV
2620 Monmouth Ave
Anchorage AK 99502

Call Sign: KL1IC
Lee J Ruble
7041 Montagne Cir
Anchorage AK 99507

Call Sign: KL7JB
Gladys L Meacock
3221 Montclaire Ct
Anchorage AK 99503

Call Sign: KL7MJ
Reed W Mc Kinney
2010 More
Anchorage AK 99504

Call Sign: KC4ICD
Karen E Haddock
6052 More Ln
Anchorage AK 99504

Call Sign: KL3DD
Jason A Copeland
8530 Moss Ct
Anchorage AK 99504

Call Sign: KL3IL
John H Pratt
1613 Mountain Man Loop
Anchorage AK 99507

Call Sign: KL0YX
Sai F Duchanin
12900 Mountain Place
Anchorage AK 99516

Call Sign: KL0YY
James N Duchanin
12900 Mountain Place
Anchorage AK 99516

Call Sign: KL0IP
Brian K Winner
1638 Mountainman Loop
Anchorage AK 99507

Call Sign: KL7GJ
Arthur T Tunley
3748 Mt Blanc Cir
Anchorage AK 99508

Call Sign: KL7VM
Alfred E Sundquist
3384 Mt Vernon Ct
Anchorage AK 99503

Call Sign: KL7ICB
John W Bains Jordan
5811 Muirwood Dr
Anchorage AK 99502

Call Sign: KL1RO
Michael C Wood
2221 Muldoon 12
Anchorage AK 99504

Call Sign: KL7GLU
Marjorie M Page
2030 Muldoon Rd
Anchorage AK 99504

Call Sign: KL1VM
Angela K Wood
2221 Muldoon Rd 12
Anchorage AK 99504

Call Sign: KL7YD
James I Callahan
2221 Muldoon Rd 247
Anchorage AK 99504

Call Sign: KL7YE
Leona M Callahan
2221 Muldoon Rd 247
Anchorage AK 99504

Call Sign: KL0OM
Gregory K Martin
104 Muldoon Rd 272
Anchorage AK 99504

Call Sign: WL7VE
James A Williams
2221 Muldoon Rd 711

Anchorage AK 99504

Call Sign: WL7GM
Terrance J Brady
2221 Muldoon Sp 611
Anchorage AK 99504

Call Sign: WL7MZ
John P Curran
31-160 Myrtle St Box 4955
Anchorage AK 99506

Call Sign: KL1FM
Michael D Hill
8300 Nadine St
Anchorage AK 99507

Call Sign: KL2XC
Kim M Peterson
5615 Naknek Ln
Anchorage AK 99516

Call Sign: AL1E
David P Oradei
7343 Nathan Dr 2
Anchorage AK 995182861

Call Sign: KC0DWD
Alice G Barnett
12610 Neher Ridge Dr
Anchorage AK 99516

Call Sign: KC5QNK
Richard R Barnett
12610 Neher Ridge Dr
Anchorage AK 99516

Call Sign: KB5DNT
Ralph E Cheek
12641 Neher Ridge Dr
Anchorage AK 99516

Call Sign: NL7ZB
Cordell W Pagh
1571 Nelchina 5B
Anchorage AK 99501

Call Sign: KL2WM
Tyler C Emmott
1601 Nelchina St 212
Anchorage AK 99501

Call Sign: KJ4ETG
Paul H Petersen

1571 Nelchina St Apt B5
Anchorage AK 99501

Call Sign: KL2DI
Robert E Ostrom
3429 Newcomb Dr
Anchorage AK 99508

Call Sign: KL2FJ
Katie H Ostrom
3429 Newcomb Dr
Anchorage AK 99508

Call Sign: N0ZKV
Robert E Ostrom
3429 Newcomb Dr
Anchorage AK 99508

Call Sign: KB8QKR
Charles S Butcher
9759 Newhaven Loop
Anchorage AK 995074429

Call Sign: NL7YF
Dwight E Hunter Mr
1428 Nichols St
Anchorage AK 99508

Call Sign: KL7D
Philip B Barber
9010 Noble Cir
Anchorage AK 99502

Call Sign: KL3CU
Bradley C Thomas
16411 Noble Point Dr
Anchorage AK 99516

Call Sign: KL1SH
Barry A Byrne
13161 Nora Dr
Anchorage AK 99515

Call Sign: KL3AJ
Kirk C Larson
6440 Norm Dr
Anchorage AK 99507

Call Sign: KC7HJM
Jeremy J Hagerman
1204 Norman St 46
Anchorage AK 99504

Call Sign: KL2AN

Robert E Stapleton Jr
1497 North Heather Meadows
Loop
Anchorage AK 99507

Call Sign: NL7PA
Richard L Langton
604 North Klevin
Anchorage AK 99548

Call Sign: AL7OB
Michael S Melum
7231 North Park Dr
Anchorage AK 99516

Call Sign: KL6M
Michael S Melum
7231 North Park Dr
Anchorage AK 99516

Call Sign: KL3GI
Paul E Fenwick
408 North Park St F
Anchorage AK 99508

Call Sign: N6SPP
Eric M Thompson
523 North Park St B
Anchorage AK 99508

Call Sign: KL1NR
Sean M Hogan
3637 North Point Dr
Anchorage AK 99502

Call Sign: KL1NO
Kenzie C Hogan
3637 North Point Dr
Anchorage AK 99502

Call Sign: KL7GRG
Donald R Meierhoff
3637 North Point Dr
Anchorage AK 99502

Call Sign: WL7OQ
Nita M Meierhoff
3637 North Point Dr
Anchorage AK 99515

Call Sign: WL7ZB
Jason W Vequist
1902 North Salem Dr
Anchorage AK 99508

Call Sign: KL1OJ
Jerry W Cartwright
2319 North Tahiti Loop
Anchorage AK 99507

Call Sign: KL2QN
John C Wojtacha
10624 Northfleet Dr
Anchorage AK 99515

Call Sign: WL7DT
Paul E Roth
1545 Northview Dr Apt F1
Anchorage AK 99504

Call Sign: WL7PR
Patricia S Roth
1545 Northview Dr Apt F1
Anchorage AK 99504

Call Sign: AL0LA
Mary D Salamanchuk
1800 Northwestern Ave
Anchorage AK 99508

Call Sign: KL7JEF
Mary D Salamanchuk
1800 Northwestern Ave
Anchorage AK 99508

Call Sign: WL7NA
Cordell T Lucia
1713 Northwestern Ave Apt B
Anchorage AK 99508

Call Sign: NL7YY
Gary L Hardwick
8330 Northwind Ave
Anchorage AK 99504

Call Sign: AL7PJ
William R Vallee
8401 Northwind Ave
Anchorage AK 99504

Call Sign: WL7LA
Al B Carraway
5070 Nottingham Way
Anchorage AK 99503

Call Sign: WL7MC
William M Carraway
5070 Nottingham Way

Anchorage AK 99503

Call Sign: AL7MJ
Daniel L Buchholz
1408 Nunaka Dr
Anchorage AK 99504

Call Sign: WL7BG
William A Williamson III
1510 Nunaka Dr
Anchorage AK 99504

Call Sign: NL7NU
John J Jacobsen
1703 Nunaka Dr
Anchorage AK 99504

Call Sign: KL2UZ
Jonathan Hanson
629 O St 203
Anchorage AK 99501

Call Sign: KL7VA
Jonathan Hanson
629 O St 203
Anchorage AK 99501

Call Sign: AL3N
Bixler P Mcclure
732 O St Apt 2
Anchorage AK 99501

Call Sign: KL3AX
Chad N Watson
311 Ocean Point Dr
Anchorage AK 99515

Call Sign: KC0GHH
Darren K Mc Laughlin
1145 Oceanview Dr
Anchorage AK 99515

Call Sign: KL2SL
Ronald C Swartz
3341 Old Muldoon Rd
Anchorage AK 99504

Call Sign: KL2ES
Theodore M Cadman
3528 Old Muldoon Rd
Anchorage AK 99504

Call Sign: KD6ACF
Jeffrey A Kopf

13300 Old Seward Hwy
Anchorage AK 99515

Call Sign: KL7BYB
Arthur N Dorsey
9191 Old Seward Hwy 3B
Anchorage AK 99515

Call Sign: KL7BL
Barbara R Luchak
6520 O'Malley Rd
Anchorage AK 99507

Call Sign: KL7BX
David J Luchak
6520 O'Malley Rd
Anchorage AK 99507

Call Sign: KL2CD
Brandon W Luchak
6520 Omally Rd
Anchorage AK 99507

Call Sign: KL2SE
Roger L Frierson
3471 Orbit Cir
Anchorage AK 99517

Call Sign: KL1KL
Edward Mooeo
1740 Orca Place
Anchorage AK 99501

Call Sign: WL7CMC
Christopher K Willey
1104 Orca St A
Anchorage AK 99501

Call Sign: KL2FN
Craig C Severson
3446 Orion Cir
Anchorage AK 99517

Call Sign: KL1OK
Donald J Thomas
1415 Otter St
Anchorage AK 99504

Call Sign: WL7AY
Charles H Iliff
804 P St 3
Anchorage AK 99501

Call Sign: NL7DN

Dennis D Strait
7937 Paine Rd
Anchorage AK 99516

Call Sign: KL2SF
William L Ennis
8690 Paine Rd
Anchorage AK 99516

Call Sign: KL2SU
Constance E Livsey
8690 Paine Rd
Anchorage AK 99516

Call Sign: KL3BI
Michael G Dennis
2633 Palmer Ct
Anchorage AK 99508

Call Sign: K5RZW
Craig A Ratchner
7230 Papago Place
Anchorage AK 99518

Call Sign: AL1T
Craig A Ratchner
7230 Papago Place
Anchorage AK 99518

Call Sign: WA0VNY
Robert W Schmidt
2006 Parkview Cir
Anchorage AK 99501

Call Sign: KL2VB
Derek C Hsieh
12851 Patrick Rd
Anchorage AK 99516

Call Sign: AL7BB
Billy B Capers
1414 Patterson St
Anchorage AK 995042745

Call Sign: KL2CO
Sean P Jensen
131 Patterson St Apt 505
Anchorage AK 99504

Call Sign: KL0QO
Gary D Cox
369 Pauline St
Anchorage AK 995041554

Call Sign: WL7CDJ
David L Filley
6930 Peck Ave
Anchorage AK 99504

Call Sign: KL2QB
Maisi Bettridge
5526 Penn Cir A
Anchorage AK 99504

Call Sign: KL2RJ
Danna Bettridge
5526 Penn Cir Apt A
Anchorage AK 99504

Call Sign: KL1KP
Kelsi Bettridge
5526 Penn Cir Apt A
Anchorage AK 99504

Call Sign: AL7OL
Wayne O Stuvick
6431 Pequod Cir
Anchorage AK 995072233

Call Sign: KB0DAM
William J Burt
3230 Peterkin 8
Anchorage AK 99508

Call Sign: KL1YX
Lamar T Ballard
6221 Petersburg St
Anchorage AK 99507

Call Sign: KL7FX
Lamar T Ballard
6221 Petersburg St
Anchorage AK 99507

Call Sign: AK0O
Timothy R Crawford II
8020 Pinebrook Cir
Anchorage AK 99507

Call Sign: WL7COE
Timothy R Crawford II
8020 Pinebrook Cir
Anchorage AK 99507

Call Sign: KL3HV
Kevin J Chase
8110 Pioneer Dr
Anchorage AK 99504

Call Sign: WL7VL
William W Powell
8450 Pioneer Dr
Anchorage AK 99504

Call Sign: KL2TW
Kevin J Mccabe
1850 Pkwy Dr
Anchorage AK 99504

Call Sign: KL2UQ
Pauline A Potter
3106 Pleasant Dr
Anchorage AK 99502

Call Sign: KL2UX
Patsy C Burgess
3106 Pleasant Dr
Anchorage AK 99502

Call Sign: WL7PN
Thomas J Burgess
3106 Pleasant Dr
Anchorage AK 99502

Call Sign: KL0QC
Florence F Busch
3116 Pleasant Dr
Anchorage AK 99502

Call Sign: NL7H
Thomas A Busch
3116 Pleasant Dr
Anchorage AK 99502

Call Sign: KL3GS
John D Gumpert Jr
12930 Plymouth Cir
Anchorage AK 99516

Call Sign: KL1IW
Pearlie M Bursey
PO Box 141573 RJ Postal
Service
Anchorage AK 99514

Call Sign: AL1W
Gordon W Hartlieb
PO Box 241864
Anchorage AK 99524

Call Sign: KL7GNN
James O Graham

PO Box 91727
Anchorage AK 995171423

Call Sign: AL7T
Doyle M Carroll
10141 Pointe Resolution Dr
Anchorage AK 995152231

Call Sign: WL7CFY
Tiffini K Jackson
15210 Pollock Dr
Anchorage AK 99516

Call Sign: KL3AP
Duwayne D Ruzicka
18711 Portugal Place
Anchorage AK 99516

Call Sign: WL7SS
William M Shaw
9838 Poseidon
Anchorage AK 99515

Call Sign: WL7BV
Lajarle M Scott
7050 Potomac Dr
Anchorage AK 99504

Call Sign: KE6DLM
Frederick S De Dios
525 Price St C
Anchorage AK 99508

Call Sign: K7OCL
James W Romerdahl
2912 Princeton Way
Anchorage AK 99508

Call Sign: KL7QQ
Donna M Romerdahl
2912 Princeton Way
Anchorage AK 99508

Call Sign: WA2BGL
Robert C Batch
6244 Prominence Pointe Dr
Anchorage AK 99516

Call Sign: KL0XQ
Jeff R Hall
9400 Prospect Dr
Anchorage AK 99516

Call Sign: KL0XR

Scott A Hall
9400 Prospect Dr
Anchorage AK 99516

Call Sign: KB7JA
John C Hall
9400 Prospect Dr
Anchorage AK 995075903

Call Sign: NL7VO
Jack Welliver
6218 Prosperity Dr
Anchorage AK 99504

Call Sign: K3FQ
Jessica C Sheldon-Hess
3211 Providence Dr
Anchorage AK 99508

Call Sign: KL7PP
Johann Bruns
3214 Purdue St
Anchorage AK 99508

Call Sign: AL7PX
Todd D Hansen
8036 Queen Victoria Dr
Anchorage AK 99518

Call Sign: KL8DW
Dennis R Walker
6341 Quiet Cir
Anchorage AK 99502

Call Sign: KC8GKK
Dennis R Walker
6341 Quiet Cir
Anchorage AK 99502

Call Sign: KL7BLF
Kathrine A Allred
3500 Rabbit Creek Rd
Anchorage AK 99516

Call Sign: KL7OW
Robert G Palmer
5700 Rabbit Crk Rd
Anchorage AK 99516

Call Sign: KL7WQ
Norman N Wiswell II
5201 Rabbitt Creek Rd
Anchorage AK 99516

Call Sign: KL3HB
Stephanie A Patton
8209 Race Cir
Anchorage AK 99504

Call Sign: WL7DN
David M Noll
2235 Radiant Cir
Anchorage AK 99501

Call Sign: KD7QAR
David M Noll
2235 Radiant Cir
Anchorage AK 99501

Call Sign: AL7JZ
David H Evans
11641 Rainbow Ave
Anchorage AK 99516

Call Sign: KL0UW
Donald M Irving
12201 Rainbow Ave
Anchorage AK 99506

Call Sign: KL7MVX
Randell W Haefka
8540 Raintree Cir
Anchorage AK 99507

Call Sign: KL2QR
Mathew C Rude
7600 Randamar Cir
Anchorage AK 99507

Call Sign: KL3HY
Michael R Tibor
7741 Randamar Cir
Anchorage AK 99507

Call Sign: KL2JX
Lori S Walkowicz-Haines
7429 Randamar Place
Anchorage AK 99507

Call Sign: AL7GZ
John H Danielsen
3601 Raspberry Rd 2C
Anchorage AK 99502

Call Sign: KL7IZS
Douglas E Lockwood
4109 Raspberry Riad
Anchorage AK 99502

Call Sign: KL2XB
James D Maclean
7833 Raymar Cir
Anchorage AK 99518

Call Sign: AL7EG
John A Taber
1901 Rebel Ridge Dr
Anchorage AK 99504

Call Sign: W3ICG
Joseph C Mixsell Jr
6212 Redtop Cir
Anchorage AK 99507

Call Sign: KL0ZB
Starla A Livengood
1210 Redwood Ct
Anchorage AK 99508

Call Sign: KL7ZR
Damian V Livengood
1210 Redwood Ct
Anchorage AK 99508

Call Sign: WL7NH
Patricia J Nightingale
2426 Redwood St
Anchorage AK 99508

Call Sign: KL7GN
Gordon J Nightingale
2426 Redwood St
Anchorage AK 995083969

Call Sign: KL1ZB
Lee A Hobart
7817 Regal Mountain Cir
Anchorage AK 99504

Call Sign: WL7BNW
Lawrence E Yerks
4280 Reka Dr
Anchorage AK 99503

Call Sign: KL7USA
Usaisc Fra Ft Richardson Ak
4280 Reka Dr
Anchorage AK 99508

Call Sign: KL3CO
John C King
4294 Reka Dr

Anchorage AK 99508

Call Sign: KL7IM
Sharon Kay
4318 Reka Dr
Anchorage AK 99508

Call Sign: KL3BW
Edward E Miller
4354 Reka Dr
Anchorage AK 995083633

Call Sign: NL7VE
John Svihra III
4112 Reka Dr 1
Anchorage AK 99508

Call Sign: WL7BVP
Michael Livingston
4650 Reka Dr 20
Anchorage AK 99508

Call Sign: KL1JH
Bernita R Boyse
4660 Reka Dr 3
Anchorage AK 99508

Call Sign: WL7CHU
Dean A Curtis
4545 Reka Dr 35
Anchorage AK 99508

Call Sign: KL1KV
Antonio J Medrano
4660 Reka Dr Apt D3
Anchorage AK 99508

Call Sign: NL7ND
Donald D Lederhos
8110 Resurrection
Anchorage AK 99504

Call Sign: KL1OZ
Donald D Lederhos
8110 Resurrection Dr
Anchorage AK 99504

Call Sign: KL0CZ
David C Ferguson
8301 Resurrection Dr
Anchorage AK 99504

Call Sign: WL7CGX
Loren S Rhyneer

3719 Rhone Cir
Anchorage AK 99508

Call Sign: KL0SU
Robert M Isbell Jr
3132 Richmond Ave Apt 7
Anchorage AK 995081082

Call Sign: W6ROW
Edward C Bosco Jr
4700 Riverton Ave
Anchorage AK 99516

Call Sign: KL1VS
Paul E Quinton
8101 Robert Dr
Anchorage AK 99516

Call Sign: KL1VU
Joshua N Paul
8101 Robert Dr
Anchorage AK 99516

Call Sign: WL7A
Thearon E Staddon
10902 Rockridge Dr
Anchorage AK 99516

Call Sign: KL0TD
Alexander F Newhall
11001 Rockridge Dr
Anchorage AK 99516

Call Sign: NL7RV
Michael E Holland
12151 Rockridge Dr
Anchorage AK 995162434

Call Sign: KL0DX
Trenton A Yates
2201 Romig Place 305
Anchorage AK 99503

Call Sign: WL7CWP
Alaska Contest Club
2003 Roosevelt
Anchorage AK 99517

Call Sign: WL7CWM
Alaska Dx Club
2003 Roosevelt Dr
Anchorage AK 99517

Call Sign: WL7CWN

Alaska Contest Club
2003 Roosevelt Dr
Anchorage AK 99517

Call Sign: KL5O
Alaska Dx Club
2003 Roosevelt Dr
Anchorage AK 99517

Call Sign: WL7CWT
Alaska Dx Club
2003 Roosevelt Dr
Anchorage AK 99517

Call Sign: KL7FH
Alaska Dx Club
2003 Roosevelt Dr
Anchorage AK 99517

Call Sign: KL1SLE
Alaska Island Runners
2003 Roosevelt Dr
Anchorage AK 99517

Call Sign: KL7FH
Francis D Hurlbut III
2003 Roosevelt Dr
Anchorage AK 99517

Call Sign: WL7KY
Christopher K Hurlbut
2003 Roosevelt Dr
Anchorage AK 99517

Call Sign: KL9A
Christopher K Hurlbut
2003 Roosevelt Dr
Anchorage AK 99517

Call Sign: WL7CVO
Faa Amateur Radio Association
2003 Roosevelt Dr
Anchorage AK 99517

Call Sign: KL7FAA
Alaska Faa Amateur Radio
Association
2003 Roosevelt Dr
Anchorage AK 99517

Call Sign: WL7CVR
Alaska Dx Club
2003 Roosevelt Dr
Anchorage AK 995172694

Call Sign: KL7CQ
Alaska Dx Club
2003 Roosevelt Dr
Anchorage AK 995172694

Call Sign: WL7CVU
Alaska Dx Club
2003 Roosevelt Dr
Anchorage AK 995172694

Call Sign: KL7DX
Alaska Dx Club
2003 Roosevelt Dr
Anchorage AK 995172694

Call Sign: AL1G
Corliss A Kimmel
2003 Roosevelt Dr
Anchorage AK 995172694

Call Sign: WL7MG
Corey L Rogers
2301 Roosevelt Dr 7
Anchorage AK 99517

Call Sign: KL0QV
Phillip Mc Guire
1806 Rosemary St
Anchorage AK 995083342

Call Sign: KL2BI
Donald F Smith
6431 Rosemont Dr
Anchorage AK 99516

Call Sign: KL2EZ
Donald F Smith
6431 Rosemont Dr
Anchorage AK 99516

Call Sign: N3QD
Micheal A Long
6900 Round Tree Dr
Anchorage AK 99507

Call Sign: NL3D
Micheal A Long
6900 Round Tree Dr
Anchorage AK 99507

Call Sign: WL7BUT
Reford G Reid
7940 Rovenna

Anchorage AK 99518

Call Sign: N3SCH
Gregory A Tartisel
1580 Russian Jack Dr 10
Anchorage AK 99508

Call Sign: KL3BT
Moses E Toyukak
153 Rusty Allen Place
Anchorage AK 99504

Call Sign: KL7ZC
Zachary M Cuddihy
8618 Sahalee Dr
Anchorage AK 99507

Call Sign: AL7I
Patrick M Cuddihy
8618 Sahalee Dr
Anchorage AK 99507

Call Sign: AL7Z
Patrick M Cuddihy
8618 Sahalee Dr
Anchorage AK 99507

Call Sign: KL7HN
Lawrence R Trotter
1458 Saint Gotthard Ave
Anchorage AK 995085052

Call Sign: AL7CD
Lindell M Mc Coy
6701 Saint Ives Place
Anchorage AK 99504

Call Sign: KL1EN
Jim E Wheeler
1725 Sanya Cir
Anchorage AK 995083524

Call Sign: KE5NLG
Robert A Cusick III
5673 Sapphire Loop
Anchorage AK 995046001

Call Sign: AL9DB
Douglas R Brower
5765 Sapphire Loop
Anchorage AK 99504

Call Sign: NK0L
Jeffrey L Brower

5765 Sapphire Loop
Anchorage AK 99504

Call Sign: W3LT
Joan R Jellison
8510 Sara Lynn Place
Anchorage AK 99502

Call Sign: W3YQ
Timothy J Jellison
8510 Sara Lynn Place
Anchorage AK 99502

Call Sign: KL7WV
Dukies Island Amateur Radio
Club
8510 Sara Lynn Place
Anchorage AK 99502

Call Sign: KL2RF
James C Anderson
12700 Saunders Rd
Anchorage AK 99516

Call Sign: WL7MH
Jerome W Watson
7030 Scalero Cir
Anchorage AK 99507

Call Sign: KL7IJR
Frank D Frost
7110 Scalero Cir
Anchorage AK 99507

Call Sign: KL7JIM
Stephen A Wilcox
3631 Scammon Bay Cir
Anchorage AK 99515

Call Sign: KL0IX
Kerwin J Faciane
9316 Sea Parrot Cir
Anchorage AK 99515

Call Sign: KL1UP
Donald J Burand II
13381 Seacloud Cir
Anchorage AK 99516

Call Sign: KL7GQC
Jimmy D Lemke
2844 Seafarer Loop
Anchorage AK 99516

Call Sign: W0EZM
Donald R Caulkins
12022 Seashore Place
Anchorage AK 99515

Call Sign: N0HYI
Donald R Caulkins
12022 Seashore Place
Anchorage AK 99515

Call Sign: N0JEN
Janelle G Caulkins
12022 Seashore Place
Anchorage AK 99515

Call Sign: NL7BF
Stephen A Pratt
3115 Seawind Dr
Anchorage AK 99516

Call Sign: KL2AL
Greg R French
2961 Seclusion Bay
Anchorage AK 99515

Call Sign: N8JCE
Peter D Wickizer
2985 Seclusion Bay Dr
Anchorage AK 99515

Call Sign: WL7CGC
Sarah E Sinclair
6840 Sequoia Cir
Anchorage AK 99516

Call Sign: KL2WN
Donna K Biagioni
7010 Serenity Cir
Anchorage AK 99502

Call Sign: WL7BNM
John E Jakobowski
10210 Sextant Cir
Anchorage AK 995152554

Call Sign: KL3GU
David J Ramos Sr
9165 Shady Bay Cir
Anchorage AK 99504

Call Sign: KL3GV
Charmaine V Ramos
9165 Shady Bay Cir
Anchorage AK 99507

Call Sign: KL3GW
Nirvana E Ramos
9165 Shady Bay Cir
Anchorage AK 99507

Call Sign: KL7JHC
Kenneth W Gilmer
3500 Shamrock
Anchorage AK 99504

Call Sign: KL7JIH
Cheryl J Gilmer
3500 Shamrock
Anchorage AK 995044247

Call Sign: KL2DL
David J Luchak
6810 Shane Place
Anchorage AK 99507

Call Sign: KC5CHO
Barbara R Luchak
6810 Shane Place
Anchorage AK 99507

Call Sign: KL0NZ
David J Luchak
6810 Shane Place
Anchorage AK 99507

Call Sign: NL7QY
David B Fuller
5331 Shaun Cir
Anchorage AK 99516

Call Sign: KL0NU
John R Norris
4631 Shelburn Place
Anchorage AK 99516

Call Sign: WL7OX
David J Gribble
12221 Shenandoah
Anchorage AK 99516

Call Sign: KL7OK
Eugene G Morris Jr
2039 Shepherdia Dr
Anchorage AK 995084043

Call Sign: KD4QJL
Michael J Cohen
2606 Shepherdia Dr

Anchorage AK 99508

Call Sign: WL7CVQ
Michael J Cohen
2606 Shepherdia Dr
Anchorage AK 99508

Call Sign: KL2EA
Mary D Hallinan
12021 Shore Cir
Anchorage AK 99515

Call Sign: KL2EB
John R Hallinan
12021 Shore Cir
Anchorage AK 99515

Call Sign: KL2BM
Rona I Florio
2020 Shore Dr
Anchorage AK 99515

Call Sign: KL2BR
Shawn A Florio
2020 Shore Dr
Anchorage AK 99515

Call Sign: KL7ROE
Rona I Florio
2020 Shore Dr
Anchorage AK 99515

Call Sign: KL7QZ
John C Bury
5142 Shorecrest Dr
Anchorage AK 99502

Call Sign: AL7LG
Robert A Hunt
14900 Sierra Way
Anchorage AK 99516

Call Sign: KL7ZO
William E Gamel
5146 Sillary Cir
Anchorage AK 99508

Call Sign: KL7ZP
Beth A Gamel
5146 Sillary Cir
Anchorage AK 99508

Call Sign: WL7RY
Gerianne O Thorsness

6840 Sky Cir
Anchorage AK 99502

Call Sign: KL3JY
Joseph M Pepe-Phelps
8501 Skyhills Dr
Anchorage AK 99502

Call Sign: KL3JZ
Gregory L Phelps
8501 Skyhills Dr
Anchorage AK 99502

Call Sign: WL7CVP
Frigid Contesters
4831 Snow Cir
Anchorage AK 995083784

Call Sign: KL4A
Frigid Contesters
4831 Snow Cir
Anchorage AK 995083784

Call Sign: NL7QL
Michael D Williams
7841 Snowview Dr
Anchorage AK 99507

Call Sign: KL2RM
Steven J Buchta
2821 Snug Harbor Cir
Anchorage AK 99507

Call Sign: KL7IYM
Joe C Ashlock
2119 Sorbus Way
Anchorage AK 99508

Call Sign: KL3BQ
Sai Sipharath
100 Sorcerer Ct
Anchorage AK 99518

Call Sign: AL7LN
John H Marton
700 South Ln St
Anchorage AK 99508

Call Sign: KL2DC
Daniel C Peterson
342 South Park St
Anchorage AK 99508

Call Sign: KL0FC

Clifford M Duncan
810 South Pine
Anchorage AK 99508

Call Sign: N6SQH
Orval T Smee
1774 South Salem
Anchorage AK 99508

Call Sign: AL1Y
James M Mounts
5801 South Tahiti Loop
Anchorage AK 99507

Call Sign: WL7NG
Christopher B Brandt
15031 South Windsor Cir
Anchorage AK 99516

Call Sign: KC7AFA
Margaret K Sparks
15800 Southpark Loop
Anchorage AK 99516

Call Sign: KC7AFC
Timothy J Sparks
15800 Southpark Loop
Anchorage AK 99516

Call Sign: NL7FD
Jerry E C Reamer
14031 Specking Ave
Anchorage AK 99515

Call Sign: KC7CMQ
Arlen D Zacharias
4510 Spenard Rd Apt 14
Anchorage AK 99517

Call Sign: K2STR
Stephen T Rust
8801 Spendlove Dr
Anchorage AK 99516

Call Sign: AL7FS
James H Larsen
3445 Spinnaker Dr
Anchorage AK 99516

Call Sign: KL7NY
Nancy C Larsen
3445 Spinnaker Dr
Anchorage AK 99516

Call Sign: KL0AP
John E Olson II
3500 Spinnaker Dr
Anchorage AK 99516

Call Sign: KL0AQ
Dianne L Olson
3500 Spinnaker Dr
Anchorage AK 99516

Call Sign: WL7QZ
Michael A Furman
3500 Spinnaker Dr
Anchorage AK 99516

Call Sign: KB6HPY
David J Fox
7511 Sportsmens Point Cir
Anchorage AK 99502

Call Sign: NL7ZY
Morris D Ferguson
7829 Spruce Rd
Anchorage AK 99507

Call Sign: KL7ZL
Joe C Maxey
7111 Spruce St
Anchorage AK 99507

Call Sign: NL7OA
Robert M S Anderson
6741 St Ives Place
Anchorage AK 99504

Call Sign: KL7IAF
Lorraine M Tessier
6044 Staedem Dr
Anchorage AK 99504

Call Sign: KL7ISX
Earl W Bell
2100 Stanford Dr
Anchorage AK 99508

Call Sign: KL7NF
Wallace S Bell
2100 Stanford Dr
Anchorage AK 99508

Call Sign: WH6KL
Terrie N J Chang
3309 Starlite Cir
Anchorage AK 99517

Call Sign: WL7COU
Michael Gartland
1841 State St
Anchorage AK 99504

Call Sign: NL7PM
Carl A Bracale Jr
6839 Stella Place
Anchorage AK 99507

Call Sign: NL7NC
John R Lawson
3731 Steller Dr
Anchorage AK 99504

Call Sign: KL2VT
Glen P Daily
3900 Steller Dr
Anchorage AK 99504

Call Sign: WL7CRL
Daryl J Carson
13144 Stephenson
Anchorage AK 99515

Call Sign: WL7AKF
Lynn S Coad
13427 Stephenson St
Anchorage AK 99515

Call Sign: KL1QQ
Monte R Handy
9224 Strathmore
Anchorage AK 99502

Call Sign: KL0KF
Charlie W Huddleston
9221 Strathmore Dr
Anchorage AK 99515

Call Sign: KL1UK
William G Fults
9305 Strathmore Dr
Anchorage AK 995021444

Call Sign: KL1UN
Pearl J Fults
9305 Strathmore Dr
Anchorage AK 995021444

Call Sign: KL7JGN
W Lloyd Fuller
9460 Strathmore Dr

Anchorage AK 99515

Call Sign: KL7LM
Vickie L Fuller
9460 Strathmore Dr
Anchorage AK 99515

Call Sign: KL7WO
Rose Anne Shoemaker
3710 Strawberry
Anchorage AK 99502

Call Sign: KL3JD
Paul H Fairchild
10141 Stroganof Dr
Anchorage AK 99507

Call Sign: AL4G
Paul H Fairchild
10141 Stroganof Dr
Anchorage AK 99507

Call Sign: N0HZF
Sally A Jaworski
2001 Sturbridge
Anchorage AK 99507

Call Sign: WB0YSG
Jim J Jaworski
2001 Sturbridge
Anchorage AK 99507

Call Sign: KL2MJ
Vincent D Ditmore
2330 Sues Way
Anchorage AK 99516

Call Sign: KL2FL
Frances M Kelly
12780 Summer Dr
Anchorage AK 99516

Call Sign: KL0DR
Richard P Dowling
12780 Summer Dr
Anchorage AK 99516

Call Sign: KL1DM
Lynnette A Werel
1519 Summit View St
Anchorage AK 99504

Call Sign: KL1DQ
Robert L Werel

1519 Summit View St
Anchorage AK 995042548

Call Sign: WL7XQ
Paul T Kiester
14101 Sun View Dr
Anchorage AK 99515

Call Sign: KL3FA
Wayne A Hughes
2231 Sunburst Cir
Anchorage AK 99501

Call Sign: WL7YY
James W Crippen
2119 Sunrise
Anchorage AK 99508

Call Sign: WL7YZ
James A Crippen
2119 Sunrise
Anchorage AK 99508

Call Sign: NL7EY
Audley E Benson
13670 Sunset View St
Anchorage AK 99515

Call Sign: KL7AGU
Dave A Fulton Sr
2306 Susitna Dr
Anchorage AK 995171145

Call Sign: KL1MY
Diane H Olson
2515 Susitna Dr
Anchorage AK 995171140

Call Sign: KL7CR
Charles R Comer
3919 Sycamore Loop
Anchorage AK 99504

Call Sign: KL3KO
Michael T Mccann Sr
4102 Taft Dr 2
Anchorage AK 99517

Call Sign: AL7IR
Gus E Mc Kenzie
3701 Taiga Dr
Anchorage AK 99516

Call Sign: WL7BTP

Bobby E Little
1716 Tamarra Cir
Anchorage AK 99508

Call Sign: KL7OX
Susan V Golds
11551 Tanglewood Lakes Cir
Anchorage AK 995161304

Call Sign: KL1AD
William J Romberg
3530 Tanglewood Place
Anchorage AK 995171500

Call Sign: KL2RH
Scott G Niwa
7444 Tarsus Dr
Anchorage AK 99502

Call Sign: KL7DWE
Joseph K Hildreth
9110 Teri Cir
Anchorage AK 99507

Call Sign: WL7CHK
William T Kluge
10221 Thimbleberry Dr
Anchorage AK 99515

Call Sign: WL7NO
James M Wiedle
10301 Thinble Berry Dr
Anchorage AK 99515

Call Sign: KL7HIU
Robert L Page
3533 Thompson
Anchorage AK 99508

Call Sign: WL7COT
Lawrence A Mock
10313 Thuja Cir
Anchorage AK 99507

Call Sign: KL1XD
Nicholas C Casler
10321 Thuja Cir
Anchorage AK 99507

Call Sign: WL7AU
William J Markley Jr
1713 Thunderbird Place
Anchorage AK 99508

Call Sign: KL7JKY
Dennis L Bickford
16840 Tideview Dr
Anchorage AK 995164831

Call Sign: WL7VB
Richard D Crain
6610 Tiffany Terr
Anchorage AK 99507

Call Sign: KL7JBT
Edward J Nelson
7534 Timber Wolf
Anchorage AK 99507

Call Sign: AL7GI
Steven E Wysong
7534 Timber Wolf Cir
Anchorage AK 99507

Call Sign: KL2YV
Francis G Andersen
7117 Timothy St
Anchorage AK 99502

Call Sign: WL7AZV
Virginia Strong
3908 Tom White Cir
Anchorage AK 99504

Call Sign: KL3CI
Christopher E Gunderson
3933 Tom White Cir
Anchorage AK 99504

Call Sign: KL7IWV
Hubert J Gellert
12831 Tracy Way
Anchorage AK 99516

Call Sign: KL7FI
Paul F Bestry
2460 Tradewind Dr
Anchorage AK 99516

Call Sign: KL7FV
Dyanne C Bestry
2460 Tradewind Dr
Anchorage AK 99516

Call Sign: KL0EO
Edythe L Lynn
7013 Trafford Ave
Anchorage AK 995041132

Call Sign: KL7EL
Edythe L Lynn
7013 Trafford Ave
Anchorage AK 995041132

Call Sign: KL0CY
John E Lynn Jr
7013 Trafford Dr
Anchorage AK 99504

Call Sign: KL7CY
John E Lynn Jr
7013 Trafford Dr
Anchorage AK 99504

Call Sign: AL7JL
Donald C Stuart
7013 Trafford Dr
Anchorage AK 99504

Call Sign: KL7IZL
Orville L Gilbert
6021 Trappers Trail
Anchorage AK 99516

Call Sign: KL1VT
Robert P Carson
12830 Trent Cir
Anchorage AK 99516

Call Sign: KL1VW
Michael P Carson
12830 Trent Cir
Anchorage AK 99516

Call Sign: KL1VX
Nathaniel R Carson
12830 Trent Cir
Anchorage AK 99516

Call Sign: WL7UL
John R Norris
4010 Truro Dr
Anchorage AK 99507

Call Sign: WL7QP
Martha R Schoenthal
2020 Tudor Hills
Anchorage AK 99507

Call Sign: WL7QO
Terry N Schoenthal
2020 Tudor Hills Dr

Anchorage AK 99507

Call Sign: KL2EK
Duane G Bessette
5351 Tudor Top Cir
Anchorage AK 99507

Call Sign: KL2FI
Nona Bessette
5351 Tudortop Cir
Anchorage AK 99507

Call Sign: KL3LB
Donald Braun
2454 Tulane Ct
Anchorage AK 99504

Call Sign: KL2VR
John H Vandervalk
11327 Tulin Park Loop
Anchorage AK 99516

Call Sign: KL2UB
Holly K Hankins
8501 Turf Ct
Anchorage AK 99504

Call Sign: WL7CLA
Christopher E Brown
8501 Turf Ct
Anchorage AK 99504

Call Sign: KL2SQ
Terry J Symonds
7217 Tyre Dr
Anchorage AK 99502

Call Sign: KL2HL
Mark D Hill
3226 Upland Dr
Anchorage AK 99504

Call Sign: WL7CGB
Christina M Croft
7435 Upper De Armoun
Anchorage AK 99516

Call Sign: WL7CNN
Mary C Kemper
8831 Upper De Armoun Rd
Anchorage AK 99516

Call Sign: WL7CNO
Steven P Kemper

8831 Upper Dearmoun Rd
Anchorage AK 99516

Call Sign: WL7CWE
Cliffside Amateur Radio
Association
9600 Vanguard Dr
Anchorage AK 995074491

Call Sign: KC7POU
Kevin M Tuning
9731 Vanguard Dr 11
Anchorage AK 99507

Call Sign: KD7AEI
Genette L Tuning
9731 Vanguard Dr 11
Anchorage AK 99507

Call Sign: WL7CHR
David W Groom
3334 Vassar
Anchorage AK 99508

Call Sign: NL7OH
John C Sheldon
3426 Vassar Dr
Anchorage AK 99508

Call Sign: WL7CEL
Carol A Sheldon
3426 Vassar Dr
Anchorage AK 99508

Call Sign: KB8JXX
Jerold L Tombleson
3558 Vassar Dr
Anchorage AK 99508

Call Sign: KB8RSX
Marla J Tombleson
3558 Vassar Dr
Anchorage AK 99508

Call Sign: WL7CSH
John Davis
13211 Venus Way
Anchorage AK 99515

Call Sign: KC4MXQ
Nathan R Soots
13400 Vern Dr
Anchorage AK 99516

Call Sign: KC4MXR
Barbara J Soots
13400 Vern Dr
Anchorage AK 99516

Call Sign: WA4SXI
Ricky A Soots
13400 Vern Dr
Anchorage AK 99516

Call Sign: KL2JE
Keith S Austin
7030 Viburnum Dr
Anchorage AK 99507

Call Sign: WL7HL
Salee V Goodman
6901 Viburnum Dr
Anchorage AK 99507

Call Sign: KL2XD
Logan L Strid
9440 Victor Rd
Anchorage AK 99515

Call Sign: KL7GSF
Dean L Strid
9440 Victor Rd
Anchorage AK 99515

Call Sign: KL1XG
Judy L Pendleton
8631 Vifor Cir
Anchorage AK 99504

Call Sign: KL1XH
Kenneth E Pendleton
8631 Vigor Cir
Anchorage AK 99504

Call Sign: KL7LR
Gene G Barnum
6471 Village Pky
Anchorage AK 99504

Call Sign: KL2NT
Rudolf Scott-Douglas Owens
1447 Virginia Ct
Anchorage AK 99501

Call Sign: AL3Q
Jeffery R Arnold
1351 W26th Ave Unit G4
Anchorage AK 99503

Call Sign: KL2CC
Noe Gonzales
200 W34th 172
Anchorage AK 99503

Call Sign: KL2XI
Arthur Milan
12201 Wagner St
Anchorage AK 99516

Call Sign: KL7DZE
George M Naumann Jr
2392 Waldron Dr
Anchorage AK 99507

Call Sign: KL2HK
William D Fleming
3100 Ward Place 28
Anchorage AK 99517

Call Sign: KL2JC
Katie A Hahn
3100 Ward Place 28
Anchorage AK 99517

Call Sign: AL2N
Michael C Wood
3100 Ward Place 18
Anchorage AK 99517

Call Sign: NL7BG
A Stephanie Oglesby
2130 Washington Ave
Anchorage AK 99515

Call Sign: KL1EO
Sarah R Oglesby
2130 Washinton Ave
Anchorage AK 99515

Call Sign: KL0LF
Christopher R Souser
6711 Weimer Dr 4
Anchorage AK 99502

Call Sign: KL3EJ
Corey N Todoroff
7075 Weimer Rd 1
Anchorage AK 99502

Call Sign: KL3LR
Shelly L Rochon
7078 Weimer Rd 8

Anchorage AK 99502

Call Sign: KL3ET
Sarah L Gollub
3424 Wentworth St
Anchorage AK 99508

Call Sign: WB0CMZ
Roger E Gollub
3424 Wentworth St
Anchorage AK 995084356

Call Sign: KL7TP
Robert C Farkas
3004 Wesleyan Dr
Anchorage AK 99508

Call Sign: KL7ITI
William R Reiter
3343 Wesleyan Dr
Anchorage AK 995084863

Call Sign: WL7G
Gunnar P Knapp
3730 Wesleyan Dr
Anchorage AK 99508

Call Sign: KL1PU
Jacob C Farkas
4817 Wesleyan Dr
Anchorage AK 99508

Call Sign: WL7WG
Paula J Anderson
3723 West 100th Ave
Anchorage AK 99515

Call Sign: KL7DLA
Grace E Dillon
923 West 11th
Anchorage AK 99501

Call Sign: KL7GU
Allen B Turner
923 West 11th
Anchorage AK 99501

Call Sign: KL4T
Roy C Gould
923 West 11th Ave Rm 407
Anchorage AK 99501

Call Sign: KL3HE
Bobbe D Seibert

905 West 12th Ave
Anchorage AK 99501

Call Sign: KL2BE
Jerry A Wertzbaugher
1111 West 12th Ave
Anchorage AK 99501

Call Sign: KL2BF
Nancy L Wertzbaugher
1111 West 12th Ave
Anchorage AK 99501

Call Sign: KL2VF
Susan C Miller
728 West 18th Ave
Anchorage AK 99503

Call Sign: KL7CI
Charles Imig
650 West 20th
Anchorage AK 99503

Call Sign: KA7JOR
Edward R Hiett
936 West 20th 1
Anchorage AK 99503

Call Sign: WL7CCQ
John C Fiorella
915 West 23rd Ave
Anchorage AK 99503

Call Sign: KL0IV
Raymond Jones
827 West 24th Ave
Anchorage AK 99503

Call Sign: KL3AN
Nathan E Proetz
133 West 24th Ave 1
Anchorage AK 99503

Call Sign: N1KDQ
Lisa Marie C Whittaker
1330 West 25th 3
Anchorage AK 99503

Call Sign: KL2TG
Mark J Dougherty
1473 West 25th Ave 108
Anchorage AK 99503

Call Sign: WB0YUL

Samuel F Shaffer
1327 West 25th Ave Unit 104
Anchorage AK 99503

Call Sign: KL7TS
Theodore J Sheffield
2631 West 27th Ave
Anchorage AK 99517

Call Sign: KL2YT
Alan H Mccutcheon
1427 West 27th Ave 30
Anchorage AK 99503

Call Sign: KL3AG
Joseph L Guyette
1040 West 27th Ave 306
Anchorage AK 99503

Call Sign: KC6RWH
Cecilio M Bituin Jr
1040 West 27th St Rm 219
Anchorage AK 99503

Call Sign: WL7BJA
William F Thomas Jr
3006 West 29th Ave
Anchorage AK 99710

Call Sign: KL1IS
Brian J Mueller
2906 West 30th St
Anchorage AK 99517

Call Sign: KL3EI
Sherry L Billings
2100 West 31st Ave
Anchorage AK 99517

Call Sign: KL7RR
Frank Jackson Jr
3011 West 31st Ave
Anchorage AK 99517

Call Sign: KL3CF
John C Marshall Jr
2808 West 33rd Ave
Anchorage AK 99517

Call Sign: KL2BP
Robert C Lee
2911 West 33rd Ave Apt 3
Anchorage AK 99517

Call Sign: KL2BT
Calex N Gonzalez
200 West 34th 172
Anchorage AK 99503

Call Sign: KL7ZT
Calex N Gonzalez
200 West 34th 172
Anchorage AK 99503

Call Sign: KL1BW
Allen D Pollard
200 West 34th 846
Anchorage AK 99503

Call Sign: AL1L
Allen D Pollard
200 West 34th 846
Anchorage AK 99503

Call Sign: KI4GCF
Richard F Dusseau
200 West 34th Ave
Anchorage AK 99503

Call Sign: KL7SFD
Richard F Dusseau
200 West 34th Ave
Anchorage AK 99503

Call Sign: KL2BQ
Kimberly A Heinrichs
200 West 34th Ave 172
Anchorage AK 99503

Call Sign: KL2RE
Brent A Howell
200 West 34th Ave 250
Anchorage AK 99503

Call Sign: KL2AY
Susan A Jensen
200 West 34th Ave 43
Anchorage AK 99503

Call Sign: N7XEB
Michael A Cady
200 West 34th Ave 505
Anchorage AK 99503

Call Sign: KL2VP
Kevin Riggan
200 West 34th Ave 1200
Anchorage AK 99503

Call Sign: AL1X
Kevin Riggan
200 West 34th Ave 1200
Anchorage AK 99503

Call Sign: WL7XX
Sandra M Niederhofer
200 West 34th Ave 215
Anchorage AK 99503

Call Sign: KL1RI
Joshua G Mcdonald
200 West 34th Ave 669
Anchorage AK 99503

Call Sign: KL1BV
Lucie A Pollard
200 West 34th Ave 846
Anchorage AK 99503

Call Sign: KG6IGS
Edward L Clair
200 West 34th St 227
Anchorage AK 99503

Call Sign: KL7BH
Arlene N Frost
3109 West 35th Ave
Anchorage AK 99503

Call Sign: KL0BF
John H Waalkes
3103 West 36th Ave
Anchorage AK 99517

Call Sign: WL7BZG
Russell A Schmieder Sr
300 West 36th Ave 14
Anchorage AK 99503

Call Sign: KL7VU
William M Caton
1701 West 37th Ave
Anchorage AK 99517

Call Sign: KL2YJ
Christopher L Rapan
525 West 3rd Ave 3
Anchorage AK 99501

Call Sign: AL3R
Christopher L Rapan
525 West 3rd Ave 3

Anchorage AK 99501

Call Sign: KL2RK
Terry S Gorlick
1501 West 41st Ave
Anchorage AK 99503

Call Sign: WL7RW
Tamara D Hamler
500 West 42nd Ave
Anchorage AK 99503

Call Sign: WL7BJB
Erldon P Gratrix
3716 West 42nd Ave
Anchorage AK 99517

Call Sign: KL2ND
Ryan S Johnson
755 West 42nd Ave 11
Anchorage AK 99503

Call Sign: KL7NR
Catherine M Moody
3062 West 42nd Ave Apt 5
Anchorage AK 995172855

Call Sign: WL7BXH
Carol L Jaynes
1509 West 45th 3
Anchorage AK 99503

Call Sign: WL7ES
Robert B Carpenter
1411 West 46th Ave
Anchorage AK 99503

Call Sign: KL7KO
Kathleen R O'Keefe
2003 West 46th Ave
Anchorage AK 99517

Call Sign: KL7MD
Michael D O'Keefe
2003 West 46th Ave
Anchorage AK 99517

Call Sign: KL1EK
Michael D O'Keefe
2003 West 46th Ave
Anchorage AK 99517

Call Sign: KL1IT
Kathleen R O'Keefe

2003 West 46th Ave
Anchorage AK 995173176

Call Sign: KL0SJ
Nick S Tonkin
1206 West 47th Ave Apt A
Anchorage AK 99503

Call Sign: KL1RX
Matthew E Childs
2301 West 48th Ave
Anchorage AK 99517

Call Sign: WL7CHL
Janet L Bolvin
733 West 4th Ave 310
Anchorage AK 99501

Call Sign: KL7HAC
Charles W Schneider
809 West 57th Ave
Anchorage AK 995181503

Call Sign: AL3J
Hitoshi Kira
329 West 5th Ave
Anchorage AK 99501

Call Sign: KL3BS
Viengpathane K Thongdy
2640 West 65th Ave
Anchorage AK 99502

Call Sign: KL3CD
David J Fison
2210 West 70th Ave
Anchorage AK 99502

Call Sign: WL7UO
Le Eric S Marvin
760 West 71st Ave
Anchorage AK 99518

Call Sign: KL7CPC
Marvin P Greene
841 West 71st Ave
Anchorage AK 99518

Call Sign: KL7JAA
Steven R Hafling
1042 West 71st Ave
Anchorage AK 995182118

Call Sign: KL3CN

Timmothy A Stephan
3830 West 72nd Ct
Anchorage AK 99502

Call Sign: NL7ZD
Daniel M Lahaie
1340 West 73rd Cir
Anchorage AK 99503

Call Sign: KL7ANV
Emitt L Soldin
806 West 74th
Anchorage AK 99518

Call Sign: NL7XR
Michael K Doyle
911 West 75th 3
Anchorage AK 99518

Call Sign: NL7AA
James N Lang
600 West 76th Ste 203
Anchorage AK 99518

Call Sign: KL7U
Lonnie R Olson
3707 West 78th
Anchorage AK 99502

Call Sign: NL7UN
Melissa M Olson
3707 West 78th
Anchorage AK 99502

Call Sign: WL7YA
Matthew A Olson
3707 West 78th
Anchorage AK 99502

Call Sign: AL7KO
Thomas F Dickson Sr
1361 West 78th Ave
Anchorage AK 99518

Call Sign: KL1UI
Nigel Guest
3320 West 78th Ave
Anchorage AK 99502

Call Sign: WL7AKU
Frank G Chalifour Sr
3224 West 80th Ave
Anchorage AK 99502

Call Sign: KL3GK
John W Pendrey V
2151 West 80th Ave 4
Anchorage AK 99502

Call Sign: KL2IM
Bryon D Skiver
3000 West 80th Unit B
Anchorage AK 99502

Call Sign: WL7CLW
Ralph O Wilkerson
3249 West 81st Ave
Anchorage AK 99502

Call Sign: KL2NC
Robert H Houtary
606 West 86th Ct
Anchorage AK 99515

Call Sign: KL3CK
Jerry A Stackhouse
731 West 88th Ave
Anchorage AK 99515

Call Sign: KA1NVZ
Thomas G Elmore
4740 West 88th Ave
Anchorage AK 99502

Call Sign: WL7GJ
Carl E Grantham
3642 West 88th Ave Apt 212
Anchorage AK 995025321

Call Sign: WL7N
Ronald M Robison
610 West 89th
Anchorage AK 99515

Call Sign: WL7COZ
Lee E Hackenberger
1200 West Diamond 703
Anchorage AK 99515

Call Sign: WL7HI
Cynthia L Squire
5400 West Dimond Blvd C10
Anchorage AK 995021320

Call Sign: KL0MP
Bruce G Knutson
1200 West Dimond Blvd
Sp1111

Anchorage AK 99515

Call Sign: AL7RE
Marcia L Knutson
1200 West Dimond Blvd
Sp1111
Anchorage AK 995151547

Call Sign: WL7HJ
Kenneth A Hales
5400 West Dimond C10
Anchorage AK 995021320

Call Sign: KL7BGZ
Neil E Thalaker
1540 West Fifteenth Ave
Anchorage AK 99501

Call Sign: KL2BK
Richard J Cardenas
117 West Harvard Ave
Anchorage AK 99501

Call Sign: KL7WIZ
Michael W Demolina
401 West International Airport
Rd 17
Anchorage AK 99518

Call Sign: KE6DUJ
Anthony M Lombardo
2875 West International Airport
Rd D106
Anchorage AK 99502

Call Sign: NL7QA
Thomas P O Neal
1317 West Northern Lights 640
Anchorage AK 99503

Call Sign: KL2BU
John K Combs
2900 West Northern Lights Blvd
4
Anchorage AK 99517

Call Sign: KD7PLK
Stephen N Phipps
1231 West Northern Lights Blvd
622
Anchorage AK 995032337

Call Sign: WL7JA
Patrick V Wilke

1231 West Northern Lights Blvd
Ste 480
Anchorage AK 99503

Call Sign: AB0IC
James M Mounts
2315 West Tudor Rd
Anchorage AK 99517

Call Sign: WL7EE
Melaine R Hurst
2315 West Tudor Rd Apt 5
Anchorage AK 99517

Call Sign: N0HJT
Douglas R Brower
4160 Westland Cr
Anchorage AK 99517

Call Sign: AL7OS
Marlene G Poulson
3950 Westland Dr
Anchorage AK 99517

Call Sign: AL7EF
Harold E Poulson
3950 Westland Dr
Anchorage AK 99517

Call Sign: KL3GY
James C Paoli
4001 Westland Dr
Anchorage AK 99517

Call Sign: KL0PV
Todd P Kelley
13591 Westwind Dr
Anchorage AK 99516

Call Sign: KL7ND
Daniel J Cismoski
13701 Westwind Dr
Anchorage AK 99516

Call Sign: WL7CFN
Charles P Allen
10000 Whale Bay Cir
Anchorage AK 99515

Call Sign: WL7DM
Marlyn A Allen
10000 Whale Bay Cir
Anchorage AK 99515

Call Sign: NL7NW
Bruce E Benson
5331 Whispering Spruce Dr
Anchorage AK 99516

Call Sign: KF5HFB
David A Rutledge
5440 Whispering Spruce Dr
Anchorage AK 99516

Call Sign: KL2VO
Bethany L Marcum
7463 White Hawk Dr
Anchorage AK 99507

Call Sign: KL7HFA
Michael F Johnnie
6905 Whitehall
Anchorage AK 995022760

Call Sign: KD0FDP
Daniel S Lann
4000 Whitfield Cir
Anchorage AK 99507

Call Sign: KD7FJY
Karen A Medkeff
4021 Whitfield Cir
Anchorage AK 99507

Call Sign: WL7BUN
Ronald G Hess
11101 Wildwood Dr
Anchorage AK 99516

Call Sign: KL2XG
Michael R Christopher
10065 William Jones Cir 2
Anchorage AK 99515

Call Sign: KL7IWM
James N Bertelson
3506 Wingate Cir
Anchorage AK 99508

Call Sign: KL2RQ
Kevin E Ehm
635 Winter Haven St
Anchorage AK 99504

Call Sign: KL7HNM
Brian D Wick
3750 Winterset Dr
Anchorage AK 99508

Anchorage AK 995172110

Call Sign: WB6MAY
Darrell A Wick
3750 Winterset Dr
Anchorage AK 99508

Call Sign: KL2MM
Mark W Heritage
4309 Wisconsin St 7
Anchorage AK 99517

Call Sign: KL7BG
Robert L Griffin
7940 Wisteria St
Anchorage AK 99502

Call Sign: NL7SV
Dian Griffin
7940 Wisteria St
Anchorage AK 99502

Call Sign: KL3BH
Shaun C Dees
7361 Woburn Cir 3
Anchorage AK 99502

Call Sign: N7JHD
John A Schwartz Jr
7301 Woburn Cir 4
Anchorage AK 99502

Call Sign: W4IGM
John W Shull Sr
1410 Wolverine
Anchorage AK 99504

Call Sign: WL7CUJ
William W Laxson III
11901 Woodbourne Cir
Anchorage AK 99516

Call Sign: KL7IPO
William W Laxson
11901 Woodbourne Cir
Anchorage AK 99516

Call Sign: KL7KB
James H Feaster
3205 Woodland Park Dr
Anchorage AK 99517

Call Sign: KL0OD
Catherine Feaster
3205 Woodland Park Dr

Call Sign: KL7LI
Norman S Lee
3305 Woodland Park Dr
Anchorage AK 99517

Call Sign: KL7WB
Alaska Weak Signal Vhf Uhf
Club
12303 Woodward Dr
Anchorage AK 99516

Call Sign: NL7TU
Jason M Bennett
12303 Woodward Dr
Anchorage AK 99516

Call Sign: KL2SP
Brett E Sarber
4340 Woronzof Dr
Anchorage AK 99517

Call Sign: KL3KS
Albert J Lorenzen
2230 Yorkshire Ln
Anchorage AK 99504

Call Sign: KL7HSU
George J Gallagher
2311 Yorkshire Ln
Anchorage AK 99504

Call Sign: NL7NO
Donald L Sheppard
6000 Yukon Rd
Anchorage AK 99516

Call Sign: NL7YM
John M Ziv II
280 Zappa Place
Anchorage AK 99504

Call Sign: KL7LED
Robert A Hufford
Anchorage AK 99504

Call Sign: KL7AI
Michael P Zeglen
Anchorage AK 99507

Call Sign: KL7MM
Harold K Clark
Anchorage AK 99509

Call Sign: KL1UH
Jason P Whipple
Anchorage AK 99509

Call Sign: KL1XC
Dawn M Rehbock
Anchorage AK 99509

Call Sign: KL2RW
James R Lavery
Anchorage AK 99509

Call Sign: K1KTQ
Alphonse V Bonito
Anchorage AK 99509

Call Sign: KL7AA
Anchorage Amateur Radio Club
Anchorage AK 99509

Call Sign: WL7CSQ
David Wallace
Anchorage AK 99509

Call Sign: WL7CSR
Harold K Clark
Anchorage AK 99509

Call Sign: WL7E
Robert J Jeffries
Anchorage AK 99509

Call Sign: KL1LW
Joshua J Howes
Anchorage AK 99510

Call Sign: KL2PH
William S Haeckler
Anchorage AK 99510

Call Sign: KL7HEY
George H Faust Jr
Anchorage AK 99510

Call Sign: WL7CJJ
Marie Catherine Thompson
Anchorage AK 99510

Call Sign: KL1KY
Leonard V Stanley
Anchorage AK 99511

Call Sign: KL3GO

Jeremiah J Mcclung
Anchorage AK 99511

Call Sign: KL3GP
Jessica G Mcclung
Anchorage AK 99511

Call Sign: KL0OC
Forest A Hayden
Anchorage AK 99511

Call Sign: KL7ZH
Barbara J Shive
Anchorage AK 99511

Call Sign: NL7BJ
Paul Jendryk
Anchorage AK 99511

Call Sign: WL7XH
Dawnda G Massey
Anchorage AK 99511

Call Sign: KL1DT
Benjamin B Hughes
Anchorage AK 99511

Call Sign: KL1EP
Todd D Engle
Anchorage AK 99511

Call Sign: N1TTX
John T Wilson Jr
Anchorage AK 99512

Call Sign: KI4SOM
Andrew J Rosenberger
Anchorage AK 99514

Call Sign: KI6HOG
William J Costello
Anchorage AK 99514

Call Sign: KL3EC
Claudia E Costello
Anchorage AK 99514

Call Sign: KL7GIQ
Claudia E Costello
Anchorage AK 99514

Call Sign: KL3HW
Herbert W Wagner
Anchorage AK 99514

Call Sign: KD4KSB
Douglas J Lawrence
Anchorage AK 99514

Call Sign: KL0QN
Rashid Stitou
Anchorage AK 99514

Call Sign: WL7KM
Elizabeth S Weekley
Anchorage AK 99514

Call Sign: KL0UT
Richard Shafer
Anchorage AK 99514

Call Sign: KL2MC
Catherine A Dwinnell
Anchorage AK 99519

Call Sign: WL7CWS
Young Ladies Radio League Of
Alaska
Anchorage AK 99519

Call Sign: KL3FD
Randy L Ditty
Anchorage AK 99519

Call Sign: KL3LH
Joyce A Creed
Anchorage AK 99519

Call Sign: KL7JIJ
James C Minton
Anchorage AK 99519

Call Sign: KL2FK
Timothy J Cowin
Anchorage AK 99520

Call Sign: WA2FXP
Robert A Briller
Anchorage AK 99520

Call Sign: KL1KU
Thomas B Fischer
Anchorage AK 99521

Call Sign: KL1LH
Grant R Fry
Anchorage AK 99521

Call Sign: KL2DY
Philip J Quinn
Anchorage AK 99521

Call Sign: KL2NE
Michael C Schader
Anchorage AK 99521

Call Sign: KL3DC
Brion J Beerle
Anchorage AK 99521

Call Sign: KJ7IR
Steve D Williamson
Anchorage AK 99521

Call Sign: NL7EV
Peter K Markvardsen
Anchorage AK 99521

Call Sign: KL2HM
Aaron K Jokela
Anchorage AK 99522

Call Sign: AL7NB
Larry L Hickman
Anchorage AK 99522

Call Sign: KL7HW
Thomas E Monroe
Anchorage AK 99522

Call Sign: NL7NN
Susan J Woods
Anchorage AK 99522

Call Sign: WL7CFF
Tiffany R Guinn
Anchorage AK 99522

Call Sign: WL7CHN
Richard A Mc Kinney
Anchorage AK 99522

Call Sign: WL7CKB
Michael R Borer
Anchorage AK 99522

Call Sign: KL1KM
Thalia J Wood
Anchorage AK 99523

Call Sign: KL1WP
Lara H Baker

Anchorage AK 99523

Call Sign: AL2R
Lara H Baker
Anchorage AK 99523

Call Sign: KL2GD
Alice L Baker
Anchorage AK 99523

Call Sign: KL2GY
Peter A Summers
Anchorage AK 99523

Call Sign: KL2RN
Kevin D Iverson
Anchorage AK 99523

Call Sign: KL2TM
Robby E Balcerzak
Anchorage AK 99523

Call Sign: KL3AU
Darrell S Taylor
Anchorage AK 99523

Call Sign: KL3CY
Neil D Gotschall III
Anchorage AK 99523

Call Sign: WL7BGX
Jeffrey W Morton
Anchorage AK 99523

Call Sign: WL7BRI
Diane Mohammadi
Anchorage AK 99523

Call Sign: KL1KO
Dayle W Lyke
Anchorage AK 99524

Call Sign: KL1XN
Christopher C Calvert
Anchorage AK 99524

Call Sign: KL2PZ
Harry R Petrie
Anchorage AK 99524

Call Sign: KL2UJ
Thomas W Bentley
Anchorage AK 99524

Call Sign: KL2VS
Frank Y Okamoto
Anchorage AK 99524

Call Sign: KL3AM
Shane C Rangel
Anchorage AK 99524

Call Sign: KL3EP
Destiny J Bradley
Anchorage AK 99524

Call Sign: KL3LD
Jared D Armstrong
Anchorage AK 99524

Call Sign: KL0ST
Pamela A Strum
Anchorage AK 99524

Call Sign: NL7IS
Jeffrey P Nowak
Anchorage AK 99524

Call Sign: WL7FH
Debora A Kerns
Anchorage AK 99524

Call Sign: KL1EE
Christopher T Gierymski
Anchorage AK 99524

Call Sign: KL3CP
Timothy M Kelly
Anchorage AK 99629

Call Sign: KL1JF
John W Wessels II
Anchorage AK 995091203

Call Sign: NL7RH
Brian E Hove
Anchorage AK 995091221

Call Sign: KL7AN
James E Sutherland
Anchorage AK 995092931

Call Sign: KL1LI
Kenneth L Martin
Anchorage AK 995100419

Call Sign: KL1NH
Richard J Helms

Anchorage AK 995100916

Call Sign: WL7CJN
Stephen K Winchell
Anchorage AK 995101352

Call Sign: AL7U
Ivar Ostbo
Anchorage AK 995101984

Call Sign: KC0GDH
Jon C Kroona
Anchorage AK 995102279

Call Sign: KL1EH
Michael J Markusen
Anchorage AK 995102281

Call Sign: KL0HP
James O Andariese
Anchorage AK 995110065

Call Sign: KL1JE
Stephen F Mckee
Anchorage AK 995110910

Call Sign: WL7XI
Michael J Massey
Anchorage AK 995111585

Call Sign: KL3CG
Sherman W Case Sr
Anchorage AK 995112295

Call Sign: KL0KB
Michael A Romanello
Anchorage AK 995112463

Call Sign: KL0QH
Walter J King
Anchorage AK 995112775

Call Sign: KL1JX
Robert A Hufford
Anchorage AK 995140691

Call Sign: KL7SKA
Robert A Hufford
Anchorage AK 995140691

Call Sign: KL7LED
Robert A Hufford
Anchorage AK 995140691

Call Sign: KL7ALZ
Geraldine L Baker
Anchorage AK 995140963

Call Sign: WL7CVD
Duane E Sherwood
Anchorage AK 995140986

Call Sign: KL7GR
Gary I Rasmussen
Anchorage AK 995141071

Call Sign: N9YD
Donald R Christensen
Anchorage AK 995142023

Call Sign: AL7GW
Donald R Christensen
Anchorage AK 995142023

Call Sign: KC7INC
Larry W Strom
Anchorage AK 995142055

Call Sign: WL7OP
Donald E Koehler
Anchorage AK 995142922

Call Sign: KL7SP
Heather C Hasper
Anchorage AK 995190341

Call Sign: KL2HH
Janet E Linnell
Anchorage AK 995190687

Call Sign: WA3CNR
Edward A Kornfield
Anchorage AK 995190873

Call Sign: KL0OI
Willie L Wright
Anchorage AK 995201732

Call Sign: WL7UZ
Michael C Schader
Anchorage AK 995211681

Call Sign: WB9JZL
Donald L Gardner
Anchorage AK 995212021

Call Sign: WL7CRR
Sallie Hogg

Anchorage AK 995212595

Call Sign: KL1PY
Tanya Y Larrabee
Anchorage AK 995212786

Call Sign: KL0PY
Rodolfo Rodriguez Worl
Anchorage AK 995221676

Call Sign: WL7ZQ
George A Seifert
Anchorage AK 995221861

Call Sign: KL0SQ
Thomas H Morse
Anchorage AK 995231003

Call Sign: KL3BY
George G Glazier
Anchorage AK 995231645

Call Sign: KL1GW
Jon Barlow
Anchorage AK 995240565

Call Sign: KV3X
D James Czech II
Anchorage AK 995241505

Call Sign: WL7BER
Norman G Kayton
Anchorage AK 995242881

Call Sign: KL1UL
Elaine R Hulse
Anchorage AK 995243762

Call Sign: NL7MC
Lisa R Holzapfel
Anchorage AK 995244553

Call Sign: AL7NC
Kazunori Watanabe
Anchorage AK 99509

Call Sign: KL7XR
John D Richards
Anchorage AK 99509

Call Sign: KL7ZR
Kathryn Y Engle
Anchorage AK 99509

Call Sign: WL7AIZ
David C Richards
Anchorage AK 99509

Call Sign: WL7BQF
Judy L Mc Clellan
Anchorage AK 99509

Call Sign: NL7ZC
Harold E Law
Anchorage AK 99510

Call Sign: WL7AW
Eva C Stevens
Anchorage AK 99510

Call Sign: KB5HEV
Jeffrey J Formica
Anchorage AK 99511

Call Sign: KL7EB
David W Stevens
Anchorage AK 99511

Call Sign: KL7IKX
Douglas P Dickinson
Anchorage AK 99511

Call Sign: NL7SF
Larry M La Grone
Anchorage AK 99511

Call Sign: WL7AKL
Daniel R Bean
Anchorage AK 99511

Call Sign: WL7GW
Barbara A Matlack
Anchorage AK 99511

Call Sign: KL7JJO
Raymond K Knefelkamp
Anchorage AK 99514

Call Sign: WL7HK
Ward C Goodman
Anchorage AK 99519

Call Sign: AL7IM
Eric D Stewart
Anchorage AK 99520

Call Sign: KL7CMQ
Charles T Coleman

Anchorage AK 99520

Call Sign: KL7FM
Robert G Norgard II
Anchorage AK 99521

Call Sign: KL7JKM
David D Simpson
Anchorage AK 99521

Call Sign: KL7VB
Harry F Gilmore
Anchorage AK 99521

Call Sign: NL7FV
Carol F Clouse
Anchorage AK 99521

Call Sign: WL7FA
Eric D Ogren
Anchorage AK 99522

Call Sign: WL7DG
William T Campbell III
Anchorage AK 99523

Call Sign: WL7GQ
John M Simpson
Anchorage AK 99523

Call Sign: AL7EM
Scott D Dennis
Anchorage AK 99524

Call Sign: WL7NB
Catherine I Gibler Moore
Anchorage AK 99524

Call Sign: N7QVH
John S Hancock
Anchorage AK 995190969

Call Sign: WL7CTO
Rozz P Lieght
Anchorage AK 99503

Call Sign: WL7BYQ
Tamara R Butaud
Anchorage AK 99509

Call Sign: KL7TI
Richard Ryan
Anchorage AK 99577

Call Sign: NL7ZH
Jim H Mc Dermott
Anchorage AK 995090026

Call Sign: AL3S
Wolf B Zemp
Anchorage AK 99510

FCC Amateur Radio Licenses in Anderson

Call Sign: KL1WE
Lucille S Farr
113 Birch St
Anderson AK 99744

Call Sign: KL0RH
Cynthia L Wright
150 Birch St
Anderson AK 99744

Call Sign: NL7XG
Larry W Flanagan
Anderson AK 99744

FCC Amateur Radio Licenses in Angoon

Call Sign: KL1GN
Stuart N Jack
Angoon AK 99820

Call Sign: KL1GO
Ozelle B Jamestown
Angoon AK 99820

Call Sign: KL1GP
Loren C Sands Jr
Angoon AK 99820

Call Sign: KL1GQ
Tonie M Vonda
Angoon AK 99820

Call Sign: KL1GR
Collin P Rielly
Angoon AK 99820

Call Sign: KL1GS
Amber E Jamestown
Angoon AK 99820

Call Sign: KL1GT
James W Parkin IV

Angoon AK 99820

Call Sign: KL1GU
Irene E Duncan
Angoon AK 99820

Call Sign: KL1GV
Carmaleeda A Estrada
Angoon AK 99820

FCC Amateur Radio Licenses in Atka

Call Sign: KL7ELO
Francis J Petrivelli
Atka Rural Branch
Atka AK 99502

FCC Amateur Radio Licenses in Atqasuk

Call Sign: KL0JK
Herman Kignak Jr
Atqasuk AK 99791

FCC Amateur Radio Licenses in Auke Bay

Call Sign: WL7CLT
Patricia A Reifenstein
4201 Auke Ln
Auke Bay AK 99821

Call Sign: WL7BJZ
Kevin J Hansen
Box 210054
Auke Bay AK 998210054

Call Sign: KL7IVY
Estol R Belflower
Box 210303
Auke Bay AK 99821

Call Sign: KL7FMX
Lorin L Nash
Box 210314
Auke Bay AK 99821

Call Sign: WL7JK
Robert W Mc Vey
Box 211413
Auke Bay AK 99821

Call Sign: AB0WS

Patrick M Cuddihy
Auke Bay AK 99821

Call Sign: KL1KC
Alan S Gross
Auke Bay AK 99821

Call Sign: KL1KQ
Lindy M Jones
Auke Bay AK 99821

Call Sign: KL1LA
Norman N Wiswell II
Auke Bay AK 99821

Call Sign: WL7EOC
Emergency Services - Se Alaska
Auke Bay AK 99821

Call Sign: AL1Z
Patrick M Cuddihy
Auke Bay AK 99821

Call Sign: KL1RW
Zachary M Cuddihy
Auke Bay AK 99821

Call Sign: AL7AZ
Patrick M Cuddihy
Auke Bay AK 99821

Call Sign: KL7EOC
Emergency Services - Se Alaska
Auke Bay AK 99821

Call Sign: AL7SE
Southeast Alaska Radio
Association
Auke Bay AK 99821

Call Sign: KL2HE
David S Miller
Auke Bay AK 99821

Call Sign: KL2UG
Ivan Hazelton
Auke Bay AK 99821

Call Sign: KL2ZP
Dalton D Fairbanks
Auke Bay AK 99821

Call Sign: KL2ZQ
Melvin D Fairbanks

Auke Bay AK 99821

Call Sign: KL3GB
Andre J Garson
Auke Bay AK 99821

Call Sign: KF7PSS
Jonathon G Folsom
Auke Bay AK 99821

Call Sign: KL3LF
Paul J Wescott
Auke Bay AK 99821

Call Sign: AL5W
Paul J Wescott
Auke Bay AK 99821

Call Sign: KL3LW
Thomas C Doran
Auke Bay AK 99821

Call Sign: KL3LX
Lois E Dworshak
Auke Bay AK 99821

Call Sign: KL0LA
Barbara J Prindle
Auke Bay AK 99821

Call Sign: KL0RW
Jacek Maselko
Auke Bay AK 99821

Call Sign: KL7AVT
Malgia Arehart Jr
Auke Bay AK 99821

Call Sign: KL7HFI
Jerry D Prindle
Auke Bay AK 99821

Call Sign: WL7BLZ
Fred A Riley
Auke Bay AK 99821

Call Sign: WL7BOU
David S Miller
Auke Bay AK 99821

Call Sign: WL7CKK
Deborah K Verrelli
Auke Bay AK 99821

Call Sign: WL7CKP
Polly A Dewey
Auke Bay AK 99821

Call Sign: KD7IMM
Jonathan W Kamler
Auke Bay AK 99821

Call Sign: KD7IMT
Darcie Neff
Auke Bay AK 99821

Call Sign: WL7CVM
Southeast Alaska Radio
Association
Auke Bay AK 99821

Call Sign: WL7QC
Robert D Dewey
Auke Bay AK 998210053

Call Sign: AL7BP
Howard M Shepherd Jr
Auke Bay AK 998210192

Call Sign: WL7S
Douglas H Alsip
Auke Bay AK 998210574

Call Sign: NL7A
Douglas H Alsip
Auke Bay AK 998210574

Call Sign: WL7CQC
Sheryl A Barnstead
Auke Bay AK 998210861

Call Sign: NL7EI
Carroll J Tamplin
Auke Bay AK 99821

Call Sign: NL7KL
Tad C Fujioka
Auke Bay AK 99821

Call Sign: W3ML
George H Reifenstein
Auke Bay AK 99821

Call Sign: WL7BJY
Elizabeth C Hansen
Auke Bay AK 99821

Call Sign: WL7BLG

Gay D Tamplin
Auke Bay AK 99821

Call Sign: WL7CK
Roy R Greening
Auke Bay AK 99821

Call Sign: WL7JJ
James M Housley
Auke Bay AK 99821

FCC Amateur Radio Licenses in Barrow

Call Sign: KL7IOD
James D Wolgemuth
Box 115
Barrow AK 99723

Call Sign: NL7L
Rolland J Thomas
Box 790
Barrow AK 99723

Call Sign: KL1NF
Robert Carrillo
Barrow AK 99723

Call Sign: K6YU
Mark E Hoffman
Barrow AK 99723

Call Sign: KL0JA
Gregory R Suriano
Barrow AK 99723

Call Sign: KL0JB
Gilbert T Simmonds Jr
Barrow AK 99723

Call Sign: KL0JJ
Richard L Lord
Barrow AK 99723

Call Sign: KL0JL
James L Contreras
Barrow AK 99723

Call Sign: KL0JN
David W Knowles
Barrow AK 99723

Call Sign: KL0JP
Joe M Lima

Barrow AK 99723

Call Sign: KL7GPS
Floyd L Davidson
Barrow AK 99723

Call Sign: NL7IW
Paul A Carr Sr
Barrow AK 99723

Call Sign: KL1BJ
Robert Carrillo
Barrow AK 99723

Call Sign: NL7HT
Robert C Sommer
Barrow AK 997232087

Call Sign: NL7LH
William D Gelvin
Barrow AK 99723

Call Sign: WL7CET
Larrie G Prociw
Barrow AK 99723

FCC Amateur Radio Licenses in Beaver

Call Sign: KL3IB
Lavern E Davison
Beaver AK 99724

FCC Amateur Radio Licenses in Beluga

Call Sign: WL7CNE
Dorothy M Jones
Beluga AK 99695

FCC Amateur Radio Licenses in Bethel

Call Sign: WL7BUS
David M Murray
Bethel AK 99559

Call Sign: KL2ZL
Shaun V Przybylski
9457A Ayaginar Dr
Bethel AK 99559

Call Sign: KL7HCI
Dwight S Lefner

255 Ayiak St
Bethel AK 99559

Call Sign: WL7BWF
Julien A Jacobs
Box 1634
Bethel AK 99559

Call Sign: AL7GB
James A Mc Curdy
Box 1681
Bethel AK 99559

Call Sign: WL7BWU
Cameron A Campbell
Box 2251
Bethel AK 99559

Call Sign: WL7BVC
Aren R Sparck
Box 267
Bethel AK 99559

Call Sign: WL7BWG
Muddassir M Aliniazee
Box 3025
Bethel AK 99559

Call Sign: WL7BTI
Joyce E Freeman
Box 40
Bethel AK 995590040

Call Sign: KM4KX
James A Strickland
3341 North Apron Rd
Bethel AK 99559

Call Sign: WL7CDW
Charles J Spindler
Phs Box 3008
Bethel AK 99559

Call Sign: KL2OZ
George T Martin
PO Box 1347 918
Bethel AK 99559

Call Sign: KL2JJ
Daniel D Albrite Jr
PO Box 64
Bethel AK 99559

Call Sign: N5RMJ

Rodney M Jones
Bethel AK 99559

Call Sign: KL1UZ
Sean T O'Leary
Bethel AK 99559

Call Sign: KL1VA
Steve D Hayden
Bethel AK 99559

Call Sign: KL2AU
Allen E Desousa
Bethel AK 99559

Call Sign: WL7CWG
Bethel Amateur Radio Club
Bethel AK 99559

Call Sign: AL7YK
Bethel Amateur Radio Club
Bethel AK 99559

Call Sign: KL2IR
Angeline T Whitman
Bethel AK 99559

Call Sign: KL2IS
Albert W Swope
Bethel AK 99559

Call Sign: KL2IT
Royle P Rogers
Bethel AK 99559

Call Sign: KL2IU
Michael F Mcintyre
Bethel AK 99559

Call Sign: KL2IV
Roger D Lowe
Bethel AK 99559

Call Sign: KL2IW
Norman H Ayagalria
Bethel AK 99559

Call Sign: KL2IX
Pete J Ebertz
Bethel AK 99559

Call Sign: KL2IY
Bruce W Claypool
Bethel AK 99559

Call Sign: KL2JA
Jeremiah E Johnson
Bethel AK 99559

Call Sign: KL2KY
Starr J Jensen
Bethel AK 99559

Call Sign: KL2KZ
Patrick B Oulton
Bethel AK 99559

Call Sign: KL2LA
Mona G Jensen
Bethel AK 99559

Call Sign: KL2LB
Ronald S Horvath
Bethel AK 99559

Call Sign: KL2LC
Joel E Malus
Bethel AK 99559

Call Sign: KL2LD
Joli B Morgan
Bethel AK 99559

Call Sign: KL2LE
Larry O Howard
Bethel AK 99559

Call Sign: KL2LF
Lori P Chikoyak
Bethel AK 99559

Call Sign: KL2LG
David J Mccormick
Bethel AK 99559

Call Sign: KL2LH
Richard J Hall III
Bethel AK 99559

Call Sign: KL2LI
Velma L Raines
Bethel AK 99559

Call Sign: KL2ML
Pamela F Conrad
Bethel AK 99559

Call Sign: KL7AED

Allen E Desousa
Bethel AK 99559

Call Sign: KL2OT
Arthur K Freitas
Bethel AK 99559

Call Sign: KL2OU
Shannon A Freitas
Bethel AK 99559

Call Sign: KL2OV
Dyle C Korthuis
Bethel AK 99559

Call Sign: KL2OW
Susan M Claypool
Bethel AK 99559

Call Sign: KL2OX
Miriam D Dillard
Bethel AK 99559

Call Sign: KL2OY
Louis I Mallette IV
Bethel AK 99559

Call Sign: KL2PB
Russ D Mcdonald
Bethel AK 99559

Call Sign: KL2PC
Conrad J Mccormick
Bethel AK 99559

Call Sign: KL2PD
Wyatt A White
Bethel AK 99559

Call Sign: KL2RA
Spencer W Hamons
Bethel AK 99559

Call Sign: KL2RB
Coryee A Hamons
Bethel AK 99559

Call Sign: KL2TV
Terry L Perry
Bethel AK 99559

Call Sign: KL2VY
James Atti
Bethel AK 99559

Call Sign: KL2VZ
Avery W Atti
Bethel AK 99559

Call Sign: KL2WA
Teresa R Markham
Bethel AK 99559

Call Sign: KL2WB
Mildred C Twitchell
Bethel AK 99559

Call Sign: KL2WC
Matthew J Martino
Bethel AK 99559

Call Sign: KL2WD
Robert M Hoehn
Bethel AK 99559

Call Sign: KL2WE
Edward N Berry
Bethel AK 99559

Call Sign: KL2WG
Sean C Armstrong
Bethel AK 99559

Call Sign: KL2WH
Brian D Watt
Bethel AK 99559

Call Sign: KL2WI
Colleen M Osterhaus
Bethel AK 99559

Call Sign: KL2WJ
Deborah G Fine
Bethel AK 99559

Call Sign: KL2WK
Anna David
Bethel AK 99559

Call Sign: KL2WL
Brian D Watt
Bethel AK 99559

Call Sign: KL2WU
Craig B Rogers
Bethel AK 99559

Call Sign: KL2YW

Pamela Lau
Bethel AK 99559

Call Sign: KL2ZI
Patrick C Jennings
Bethel AK 99559

Call Sign: KL2ZK
Joseph E Shawler
Bethel AK 99559

Call Sign: KL2ZM
Robert J Gregory
Bethel AK 99559

Call Sign: KL3DF
Carlos L Breaux
Bethel AK 99559

Call Sign: KL3DG
Marvin C Hamilton
Bethel AK 99559

Call Sign: KL3EU
Clifford L Geimer
Bethel AK 99559

Call Sign: KL3EW
Justin A Wintersteen
Bethel AK 99559

Call Sign: KL3EX
Justin Brandt
Bethel AK 99559

Call Sign: KL3EY
Ralph E Monteith
Bethel AK 99559

Call Sign: KA1NCN
David A Case
Bethel AK 99559

Call Sign: KL7NZ
Bruce R Perry Sr
Bethel AK 99559

Call Sign: NL7NE
Joyce M Straight
Bethel AK 99559

Call Sign: WL7BCT
Mark E Springer
Bethel AK 99559

Call Sign: WL7CEB
Robert C Ellsworth
Bethel AK 99559

Call Sign: WL7COJ
Dean R Swope
Bethel AK 99559

Call Sign: KL0YI
Joseph E Seibert
Bethel AK 99559

Call Sign: AL1F
Joseph E Seibert
Bethel AK 99559

Call Sign: W8PVZ
Ronald S Horvath
Bethel AK 995590885

Call Sign: W8MDD
Miriam D Dillard
Bethel AK 995590885

Call Sign: NL7SP
Kenneth W Eggleston
Bethel AK 995591045

Call Sign: NL7WZ
Suzanne L Angstman
Bethel AK 99559

Call Sign: WL7BTJ
Hansel L Mathlaw
Bethel AK 99559

Call Sign: WL7BUP
Ryan J Balliet
Bethel AK 99559

Call Sign: WL7BUQ
Jonathan Squire
Bethel AK 99559

Call Sign: WL7BUR
David M Ausdahl II
Bethel AK 99559

Call Sign: WL7BVD
Jason Peebles
Bethel AK 99559

Call Sign: WL7BVG

Samuel M Patten Jr
Bethel AK 99559

Call Sign: WL7BWH
Robert E Aloysius Jr
Bethel AK 99559

Call Sign: WL7BWI
Edwin D Hahn
Bethel AK 99559

Call Sign: WL7BWL
Joshua D Morris
Bethel AK 99559

Call Sign: WL7BWM
Yvonne L Mockta
Bethel AK 99559

Call Sign: WL7BWN
Denise E Campbell
Bethel AK 99559

Call Sign: WL7BWO
Sterling T Graham
Bethel AK 99559

Call Sign: WL7BWQ
Brandon G Power
Bethel AK 99559

Call Sign: WL7BWT
Sara M Ellsworth
Bethel AK 99559

Call Sign: WL7BWX
Jaclyn A Mojin
Bethel AK 99559

Call Sign: WL7CAE
Mary C Rearden
Bethel AK 99559

Call Sign: WL7CAF
Connie J Peter
Bethel AK 99559

Call Sign: WL7CAH
Michelle E Grant
Bethel AK 99559

Call Sign: WL7CAI
Michael J Franks
Bethel AK 99559

Call Sign: WL7CAK
Rebekah A Peter
Bethel AK 99559

Call Sign: WL7CAL
Maria K Maze
Bethel AK 99559

Call Sign: WL7CAM
Jacques L Longpre
Bethel AK 99559

Call Sign: WL7CAN
Abatch Hamilton
Bethel AK 99559

Call Sign: WL7CAO
Andrew P Angstman
Bethel AK 99559

Call Sign: WL7CAS
Matthew H Peter
Bethel AK 99559

Call Sign: WL7CAT
Tracey L Anderson
Bethel AK 99559

Call Sign: WL7CAU
Beth M Rearden
Bethel AK 99559

Call Sign: WL7CDM
Greg E Stoddard
Bethel AK 99559

Call Sign: WL7CDN
Dacota D Brown
Bethel AK 99559

Call Sign: WL7CDO
Charles E Burkey Jr
Bethel AK 99559

Call Sign: WL7CDP
Patricia L Burkey
Bethel AK 99559

Call Sign: WL7CDQ
Randy L Burkey
Bethel AK 99559

Call Sign: WL7CDR

Skye M Campbell
Bethel AK 99559

Call Sign: WL7CDS
Katie A Ellsworth
Bethel AK 99559

Call Sign: WL7CDT
John L Hastie
Bethel AK 99559

Call Sign: WL7CDU
Jeremiah A Kacyon
Bethel AK 99559

Call Sign: WL7CDV
Becky L Meyers
Bethel AK 99559

Call Sign: WL7CDX
Travis E Glessing
Bethel AK 99559

Call Sign: WL7CFC
Rachel M Chamberlain
Bethel AK 99559

Call Sign: WL7CFD
Patrick W Jones
Bethel AK 99559

Call Sign: WL7CFE
Christopher A White
Bethel AK 99559

Call Sign: WL7CFG
Howard R Wassilie
Bethel AK 99559

Call Sign: WL7CFH
Sharon A Mojin
Bethel AK 99559

FCC Amateur Radio Licenses in Big Lake

Call Sign: KG6KGV
James M Brooks
Box 520463
Big Lake AK 99652

Call Sign: KL7GAM
Wallace R Comeaux
15181 Dogwood Cr

Big Lake AK 99652

Call Sign: KL0YN
Robert A Sherrer
13912 Kluane Dr
Big Lake AK 99652

Call Sign: KL0YQ
Tammi A Sherrer
13912 Kluane Dr
Big Lake AK 99652

Call Sign: WB6SWE
Virginia K Croner
2390 South Park Rd
Big Lake AK 99652

Call Sign: AL7FJ
Shari K Macgregor
16582 West Macgregor Cir
Big Lake AK 99652

Call Sign: KL1OT
Frank A Chamberlain
Big Lake AK 99652

Call Sign: KL1OU
Debbie L Underwood
Big Lake AK 99652

Call Sign: KL1TV
Thomas M Gillett
Big Lake AK 99652

Call Sign: KL1YO
Kevin S Brooks
Big Lake AK 99652

Call Sign: KL2CN
William F Gamble
Big Lake AK 99652

Call Sign: KL2CP
William E Morrow
Big Lake AK 99652

Call Sign: KL7OU
Debbie L Underwood
Big Lake AK 99652

Call Sign: WL7O
Frank A Chamberlain
Big Lake AK 99652

Call Sign: KL2HA
Stephen C Hoff
Big Lake AK 99652

Call Sign: KL2QU
Jeffery R Arnold
Big Lake AK 99652

Call Sign: KL3AZ
Charles D Phillips
Big Lake AK 99652

Call Sign: KL3KM
William L Morgan
Big Lake AK 99652

Call Sign: KL7GID
Eugene M Mockerman
Big Lake AK 99652

Call Sign: KL7TK
James B Leach
Big Lake AK 99652

Call Sign: KY7J
Kenneth E Cole Jr
Big Lake AK 99652

Call Sign: N7WUY
Maria R Northcutt
Big Lake AK 99652

Call Sign: NL7WI
Sarah A Leach
Big Lake AK 99652

Call Sign: WL7CMD
Dawn E Deiser
Big Lake AK 99652

Call Sign: KL1IV
Todd A Richardson
Big Lake AK 99652

Call Sign: KA7LUZ
Peggy A Cole
Big Lake AK 996520135

Call Sign: KL7JHG
Jean B Comeaux
Big Lake AK 996521726

Call Sign: KL7HFQ
Roger K Hansen

Big Lake AK 99652

Call Sign: N3HEG
Patrick A Dalton
Big Lake AK 99652

Call Sign: WL7BOA
Robert L Alvord
Big Lake AK 99652

Call Sign: WL7BSB
Gordon B Mac Williams
Big Lake AK 99652

Call Sign: WL7BUK
Gregory W Krapff
Big Lake AK 99652

Call Sign: WL7CAD
Alice L Mockerman
Big Lake AK 99652

FCC Amateur Radio Licenses in Cantwell

Call Sign: NL7MX
Bernice Sheldon
Box 154
Cantwell AK 99729

Call Sign: KL0HE
Aase K Dane
Cantwell AK 99729

FCC Amateur Radio Licenses in Central

Call Sign: KL2GS
Mclaren C Carter Jr
Central AK 99730

Call Sign: KL2ZC
Linda J Carter
Central AK 99730

FCC Amateur Radio Licenses in Chickaloon

Call Sign: KL3EZ
Steven H Hudson
Chickaloon AK 99674

Call Sign: KL3KU
Darlene F Lust

Chickaloon AK 99674

Call Sign: KL7HHR
Albert L Haynes
Chickaloon AK 99674

Call Sign: KL7B
Charles R Hammond
Chicken AK 99732

Call Sign: KL1WV
Darcy H Hammond
Chicken AK 99732

Call Sign: WL7VO
Charles R Hammond
Chicken AK 99732

Call Sign: WL7VP
Robin L Hammond
Chicken AK 99732

Call Sign: KL1BU
Marie B Fichtelman
Chicken AK 99732

Call Sign: WL7GMT
Marie B Fichtelman
Chicken AK 99732

Call Sign: WL7CTR
Earl L Schene
Chicken AK 997320066

Call Sign: KL7RY
Robert L Livingston
Chigmik AK 99564

Call Sign: KL7IOL
Richard E Dennis
HC 01 Box 158
Chistochina AK 99586

Call Sign: WL7YF
Barrie D Shepherd
Mile 15 Mc Carty Rd
Chitina AK 99566

Call Sign: KB7PUY
Vicky Stephens
23107 Barbara St
Chugiak AK 99567

Call Sign: KL3LK
Theodore F Freitag
19439 Beverly 3
Chugiak AK 99567

Call Sign: WL7EK
Daryl A Douthat
Box 38
Chugiak AK 99567

Call Sign: KL7CG
Carl A Nelson
Box 670671
Chugiak AK 99567

Call Sign: KL0BA
Steve E King
20235 Chugach Park Dr
Chugiak AK 99567

Call Sign: KL1RU
Michael S Kahler
21435 Ginger Lee Dr
Chugiak AK 99567

Call Sign: KM4OE
Mark A Davis
27333 Golden Eagle Ct
Chugiak AK 99567

Call Sign: KC4OPI
Margaret L Davis
27333 Golden Eagle Ct
Chugiak AK 99567

Call Sign: AL7ML
Robin L Smith
27345 Golden Eagle Ct

Chugiak AK 995675725

Call Sign: NL7TL
John M Carr
21249 Gorsuch St 2
Chugiak AK 99567

Call Sign: WL7CRS
Jason J Morgan
23627 Greatland Dr
Chugiak AK 99567

Call Sign: KL3DM
Dean A Lang
23105 Green Garden Dr
Chugiak AK 99567

Call Sign: WL7BWE
Jay C Friesen
HC 78 Box 1023
Chugiak AK 99567

Call Sign: WL7BAP
Richard L Runyan
HC80 Box 5840
Chugiak AK 99567

Call Sign: NL7NR
Roger R Patch
23745 Immelman Cir
Chugiak AK 99567

Call Sign: NL7NS
Janet D Patch
HC 80 Box 309 Immelman Cr
Chugiak AK 99567

Call Sign: KL1KW
David C Dunckle
21131 Jayhawk Dr
Chugiak AK 99567

Call Sign: KL2TC
Allen H Koenig
21313 Jayhawk Dr
Chugiak AK 99567

Call Sign: KL1KD
Lance A Cluff
24821 Jesse Lee Ct
Chugiak AK 99567

Call Sign: KC5IBS
Troy K Laird

22733 Mc Manus Dr
Chugiak AK 99567

Call Sign: KD5DNA
Harold H Wingo
22349 Mirror Lake Dr
Chugiak AK 99567

Call Sign: AL7FI
Rachel L Runyan
21551 Old Glenn Hwy
Chugiak AK 995675632

Call Sign: KL7EML
Larry L Ledlow Sr
16533 Old Glenn Hwy Sp 7
Chugiak AK 99567

Call Sign: AL7JQ
Timothy R Dean
SR 2 Box 4487 Park Dr
Chugiak AK 99567

Call Sign: KL3EG
Waldo C Holden III
16241 Parksville Dr
Chugiak AK 99567

Call Sign: WL7CNB
Shannon P Wold
18215 Poplar St
Chugiak AK 99567

Call Sign: WL7CNC
Nancy A Wold
18215 Poplar St
Chugiak AK 99567

Call Sign: WL7BWY
Daniel T Hepler
22630 Sherman St
Chugiak AK 99567

Call Sign: KL7KP
Alan F Kukla
20414 Stephen Cir
Chugiak AK 99567

Call Sign: KL1FG
Darrell D Holmstrom
24629 Teal Loop
Chugiak AK 99567

Call Sign: KL7DTH

Charles L Wareham
24865 Teal Loop
Chugiak AK 99567

Call Sign: WL7FF
Shawn M Odell
HC 79 Box 206 Thunderbird Dr
Chugiak AK 99567

Call Sign: WL7CTM
Garrick A Olsen
19840 Tulwar Dr
Chugiak AK 99567

Call Sign: KL7WH
Donna J Jones
19901 Tulwar Dr
Chugiak AK 99567

Call Sign: KL2HN
Arthur P Bowen
Chugiak AK 99567

Call Sign: KL2LO
Randy Lissey
Chugiak AK 99567

Call Sign: KL2QA
Kayleigh S Gilbert
Chugiak AK 99567

Call Sign: KL7KSG
Kayleigh S Gilbert
Chugiak AK 99567

Call Sign: KL2QL
Kimberly D Middleton
Chugiak AK 99567

Call Sign: KL2RX
John V Rockwell
Chugiak AK 99567

Call Sign: KL2VG
Roxanne V Sidebottom
Chugiak AK 99567

Call Sign: KL2VH
Anita M Sidebottom
Chugiak AK 99567

Call Sign: KL3ES
Sammy L Cohen
Chugiak AK 99567

Call Sign: KL3FJ
Paul E Vaona
Chugiak AK 99567

Call Sign: KL3HJ
Jesse W Stone
Chugiak AK 99567

Call Sign: AL4B
Larry J Andersen
Chugiak AK 99567

Call Sign: KB9JDV
Gerald L Buttitta
Chugiak AK 99567

Call Sign: KE4EPS
Judie M Block
Chugiak AK 99567

Call Sign: KL7CC
James B Wiley
Chugiak AK 99567

Call Sign: KL7EI
Jennifer R Nelson
Chugiak AK 99567

Call Sign: KL7FN
Cleo J Morris
Chugiak AK 99567

Call Sign: KL7IXT
John M Barbarick
Chugiak AK 99567

Call Sign: KL7UQ
Francis J Soltis
Chugiak AK 99567

Call Sign: NL7NT
Gary R Kosto
Chugiak AK 99567

Call Sign: NL7QU
Frederick A Sawyer
Chugiak AK 99567

Call Sign: NL7QZ
Charles E Tetreault
Chugiak AK 99567

Call Sign: NL7RG

Shirley A Kosto
Chugiak AK 99567

Call Sign: WL7ABC
Anthony J Spangler
Chugiak AK 99567

Call Sign: WL7ATC
George Kobelnyk
Chugiak AK 99567

Call Sign: WL7BKN
Michael F Soltis
Chugiak AK 99567

Call Sign: WL7BMV
David P Holloway
Chugiak AK 99567

Call Sign: WL7BZU
Sherrie L Soltis
Chugiak AK 99567

Call Sign: WL7CPF
Kenneth L Pitts
Chugiak AK 99567

Call Sign: WL7CSU
Paul A Heater
Chugiak AK 99567

Call Sign: WL7GP
Denise M Marsh
Chugiak AK 99567

Call Sign: WL7HH
Richard E Falk
Chugiak AK 99567

Call Sign: WL7PE
David F Mc Cormick
Chugiak AK 99567

Call Sign: WL7RR
Carol L Douthat
Chugiak AK 99567

Call Sign: WL7ZM
Susan D Hall
Chugiak AK 99567

Call Sign: KG4JMW
William C Stevens Jr
Chugiak AK 99567

Call Sign: WL7CVF
Alaska Ares
Chugiak AK 99567

Call Sign: WL7CVG
Alaska Ares
Chugiak AK 99567

Call Sign: KL1FN
Cara D Spearman
Chugiak AK 99567

Call Sign: KD0CLU
Angus M Gilbert
Chugiak AK 995670170

Call Sign: KL7AMG
Angus M Gilbert
Chugiak AK 995670170

Call Sign: KL7JTG
Joel T Gilbert
Chugiak AK 995670170

Call Sign: KL7LJG
Laura J Gilbert
Chugiak AK 995670170

Call Sign: KL1EF
Joel T Gilbert
Chugiak AK 995670170

Call Sign: KL1HR
Laura J Gilbert
Chugiak AK 995670170

Call Sign: AL7HF
Frank M Hall
Chugiak AK 995670245

Call Sign: AL0R
Warren K Weldon
Chugiak AK 995670456

Call Sign: KL0TO
Warren K Weldon
Chugiak AK 995670456

Call Sign: AL0R
Warren K Weldon
Chugiak AK 995670456

Call Sign: K9ZW

Warren K Weldon
Chugiak AK 995670456

Call Sign: NL7AC
Deborah J Soltis
Chugiak AK 995670670

Call Sign: KL0ZR
Deborah J Soltis
Chugiak AK 995670670

Call Sign: KL7IZJ
Deanna Barbarick
Chugiak AK 995670841

Call Sign: KL0ZQ
James D Walcutt
Chugiak AK 995671014

Call Sign: NL7OD
Gary E Sherman
Chugiak AK 995671222

Call Sign: KL0DV
John W Peters
Chugiak AK 995672096

Call Sign: KL3CB
Theron C Wilson
Chugiak AK 996571245

Call Sign: AL7PN
Lois I Harter
Chugiak AK 99567

Call Sign: KL5E
Robert J Engberg
Chugiak AK 99567

Call Sign: KL7FKF
John A Steeby
Chugiak AK 99567

Call Sign: NL7ZI
Gerald E Sherman
Chugiak AK 99567

Call Sign: WL7BKO
Mary K Soltis
Chugiak AK 99567

Call Sign: WL7BRS
Claude R Lisenbee Jr
Chugiak AK 99567

Call Sign: WL7BZP
Andrew J Soltis
Chugiak AK 99567

Call Sign: WL7DX
Judith F Ramage
Chugiak AK 99567

Call Sign: WL7FM
James D Bruchie
Chugiak AK 99567

Call Sign: WL7MF
Vicki L Sherman
Chugiak AK 99567

Call Sign: WL7MS
Christina M Sherman
Chugiak AK 99567

Call Sign: WL7QI
Mary E Heater
Chugiak AK 99567

Call Sign: NL7J
Dale M Heater
Chugiak AK 995670197

FCC Amateur Radio Licenses in Clam Gulch

Call Sign: KL7JHR
Dennis K Ogren
72590 Sterling Hwy
Clam Gulch AK 99568

Call Sign: KL7KL
Martha E Ogren
72590 Sterling Hwy
Clam Gulch AK 99568

Call Sign: WL7AHY
James E Russell
Clam Gulch AK 99568

Call Sign: NL7OW
Thomas M Corbitt
Clam Gulch AK 99568

FCC Amateur Radio Licenses in Clear

Call Sign: KB1FCX

Jacob A Noll
200 A St Stop 123
Clear AK 99704

Call Sign: KL0MM
Thomas E Wright II
200 A St Stop 207
Clear AK 99704

Call Sign: NL7YQ
John A Roginski
Box 613
Clear AK 99704

FCC Amateur Radio Licenses in College

Call Sign: WL7BQW
Thomas M Clark
Box 80106
College AK 99708

Call Sign: KL7DIY
Robert P Merritt
Box 80627
College AK 99701

Call Sign: KL7JAV
Daniel L Osborne
College AK 99708

Call Sign: NL7XY
Jon Bolles
College AK 99708

Call Sign: WA6IQF
Keith E Pollock
College AK 99708

Call Sign: WL7BVW
Richard L Blackmer
College AK 99708

Call Sign: AL7KU
Gilbert D Monroe
College AK 99708

Call Sign: WL7OV
Bernice L Bentley
College AK 99708

Call Sign: WL7QM
Wesley A Bentley
College AK 99708

FCC Amateur Radio Licenses in Cooper Landing

Call Sign: NL7DZ
Keith F Freeman
Box 663
Cooper Landing AK 99572

Call Sign: WL7FK
Karen F Freeman
Box 663
Cooper Landing AK 99572

Call Sign: KL7PL
Kathleen M Freeman
20197 Sterling Hwy
Cooper Landing AK 99572

Call Sign: KL6A
Communications Associates
Radio Club
Cooper Landing AK 99572

Call Sign: KL7GGT
Dennis B Gleason
Cooper Landing AK 99572

Call Sign: WL7CMI
Aaron P Dye
Cooper Landing AK 99572

Call Sign: KL7TF
Thomas R Farrington
Cooper Landing AK 99572

Call Sign: NL7DE
Rose C Banse
Cooper Landing AK 99572

Call Sign: NL7KV
Justin M Freeman
Cooper Landing AK 99572

Call Sign: NL7LO
Joshua M Freeman
Cooper Landing AK 99572

Call Sign: WL7FP
John F Freeman
Cooper Landing AK 99572

FCC Amateur Radio Licenses in Cooper Center

Call Sign: KL1RH
Harry J Termin
HC 60 Box 115E
Copper Center AK 99573

Call Sign: NL7ZW
Eric J Nashlund
HC 60 Box 271
Copper Center AK 99573

Call Sign: NL7UL
Theodore M Hesser
HC 60 Box 289
Copper Center AK 99573

Call Sign: KL1SO
Judith B Termin
HC60 Box 115E
Copper Center AK 99573

Call Sign: N7MKL
Robert E Cooley
HC60 Box 142
Copper Center AK 99573

Call Sign: KL2JF
Allan H Sainsbury
HC60 Box 221D
Copper Center AK 99573

Call Sign: KL7GLS
Michael J Swisher
Mile 5 Old Edgerton Hwy
Copper Center AK 99573

Call Sign: WL7JI
Linda J Perry Plake
Copper Center AK 99573

FCC Amateur Radio Licenses in Cordova

Call Sign: KL2XZ
Richard W Groff
201 Whiskey Ridge Rd
Cordova AK 99574

Call Sign: WL7CWV
Copper River Cw Club
Cordova AK 99574

Call Sign: KL2SA
Jennifer L Green

Cordova AK 99574

Call Sign: KL2SI
Susan E Jensen
Cordova AK 99574

Call Sign: KL2XL
Faith L Barnes
Cordova AK 99574

Call Sign: KL2XM
Robert W Behrends
Cordova AK 99574

Call Sign: KL2XN
Joan D Behrends
Cordova AK 99574

Call Sign: KL2XO
Toni I Bocci
Cordova AK 99574

Call Sign: KL2XP
Bradley A Sapp
Cordova AK 99574

Call Sign: KL2XQ
Reuben B Brown
Cordova AK 99574

Call Sign: KL2XR
Michael R Butler
Cordova AK 99574

Call Sign: KL2XS
Austin F Carter
Cordova AK 99574

Call Sign: KL2XT
Jesse H Carter
Cordova AK 99574

Call Sign: KL2XU
William L Crawford
Cordova AK 99574

Call Sign: KL2XV
Pam T Crawford
Cordova AK 99574

Call Sign: KL2XW
Oscar Del Pino
Cordova AK 99574

Call Sign: KL2XX
Susan E Farzan
Cordova AK 99574

Call Sign: KL2XY
Jason E Fischer
Cordova AK 99574

Call Sign: KL2YA
Jonathan L Syder
Cordova AK 99574

Call Sign: KL2YB
Samuel K Zamudio
Cordova AK 99574

Call Sign: KL2YC
Melanie M O Brien
Cordova AK 99574

Call Sign: KL2YE
Michael W Hicks
Cordova AK 99574

Call Sign: KL0PW
Malia Y Vansant
Cordova AK 99574

Call Sign: KL0ZZ
Lyndall Aston
Cordova AK 99574

Call Sign: KL1AF
Michael P Mccarthy
Cordova AK 99574

Call Sign: KL1AL
Ralph G Bullis
Cordova AK 99574

Call Sign: AL7G
James P Vansant III
Cordova AK 99574

Call Sign: WL7BXL
William A Bauer III
Cordova AK 99574

Call Sign: WL7CBC
Michael S Cunningham
Cordova AK 99574

Call Sign: WL7CBH
Charles E Trowbridge

Cordova AK 99574

Call Sign: WL7CAX
Patricia M Schnoor
Box 2426
Cordova AK 99574

Call Sign: KL7HLM
Charles A Irvine
Box 319
Cordova AK 99574

Call Sign: WL7CAY
John R Carli
Box 766
Cordova AK 99574

Call Sign: KL2VC
Florian Orley
Cordova AK 99574

FCC Amateur Radio Licenses in Craig

Call Sign: KG6YDX
John G Larsen
Craig AK 99921

Call Sign: KL2AX
John G Larsen
Craig AK 99921

Call Sign: N7RVE
Stephen E Gianarelli
Craig AK 99921

Call Sign: WB7WSQ
Allen E Hoffman
Craig AK 99921

Call Sign: WL7CSO
Harold D Sheppard
Craig AK 99921

FCC Amateur Radio Licenses in Delta Junction

Call Sign: WL7CLH
Margaret S A Stevens
Mi 1344 Ak Hwy Hc 62 Box
5040
Delta Junction AK 99737

Call Sign: KD7HBC

Michael L Prestegard
2505 East Taxiway
Delta Junction AK 997370690

Call Sign: WL7JB
Roy C Bowdre
4543 Jack Warren Rd
Delta Junction AK 99737

Call Sign: AB7YB
Adina D Holbrook
2192 Piper Ln
Delta Junction AK 99737

Call Sign: KD4DQJ
Brian D Gay
Strawberry Rd
Delta Junction AK 99737

Call Sign: KL0EC
James M Wilcox
Box 198
Delta Junction AK 99737

Call Sign: KL7JFX
Harvey L Anderson
Box 981
Delta Junction AK 99737

Call Sign: WL7BJN
Ray E Andreassen
HC 06 Box 4859
Delta Junction AK 99737

Call Sign: KL2YD
Edna E Leedy
HC 60 4035
Delta Junction AK 99737

Call Sign: KL2FZ
Melody B Holbrook
HC 60 Box 3240
Delta Junction AK 99737

Call Sign: KL7IXF
Phillip L Holbrook
HC 60 Box 3240
Delta Junction AK 99737

Call Sign: WL7CKF
Aaron M Holbrook
HC 60 Box 3240
Delta Junction AK 99737

Call Sign: WL7CSS
Jesse A Holbrook
HC 60 Box 3240
Delta Junction AK 99737

Call Sign: WL7QY
Bethel J Holbrook
HC 60 Box 3240
Delta Junction AK 99737

Call Sign: WL7RP
Benjamin P Holbrook
HC 60 Box 3645
Delta Junction AK 99737

Call Sign: KL0XD
Brantly D Bailey
HC 60 Box 4220
Delta Junction AK 99737

Call Sign: WL7CTW
Beth C Abbott
HC 60 Box 4225
Delta Junction AK 99737

Call Sign: WL7CPP
Terry L Griffith
HC 60 Box 4300
Delta Junction AK 99737

Call Sign: AL7QT
Peter Kruger Larsen
HC 62 Box 5040
Delta Junction AK 99737

Call Sign: WL7CLK
Lev A Kuznetsov
HC 62 Box 5040
Delta Junction AK 99737

Call Sign: NL7EJ
William A Trotter
HC 62 Box 5220
Delta Junction AK 99737

Call Sign: WL7CON
Flori Stoeber
HC 62 Box 5220
Delta Junction AK 997379601

Call Sign: KD7DIG
Andrea S Holbrook
HC 62 Box 5335
Delta Junction AK 99737

Call Sign: NL7TT
Brenda L Sutherland
HC 62 Box 5670
Delta Junction AK 99737

Call Sign: WL7CCO
Arles C Sutherland
HC 62 Box 5670
Delta Junction AK 99737

Call Sign: KL0BE
Charles E Abbott
HC60 Box 4225
Delta Junction AK 99737

Call Sign: WL7CST
Ruth A Abbott
HC60 Box 4225
Delta Junction AK 99737

Call Sign: KL7IDA
William J Stevens
HC62 Box 5040
Delta Junction AK 99737

Call Sign: AL7QF
Jonathan A Riche
PO Box 1229
Delta Junction AK 99737

Call Sign: KL1OW
Vernon L Gebauer
Delta Junction AK 99737

Call Sign: KL1QH
Rebekah Holbrook
Delta Junction AK 99737

Call Sign: KL1QT
Rebekah H Holbrook
Delta Junction AK 99737

Call Sign: KL1QN
Jadon Holbrook
Delta Junction AK 99737

Call Sign: WL7CWA
Grizzly Amateur Radio Club
Delta Junction AK 99737

Call Sign: KL1UU
Shawn Behr
Delta Junction AK 99737

Call Sign: KL2AV
Brian K Corty
Delta Junction AK 99737

Call Sign: KL2CW
Coby C Haas
Delta Junction AK 99737

Call Sign: KL2NL
Jeffrey Kinsman
Delta Junction AK 99737

Call Sign: KL2QP
Eathon C Gebauer
Delta Junction AK 99737

Call Sign: KL2WQ
Daniel P Holbrook
Delta Junction AK 99737

Call Sign: AL7PQ
Joel P Holbrook
Delta Junction AK 99737

Call Sign: KA7YEY
John B Lewis III
Delta Junction AK 99737

Call Sign: KL0EA
Kenneth E Farrow
Delta Junction AK 99737

Call Sign: KL0EB
Joanna F Holbrook
Delta Junction AK 99737

Call Sign: KL0EW
Tommy C Bowdre
Delta Junction AK 99737

Call Sign: KL0EZ
Carole L Bowdre
Delta Junction AK 99737

Call Sign: KL0FB
James F Watford
Delta Junction AK 99737

Call Sign: KL0KK
Sharon K Bowdre
Delta Junction AK 99737

Call Sign: KL0RB

Josiah S Holbrook
Delta Junction AK 99737

Call Sign: N7TBU
Jeffrey Kinsman
Delta Junction AK 99737

Call Sign: NL7HW
John I Marhanka Jr
Delta Junction AK 99737

Call Sign: WL7ACA
Garald R Hobbs
Delta Junction AK 99737

Call Sign: WL7CJL
Rhoda M Mcnabb
Delta Junction AK 99737

Call Sign: WL7JY
Rachel P Holbrook
Delta Junction AK 99737

Call Sign: KL0WI
Stephanie J Wilcox
Delta Junction AK 99737

Call Sign: KL0WJ
Esther J Holbrook
Delta Junction AK 99737

Call Sign: KL0WM
James A Wilcox
Delta Junction AK 99737

Call Sign: KL0WZ
Tisa F Hirschel
Delta Junction AK 99737

Call Sign: KL0XC
Heather D Hirschel
Delta Junction AK 99737

Call Sign: KL0OY
Roger W Fleming
Delta Junction AK 997370484

Call Sign: KL7CVB
Goldman C Bandy
Delta Junction AK 99737

Call Sign: WL7BOK
Susan D Miller
Delta Junction AK 99737

FCC Amateur Radio Licenses in Denali National Park

Call Sign: KL1VB
Suann N Sauvey
Denali National Park AK 99755

Call Sign: KE7ZOD
Dean S Maschner
Denali National Park AK 99755

Call Sign: KL3ED
Dean S Maschner
Denali National Park AK 99755

Call Sign: KE8RO
Phillip L Sauvey
Denali National Park AK 99755

Call Sign: KC7UWA
Mary E Pinter
Denali National Park AK 99755

Call Sign: KC8CSD
Sean R Fielding
Denali National Park AK
997550182

Call Sign: KC8JCS
Malinda S Emahiser
Denali National Park AK
997550182

FCC Amateur Radio Licenses in Dillingham

Call Sign: KL7FHE
William A Crow
Box 244
Dillingham AK 99576

Call Sign: KB5GAH
Steven W Huddleston
Box 832
Dillingham AK 99576

Call Sign: KL3IH
Arnold E Watland
Dillingham AK 99576

Call Sign: AL7KA
Michael O Megli
Dillingham AK 99576

Call Sign: KL7GAJ
Joseph Chuckwuk
Dillingham AK 99576

Call Sign: WA0LKT
William L Johnson
Dillingham AK 99576

Call Sign: WL7BBX
Paul FrIIs Mikkelsen
Dillingham AK 99576

Call Sign: WL7BVH
Drew G Cherry
Dillingham AK 99576

FCC Amateur Radio Licenses in Dot Lake

Call Sign: KL1OM
Kathleen A Ashcraft
13613 Alaska Hwy
Dot Lake AK 99737

Call Sign: KL1KF
Andrea N Frederick
Dot Lake AK 99737

Call Sign: KL1KG
David K Frederick
Dot Lake AK 99737

Call Sign: KL1KT
Jesse K Frederick
Dot Lake AK 99737

FCC Amateur Radio Licenses in Douglas

Call Sign: KL7IG
Charles M Gray Jr
2110A 2nd St
Douglas AK 99824

Call Sign: N7HGA
Tommy D Ronsse
751 4th St
Douglas AK 99824

Call Sign: NL7NG
Robert D Montag
515 5th St
Douglas AK 99824

Call Sign: KL0TP
Lynne K Stevens
633 5th St
Douglas AK 99824

Call Sign: KL0SH
Ben M Ewing
656 Alta Ct
Douglas AK 99824

Call Sign: WL7YL
Matthew W Highley
1717 Douglas Hwy 11
Douglas AK 99824

Call Sign: WL7QB
Donald M Bullock Jr
900 First St 9
Douglas AK 99824

Call Sign: WL7BPL
David J Plotnick
1511 Second St
Douglas AK 99824

Call Sign: KL3JX
Robin F Lown
307 St Anns Ave
Douglas AK 99824

Call Sign: KL7GDF
Kenneth R Gehring
Douglas AK 99824

Call Sign: KL7HFV
Byron T Kinney
Douglas AK 99824

Call Sign: N7FOR
G Carl Schrader
Douglas AK 99824

Call Sign: WL7CMT
Eric P Bailey
Douglas AK 99824

Call Sign: WL7QF
John M Stone
Douglas AK 99824

Call Sign: KL1FA
Robert E Kindred
Douglas AK 998240848

Call Sign: KL7AK
Richard A Kaplan
Douglas AK 99824

Call Sign: WL7BKD
Joseph Akagi Sr
Box 1036
Douglas AK 99824

Call Sign: WL7BL
Samuel S Connor
Douglas AK 99824

FCC Amateur Radio Licenses in Dutch Harbor

Call Sign: NL8F
Timothy J Tilleman
Dutch Harbor AK 99692

Call Sign: KA7VCR
Jan M Tilleman
Dutch Harbor AK 99692

Call Sign: KL0TR
Linda L Ensign
Dutch Harbor AK 99692

Call Sign: NO7F
Timothy J Tilleman
Dutch Harbor AK 99692

Call Sign: KD0RJT
Rosalyn J Glorso
Dutch Harbor AK 996921242

Call Sign: WL7CWR
Russian Robinson Club
Mac Enterprises
Dutch Harbor AK 99692

Call Sign: KL7RRC
Russian Robinson Club
Mac Enterprises
Dutch Harbor AK 99692

FCC Amateur Radio Licenses in Eagle

Call Sign: WL7AVH
John W Ostrander
4th & Amundson St
Eagle AK 99738

Call Sign: WL7AVF
Betty A Borg
426 Third St
Eagle AK 99738

Call Sign: KL1YT
David R Helmer
Eagle AK 99738

Call Sign: KL1YV
David R Helmer
Eagle AK 99738

Call Sign: KL2FR
Daniel W Helmer
Eagle AK 99738

Call Sign: KL2FS
Joel R Helmer
Eagle AK 99738

Call Sign: NL7SS
Joyce A Worner
Eagle AK 99738

Call Sign: WL7AVG
John A Borg
Eagle AK 99738

Call Sign: WL7SU
Lori M Richards
Eagle AK 99738

Call Sign: WL7BZX
Ralph E Helmer
Eagle AK 997380006

Call Sign: AL7HT
Mark S Richards
Eagle AK 99738

Call Sign: WL7CGV
Donald M Watson
Eagle AK 99738

FCC Amateur Radio Licenses in Eagle River

Call Sign: KL7STE
Michael E Johnson Mr
14741 B Terrace Ln
Eagle River AK 99577

Call Sign: KA7STE
Michael E Johnson
14741 B Terrace Ln
Eagle River AK 99577

Call Sign: KL2YX
Thane E Shipley
11154 Aberdeen Cir
Eagle River AK 99577

Call Sign: KC8UGT
Adam D Henry
17416 Adams Ln
Eagle River AK 99577

Call Sign: WL7KW
Andrew R Duprey
9347 Agattu Cir
Eagle River AK 99577

Call Sign: WL7CQL
John F Woyte
13352 Alex Cir
Eagle River AK 995776714

Call Sign: N4WWT
Forrest A Booker
9912 Amchitka Cir
Eagle River AK 99577

Call Sign: KL0EN
Ersa W Kelley Jr
19067 Andreanof Dr
Eagle River AK 99577

Call Sign: KL3BO
Daen J Musick-Slater
11427 Aurora St
Eagle River AK 99577

Call Sign: KL1RD
Richard A Benson
19130 Babrof Dr
Eagle River AK 99577

Call Sign: N7YRW
Daniel R Wiese
17506 Baronoff Ave
Eagle River AK 99577

Call Sign: KL1TY
Shane A Taylor
17411 Beaujolais Cir
Eagle River AK 99577

Call Sign: AL2W
Shane A Taylor
17411 Beaujolais Cir
Eagle River AK 99577

Call Sign: KB3AQW
Laura J Hoffman
17711 Beaujolais Cir
Eagle River AK 99577

Call Sign: KL3BR
Kevin K Slayden
17691 Beaujolais Dr
Eagle River AK 99577

Call Sign: KC0PSZ
Chad M Mcilheran
17741 Beaujolais Dr
Eagle River AK 99577

Call Sign: AL7CE
Terry K Reynolds
17800 Beaujolais Dr
Eagle River AK 99577

Call Sign: KL7SZ
Linda J Reynolds
17800 Beaujolais Dr
Eagle River AK 99577

Call Sign: KL0XZ
Jeannine J Alley
17900 Beaujolais Dr
Eagle River AK 99577

Call Sign: KL2NI
Paul R Arasz
11416 Borealis St
Eagle River AK 99577

Call Sign: KL2YS
John A Godsey
11505 Borealis St
Eagle River AK 99577

Call Sign: AL7AJ
Arun J Jain
12110 Business Blvd Ste 6 Pmb
337
Eagle River AK 99577

Call Sign: AL7MY
George T Fagan Jr

10231 Caribou
Eagle River AK 99577

Call Sign: KL1ES
Dakota Stuart
16510 Centerfield Dr D-10
Eagle River AK 99577

Call Sign: KL7IO
Lynne L Duncan
10820 Chain Of Rock St
Eagle River AK 99577

Call Sign: W0NVD
Everett A Thomas
10534 Chatanika Loop
Eagle River AK 99577

Call Sign: KL2QC
Marco P Morimanno
18908 Chichagof Loop
Eagle River AK 99577

Call Sign: KL2RO
Gary L Winborg
19031 Citation
Eagle River AK 99577

Call Sign: KA7PUB
Robert S Fisher
10208 Colville St
Eagle River AK 99577

Call Sign: WL7CUC
Eric L Kahle
16307 Copper Mtn Cir
Eagle River AK 99577

Call Sign: AL7FM
Wendell B Bruckner
12128 Curtis Cir
Eagle River AK 99577

Call Sign: KL7BBO
Donald J Bruckner
12128 Curtis Cir
Eagle River AK 995770389

Call Sign: NL7TJ
Melinda L Tomazevic
9826 Dinaaka
Eagle River AK 99577

Call Sign: NL7KJ

Thomas A Tomazevic
9826 Dinaaka Dr
Eagle River AK 99577

Call Sign: AL7PH
Kim S Kjaersgaard
19980 Driftwood Bay Dr
Eagle River AK 99577

Call Sign: KL1CN
Michael A Page
9504 Dundas Cir
Eagle River AK 99577

Call Sign: KL7ZN
Clare L Jaeger
10227 Eagle River Ln
Eagle River AK 99577

Call Sign: KL7ZX
Shirley M Gabbert
20711 Eagle River Rd
Eagle River AK 99577

Call Sign: NL7SZ
Larry L Moran
23307 Eagle River Rd
Eagle River AK 99577

Call Sign: KL3BZ
Robert G Elder
32580 Eagle River Rd
Eagle River AK 99577

Call Sign: KL2PK
Phillip J Watson
18949 Elnora
Eagle River AK 99577

Call Sign: KL7PK
Phillip J Watson
18949 Elnora
Eagle River AK 99577

Call Sign: KL2YP
Andrew L Matlock
12332 End St 103
Eagle River AK 99577

Call Sign: KL3LQ
Michael J Poplin
11809 Falklands Loop
Eagle River AK 99577

Call Sign: KL3LO
Kevin M Palmatier
11815 Falklands Loop
Eagle River AK 99577

Call Sign: KL5T
Larry K Petty
21440 Falling Water Cir
Eagle River AK 99577

Call Sign: KL2MH
Zack R Colbert
13856 Fire Creek Trail
Eagle River AK 99577

Call Sign: W7ICI
Robert J Lupo Sr
11423 Fireball St
Eagle River AK 995777868

Call Sign: KL7ITD
Midori S Sylvia
18727 First St
Eagle River AK 995778350

Call Sign: KL2RI
Robert M Clay
10917 Gakona Cir
Eagle River AK 99577

Call Sign: KL3CE
Arthur C Saltmarsh
11859 Galloway Loop
Eagle River AK 99577

Call Sign: KL2SJ
Gary L Johnson
10218 Genor St
Eagle River AK 99577

Call Sign: KL7GJ
Gary L Johnson
10218 Genor St
Eagle River AK 99577

Call Sign: KL2SM
Sherry L Price
10218 Genora St
Eagle River AK 99577

Call Sign: KL2VE
Matthew L Johnson
10218 Genora St
Eagle River AK 99577

Call Sign: N3SNQ
Lisa D Wardle
18651 Gibens Cir
Eagle River AK 99577

Call Sign: KL3ID
Martin A Foreman
19941 Grant Cir
Eagle River AK 99577

Call Sign: KL3IE
Micah O Foreman
19941 Grant Cir
Eagle River AK 99577

Call Sign: KL2VD
Dennis L Gum
9901 Greenhouse St
Eagle River AK 99577

Call Sign: NL7XL
Mack H Humphery
11031 Gulkana Cir
Eagle River AK 99577

Call Sign: WL7BVU
Nancy J Taylor
11508 Heritage Ct 700
Eagle River AK 99577

Call Sign: KB7RQP
Jacqueline A Curtis
19918 Highland Ridge Dr
Eagle River AK 99577

Call Sign: N7YKY
George W Curtis Jr
19918 Highland Ridge Dr
Eagle River AK 99577

Call Sign: KD7BYJ
Richard L Wells
20151 Highland Ridge Dr
Eagle River AK 99577

Call Sign: KL7MI
Ross C Oliver
4730 Hiland Rd
Eagle River AK 99577

Call Sign: NL7AO
Robert F Brooks
16403 Home Place Apt 25

Eagle River AK 99577

Call Sign: N5ZDI
James N Wales
13791 Hunterwood Ln
Eagle River AK 99577

Call Sign: KL1QJ
Jory R Moon
17833 James Way
Eagle River AK 99577

Call Sign: KL4E
Craig V Bledsoe
18811 Jamie Dr
Eagle River AK 99577

Call Sign: KL0ER
Bradley J Husberg
17239 Kantishna Dr
Eagle River AK 99577

Call Sign: KL7IMD
James C Hilton
17824 Kantishna Dr
Eagle River AK 99577

Call Sign: NL7AV
Susan G Hilton
17824 Kantishna Dr
Eagle River AK 995778231

Call Sign: KD9LE
Everett L Harper
17936 Kantishna Dr
Eagle River AK 99577

Call Sign: K6MHO
Michael W Sweeley
11048 Kaskanak Dr
Eagle River AK 99577

Call Sign: N7XXA
Deborah S Sweeley
11048 Kaskanak Dr
Eagle River AK 99577

Call Sign: KL7AS
Michael W Sweeley
11048 Kaskanak Dr
Eagle River AK 99577

Call Sign: KL2EL
Sheila M Van Weel

10831 Klutina Cir
Eagle River AK 99577

Call Sign: KE7EPZ
Pieter M Van Weel
10831 Klutina Cir
Eagle River AK 99577

Call Sign: KL2CR
Pieter M Van Weel
10831 Klutina Cir
Eagle River AK 99577

Call Sign: WL7AC
John D Bronner
13336 Konrad Dr
Eagle River AK 99577

Call Sign: WL7AZ
Beverly J Bronner
13336 Konrad Dr
Eagle River AK 99577

Call Sign: KL3HG
Stanislaw Lewak
8538 Lassen Cir
Eagle River AK 99577

Call Sign: NL7LA
Timothy A Halstead
10316 Lee St
Eagle River AK 99577

Call Sign: KL2PW
Robert J Arnold
20433 Lucas Ave
Eagle River AK 99577

Call Sign: KL2CE
Pamela M Weaver
20608 Lucas Ave
Eagle River AK 99577

Call Sign: KL7KR
Thomas B Quimby
18110 Mac Laren St
Eagle River AK 99577

Call Sign: AL7JK
William J Raynsford
18730 Man O War Rd
Eagle River AK 99577

Call Sign: KL0BL

Christian Meer
18730 Man O War Rd
Eagle River AK 99577

Call Sign: KL3JH
Pat Gionson Jr
18807 Man-O-War Rd
Eagle River AK 99577

Call Sign: AL7BG
S E Thomas
16422 Marcus St
Eagle River AK 995777616

Call Sign: N5ATD
Charles D Moore
17305 Meadow Creek
Eagle River AK 99577

Call Sign: WL7WS
Gregory E Hoch
17104 Meadow Creek Dr
Eagle River AK 99577

Call Sign: AL7ON
Richard C Turcic
17204 Meadow Creek Dr
Eagle River AK 99577

Call Sign: KL2UD
Noah L Miller
17444 Meadow Creek Dr
Eagle River AK 99577

Call Sign: KL7IIS
David R Buchanan
17505 Meadow Creek Dr
Eagle River AK 99577

Call Sign: KL2SS
Mark D Halterman
17928 Meadow Creek Dr
Eagle River AK 99577

Call Sign: NN5H
Thomas L Blackley Jr
18859 Mills Bay Cir
Eagle River AK 99577

Call Sign: KL7DC
William H Woolett
18113 Misty Falls
Eagle River AK 99577

Call Sign: NL7AC
William H Woolett
18113 Misty Falls
Eagle River AK 99577

Call Sign: KL1JC
Patrick S Woolett
18113 Misty Falls Cir
Eagle River AK 99577

Call Sign: KL7CT
Gail L Woolett
18122 Misty Falls Cir
Eagle River AK 99577

Call Sign: N7FCT
Gail L Woolett
18122 Misty Falls Cir
Eagle River AK 99577

Call Sign: KF7NKD
Danny J Hull
31343 Misty Mountain Cir
Eagle River AK 99577

Call Sign: KL7AR
Michael W Sweeley
12341 Mountain Ash Dr
Eagle River AK 99577

Call Sign: KL7JS
Deborah S Sweeley
12341 Mountain Ash Dr
Eagle River AK 99577

Call Sign: WB7WSK
Thomas D Christensen
18503 Neumann Cir
Eagle River AK 99577

Call Sign: AL7IX
James B Eaves
20322 New England Dr
Eagle River AK 995777114

Call Sign: KL7LS
Charles E Brazil
17517 North Juanita Loop
Eagle River AK 99577

Call Sign: KL3BB
James H Mcafee IV
19631 North Mitkof Loop
Eagle River AK 99577

Call Sign: KL2ET
Keith D Howard
18129 North Parkview Terrace
Loop
Eagle River AK 99577

Call Sign: KL2YY
Joseph A Cerullo
13900 Old Glenn Hwy 49
Eagle River AK 99577

Call Sign: NL7NQ
Ernest M Scheidler
12238 Osborne
Eagle River AK 99577

Call Sign: KL2UT
Edward F Deforest
19531 Ostoria Cir
Eagle River AK 99577

Call Sign: WL7BN
Jerry E Coppess
19532 Ostovia Cl
Eagle River AK 99577

Call Sign: WL7XP
Christopher F Eaves
19444 Ostovia Cr
Eagle River AK 99577

Call Sign: WL7CKC
Richard L Ayers
10452 Palos Verde
Eagle River AK 99577

Call Sign: KL1ZF
Becky D Barney
17311 Palos Verdes Dr
Eagle River AK 99577

Call Sign: AL7RA
Douglas E Lockwood II
17406 Palos Verdes Dr
Eagle River AK 99577

Call Sign: KL1YK
Theodore P Kohlstedt
16938 Park Place St Apt 1
Eagle River AK 99577

Call Sign: KL3BG
Daniel J Crawford

9507 Puffin Cir
Eagle River AK 99577

Call Sign: KL0YO
Patrick J Tipton
17602 Rachel
Eagle River AK 99577

Call Sign: KL0ZY
David M Tipton
17602 Rachel Cir
Eagle River AK 99577

Call Sign: KL2VM
Phyllis L Goodwin
16706 Riddell Cir
Eagle River AK 99577

Call Sign: WL7CLP
John J Moore
9825 Saaya Cir
Eagle River AK 99577

Call Sign: KL1CU
Michael C Masters
19809 Samalga Cir
Eagle River AK 99577

Call Sign: KL1HN
Ronald E Mcnaughton
17757 Sanctuary Dr
Eagle River AK 995778220

Call Sign: KL7WA
Barry F Yates
17809 Sanctuary Dr
Eagle River AK 99577

Call Sign: KL7X
Michael T Turner
18145 Sanctuary Dr
Eagle River AK 99577

Call Sign: KL0AC
Jason A Dolph
18733 Sarichef Loop
Eagle River AK 99577

Call Sign: K2MO
Art R Gray
19015 Sarichef Loop
Eagle River AK 99577

Call Sign: KL0DW

Eric O Rogers
13914 Savage Dr
Eagle River AK 995777509

Call Sign: WL7YG
Gary R Wheeler
9834 Saya Cir
Eagle River AK 99577

Call Sign: N7AOV
Erik P Kohler
8730 Sonora Cir
Eagle River AK 99577

Call Sign: AL7NH
Terry W Clark
12015 Springbrook Dr
Eagle River AK 99577

Call Sign: KL2SH
Bong K Yoon
10442 Stewart Dr
Eagle River AK 99577

Call Sign: KL2BJ
Wayne R Marquis
17401 Stonewood Place
Eagle River AK 99577

Call Sign: KL2XJ
W L Pat Patterson
9711 Takli Cir
Eagle River AK 99577

Call Sign: WL1PP
W L Pat Patterson
9711 Takli Cir
Eagle River AK 99577

Call Sign: WL7CRQ
Travis W From
18315 Tedrow Cir
Eagle River AK 99577

Call Sign: KL2GI
Douglas L Dortch Jr
18207 Tedrow Dr
Eagle River AK 99577

Call Sign: KL1JS
Craig N Christensen
17546 Teklanika
Eagle River AK 99577

Call Sign: KL1CM
Gary L Eichhorn
17943 Teklanika Dr
Eagle River AK 99577

Call Sign: KL7TQ
Mark J Kelliher
11317 Terrace Hills Dr
Eagle River AK 99577

Call Sign: NL7EA
Hannelore Kelliher
11317 Terrace Hills Dr
Eagle River AK 99577

Call Sign: KL7GG
C Melvin Bowns
23708 The Clearing Dr
Eagle River AK 99577

Call Sign: KL7ZZ
John D Calhoun
19910 Third St
Eagle River AK 99577

Call Sign: KC0NFH
Daniel P Kozak
17330 Toakoana Dr
Eagle River AK 99577

Call Sign: WL7KX
Robert C Beneda
17703 Toakoanna Way
Eagle River AK 99577

Call Sign: KL5R
Bill L Young
19219 Trail Bay Dr
Eagle River AK 99577

Call Sign: W7RVY
Bill L Young
19219 Trail Bay Dr
Eagle River AK 99577

Call Sign: NL7NP
Ronald B Lewis
11021 Tsusena Cir
Eagle River AK 99577

Call Sign: KC5BNN
Ronald B Lewis
11021 Tsusena Cir
Eagle River AK 99577

Call Sign: KL0YD
Sean M Trimble
18430 Uper Skyline Dr
Eagle River AK 99577

Call Sign: KL7DC
Steven J Gehring
19008 War Admiral Rd
Eagle River AK 99577

Call Sign: KL7TJ
Maeve M Ryan
9223 West Parkview Ter Loop
Eagle River AK 99577

Call Sign: KL2SK
Helen E Haverty
9116 West Parkview Terrace
Loop
Eagle River AK 99577

Call Sign: KL3BP
Albert E Ostrowski
9456 West Parkview Terrace
Loop
Eagle River AK 99577

Call Sign: KL1VP
Marco A Gutierrez
25949 White Spruce Dr
Eagle River AK 99577

Call Sign: KL2AM
Brandon L Cory
10022 Wildwood St
Eagle River AK 99577

Call Sign: KL7CA
Leonard E Andrews Jr
11304 Wood River Way
Eagle River AK 99577

Call Sign: WL7BZD
Michael G Clemens
9928 Wren Ln
Eagle River AK 99577

Call Sign: KL7PC
Robert N Gunson
16712 Yellowstone Cir
Eagle River AK 99577

Call Sign: KL1MP

Lynda Dagley
Eagle River AK 99577

Call Sign: KL1MQ
Eric C Lindboe
Eagle River AK 99577

Call Sign: KL1ZD
Lawrence J Weeks
Eagle River AK 99577

Call Sign: WL7AK
Lawrence J Weeks
Eagle River AK 99577

Call Sign: KL2GM
Christopher Cheng
Eagle River AK 99577

Call Sign: KL2GO
Paul J Gambish
Eagle River AK 99577

Call Sign: KL2KL
Christopher Cheng
Eagle River AK 99577

Call Sign: KL2TN
Miller Katzenberg
Eagle River AK 99577

Call Sign: KL6MK
Miller Katzenberg
Eagle River AK 99577

Call Sign: KL2UO
James H Mitchell
Eagle River AK 99577

Call Sign: KL2UP
Lorinda L Mitchell
Eagle River AK 99577

Call Sign: KL2ZH
Scott T Mc Comb
Eagle River AK 99577

Call Sign: KL7STM
Scott T Mc Comb
Eagle River AK 99577

Call Sign: KF5HJC
Jolly M Tangog
Eagle River AK 99577

Call Sign: KF7LEX
Shelah M Tangog
Eagle River AK 99577

Call Sign: KB7IKX
Ellen K Vickrey
Eagle River AK 99577

Call Sign: KD4MEY
Scott T Mc Comb
Eagle River AK 99577

Call Sign: KL0EV
Richard D Floyd
Eagle River AK 99577

Call Sign: KL0NF
Douglas C Norman
Eagle River AK 99577

Call Sign: KL7BHH
Wendell E Lane
Eagle River AK 99577

Call Sign: KL7FHF
Jon M Girard
Eagle River AK 99577

Call Sign: KL7GGW
Terry D Mobley
Eagle River AK 99577

Call Sign: NL7WV
Jana A Erickson
Eagle River AK 99577

Call Sign: NL7WW
John E Murray
Eagle River AK 99577

Call Sign: WL7CJP
Kevin J Scott
Eagle River AK 99577

Call Sign: KL0VL
Jack M Hayden
Eagle River AK 99577

Call Sign: AL0V
Thomas S Teallow
Eagle River AK 99577

Call Sign: KL0ZV

Leonard E Andrews Jr
Eagle River AK 99577

Call Sign: KL0OW
Corliss A Kimmel
Eagle River AK 995770965

Call Sign: KA4SKZ
Robert J Gryder
Eagle River AK 99577

Call Sign: WL7CDE
Matthew T Mannhardt
Eagle River AK 99577

Call Sign: KL0YJ
Mark A Stadsklev
HC 85 Box 9206
Eagle River AK 995779401

FCC Amateur Radio Licenses in Edna Bay

Call Sign: KC7DRF
Jere A Crew
Edna Bay AK 99950

FCC Amateur Radio Licenses in Eielson AFB

Call Sign: KB7YJG
Angela M Vincent
5433 B Sundog Ct
Eielson AFB AK 99702

Call Sign: KL0LT
John E Hall
49870 Bering Ave
Eielson AFB AK 99702

Call Sign: WL7CIB
Alison J Sanford
651-D Bering Ave
Eielson AFB AK 99702

Call Sign: WL7MI
Michael J Millard
5090 C Apollo Cir
Eielson AFB AK 99702

Call Sign: KL1LU
Joseph P Kelly
5274 C Broadway
Eielson AFB AK 99702

Call Sign: KL0CG
Gary R Olson Jr
4948 C Columbia Ave
Eielson AFB AK 99702

Call Sign: KC9FJE
Mykal J Anstrom
2322 Central Ave Unit 17
Eielson AFB AK 99702

Call Sign: AL4F
Peter M Johnson
2470B Misty Fjord Ct
Eielson AFB AK 99702

Call Sign: KG6HTN
Kyle Raihala
726 Seward Ave Apt 13
Eielson AFB AK 99702

Call Sign: KB7YJF
Donald R Vincent
5433 B Sundog Ct
Eielson AFB AK 99702

Call Sign: KL0UB
Kenneth W Holden
Eielson AFB AK 99702

FCC Amateur Radio Licenses in Elmendorf AFB

Call Sign: KL2WV
James N Martineau
4023C Blake Ave
Elmendorf AFB AK 99506

Call Sign: KL2GH
Scott M Herbert
6967 D Campos Ave
Elmendorf AFB AK 99506

Call Sign: KL2YU
Daniel S Poe
6984 B Campos Ave
Elmendorf AFB AK 99506

Call Sign: WL7LQ
John M Dorgan
21-367B Citrus Ave
Elmendorf AFB AK 99506

Call Sign: KL3JA

Howard S Bergeron
7923 Anderson Cir C
Elmendorf AFB AK 99506

Call Sign: AI4YW
Paul K Routhier
3894-D Beach Ct
Elmendorf AFB AK 99506

Call Sign: KL3EN
Kelly J Wetzel Sr
4077 Bullard Ave D
Elmendorf AFB AK 99506

Call Sign: KB9ZSZ
Paul L Tucker
7053 Chennault Ave Unit 1567
Elmendorf AFB AK 99506

Call Sign: WL7CWQ
477Th Fighter Group Arc
8111 Craw Ave Unit 3000
Elmendorf AFB AK 99506

Call Sign: KL2WW
Jeffery P Steinke
8119 Dethlefgen Ave 4320
Elmendorf AFB AK 99506

Call Sign: KL2XII
Jason L Franks
8119 Dethlefsen Ave
Elmendorf AFB AK 99506

Call Sign: KL2VV
Stephanie Munoz
8119 Dethlefsen Ave 405
Elmendorf AFB AK 99506

Call Sign: KL2WY
Tracy D Smith
8119 Dethlefsen Dr 459
Elmendorf AFB AK 99506

Call Sign: KF4YFD
John A Phelps
8128 Doolittle Ave Unit 662
Elmendorf AFB AK 99506

Call Sign: KL2YL
Meghan M Samek
4198 Fairchild Ave E
Elmendorf AFB AK 99506

Call Sign: KC9JDB
Jeffrey R Hartzell
3902 Graveline Ct Unit E
Elmendorf AFB AK 99506

Call Sign: KL1QK
Julie A Hayford
9423 Luke Ave E
Elmendorf AFB AK 99506

Call Sign: KD7HXF
Gregg R Hayford
9423 Luke Ave Unit E
Elmendorf AFB AK 99506

Call Sign: KL7AF
477Th Fighter Group Arc
7403 A Metzger Ave
Elmendorf AFB AK 99506

Call Sign: KL3EH
Scott K Jackson
7413 Metzger Ave B
Elmendorf AFB AK 99506

Call Sign: KB7ARS
Shawn J Sundseth
5742 Staffan Ct Unit C
Elmendorf AFB AK 995064549

Call Sign: WL7CPY
Ronnie G Hunemuller
Elmendorf AFB AK 99506

Call Sign: KL3HD
Enoch K Wong
Elmendorf AFB AK 99506

Call Sign: KC7FUY
Jeffery L Stidham
Elmendorf AFB AK 995066105

Call Sign: NL7KY
Albert Arruda
Elmendorf AFB AK 99506

Call Sign: N7MGT
Donald E Koehler
Box 382
Elmendorf AFB AK 99506

**FCC Amateur Radio Licenses
in Emmonak**

Call Sign: KL1AO
Philip J Covlasky
Emmonak AK 99581

Call Sign: KL1AP
Evan B Charles
Emmonak AK 99581

Call Sign: KL1AQ
Jonathan F Hunt
Emmonak AK 99581

Call Sign: AL7OM
Marilyn F Dennis
Emmonak AK 99581

**FCC Amateur Radio Licenses
in Ester**

Call Sign: WL7SM
Donald C Meares
3806 Nenaza Hwy Box 9
Ester AK 99725

Call Sign: NL7KM
Dorothy J Guritz
Ester AK 99725

Call Sign: WL7BLL
Jeanne C Laurencelle
Ester AK 99725

Call Sign: WL7CNV
Jebidiah R Timm
Ester AK 99725

Call Sign: WL7WI
Daniel G Benn
Ester AK 99725

Call Sign: KL1DS
Robert L Biehl
Ester AK 99725

Call Sign: KC7FWK
Dean T Jazzo
Ester AK 997250412

Call Sign: AL7LC
Dennis G Quinn
Ester AK 99725

Call Sign: KL7IAA
Robert E Guritz

Box 73
Ester AK 99725

**FCC Amateur Radio Licenses
in Excursion Inlet**

Call Sign: WL7BPO
Charles E Hill
Excursion Inlet Cannery
Excursion Inlet AK 99850

Call Sign: KL7WJ
Debora L Gordon
Excursion Inlet South
Excursion Inlet AK 998500090

**FCC Amateur Radio Licenses
in Fairbanks**

Call Sign: N5NXG
John E Harrison
2061A 30th Ave
Fairbanks AK 997017317

Call Sign: KL0LZ
Abe Krejci
29D Eureka Ave
Fairbanks AK 99701

Call Sign: KL0MA
Rebekah R Krejci
29D Eurekah Ave
Fairbanks AK 99701

Call Sign: KC8BKP
Philip D Nace
1429 B Farmers Loop Rd
Fairbanks AK 99709

Call Sign: WL7CCP
Matthew B Gillies
1220 10th Ave
Fairbanks AK 99701

Call Sign: KL2TU
Samuel J Vanderwaal
1206 16th Ave
Fairbanks AK 99701

Call Sign: KL0HA
Stephanie L Masek
701 17th Ave
Fairbanks AK 99701

Call Sign: WL7FR
Otis D Shelley
1120 23rd Ave Apt A
Fairbanks AK 997016803

Call Sign: KL0BD
Brad S Gordon
1202 27th Ave
Fairbanks AK 99701

Call Sign: WL7CIQ
Juan A Goula
1219 27th Ave
Fairbanks AK 99701

Call Sign: WL7HO
Dennis J Rundle
1516 27th Ave Apt 4
Fairbanks AK 99701

Call Sign: KL0IA
Dolores J Baker
1209 3rd Ave
Fairbanks AK 99701

Call Sign: KL0IQ
Mary C Ruzich
1505 3rd Ave
Fairbanks AK 99701

Call Sign: WL7BK
Larry I Dunlap Mr
455 3rd Ave Apt 419
Fairbanks AK 99701

Call Sign: KL2GW
Charles E Haller
455 3rd Ave 228
Fairbanks AK 99701

Call Sign: KA2KIA
Evan D Roberts
1311 4th Ave
Fairbanks AK 99701

Call Sign: WL7YS
Jason C Updike
155 8th Ave
Fairbanks AK 99701

Call Sign: KL7YU
Roderick D Mitchell
691 8th Ave
Fairbanks AK 99701

Call Sign: KL0YU
Roderick D Mitchell
691 8th Ave
Fairbanks AK 99701

Call Sign: WL7PI
Kenneth C Mercer
1271 9th Ave Apt207
Fairbanks AK 99701

Call Sign: KL0LU
Kurt C Helms
201 A St
Fairbanks AK 99701

Call Sign: WL7CRD
David H De Voe
6315 Abraham Rd
Fairbanks AK 99709

Call Sign: WL7CRE
Carol E De Voe
6315 Abraham Rd
Fairbanks AK 99709

Call Sign: KL0MR
Raymond C Solomon Sr
3258 Adams Dr Apt B
Fairbanks AK 99709

Call Sign: WL7CGN
Joel R Renner
969 Agnes Ln
Fairbanks AK 99705

Call Sign: N7UEF
Robinson E Duffy
1360 Airport Way 1E3
Fairbanks AK 99701

Call Sign: KL0MT
Scott D Ahlstrom
102 Allegheny Way
Fairbanks AK 99709

Call Sign: WL7CBT
Christopher R Jasperson
126 Allegheny Way
Fairbanks AK 99709

Call Sign: WL7OB
Jimmy B Jasperson
126 Allegheny Way

Fairbanks AK 99709

Call Sign: KL7ISH
Willard C Simmons
1901 Alston Rd
Fairbanks AK 997095308

Call Sign: KC8MVW
Billy J Brookins
824 Amanita
Fairbanks AK 99712

Call Sign: KL3HP
Christine A Mccabe
824 Amanita Rd
Fairbanks AK 99712

Call Sign: N0WGG
Timothy G Miner
5190 Amherst Dr 41
Fairbanks AK 99709

Call Sign: KL2KJ
Melissa C Miner
5190 Amherst Dr 41
Fairbanks AK 99709

Call Sign: AL7GL
Tury G Anderson
5380 Anderson Rd
Fairbanks AK 99706

Call Sign: WL7UJ
William B Wilkerson Jr
809 Andrew St
Fairbanks AK 997011501

Call Sign: KL1TL
Christopher M Howard
343 Archives Alley
Fairbanks AK 99712

Call Sign: WL7CIH
Hal F Meyer
4250 Aspenwood Dr
Fairbanks AK 99709

Call Sign: WL7ZX
Joshua S Lott
811 Austin
Fairbanks AK 99701

Call Sign: KL0ZU
Dennis W Stuller

817 Austin St
Fairbanks AK 99707

Call Sign: KL0FY
Willis A Snipes
1212 29 Ave 1
Fairbanks AK 99701

Call Sign: NH6UG
Rachel K Lenore
1142 Bainbridge Blvd
Fairbanks AK 99701

Call Sign: AL7FG
Dianne L Marshall
972 Ballaine Rd
Fairbanks AK 99709

Call Sign: KL7KC
Arctic Amateur Radio Club
972 Ballaine Rd
Fairbanks AK 99709

Call Sign: KL7XO
Steven A Estes
972 Ballaine Rd
Fairbanks AK 99709

Call Sign: NL7QK
Betty A Marshall
972 Ballaine Rd
Fairbanks AK 99709

Call Sign: KL0YW
Maxwell M Estes
972 Ballaine Rd
Fairbanks AK 99709

Call Sign: KL7MAX
Maxwell M Estes
972 Ballaine Rd
Fairbanks AK 99709

Call Sign: KL7YX
Charles E Dennis
138 Baranof
Fairbanks AK 99701

Call Sign: WL7LF
Jane M Dennis
138 Baranof
Fairbanks AK 99701

Call Sign: WL7AOT

Glen A Abel
405 Baranof Ave
Fairbanks AK 997013209

Call Sign: WL7KA
Michael C Gott
1724 Barnswallow Way
Fairbanks AK 99709

Call Sign: AL7AD
Joseph M Killion
804 Bennett Rd
Fairbanks AK 99712

Call Sign: KL0HF
Patricia C Costello
962 Bennett Rd
Fairbanks AK 99712

Call Sign: WL7CRF
Paul C Costello
962 Bennett Rd
Fairbanks AK 99712

Call Sign: KL7HCF
Richard F Lord
609 Bentley Dr
Fairbanks AK 99701

Call Sign: AH0H
Masayuki Kobayashi
829 Birch Hill Rd
Fairbanks AK 99712

Call Sign: NL7HU
William H Mc Laughlin
1412 Birchwood Dr
Fairbanks AK 99709

Call Sign: KL7DZ
Richard G Zdanovec
1453 Birchwood Dr
Fairbanks AK 99709

Call Sign: KL7DCO
Richard W Hecht
119 Bridget Ave
Fairbanks AK 997011516

Call Sign: WL7ARA
Obert Friborg
2058 Bridgewater Dr
Fairbanks AK 99709

Call Sign: NP2LM
Rodney R Platzke
2085 Bridgewater Dr
Fairbanks AK 99709

Call Sign: NL7KF
Alan L Hoza
246 Brighton Dr
Fairbanks AK 997121283

Call Sign: KL1SG
Dean C Phillips Jr
465 Bullion Dr
Fairbanks AK 99712

Call Sign: WL7CQO
Wendy J Ray
607 Bullion Dr
Fairbanks AK 99712

Call Sign: WL7CQP
Ryan N Ray
607 Bullion Dr
Fairbanks AK 99712

Call Sign: WL7PH
Scott R Ray
607 Bullion Dr
Fairbanks AK 99712

Call Sign: KL7IGR
Gordon R Comings
1516 Buttercup St
Fairbanks AK 99701

Call Sign: KL7IEH
Jaimie C Weidner
5479 C H S R
Fairbanks AK 997123507

Call Sign: KL0CM
Helen R Brown
409 C St
Fairbanks AK 99701

Call Sign: KL7CUS
Frederic E Brown
409 C St
Fairbanks AK 99701

Call Sign: WL7CIS
Henry W Grant
604 Cambridge Dr
Fairbanks AK 997096758

Call Sign: WL7CKH
Brian D Grant
604 Cambridge Dr
Fairbanks AK 997096758

Call Sign: KL1JN
Clifford H Cole
1994 Camomile Ln
Fairbanks AK 99712

Call Sign: WL7ARN
June A Cook
1702 Carr Ave
Fairbanks AK 99709

Call Sign: WD6DZM
Jack V Rowe
1165 Cartleb Rd
Fairbanks AK 997123061

Call Sign: WL7HY
John W Barsi
795 Chena Hills Dr
Fairbanks AK 99709

Call Sign: KL7FAL
Rudolph C Domke
2391 Chena Hot Springs Rd
Fairbanks AK 99712

Call Sign: AL7NG
John W Kalmbacher
3070 Chena Hot Springs Rd
Fairbanks AK 99712

Call Sign: NL7YJ
Jane F Kalmbacher
3070 Chena Hot Springs Rd
Fairbanks AK 99712

Call Sign: KL1YQ
George R Kirchner
3090 Chena Hot Springs Rd
Fairbanks AK 99712

Call Sign: KL7DH
Darrel E Harpham
3325 Chena Hot Springs Rd
Fairbanks AK 99712

Call Sign: KL7QOL
David S Grauman
591 Chena Ridge Rd

Fairbanks AK 99709

Call Sign: WL7CPK
William R Wakefield
1075 Chena Ridge Rd
Fairbanks AK 997092602

Call Sign: WL7OF
Birch A Badger
1235 Chena Ridge Rd
Fairbanks AK 99709

Call Sign: KL1PC
Mark J Sisinyak Jr
1239 Chena Ridge Rd
Fairbanks AK 99709

Call Sign: NL7KC
John T Adams
1407 Chena Ridge Rd
Fairbanks AK 99709

Call Sign: AL7JD
David R Carlstrom
1739 Chena Ridge Rd
Fairbanks AK 99709

Call Sign: KL7BI
Glen H Greeley
4697 Chena Small Tracts Rd
Fairbanks AK 99709

Call Sign: NL7ZK
Kevin K O Connor
2380 Chief John Dr
Fairbanks AK 99708

Call Sign: KL2EX
Travis L Booms
1245 Chili Pepper Ct
Fairbanks AK 99709

Call Sign: KL0VN
William E Dewey
5122 Chilkoot Dr
Fairbanks AK 997093136

Call Sign: KL0XN
William E Dewey
5122 Chilkoot Dr
Fairbanks AK 997093136

Call Sign: NL7HI
James P Dixon

3114 Chinook Dr
Fairbanks AK 997094042

Call Sign: KL1AY
Gerry Ostrow
3412 College Rd
Fairbanks AK 99709

Call Sign: WL7BZY
Lauren E Ruff
123 Concordia Dr
Fairbanks AK 99709

Call Sign: KL1LJ
Lorinda R Lhotka
867 Constitution Dr
Fairbanks AK 99709

Call Sign: AL7LM
Kyle T Franks
1173 Coppet
Fairbanks AK 99709

Call Sign: KL0TU
Linda L Tilman
1105 Coppet St
Fairbanks AK 997054722

Call Sign: KL0RA
Warren D Tilman
1105 Coppet St
Fairbanks AK 997094722

Call Sign: WL7CPU
William E Anker
1586 Coyote Trail
Fairbanks AK 997096009

Call Sign: WL7OO
Leslie A Knoll
193 Crest Dr
Fairbanks AK 99712

Call Sign: KC7ZKF
Amy L Hoger
895 Crestwood
Fairbanks AK 99712

Call Sign: KK7IV
Kevin D Hoger
895 Crestwood Ave
Fairbanks AK 99712

Call Sign: KL7N

Scott S Diseth
985 Crocus Way
Fairbanks AK 997121355

Call Sign: KL1XV
Boris R Bracio
346 Crystal Rd
Fairbanks AK 99712

Call Sign: AL7BH
Roger B Burns
2559 Dale Rd
Fairbanks AK 99709

Call Sign: KL0SO
Jack A Lanam
5002 Dartmouth 17
Fairbanks AK 99709

Call Sign: KL2TL
Victor B Dasher
2380 Davendot Ln
Fairbanks AK 99709

Call Sign: KL7EBF
Charles R Clark
3187 Davis Rd
Fairbanks AK 99709

Call Sign: AL7DP
Kenneth R Allen
3040 Davis Rd - Apt A29
Fairbanks AK 99709

Call Sign: AL7CL
Michael J Graham
5131 Decathlon Ave
Fairbanks AK 997094516

Call Sign: KL0WU
Mark J Neidhold
1308 Denali Way
Fairbanks AK 997014140

Call Sign: KL0RR
Wayne E Fralick
1311 Denali Way
Fairbanks AK 99701

Call Sign: WL7UU
Raymond E Wise
1018 Dogwood St 302
Fairbanks AK 99709

Call Sign: WL7CEW
Becky A Mease
1001 Dolly Varden Ln
Fairbanks AK 99709

Call Sign: WL7CBE
Sandra L Calvillo
4513 Drake St
Fairbanks AK 99709

Call Sign: KL7TC
William E Hunstein
4586 Drake St
Fairbanks AK 99709

Call Sign: WL7CBR
Ian M Sink
4894 Drake St
Fairbanks AK 99709

Call Sign: WL7CIM
Elizabeth F King
363 Droz Dr
Fairbanks AK 99701

Call Sign: NL7FB
Douglas C Hummel
510 Dunbar Ave
Fairbanks AK 99701

Call Sign: WL7CTZ
The A Team
3928 Dunlap Ave
Fairbanks AK 99709

Call Sign: KL7AM
Robert M Hisamoto
3985 Dunlap Ave
Fairbanks AK 99709

Call Sign: WL7BNX
Louisa B Hisamoto
3985 Dunlap Ave
Fairbanks AK 99709

Call Sign: WL7TO
Alan D Lahti
4019 Dunlap Ave
Fairbanks AK 99709

Call Sign: KL0TZ
Louis J Maloney III
4049 Dunlap Ave
Fairbanks AK 99709

Call Sign: WL7CRK
Craig T Bakalar
402 E St 6
Fairbanks AK 99701

Call Sign: KC6TVL
Matthew H Glover
402 E St Apt 1
Fairbanks AK 99701

Call Sign: WL7CPT
Lawrence A Bendall
2110 Eagan Ave
Fairbanks AK 99701

Call Sign: KL1LM
Sheldon F Maier
276 Eagle Ridge Rd
Fairbanks AK 99712

Call Sign: KL1CJ
Janne H Maier
276 Eagle Ridge Rd
Fairbanks AK 99712

Call Sign: KL1SQ
Emma J Honea
312 East Birch Hill Rd
Fairbanks AK 99712

Call Sign: KL1TE
Patrick J Honea
312 East Birch Hill Rd
Fairbanks AK 99712

Call Sign: KL2SZ
Gary V Kendall
1048 East Chena Hills
Fairbanks AK 99709

Call Sign: WB5WAF
Ali E Fant
3215 East College Rd
Fairbanks AK 99709

Call Sign: KL0PF
Kenneth R Klopf
1191 Eastwood Ln
Fairbanks AK 99712

Call Sign: KL7GBG
Carol R Klopf
1191 Eastwood Ln

Fairbanks AK 99712

Call Sign: NL7OU
Adam J Overton
3281 Edby Rd
Fairbanks AK 99709

Call Sign: N0AJW
Joan Soutar
3281 Edby Rd
Fairbanks AK 997092657

Call Sign: N0SN
Aaron L Overton
3281 Edby Rd
Fairbanks AK 997092657

Call Sign: KL7HT
Melfred Lofthus
1913 Esquire Ave
Fairbanks AK 99709

Call Sign: KL2GE
Malia D Johnson
613 Eton Rd
Fairbanks AK 99709

Call Sign: NL7QH
Mary M Worrall
120 Eureka Ave
Fairbanks AK 99701

Call Sign: WL7BZK
Michael Y Stepantsev
205 Eureka Ave
Fairbanks AK 99701

Call Sign: WL7CFQ
Nickolas W Gostry
205 Eureka Ave
Fairbanks AK 99701

Call Sign: WL7BGL
Linda M Carter
1056 Evergreen St
Fairbanks AK 99709

Call Sign: WL7UE
Ray S Brooks
1512 Evergreen St
Fairbanks AK 99709

Call Sign: AL7BJ
Rex E Keirn Sr

759 Fabian Dr
Fairbanks AK 99712

Call Sign: WL7CIN
Rachel E C Keirn
759 Fabian Dr
Fairbanks AK 99712

Call Sign: WL7GL
Fabian J N Keirn
759 Fabian Dr
Fairbanks AK 99712

Call Sign: WL7JD
Janet M Keirn
759 Fabian Dr
Fairbanks AK 99712

Call Sign: WL7VQ
Richard C Keirn
759 Fabian Dr
Fairbanks AK 99712

Call Sign: WL7GK
Robert E Kreiser
409 Fairbanks St
Fairbanks AK 99709

Call Sign: KL1ST
Cole B Kreiser
409 Fairbanks St
Fairbanks AK 997093450

Call Sign: KL7JY
Paul E Mercer Jr
425 Fairbanks St
Fairbanks AK 99709

Call Sign: WL7CME
Benjamin P Mercer
425 Fairbanks St
Fairbanks AK 99709

Call Sign: WL7MQ
Veldon B Speed
660 Fairbanks St   Unit C3
Fairbanks AK 99709

Call Sign: WL7CAG
Cathleen L Hepler
658 Fairbanks St B-5
Fairbanks AK 99709

Call Sign: KL1RS

Stanley R Speed
660 Fairbanks St C3
Fairbanks AK 99709

Call Sign: KL0GR
Miranda L Suttles
5231 Fairchild Ave
Fairbanks AK 99709

Call Sign: WL7RU
Stacey M Eggers
5231 Fairchild Ave
Fairbanks AK 99709

Call Sign: WL7CLF
Claudia J Tessier
439 Fairway Dr
Fairbanks AK 99709

Call Sign: WL7HA
George T Lampe
320 Farewell
Fairbanks AK 99701

Call Sign: WL7CRA
Mikel D Gasaway
229 Farewell Ave
Fairbanks AK 99701

Call Sign: KL2ZD
Ambrose L Mazion Sr
316 Farewell Ave
Fairbanks AK 99701

Call Sign: WL7TQ
Michael R Leake
228 Farmers Loop Ext
Fairbanks AK 99712

Call Sign: KL0CH
Richard J L Keeler
1374 Farmers Loop Rd
Fairbanks AK 99709

Call Sign: NL7XH
John Benevento
1374 Farmers Loop Rd
Fairbanks AK 99709

Call Sign: WL7CIZ
Sally I Benevento
1374 Farmers Loop Rd
Fairbanks AK 99709

Call Sign: KL0GM
Cynthia E Wilde Sullivan
1464 Farmers Loop Rd
Fairbanks AK 99709

Call Sign: KL0MK
Damien R Wilde
1464 Farmers Loop Rd
Fairbanks AK 99709

Call Sign: WL7CAA
Erik R Schoen
475 Forest Hills Ct
Fairbanks AK 99709

Call Sign: KL0UZ
Clifford D Cullings
480 Forest Hills Ct
Fairbanks AK 99709

Call Sign: AL0T
Clifford D Cullings
480 Forest Hills Ct
Fairbanks AK 99709

Call Sign: WL7S
Clifford D Cullings
480 Forest Hills Ct
Fairbanks AK 99709

Call Sign: KD7FGL
Clay W Shepherd
3095 Forrest Dr
Fairbanks AK 997095742

Call Sign: N6UPV
Paula J Shepherd
3095 Forrest Dr
Fairbanks AK 997095742

Call Sign: WL7WJ
Peter W Kristeller
172 Frog Pond Cir
Fairbanks AK 99712

Call Sign: WL7WQ
Justin E Strawther
1410 Garay St
Fairbanks AK 99709

Call Sign: WL7CTJ
Michael H Parcell
1456 Gateway Dr
Fairbanks AK 99709

Call Sign: KL7JI
Elden W Pederson
3875 Geist Rd
Fairbanks AK 99709

Call Sign: KL1NU
Myles S Thomas
3875 Geist Rd E-331
Fairbanks AK 99709

Call Sign: KL2KK
Larry W Field
3875 Geist Rd Pmb 191
Fairbanks AK 99709

Call Sign: WL7KC
Christophe Y Berthomier
4001 Geist Rd Ste 12
Fairbanks AK 99709

Call Sign: KL1BX
Benjamin C Johnson III
3875 Geist Rd Ste E 276
Fairbanks AK 99709

Call Sign: KL7PI
Netia I Pederson
3875 Geist Rd Ste E 343
Fairbanks AK 99709

Call Sign: KL0YT
William F Peacock
3875 Geist Rd Ste E Box 241
Fairbanks AK 99709

Call Sign: KL1DP
Connie A Sutten
3875 Geist Rd Ste E Box 362
Fairbanks AK 99709

Call Sign: KL1IA
Galen Sutten
3875 Geist Rd Ste E Box 362
Fairbanks AK 99709

Call Sign: KL7IAU
Carl P Jeglum
3875 Geist Rd Ste E305
Fairbanks AK 99709

Call Sign: WL7ARX
Joel H Braun Sr
1016 Gilmore St

Fairbanks AK 99701

Call Sign: KL2WR
Ruth J Knapman
1280 Gilmore Trail
Fairbanks AK 99712

Call Sign: KL2WS
Larry N Knapman
1280 Gilmore Trail
Fairbanks AK 99712

Call Sign: KL7EV
William G Eubank
705 Ginko
Fairbanks AK 997093633

Call Sign: WL7CEP
William P Gertz
537 Glacier Ave
Fairbanks AK 99701

Call Sign: AL7OU
Paul D Mane
324 Gloria Ave
Fairbanks AK 99701

Call Sign: WL7TP
Brian G Lawson
2820 Gold Hill Rd
Fairbanks AK 99709

Call Sign: WL7CQS
Kathleen M Lawson
2820 Gold Hill Rd
Fairbanks AK 997092319

Call Sign: WL7CIV
Gregory E Egan
981 Gold Mine Trail
Fairbanks AK 99712

Call Sign: WL7CJH
Catherine G Egan
981 Gold Mine Trl
Fairbanks AK 99712

Call Sign: KL2YI
Jesse M Frey
675 Gold Vein Rd
Fairbanks AK 99712

Call Sign: KL1DE
Martin J Hall

872 Goldfinch Rd
Fairbanks AK 99709

Call Sign: KL7ELR
John J Eubank Jr
2512 Goldhill Rd
Fairbanks AK 997092313

Call Sign: KL0QA
Raoul A Chapman
2967 Goldhill Rd
Fairbanks AK 99709

Call Sign: KL0YR
Carmen L Brooks
390 Goldstream Rd
Fairbanks AK 99712

Call Sign: KL1HM
Bittner A Brooks
390 Goldstream Rd
Fairbanks AK 99712

Call Sign: KL1SR
Mckenzie C Brooks
390 Goldstream Rd
Fairbanks AK 99712

Call Sign: KL2DA
Blaze W Brooks
390 Goldstream Rd
Fairbanks AK 99712

Call Sign: WL7CPS
Ronald A Brooks
390 Goldstream Rd
Fairbanks AK 997121007

Call Sign: KL7HON
Shirley A Liss
2749 Goldstream Rd
Fairbanks AK 997096066

Call Sign: K7KK
James H Maynard
684 Gradelle Ave
Fairbanks AK 99709

Call Sign: WL7BMZ
Susan E Fisher
1379 Great View Ln
Fairbanks AK 99712

Call Sign: KL7IXW

Ward M Merdes
1351 Greatview Ln
Fairbanks AK 99712

Call Sign: WL7CIR
Leroy A Gross
2445 Green Acres Dr
Fairbanks AK 99712

Call Sign: KL1RL
Justin E Burket
1530 Gunning Dr
Fairbanks AK 99712

Call Sign: KL7IGX
Mary L Bishop
1555 Guss Grind
Fairbanks AK 99709

Call Sign: KL0GN
Dorothy M Wilde
365 Hagelbarger Ave
Fairbanks AK 997121916

Call Sign: KL0WG
Michael B Hyatt
375 Hagelbarger Ave
Fairbanks AK 99712

Call Sign: KL7IRT
Berton J Curwen
511 Hagelbarger Ave
Fairbanks AK 99712

Call Sign: KL7DTE
Harold J Bacon
235 Haines
Fairbanks AK 99701

Call Sign: WL7CGO
Brandon P Moore
1462 Hans Way
Fairbanks AK 99709

Call Sign: WL7CLN
Greg D Aldrich
1466 Hans Way
Fairbanks AK 99709

Call Sign: WL7CNH
Jeff D Aldrich
1466 Hans Way
Fairbanks AK 99709

Call Sign: WL7ZZ
James W Aldrich
1466 Hans Way
Fairbanks AK 99709

Call Sign: KL7IGO
Joseph G Hawkins Jr
3680 Hardluck Dr
Fairbanks AK 99709

Call Sign: KL0RP
Donald R La Faver
23 Harriet St Apt 3
Fairbanks AK 99701

Call Sign: KL0GX
William C O Halloran
4741 Harvard Cir
Fairbanks AK 99709

Call Sign: KL0GY
Patricia G O Halloran
4741 Harvard Cir
Fairbanks AK 99709

Call Sign: KL0GZ
Brian W O Halloran
4741 Harvard Cir
Fairbanks AK 99709

Call Sign: WL7CBV
Daniel S Clautice
1465 Haus Way
Fairbanks AK 99709

Call Sign: WL7BTB
Leo J Kerin
232 Henderson Rd
Fairbanks AK 99709

Call Sign: WL7BTC
Britton L Kerin
232 Henderson Rd
Fairbanks AK 99709

Call Sign: KL1TR
Zachary A Canright
461 Herning
Fairbanks AK 99712

Call Sign: AL2S
Zachary A Canright
461 Herning
Fairbanks AK 99712

Call Sign: KL1TS
Jared Canright
461 Herning Rd
Fairbanks AK 99712

Call Sign: WL7CBS
Andrew L Foley
111 Hickory Dr
Fairbanks AK 99709

Call Sign: WL7BQK
Robert E Boswell
795 High Grade Way
Fairbanks AK 99712

Call Sign: KL7ENY
Robert W Taylor
1922 Hilling Ave
Fairbanks AK 99709

Call Sign: KL7IVN
Richard H Morgan
573 Hilltop Ave
Fairbanks AK 99709

Call Sign: WL7OG
Caitlin A Warbelow
1530 Holy Cross
Fairbanks AK 99709

Call Sign: WL7OH
Arthur W Warbelow
1530 Holy Cross
Fairbanks AK 99709

Call Sign: WL7SZ
Ernst S Boyd
685 Indiana Ave
Fairbanks AK 99709

Call Sign: WL7CQI
William F Buchanan
2246 Jack St
Fairbanks AK 99709

Call Sign: KL0OK
Seth W Johnson
289 Jade St
Fairbanks AK 99712

Call Sign: WL7CTF
Jason S Gustin
3278 Jefferson Dr

Fairbanks AK 99709

Call Sign: WL7NT
Roger L Asbury Jr
649 Jennie Ln E3
Fairbanks AK 99709

Call Sign: KL7JZ
James M Romersberger
1016 John Kalinas Rd
Fairbanks AK 99712

Call Sign: NL7VB
Virgil W Hoppe
1001 Joyce Dr
Fairbanks AK 99701

Call Sign: WL7CEC
Woodrow A Knapp
133 Kantishna Way
Fairbanks AK 99701

Call Sign: AL4E
Charles T Miller
769 Karluk Ct
Fairbanks AK 99701

Call Sign: KL7BVY
Ernest J Watson
1040 Kellum St
Fairbanks AK 99701

Call Sign: WL7AYG
Gene H Shafer
1823 Kennedy St
Fairbanks AK 99709

Call Sign: KL1BF
Randy L Davis
1828 Kennedy St
Fairbanks AK 99709

Call Sign: KL0IS
Katherine L Babcock
423 Ketchikan Ave
Fairbanks AK 99701

Call Sign: AL7QY
Myron F Babcock
423 Ketchikan Ave
Fairbanks AK 997013736

Call Sign: KL7YY
Myron F Babcock

430B Ketchikan Ave
Fairbanks AK 997013736

Call Sign: NL7YX
Dale S Baker
1880 Kettiwake Dr
Fairbanks AK 99709

Call Sign: WL7BFX
Aquila W Baker Jr
1880 Killiwake Dr
Fairbanks AK 99709

Call Sign: NL7X
Duane M Cook
630 Kilo Ct
Fairbanks AK 997110366

Call Sign: KL3AC
Peter Williams
1835 Kittiwake Dr
Fairbanks AK 99709

Call Sign: KL0GW
Shanna K Patterson
1883 Kittiwake Dr
Fairbanks AK 99709

Call Sign: WL7CQR
John H Patterson
1883 Kittiwake Dr
Fairbanks AK 99709

Call Sign: KJ7FX
Daniel C Hall
1664 Kivalina St
Fairbanks AK 99709

Call Sign: KL0UE
Susan P Englebrecht
218 Kody
Fairbanks AK 99701

Call Sign: KL0QS
Gregg D Eschright
218 Kody Dr
Fairbanks AK 99701

Call Sign: KL7GGP
Harley D Shield
928 Kokomo St
Fairbanks AK 99712

Call Sign: KL7AVD

Voice Of Alaska Radio Club
903 Koyukuk Dr
Fairbanks AK 997757320

Call Sign: KL7KT
William L Johnson
3239 La Ree Way
Fairbanks AK 99709

Call Sign: WL7IO
Matthew A Johnson
3269 La Ree Way
Fairbanks AK 99709

Call Sign: W7USB
Neal B Brown
1569 La Rue Ln
Fairbanks AK 99709

Call Sign: WL7NZ
Neal B Brown
1569 La Rue Ln
Fairbanks AK 99709

Call Sign: KD6DLB
Larry J Ellsworth
215 Ladd Ave Apt E
Fairbanks AK 99701

Call Sign: WL7KU
Robert M Burke
2012 Lakeview Ter
Fairbanks AK 99701

Call Sign: WL7CUR
James W Firmin
2077 Lakeview Ter
Fairbanks AK 99701

Call Sign: NL7GM
Kenneth E Wooten
892 Landon Ln
Fairbanks AK 99712

Call Sign: AL7GT
Roger T Sperl
1416 Lathrop
Fairbanks AK 99701

Call Sign: NL7OV
Barbara J Sperl
1416 Lathrop
Fairbanks AK 99701

Call Sign: KL7IVO
James M Joy
1045 Lathrop St
Fairbanks AK 99701

Call Sign: K9YYG
Roger J Halmstad
3411 Lills Way
Fairbanks AK 997092836

Call Sign: WL7BUG
Walter R Johnson
2593 Lingonberry Ln
Fairbanks AK 99709

Call Sign: KL7QE
David C Munson Sr
1925 Lisga St
Fairbanks AK 99701

Call Sign: WL7AUF
Sharon A Munson
1925 Lisga St
Fairbanks AK 99701

Call Sign: WL7CPQ
Joseph W Gillis
1365 Little Fox Trail
Fairbanks AK 997121823

Call Sign: WL7GX
Jerry L Cates
1271 Lois Ln
Fairbanks AK 99712

Call Sign: KH6IHS
Richard W Cowles
448 Lone Pine
Fairbanks AK 99701

Call Sign: WL7CBF
Colin L Read
653 Love Rd
Fairbanks AK 99708

Call Sign: WL7YT
Thomas F Paragi
1271 Lowbush Ln
Fairbanks AK 997096039

Call Sign: AL2A
Chet Higa
4600 Lundeberg Rd
Fairbanks AK 99712

Call Sign: KL1IB
Chet Higa
4600 Lundeberg Rd
Fairbanks AK 99712

Call Sign: KL2AW
Scott W Bracy
4610 Lundeberg Rd
Fairbanks AK 99712

Call Sign: KL2AJ
Alison R Spees
4610 Lundeberg Rd
Fairbanks AK 99712

Call Sign: AL7NO
Robert D Shankle Jr
1370 Macfarland St
Fairbanks AK 99709

Call Sign: KL1BY
Jim J Masek
1501 Marika Apt 5
Fairbanks AK 99709

Call Sign: WL7AYR
Susan F Vicente
3752 Mariposa Ln
Fairbanks AK 99709

Call Sign: KL7OH
Charles C Newberg Sr
472 Marshall Dr
Fairbanks AK 99712

Call Sign: KL0CI
Frank J De Nardo
731 Mcgrath Rd
Fairbanks AK 99712

Call Sign: AL0W
Frank J De Nardo
731 Mcgrath Rd
Fairbanks AK 99712

Call Sign: WL7CPI
Ronald D Rasmussen
445 Mckinley View Dr
Fairbanks AK 99712

Call Sign: WL7BED
Joyce J Bennett
4458 Melan Dr

Fairbanks AK 99712

Call Sign: KL0CN
Anthony L Blanford
4557 Melan Dr
Fairbanks AK 99712

Call Sign: KE4ITP
Walter W Mullen Jr
4555 Melan Dr N
Fairbanks AK 99712

Call Sign: WL7SY
Robert L Bowdoin
991 Miller Hill Ext
Fairbanks AK 99709

Call Sign: NL7WO
Kevin C Abnett
1216 Miller Hill Extension
Fairbanks AK 99708

Call Sign: NL7F
William J Beam
774 Miners Ct
Fairbanks AK 997121340

Call Sign: KL1JZ
Andrew B Crabb
1724 Moose Trail
Fairbanks AK 99709

Call Sign: KL1LK
Amie M Crabb
1724 Moose Trail
Fairbanks AK 99709

Call Sign: KL1LL
Hannah S Bailey
1724 Moose Trail
Fairbanks AK 99709

Call Sign: KG7EH
Ernest P Crabb
1724 Moose Trail
Fairbanks AK 99709

Call Sign: WL7PJ
Martin E Hartman
168 Mountain View Dr
Fairbanks AK 99712

Call Sign: KL2SY
David P Costello

4465 Murphy Dome Rd
Fairbanks AK 99709

Call Sign: KL1AG
Paul R Lhotka
4505 Murphy Dome Rd
Fairbanks AK 99709

Call Sign: KL7ARU
Celia M Hunter
1819 Muskox Trail
Fairbanks AK 99709

Call Sign: KB5QOH
Durell Smith
667 Nine Mile Hill Rd
Fairbanks AK 99712

Call Sign: KL7BIA
Robert L Benish
2890 North Kobuk Ave
Fairbanks AK 99709

Call Sign: AD4BL
Linda G Mullen
4555 North Melan Dr
Fairbanks AK 99712

Call Sign: KL0HD
Carol J Hammond
1389 North Rader Dr
Fairbanks AK 99709

Call Sign: WL7CQX
William R Hammond
1389 North Rader Dr
Fairbanks AK 99709

Call Sign: WL7AE
Kenneth R Schwartz
480 North Slope Ln
Fairbanks AK 99709

Call Sign: NL7SL
Andrew J Wareham
2641 North Steese
Fairbanks AK 99712

Call Sign: KL0VY
Daniel L Hickman
2086 North Van Horn Ct
Fairbanks AK 99701

Call Sign: KL1MZ

Rhees E Burket
1119 Northwood Ln
Fairbanks AK 99712

Call Sign: WL7TA
Sean D Carlisle
1303 O Connor Rd 14
Fairbanks AK 99701

Call Sign: WL7CRG
Deborah L Treb
1303 O'Conner Rd Lot 26A
Fairbanks AK 997011580

Call Sign: AL1S
Deborah L Treb
1303 O'Conner Rd Lot 26A
Fairbanks AK 997011580

Call Sign: KL7GCC
James R Marsh
711 Old Cat Trail
Fairbanks AK 99709

Call Sign: KL2KX
Larry A Lysne
2482 Old Chena Ridge Rd
Fairbanks AK 99709

Call Sign: KB0CCW
Larry A Lysne
2482 Old Chena Ridge Rd
Fairbanks AK 99709

Call Sign: KL3IY
Thomas A Narow
1787 Old Pioneer Way
Fairbanks AK 99709

Call Sign: KL1BA
Donald J Aycock
330 Old Steese Hwy 300
Fairbanks AK 99701

Call Sign: KL8T
William L Morrow
330 Old Steese Hwy 763
Fairbanks AK 99701

Call Sign: WL7AZR
Benjamin J Halvorsen
607 Old Steese Hwy Pmb 411
Ste B
Fairbanks AK 99701

Call Sign: KL1AA
Joyce T O Beirne
607 Old Steese Hwy Ste B Pmb
203
Fairbanks AK 99701

Call Sign: KL7IHT
Sandra G Dauenhauer
507 Ookpik Way
Fairbanks AK 99709

Call Sign: WL7BUE
Delmar G Johnson
1301 Overhill Dr
Fairbanks AK 99709

Call Sign: WL7NL
Michael E Hoefer
1363 Overhill Dr
Fairbanks AK 99709

Call Sign: WL7OJ
Judith F Reece
4731 Palo Verde
Fairbanks AK 99709

Call Sign: WL7CEN
Brittany E Burrows
4894 Palo Verde
Fairbanks AK 99709

Call Sign: KL0OZ
Robert D Fath Sr
5165 Palo Verde Ave
Fairbanks AK 99709

Call Sign: WL7CRC
Anna M Fath
5165 Palo Verde Ave
Fairbanks AK 99709

Call Sign: WL7CAP
Austin D Swift
4851 Palo Verde Dr
Fairbanks AK 99709

Call Sign: KL0IM
Kathleen A Bue
387 Pay Streak Dr
Fairbanks AK 99712

Call Sign: KL0JU
Fredrick J Bue

387 Pay Streak Dr
Fairbanks AK 99712

Call Sign: WL7CHO
Keith E Palchikoff
329 Paystreak Dr
Fairbanks AK 99712

Call Sign: KL0XO
Keith E Palchikoff
329 Paystreak Dr
Fairbanks AK 99712

Call Sign: KL1BO
Nicolas F Miramontes
238 Pearl Dr
Fairbanks AK 99712

Call Sign: AL7XT
Scott A Mc Donnell
238 Pearl Dr
Fairbanks AK 99712

Call Sign: KL1DF
Alyssa N Miramontes
238 Pearl Dr
Fairbanks AK 99712

Call Sign: KB0ROF
Mark L Mac Donald
2228 Penrose Ln
Fairbanks AK 99709

Call Sign: WL7HU
Kenneth P Severin
2235 Penrose Ln
Fairbanks AK 99709

Call Sign: KL0VC
Dan P Scannell
296 Peregrine Dr
Fairbanks AK 99712

Call Sign: KL0XB
Chuck A Mcdonald
1440 Pickering Dr
Fairbanks AK 99709

Call Sign: KL0VF
Sherryll L Mcdonald
1440 Pickering Dr
Fairbanks AK 997092668

Call Sign: KL0BI

Terry L Marsh
1327 Polar Dr
Fairbanks AK 99712

Call Sign: WL7CBU
Douglas C Knight
4913 Princeton Dr
Fairbanks AK 99709

Call Sign: NL7QG
John S Murray
1129 Propwash Dr
Fairbanks AK 99709

Call Sign: KL0SF
Gail Kaufman Lindh
589 Prospectors Trail
Fairbanks AK 99712

Call Sign: KL0TT
Jan L Lindh
589 Prospectors Trail
Fairbanks AK 99712

Call Sign: AL7RP
Jan L Lindh
589 Prospectors Trail
Fairbanks AK 99712

Call Sign: AL0S
Jan L Lindh
589 Prospectors Trail
Fairbanks AK 99712

Call Sign: KA6PTO
Eddie R Lee
4152 Rabbit Run
Fairbanks AK 99709

Call Sign: WL7AJG
Robert K Teel III
288 Rambling Rd 74
Fairbanks AK 99701

Call Sign: KL0KL
Maryanne Allan
443 Ramola St
Fairbanks AK 99709

Call Sign: NJ5O
James H Giles
1918 Raven Dr
Fairbanks AK 99709

Call Sign: KF6EJR
Holly M Proell
2011 Red Berry Rd
Fairbanks AK 99709

Call Sign: KL0CJ
David De Nardo
109 Rhubarb Dr
Fairbanks AK 99712

Call Sign: KL0VA
William D Baranauskas
165 Rhubarb Dr
Fairbanks AK 99712

Call Sign: KL7GNG
Tom M Walyer
1909 Ridge Run
Fairbanks AK 99712

Call Sign: WL7CLD
Duane J Metz
3310 Riverside Dr 1
Fairbanks AK 99709

Call Sign: WL7CII
Joan L Mc Inerney
2811 Riverview Dr
Fairbanks AK 99709

Call Sign: KL1AW
Stephen T Paskvan
3275 Riverview Dr
Fairbanks AK 99709

Call Sign: WL7CIE
John E Orbeck
3278 Riverview Dr
Fairbanks AK 99709

Call Sign: NL7KW
Dennis J Stephens
3140 Roden Ln
Fairbanks AK 99709

Call Sign: WL7WR
James R Waldo
3414 Rosie Creek Rd
Fairbanks AK 99709

Call Sign: WL7JZ
Samuel J Haas
3760 Rosie Creek Rd
Fairbanks AK 99709

Call Sign: WL7MK
Carol L Haas
3760 Rosie Creek Rd
Fairbanks AK 99709

Call Sign: WL7BFL
Jay K Williams
428 Samiel Ct
Fairbanks AK 99709

Call Sign: AL7RT
Dan Hunt
450 Samiel Ct
Fairbanks AK 99709

Call Sign: K5WXN
Dan Hunt
450 Samiel Ct
Fairbanks AK 99709

Call Sign: KA0OVR
Renee J Mc Key
581 Sandpiper Dr
Fairbanks AK 99709

Call Sign: NL7QJ
Clarence E Mc Key Jr
581 Sandpiper Dr
Fairbanks AK 99709

Call Sign: WL7CKG
Diann M Aldrich
593 Sandpiper Dr
Fairbanks AK 997096656

Call Sign: KL1DX
Jason A Karella
3405 Sandvick
Fairbanks AK 99709

Call Sign: WL7SX
Teddy W Baxter
344 Scenic Hills Ct
Fairbanks AK 99712

Call Sign: KL2KB
Tim W Childs
1525 Scenic Loop
Fairbanks AK 99709

Call Sign: KL0XU
Nicholas I Covell
764 Senate Dr

Fairbanks AK 99712

Call Sign: NL7Q
Gary F Chamberlain
1219 Shypoke Dr
Fairbanks AK 99709

Call Sign: WL7AYA
Gary F Chamberlain
1219 Shypoke Dr
Fairbanks AK 99709

Call Sign: KL1QM
Jeremy E Bennis
1280 Shypoke Dr
Fairbanks AK 99709

Call Sign: WL7ZW
Lowell F North
1241 Silverberry Dr
Fairbanks AK 99712

Call Sign: KL7AY
Charles R Johnson
2382 Skiland Rd
Fairbanks AK 997121749

Call Sign: NL7RJ
Robert B Harte
1330 Skinner Dr
Fairbanks AK 99709

Call Sign: WL7TE
Marc J Dumas
1166 Skyline Dr
Fairbanks AK 99712

Call Sign: WL7TW
Lisa M Penalver
1166 Skyline Dr
Fairbanks AK 99712

Call Sign: KL0ME
Robert A Parsons
440 Skyridge
Fairbanks AK 99712

Call Sign: KL0MD
Jennifer A Parsons
440 Skyridge Rd
Fairbanks AK 99712

Call Sign: KL1GZ
Mary K Parsons

440 Skyridge Rd
Fairbanks AK 99712

Call Sign: KL7EUY
Dwight E Morris
206 Slater Dr
Fairbanks AK 997013430

Call Sign: KL7TA
William F St George
228 Slater Dr
Fairbanks AK 99701

Call Sign: WL7BBQ
Jane L St George
228 Slater Dr
Fairbanks AK 99701

Call Sign: WL7BPQ
Leanne M Olmstead
674 Slater Dr E
Fairbanks AK 99901

Call Sign: NL7QF
Thomas L Bruner
216 Slater St
Fairbanks AK 99701

Call Sign: WL7SL
Calvin L Skaugstad
942 Sluice Box Rd
Fairbanks AK 99712

Call Sign: KL7JAT
Michael D Mc Cann
793 Smallwood Trail
Fairbanks AK 99712

Call Sign: WL7CLG
David A Stoots
3445 Snow Flake Ln
Fairbanks AK 99709

Call Sign: KL0BM
David D Hiatt
135 Snowy Owl Ln
Fairbanks AK 99712

Call Sign: KL0LR
Tiffany E Deeter
135 Snowy Owl Ln
Fairbanks AK 997121241

Call Sign: WL7CSV

Denise C Hiatt
135 Snowy Owl Ln
Fairbanks AK 997121241

Call Sign: KL0LQ
Chad D Carscallen
292 Snowy Owl Ln
Fairbanks AK 99712

Call Sign: WL7CTI
George G Bird
297 Snowy Owl Ln
Fairbanks AK 99712

Call Sign: KL2ZD
James G Farnham
369 Snowy Owl Ln
Fairbanks AK 99712

Call Sign: WL7CQM
Tobe A Sanford
384 Snowy Owl Ln
Fairbanks AK 99712

Call Sign: AL7N
Lake E Trump
2950 South Kobuk Ave
Fairbanks AK 997095126

Call Sign: WL7HQ
Pamela M Tinsley
1609 Southern Ave Apt B
Fairbanks AK 99709

Call Sign: KC7QDV
Roger A Smith
3773 Spinach Creek Rd
Fairbanks AK 99708

Call Sign: KL3CT
Troy M Hicks
820 Spudwood Rd
Fairbanks AK 99712

Call Sign: KL1TQ
Thomas R Edwards
1199 Stack Rd
Fairbanks AK 99709

Call Sign: WL7CHY
Walker S Wheeler
4461 Stanford
Fairbanks AK 99709

Call Sign: KL2TZ
Tyler M Davis
4440 Stanford Dr
Fairbanks AK 99709

Call Sign: WL7BRY
Milton R Desrochers
536 Steele Creek Rd
Fairbanks AK 99712

Call Sign: KL7FAP
Frederick E Wirth Jr
638 Steele Creek Rd
Fairbanks AK 99712

Call Sign: WB0ZKJ
Kanza R Easterly Keill
641 Steele Creek Rd
Fairbanks AK 99712

Call Sign: KL2OM
Branden L Scram
1211 Steele Creek Rd
Fairbanks AK 99712

Call Sign: KA6PJV
Karen G Kiele
1232 Steele Creek Rd
Fairbanks AK 99712

Call Sign: KC7MIJ
Renee G Kiele
1232 Steele Creek Rd
Fairbanks AK 99712

Call Sign: KC7TYT
Angela D Kiele
1232 Steele Creek Rd
Fairbanks AK 99712

Call Sign: KJ7MY
Jan E Kiele
1232 Steele Creek Rd
Fairbanks AK 99712

Call Sign: KL3JV
Robert M Frederick
1366 Steele Creek Rd
Fairbanks AK 99712

Call Sign: KL3KQ
Philemon R Frederick
1366 Steele Creek Rd
Fairbanks AK 99712

Call Sign: WL7CER
Kevin B Sauer
86 Steelhead St
Fairbanks AK 99709

Call Sign: WL7BKH
Samuel A Mc Querry
Steese Branch
Fairbanks AK 99710

Call Sign: KL2ZA
Jay G Helmericks
2290 Steese Hwy
Fairbanks AK 99712

Call Sign: KL0RL
Dennis V Schmit
2303 Steese Hwy
Fairbanks AK 99712

Call Sign: KL7QT
Duncan R Edwards
1199 Stock Rd
Fairbanks AK 99709

Call Sign: KL0ML
Bonnie I Williams
1335 Sunny Slope Rd
Fairbanks AK 99709

Call Sign: KL7DW
David L Williams
1335 Sunny Slope Rd
Fairbanks AK 99709

Call Sign: WB5ZOD
David L Welch
1233 Sutton Loop
Fairbanks AK 99701

Call Sign: NL7Y
Gary A Pearse
1700 Tamarack St
Fairbanks AK 99709

Call Sign: WL7XS
Kathleen R Pearse
1700 Tamarack St
Fairbanks AK 99709

Call Sign: WL7CXB
Uaf Satellite
306 Tanana Loop

Fairbanks AK 99775

Call Sign: WL7CIC
David R Roberts
2821 Tatem Dr
Fairbanks AK 99709

Call Sign: KL0CL
George Colette
146 third Ave
Fairbanks AK 99701

Call Sign: WL7XT
Jay P Langton
3030 Tinkers Ln
Fairbanks AK 99762

Call Sign: KF6ZKW
Kieran M Gleason
2170 Toboggan Ln
Fairbanks AK 99709

Call Sign: WL7SW
John T Bailey Jr
4563 Tolovana Dr
Fairbanks AK 997093412

Call Sign: KL2CX
Jason M Banks
48 A Trinidad Dr
Fairbanks AK 99709

Call Sign: KL2CZ
James L Rieve II
48 A Trinidad Dr
Fairbanks AK 99709

Call Sign: WB2IKA
Hilmar A Maier
2140 Twin Flower Dr
Fairbanks AK 99709

Call Sign: KL0OO
Wendell M Wassmann
960 Union Dr
Fairbanks AK 99709

Call Sign: KE4LJR
Loren A Dobberpuhl
875 University Ave
Fairbanks AK 99709

Call Sign: KL2LV
Michael A Cross

895 University Ave 1
Fairbanks AK 99709

Call Sign: KL1NV
Oshawa L Laney
1733 University Ave Apt F66
Fairbanks AK 99709

Call Sign: KL0RK
Cherie S Silapaswan
1737 University Ave Apt G 53
Fairbanks AK 99709

Call Sign: KL1NT
Alexis O Diaz
1725 University Ave D-3
Fairbanks AK 99709

Call Sign: KL7IFM
Arlin R Hogenson
450 Valley View Dr
Fairbanks AK 99712

Call Sign: WL7XY
Peggy V Beagle
3580 Vanhorn Rd
Fairbanks AK 99706

Call Sign: WL7BIT
Edward W Curry
940 Vide Way
Fairbanks AK 99701

Call Sign: KL7EDK
Jerrold M Curry
940 Vide Way
Fairbanks AK 99712

Call Sign: NL7RF
Randy J Brown
865 Viridian
Fairbanks AK 99708

Call Sign: WL7BTR
Karen E Kallen Brown
865 Viridian
Fairbanks AK 99708

Call Sign: KL7US
Gerald L Lizotte
304 Wedgewood Dr Apt A-47
Fairbanks AK 997011635

Call Sign: AL7KT

Albert N Milliron
405 Wedgewood Dr Apt J31
Fairbanks AK 99701

Call Sign: WL7UF
David S Hauger
330 Wedgewood Dr E3
Fairbanks AK 99701

Call Sign: AL7PW
Edward A Zawadzki
1125 West Chena Hills Dr
Fairbanks AK 99709

Call Sign: WL7BS
Orwin B Westwick
1310 Westwick Dr
Fairbanks AK 99712

Call Sign: KL0AW
Daniel D Foreman IV
1274 Wideview Rd
Fairbanks AK 99709

Call Sign: WB4LMK
Frederick J Schramm
451 Wilcox Ave
Fairbanks AK 99709

Call Sign: NL7AB
Muriel A Scott
605 Wilcox Ave
Fairbanks AK 997093628

Call Sign: KL1CP
Mark P Mowery
545 Wild Horse Ln
Fairbanks AK 99709

Call Sign: KL3ER
Matthew Cooper
995 Willow Grouse Rd
Fairbanks AK 99712

Call Sign: KL3OC
Matthew Cooper
995 Willow Grouse Rd
Fairbanks AK 99712

Call Sign: KL0MB
Mark R Mac Farlane
1103 Willow Grouse Rd
Fairbanks AK 99712

Call Sign: KL2WO
Alan M Armbruster
1637 Willow St
Fairbanks AK 99709

Call Sign: KL0BJ
Gary S Jones
748 Winch Rd
Fairbanks AK 99712

Call Sign: WL7BFM
Tonya M Schlentner
1398 Windfall Way
Fairbanks AK 99709

Call Sign: NL7YT
Daniel R Baltrum
3400 Wolf Run
Fairbanks AK 99709

Call Sign: NL7MK
Tovan L Adams
1893 Woodbine Dr
Fairbanks AK 99709

Call Sign: AL7MU
Randy H Hesser
228 Woodridge St Unit 3
Fairbanks AK 99709

Call Sign: AL7EN
Russell D Amerson
490 Wright Ln
Fairbanks AK 99712

Call Sign: WL7JT
Margaret E Clements
510 Yak Rd Apt 860D
Fairbanks AK 99709

Call Sign: KL0VJ
Nicholas G Schmidt
510 Yak Rd Apt 862D
Fairbanks AK 99709

Call Sign: WL7CBW
Bryan D Davis
218 Yale Way
Fairbanks AK 99709

Call Sign: WL7CHX
Rosita D Wilburn
218 Yale Way
Fairbanks AK 99709

Call Sign: KL2CY
Richard M Timm
240 Yale Way
Fairbanks AK 99709

Call Sign: KL7BDW
William W Mendenhall
1907 Yankovich Rd
Fairbanks AK 997096540

Call Sign: KL7HNT
Harvey W Davis
4038 Yvonne Ave
Fairbanks AK 99709

Call Sign: KL1WL
Jan H Julian
Fairbanks AK 99705

Call Sign: KL1JP
Daniel M Wietchy
Fairbanks AK 99706

Call Sign: KL1OQ
George E Stevens
Fairbanks AK 99706

Call Sign: KL1SU
Alyssa Quaile
Fairbanks AK 99706

Call Sign: KL1TB
Bill Boucher
Fairbanks AK 99706

Call Sign: KL1TD
Morgan Hostina
Fairbanks AK 99706

Call Sign: KL1TJ
Michael P Hostina
Fairbanks AK 99706

Call Sign: KL2MR
Martha E Thomas
Fairbanks AK 99706

Call Sign: KL3FO
Laureen M Hege
Fairbanks AK 99706

Call Sign: KL3JW
Jason A Dennis

Fairbanks AK 99706

Call Sign: KL3KX
Annlouia Smith
Fairbanks AK 99706

Call Sign: AL7HV
Wayne J Calkin Sr
Fairbanks AK 99706

Call Sign: KL7FY
Carrie A Rosengren
Fairbanks AK 99706

Call Sign: KL7HJF
Warren D Wurm
Fairbanks AK 99706

Call Sign: KL7NO
Albert E Noe
Fairbanks AK 99706

Call Sign: NL7SD
Duane E Widdis
Fairbanks AK 99706

Call Sign: WL7ATL
Richard L Gaffi
Fairbanks AK 99706

Call Sign: WL7CSB
Allen R Nussbaumer
Fairbanks AK 99706

Call Sign: WL7LU
Roger F Weggel
Fairbanks AK 99706

Call Sign: WL7UB
Richard C Sullivan
Fairbanks AK 99706

Call Sign: KL1YU
Frances J Collins
Fairbanks AK 99707

Call Sign: KL1YW
Frances J Collins
Fairbanks AK 99707

Call Sign: KL2KH
Jeremy M Stepp
Fairbanks AK 99707

Call Sign: KL7R
Dale E Pelzer
Fairbanks AK 99707

Call Sign: KL7DFL
Donald F Logan
Fairbanks AK 99707

Call Sign: KL7V
Dale D Powell Jr
Fairbanks AK 99707

Call Sign: AL7MG
Bruce Congleton
Fairbanks AK 99707

Call Sign: AL7MI
Michael R Rice
Fairbanks AK 99707

Call Sign: AL7Z
Donald R Etheredge
Fairbanks AK 99707

Call Sign: KL0CD
Charles H Scheer
Fairbanks AK 99707

Call Sign: KL0EP
Robert G Homoleski
Fairbanks AK 99707

Call Sign: KL0LY
Rosa L Jadczak
Fairbanks AK 99707

Call Sign: KL1R
Dale E Pelzer
Fairbanks AK 99707

Call Sign: KL7JAU
Steven M Gudschinsky
Fairbanks AK 99707

Call Sign: KL7RE
William L Eaves
Fairbanks AK 99707

Call Sign: KL7YY
Mike S Hunstein
Fairbanks AK 99707

Call Sign: NL7BB
Robert A Halvorsen

Fairbanks AK 99707

Call Sign: NL7DU
Christie A Pelzer
Fairbanks AK 99707

Call Sign: NL7GS
Glenn Estabrook
Fairbanks AK 99707

Call Sign: W2DLS
David L Smith
Fairbanks AK 99707

Call Sign: WL7BGS
Karen L Kohout
Fairbanks AK 99707

Call Sign: WL7CDK
Jeffrey Anderson
Fairbanks AK 99707

Call Sign: WL7CIT
James E Gibertoni
Fairbanks AK 99707

Call Sign: WL7CPN
David E Ways
Fairbanks AK 99707

Call Sign: WL7CQY
Chad E Gudschinsky
Fairbanks AK 99707

Call Sign: WL7CTV
Harmony A Posey
Fairbanks AK 99707

Call Sign: WL7IJ
Fred L Brantingham
Fairbanks AK 99707

Call Sign: WL7TX
Donald H Piatt
Fairbanks AK 99707

Call Sign: WL7YV
Marty E Brantingham
Fairbanks AK 99707

Call Sign: WL7ZY
Eugene H Culp
Fairbanks AK 99707

Call Sign: KL0WO
Maureen E Dey
Fairbanks AK 99707

Call Sign: KL0WP
Donald F Logan
Fairbanks AK 99707

Call Sign: KL0WS
Paul D Korchin
Fairbanks AK 99707

Call Sign: KL1AI
Stuller L Conceicao
Fairbanks AK 99707

Call Sign: AL7Y
Dale D Powell Jr
Fairbanks AK 99707

Call Sign: KL1OO
Bradley D Snow
Fairbanks AK 99708

Call Sign: KL1OY
Christa L Matthews
Fairbanks AK 99708

Call Sign: KL1PF
Scott F Rosengren
Fairbanks AK 99708

Call Sign: KL1PK
Monte R Ervin
Fairbanks AK 99708

Call Sign: KL7RB
Robert F Brown
Fairbanks AK 99708

Call Sign: KL1TA
Ben Schroeder
Fairbanks AK 99708

Call Sign: KL1TH
Glenn P Walston
Fairbanks AK 99708

Call Sign: KL1VZ
Tacy L Magill
Fairbanks AK 99708

Call Sign: KL1WA
Ross L Novak

Fairbanks AK 99708

Call Sign: W7EIK
Tracy L Magill
Fairbanks AK 99708

Call Sign: KL1XE
Steve A Anderson
Fairbanks AK 99708

Call Sign: KL2EG
Brian J Mader
Fairbanks AK 99708

Call Sign: KL2MD
Cody D White
Fairbanks AK 99708

Call Sign: KL2MS
Patrick O Bartolatz-Sawyer
Fairbanks AK 99708

Call Sign: KL2SX
Michael C Anderson
Fairbanks AK 99708

Call Sign: KL2UK
Samuel Joseph
Fairbanks AK 99708

Call Sign: KL2UM
Joanna E Roth
Fairbanks AK 99708

Call Sign: KL2WP
Stuart C Edgerton
Fairbanks AK 99708

Call Sign: KL2YK
Abraham P Christenson
Fairbanks AK 99708

Call Sign: KL3DO
Eric R Proell
Fairbanks AK 99708

Call Sign: KL3DP
Austin T Roberts
Fairbanks AK 99708

Call Sign: KL3DR
Roberta W Fraser
Fairbanks AK 99708

Call Sign: KL3IQ
David A Huckaby Jr
Fairbanks AK 99708

Call Sign: KL3JP
Denise L Thorsen
Fairbanks AK 99708

Call Sign: AD6GC
Michael B Carlsen
Fairbanks AK 99708

Call Sign: AL7AF
Leonard G Coursey
Fairbanks AK 99708

Call Sign: AL7EA
Linda M Baker
Fairbanks AK 99708

Call Sign: KC0CWG
Mary Beth E Groves
Fairbanks AK 99708

Call Sign: KE6SEF
Steve R Cox
Fairbanks AK 99708

Call Sign: KL0CC
Jeff T Meierotto
Fairbanks AK 99708

Call Sign: KL0FV
Steven L Leclerc Jr
Fairbanks AK 99708

Call Sign: KL0GS
John R Stowman
Fairbanks AK 99708

Call Sign: KL0GV
Shaun M Patterson
Fairbanks AK 99708

Call Sign: KL0HC
Lloyd K Lovin
Fairbanks AK 99708

Call Sign: KL0HL
Steven C Leclerc
Fairbanks AK 99708

Call Sign: KL0MU
Kathleen R Miller

Fairbanks AK 99708

Call Sign: KL0QI
Tyler K Freeman
Fairbanks AK 99708

Call Sign: KL0SD
Keith A Mueller
Fairbanks AK 99708

Call Sign: KL0UG
Andrew J Chapman
Fairbanks AK 99708

Call Sign: KL7DJI
Robert F Brown
Fairbanks AK 99708

Call Sign: KL7HOO
Dwight M West
Fairbanks AK 99708

Call Sign: KL7HY
David A Rohwer
Fairbanks AK 99708

Call Sign: KL7IKQ
Celia M Rohwer
Fairbanks AK 99708

Call Sign: KL7JHE
Nancy C Reagan
Fairbanks AK 99708

Call Sign: KL7JJA
Rodney A Combellick
Fairbanks AK 99708

Call Sign: N7FXE
Michael S Mc Graw
Fairbanks AK 99708

Call Sign: NL7DX
Norman C Piispanen
Fairbanks AK 99708

Call Sign: WL7BVX
Walter L Rutherford
Fairbanks AK 99708

Call Sign: WL7CIL
Julie A Krol
Fairbanks AK 99708

Call Sign: WL7CIO
Ian A Hegdal
Fairbanks AK 99708

Call Sign: WL7CQV
Scott W Heidorn
Fairbanks AK 99708

Call Sign: WL7CQW
Rita M Heidkamp
Fairbanks AK 99708

Call Sign: WL7CRH
George A Aplustill
Fairbanks AK 99708

Call Sign: WL7CTH
Ian K Commissiong
Fairbanks AK 99708

Call Sign: WL7CTS
Trish A T Patterson
Fairbanks AK 99708

Call Sign: WL7QL
Longin Krol
Fairbanks AK 99708

Call Sign: WL7QW
Danielle J Vivlamore
Fairbanks AK 99708

Call Sign: WL7RQ
Craig A Helmuth
Fairbanks AK 99708

Call Sign: WL7TK
Andrea B Johnson
Fairbanks AK 99708

Call Sign: WL7TS
David C Matthews
Fairbanks AK 99708

Call Sign: WL7TU
Richard W Miers
Fairbanks AK 99708

Call Sign: WL7UA
Kenneth E Stichter
Fairbanks AK 99708

Call Sign: WL7WP
Jeffrey L Levison

Fairbanks AK 99708

Call Sign: WL7ZR
David A Bettez
Fairbanks AK 99708

Call Sign: KL0XA
Peter J Chapman
Fairbanks AK 99708

Call Sign: KL0ZD
Martha K Baldridge
Fairbanks AK 99708

Call Sign: KL1BB
Daniel J Hancock
Fairbanks AK 99708

Call Sign: KL1BC
David L Dausel
Fairbanks AK 99708

Call Sign: KL1BD
Percy W Houts
Fairbanks AK 99708

Call Sign: KL1BG
Lee H Kelley
Fairbanks AK 99708

Call Sign: KL1BN
Thelma J Childers
Fairbanks AK 99708

Call Sign: KL1EJ
Sharon J Walsh
Fairbanks AK 99708

Call Sign: KL1GH
Gary E Hampton
Fairbanks AK 99708

Call Sign: KC2PIO
Ashton M Gasper-Scavette
Fairbanks AK 99709

Call Sign: KL7PIO
Ashton M Gasper-Scavette
Fairbanks AK 99709

Call Sign: K3CLK
Eugene E Augustin
Fairbanks AK 99709

Call Sign: KL1JO
Michael E Schwietert
Fairbanks AK 99710

Call Sign: KL1PG
Alan Compare
Fairbanks AK 99710

Call Sign: KL1PH
Crystal M Hoke
Fairbanks AK 99710

Call Sign: KL2AB
Linda E Conley
Fairbanks AK 99710

Call Sign: KL0CT
Olga M Krejci
Fairbanks AK 99710

Call Sign: KL0DP
Daniel W Schwietert
Fairbanks AK 99710

Call Sign: KL0FU
Paul T Lord
Fairbanks AK 99710

Call Sign: KL0GT
Randolph C Settje
Fairbanks AK 99710

Call Sign: KL0LE
Alexander P Cryan
Fairbanks AK 99710

Call Sign: KL7DDB
Florence R Collins
Fairbanks AK 99710

Call Sign: KL7JLF
Herbert E Walls
Fairbanks AK 99710

Call Sign: KL7MB
Kathleen F Romersberger
Fairbanks AK 99710

Call Sign: NL7ML
Charles E Collins
Fairbanks AK 99710

Call Sign: NL7MN
Clara M Collins

Fairbanks AK 99710

Call Sign: WD9HYW
Warren K Compton
Fairbanks AK 99710

Call Sign: AL7RO
Alexander P Cryan
Fairbanks AK 99710

Call Sign: KL0WK
Thomas A Benson
Fairbanks AK 99710

Call Sign: KL0WL
Bianca N Benson
Fairbanks AK 99710

Call Sign: AL7EX
Alexander P Cryan
Fairbanks AK 99710

Call Sign: KL1BE
Constance B Ledlow
Fairbanks AK 99710

Call Sign: KL1BP
Floyd R Wright Sr
Fairbanks AK 99710

Call Sign: KL1CK
Marie L Peacock
Fairbanks AK 99710

Call Sign: KL1HB
Peter A Burokas
Fairbanks AK 99710

Call Sign: KL1HI
Christopher K Badger
Fairbanks AK 99710

Call Sign: KL7YO
Nicholas D Olson
Fairbanks AK 99711

Call Sign: WL7CKE
Jeannine E Wheeler
Fairbanks AK 99711

Call Sign: WL7CQZ
Julius C Givens
Fairbanks AK 99711

Call Sign: WL7CRV
Thomas M Kohler
Fairbanks AK 99711

Call Sign: WL7TI
Erik B Hansen
Fairbanks AK 99711

Call Sign: KL1SC
Michael R Breese
Fairbanks AK 99775

Call Sign: KL1TF
Hays H Boughan
Fairbanks AK 99775

Call Sign: KL2NP
Meghan L Tillapaugh
Fairbanks AK 99775

Call Sign: KL2TI
Alex J Arneson
Fairbanks AK 99775

Call Sign: KL3EM
Kathryn R Burns
Fairbanks AK 99775

Call Sign: KF7OFW
Samuel A McIntosh
Fairbanks AK 99775

Call Sign: KL3IR
Evelyn E Jackson
Fairbanks AK 99775

Call Sign: NL7YD
Lee Rice
Fairbanks AK 99775

Call Sign: WL7BTO
Matthew D Sill
Fairbanks AK 99775

Call Sign: WL7CIP
Jay M Gulledge
Fairbanks AK 99775

Call Sign: WL7CQU
Reid E Hermann
Fairbanks AK 99775

Call Sign: KL0IR
Michelle Hawkins

Fairbanks AK 997060342

Call Sign: KL0MI
Edna F Varner
Fairbanks AK 997060566

Call Sign: KL0MH
Fred P Thruston Jr
Fairbanks AK 997061100

Call Sign: KB7LJZ
Robert S Christian
Fairbanks AK 997070311

Call Sign: KL0LW
Marlis R Homoleski
Fairbanks AK 997071346

Call Sign: WL7TY
Terry A Preston
Fairbanks AK 997071559

Call Sign: KL0TW
Clipper Z Ordiway
Fairbanks AK 997072350

Call Sign: KL0MG
Jeffrey A Schend Sr
Fairbanks AK 997073791

Call Sign: KL0RI
Aileen M Witrosky
Fairbanks AK 997080124

Call Sign: KL1BI
Theodore F Fathauer
Fairbanks AK 997080210

Call Sign: WL7TL
Gary L Johnson
Fairbanks AK 997080606

Call Sign: KL0UR
C W Scholle
Fairbanks AK 997081011

Call Sign: KL0YV
James N Baldridge
Fairbanks AK 997081055

Call Sign: AL1I
James N Baldridge
Fairbanks AK 997081055

Call Sign: WL7BOF
James B Chapman
Fairbanks AK 997081513

Call Sign: KL7BR
Richard W Briggs
Fairbanks AK 997081755

Call Sign: KL1JR
Steve C Adams
Fairbanks AK 997081814

Call Sign: KL0DO
Marguerite A Matthews
Fairbanks AK 997082024

Call Sign: NL7BA
Michelle G Combellick
Fairbanks AK 997082422

Call Sign: KL7DUJ
William D Tanner
Fairbanks AK 997082582

Call Sign: KL7LF
Joe Voelkelt
Fairbanks AK 997082808

Call Sign: WL7AD
Gael D Baxley
Fairbanks AK 997083406

Call Sign: AL0J
Joseph W Miller
Fairbanks AK 997083440

Call Sign: AL7E
Marvin D Foglesong
Fairbanks AK 997083597

Call Sign: AL7OV
Linda K Foglesong
Fairbanks AK 997083597

Call Sign: KL7JM
Arthur J Movius
Fairbanks AK 997083992

Call Sign: WL7RA
Betsy Tozzi
Fairbanks AK 997084665

Call Sign: KL0LX
Charles K Hunt

Fairbanks AK 997085287

Call Sign: WL7CUZ
Alaska Qrp Club
Fairbanks AK 997100079

Call Sign: KL1BH
Carl B Brooks
Fairbanks AK 997100131

Call Sign: KL1HH
Judy K Badger
Fairbanks AK 997100223

Call Sign: WL7CWF
Two Rivers Contest Club
Fairbanks AK 997100654

Call Sign: KL2R
Two Rivers Contest Club
Fairbanks AK 997100654

Call Sign: N1TX
Larry L Ledlow Jr
Fairbanks AK 997100654

Call Sign: KL0UF
Susan M Ault
Fairbanks AK 997110211

Call Sign: KL6C
Elaine C Larson
Fairbanks AK 997110593

Call Sign: N6PU
Elaine C Larson
Fairbanks AK 997110593

Call Sign: KL2EW
Christian Petrich
Fairbanks AK 997750221

Call Sign: KG4HJM
Christian Petrich
Fairbanks AK 997750221

Call Sign: KL1KR
Stephen R Carter
Fairbanks AK 997750527

Call Sign: KL0RS
Eric R Darnel
Fairbanks AK 997750635

Call Sign: WL7CJF
Jeffrey F Kulawiak
Fairbanks AK 997750661

Call Sign: KL3JR
Patrick C Wade
Fairbanks AK 997751537

Call Sign: KL3JQ
Wyatt C Rehder
Fairbanks AK 997753541

Call Sign: KL1JM
Raj Kombiyil
Fairbanks AK 997757320

Call Sign: WL7CVJ
Wsfo Fairbanks Skywarn
Fairbanks AK 997757345

Call Sign: KL7FWX
Wsfo Fairbanks Skywarn
Fairbanks AK 997757345

Call Sign: KL7GL
Michael F Drury
Fairbanks AK 99706

Call Sign: KL7KS
Samuel K Medsker
Fairbanks AK 99706

Call Sign: WL7CEX
Carey T Seward
Fairbanks AK 99706

Call Sign: WL7KB
Terrance A Dalton
Fairbanks AK 99706

Call Sign: AL7KB
Dale D Powell Jr
Fairbanks AK 99707

Call Sign: KA0YPV
Clarence M Douthett
Fairbanks AK 99707

Call Sign: KL7XD
Edward S Hunstein
Fairbanks AK 99707

Call Sign: NL7OQ
Morgan Sanders

Fairbanks AK 99707

Call Sign: WL7AJ
Clark D Williams
Fairbanks AK 99707

Call Sign: WL7BLV
David M Chamberlin
Fairbanks AK 99707

Call Sign: WL7BSR
David E Luce
Fairbanks AK 99707

Call Sign: WL7BSS
Janice F Luce
Fairbanks AK 99707

Call Sign: WL7BUZ
Robert D Murton
Fairbanks AK 99707

Call Sign: WL7BYI
Michael D Wilks
Fairbanks AK 99707

Call Sign: WL7DI
Charles F Chase III
Fairbanks AK 99707

Call Sign: WL7HW
Wesley G Graf
Fairbanks AK 99707

Call Sign: WL7ML
Mario O Gho
Fairbanks AK 99707

Call Sign: WL7PQ
Sandra K Hunstein
Fairbanks AK 99707

Call Sign: K0NIK
Todd F Nichols
Fairbanks AK 99708

Call Sign: KL7AZ
Florence R Weber
Fairbanks AK 99708

Call Sign: KL7B
Richard Attwood
Fairbanks AK 99708

Call Sign: KL7HAE
James F O Kelley
Fairbanks AK 99708

Call Sign: KL7HAN
Frank Abegg III
Fairbanks AK 99708

Call Sign: KL7HJH
Joanne E Groves
Fairbanks AK 99708

Call Sign: KL7HOP
Marilyn J West
Fairbanks AK 99708

Call Sign: N5OPR
Ravonna G Martin
Fairbanks AK 99708

Call Sign: NL7ED
Guy C Tytgat
Fairbanks AK 99708

Call Sign: NL7QV
Melissa A Pearson
Fairbanks AK 99708

Call Sign: NL7VN
Jo Roberts
Fairbanks AK 99708

Call Sign: WL7AZQ
Earl C Smith
Fairbanks AK 99708

Call Sign: WL7BZZ
Sara R Harriger
Fairbanks AK 99708

Call Sign: WL7CED
Dale A Greeley
Fairbanks AK 99708

Call Sign: WL7CEE
Samuel J Hirt
Fairbanks AK 99708

Call Sign: WL7CEI
Virginia L Bedford
Fairbanks AK 99708

Call Sign: WL7CEM
Janine M Welp

Fairbanks AK 99708

Call Sign: WL7CEO
Seth D Adams
Fairbanks AK 99708

Call Sign: WL7CFB
Zarin C Taylor
Fairbanks AK 99708

Call Sign: WL7CFS
Daniel M Adams
Fairbanks AK 99708

Call Sign: WL7CGK
Nicholas A Oswood
Fairbanks AK 99708

Call Sign: WL7HR
John N Taylor
Fairbanks AK 99708

Call Sign: WL7HS
Joanne M Smothermon
Fairbanks AK 99708

Call Sign: WL7HT
Charles C Smothermon III
Fairbanks AK 99708

Call Sign: WL7HV
David B Hoffman
Fairbanks AK 99708

Call Sign: WL7HX
Judith M Gouwens
Fairbanks AK 99708

Call Sign: WL7NC
Herbert S Chesney
Fairbanks AK 99708

Call Sign: WL7OD
La Rita A Chapman Mann
Fairbanks AK 99708

Call Sign: WL7OI
Steven N Storo
Fairbanks AK 99708

Call Sign: WL7OL
Nathan J Adams
Fairbanks AK 99708

Call Sign: WL7OY
Laurie A Chavasse
Fairbanks AK 99708

Call Sign: WL7OZ
Aidan E Chavasse
Fairbanks AK 99708

Call Sign: WL7PG
James J Vohden
Fairbanks AK 99708

Call Sign: WL7QK
Jane E Vohden
Fairbanks AK 99708

Call Sign: WL7OM
Brian C Henry
Fairbanks AK 99709

Call Sign: KL7TR
Thomas D Roberts
Fairbanks AK 99710

Call Sign: WL0JM
James W Matthews
Fairbanks AK 99710

Call Sign: NL7CY
Cyril Linek
Fairbanks AK 99711

Call Sign: WL7CX
Leo Bettinger
Fairbanks AK 99711

Call Sign: WL7EG
Daniel E Bettinger
Fairbanks AK 99711

Call Sign: WL7JQ
Donna L Bettinger
Fairbanks AK 99711

Call Sign: WL7LG
Mary E Bettinger
Fairbanks AK 99711

Call Sign: WL7RX
Beverly G Wilson
Fairbanks AK 99711

Call Sign: NL7WU
Jan L Bishop

Fairbanks AK 99725

Call Sign: NL7VM
Walter A Lindley
Fairbanks AK 997081491

Call Sign: KL7AQC
Alaska Qrp Club
Fairbanks AK 997100079

Call Sign: NL7HR
David D Straight
Box 10158
Fairbanks AK 99710

Call Sign: WL7BSU
Dawn M Straight
Box 10158
Fairbanks AK 99710

Call Sign: KL7QD
Frank P Canha
Box 1326
Fairbanks AK 99707

Call Sign: KL7YW
Edward J Bush
Box 352
Fairbanks AK 99707

Call Sign: NL7YS
Ida L Knaebel
Box 58358
Fairbanks AK 99711

Call Sign: WL7VY
Paul M Jagow
Box 72557
Fairbanks AK 99707

Call Sign: AL7EO
Brian W Phillips
Box 80141
Fairbanks AK 99708

Call Sign: KL7YC
Arvid W Weflen
Box 80311
Fairbanks AK 99708

Call Sign: KL7AG
Albert F Weber
Box 80745
Fairbanks AK 99708

Call Sign: KL7GW
Gary D Hagestead
Box 81276
Fairbanks AK 99708

Call Sign: KL7ZM
Leonard Kamerling
Box 81323
Fairbanks AK 99708

Call Sign: KL7IZM
Leonard Kamerling
Box 81323
Fairbanks AK 99708

Call Sign: AL7FQ
Billy G Connor
Box 82551
Fairbanks AK 99708

Call Sign: NL7YR
Alan J Chuculate
Box 83305
Fairbanks AK 99708

Call Sign: KF4DFW
John J O Connor
General Delivery
Fairbanks AK 99701

Call Sign: KA2TJZ
Randall C Stein
PO Box 74701
Fairbanks AK 997074701

Call Sign: WL7CES
Timothy O Leghorn Jr
Uaf
Fairbanks AK 99775

Call Sign: KL3EL
William D Webb
Univ Of Alaska
Fairbanks AK 99775

Call Sign: KL3FY
William D Webb
Univ Of Alaska
Fairbanks AK 99775

Call Sign: KL7ITE
Ray R Collins
Fairbanks AK 99707

FCC Amateur Radio Licenses in Flat

Call Sign: KL7HPU
Kathleen M Agoff
General Delivery
Flat AK 99584

FCC Amateur Radio Licenses in Fort Greely

Call Sign: N9UOM
Randi W Owen
814D Third St
Fort Greely AK 99731

Call Sign: WA7NGX
Steven M Schneider
830 East 3rd St
Fort Greely AK 99731

Call Sign: WH6CYY
William H Mac Kinnon Jr
Fort Greely AK 99731

Call Sign: WD4TW
Timothy D Weathers
Fort Greely AK 99731

Call Sign: WL7CVZ
Fort Greely Amateur Radio
Club
Fort Greely AK 99731

FCC Amateur Radio Licenses in Fort Richardson

Call Sign: WL7GB
Johnny T Rowe Jr
6118D 6th St
Fort Richardson AK 99505

Call Sign: KD5QPD
Jason J Proffitt
324A Gulkana
Fort Richardson AK 99505

Call Sign: NL7LX
Curtis E Damien
263G Chilkoot Ave
Fort Richardson AK 99505

Call Sign: KL1QO

Jonathan D Zeppa
130 Iliamna Ave B
Fort Richardson AK 995051027

Call Sign: KL2MZ
Matthew L Palmer
Fort Richardson AK 99505

Call Sign: KL1HL
Julius L Taylor
Fort Richardson AK 99505

Call Sign: KL3CL
Michael J Helbig
Fort Richardson AK 99505

Call Sign: KL0NE
Rick R Renaud
Fort Richardson AK 99505

Call Sign: NL7IG
Gary G Wall
Fort Richardson AK 99505

FCC Amateur Radio Licenses in Fort Wainwright

Call Sign: KE7LDS
Leland J Haroldsen
1210 600th St 8
Fort Wainwright AK 99703

Call Sign: WL7CHM
Joseph J Lee
Bldg 3718 D Trp 4-9 Cav
Fort Wainwright AK 99703

Call Sign: WL7CS
Kenneth B Muse
Hhc 6th Eng Bn
Fort Wainwright AK 99707

Call Sign: KL0UC
Jon S Esch
3409 Lorraine Ave Box 476
Fort Wainwright AK 99703

Call Sign: KL1MK
Bryan R Bennett
3010 Montgomery Rd Box 281
Fort Wainwright AK 99703

Call Sign: KL3JC
John M Cooper

1330A Normandy Ct
Fort Wainwright AK 99703

Call Sign: KL1PD
Scott H Foster
1036 Vannatta Crt
Fort Wainwright AK 99703

Call Sign: KL1SW
Otto W Wendt IV
4381 White St L
Fort Wainwright AK 99703

Call Sign: KL1OP
Mary D Mitchell
Fort Wainwright AK 99703

Call Sign: KL1PN
Roderick D Mitchell Jr
Fort Wainwright AK 99703

Call Sign: KL1Y
Roderick D Mitchell
Fort Wainwright AK 99703

Call Sign: W2FF
Timothy J Petersen
Fort Wainwright AK 99703

Call Sign: KL7OC
Brett L Landis
Fort Wainwright AK 99703

Call Sign: AB7SB
Brett L Landis
Fort Wainwright AK 99703

Call Sign: WL7CQQ
Kelly D Philbrick
Fort Wainwright AK 99703

Call Sign: KL1FD
Zaquary L Mitchell
Fort Wainwright AK 99703

Call Sign: KL7FGA
Fort Greely Amateur Radio
Club
Fort Wainwright AK 99703

Call Sign: KL1TI
Monte G Landis
Fort Wainwright AK 99703

Call Sign: KL1YF
Monte G Landis
Fort Wainwright AK 99703

Call Sign: KL0RJ
Paul C Smith
Fort Wainwright AK 99703

Call Sign: WL7UK
William H Philbrick
Fort Wainwright AK 997030323

FCC Amateur Radio Licenses in Fritz Creek

Call Sign: WL7M
Joseph C Hannigan
Fritz Creek AK 99603

FCC Amateur Radio Licenses in Gakona

Call Sign: KL0NV
Jan M Bullock
HC 01 Box 479
Gakona AK 99586

Call Sign: KL0NT
James F Bullock Jr
HC 03 Box 479
Gakona AK 995869704

Call Sign: KL7ERP
Haarp Amateur Radio Club
Milepost 113
Gakona AK 99586

FCC Amateur Radio Licenses in Galena

Call Sign: AE5EX
Scott A Betterton
Galena AK 99741

Call Sign: AL3H
Scott A Betterton
Galena AK 99741

Call Sign: AL2J
R Justin Huber
Galena AK 99741

Call Sign: KL1EI
Timothy J Bodony

Galena AK 99741

Call Sign: AA8FY
R Justin Huber
Galena AK 997410131

Call Sign: KA7DCK
Michael J Rath
Galena AK 99741

<table>
<tr><td>FCC Amateur Radio Licenses
in Gambell</td></tr>
</table>

Call Sign: KL2FV
Derek D Angi
Gambell AK 99742

<table>
<tr><td>FCC Amateur Radio Licenses
in Girdwood</td></tr>
</table>

Call Sign: KJ6HF
Victor M Martin
Alpine & Okemo
Girdwood AK 995870735

Call Sign: KL1JB
Elizabeth A Davidson
Girdwood AK 99587

Call Sign: KL1NE
Brandi L Morgan
Girdwood AK 99587

Call Sign: KL1SK
Russell P Andrew
Girdwood AK 99587

Call Sign: AL2T
Carl C Madson
Girdwood AK 99587

Call Sign: KL2NV
Kevin M Opalka
Girdwood AK 99587

Call Sign: KL2ST
Gary H Wilson
Girdwood AK 99587

Call Sign: KL2XE
Peter W Bellino
Girdwood AK 99587

Call Sign: KL3FH

Robert L Bridges
Girdwood AK 99587

Call Sign: AL3Z
Robert L Bridges
Girdwood AK 99587

Call Sign: KC7BLD
Carl C Madson
Girdwood AK 99587

Call Sign: WL7CQG
Everett M House
Girdwood AK 99587

Call Sign: WL7V
Douglas J Stern
Girdwood AK 995870055

Call Sign: KL1KS
Joseph C O Donnell
Girdwood AK 995870726

Call Sign: WL7CUV
Joseph C O Donnell
Girdwood AK 995870726

Call Sign: KL7LE
James S Graves
Girdwood AK 99587

Call Sign: N7JAY
Joseph A Motter
Girdwood AK 99587

<table>
<tr><td>FCC Amateur Radio Licenses
in Glennallen</td></tr>
</table>

Call Sign: KL7BGR
John M Berner
523 1868 Glenn Hwy
Glennallen AK 995880303

Call Sign: AL7S
Daniel J Krushensky
Mile 1285 Glenn Hwy Hc1
Glennallen AK 995889501

Call Sign: KA1MNG
Cynthia G Swehla
College Rd Box 289
Glennallen AK 99588

Call Sign: KL3FX

Kristy A Wasilewski
HC01 Box 1925
Glennallen AK 99588

Call Sign: KL3FZ
David R Wasilewski
HC01 Box 1925
Glennallen AK 99588

Call Sign: WL7US
Robert D St John Jr
HC01 Box 2235
Glennallen AK 99588

Call Sign: NL7IK
Tonia K Alexander
Long Lake Mc Carthy
Glennallen AK 99588

Call Sign: NL7IL
Steve T Alexander
Long Lake Mc Carthy
Glennallen AK 99588

Call Sign: KL2IN
Mark H Roti
Glennallen AK 99588

Call Sign: KE6QFE
Katherine A Dorsey
Glennallen AK 99588

Call Sign: KL0BK
Thomas H Person
Glennallen AK 99588

Call Sign: KL0KY
Kevin L Dorsey
Glennallen AK 99588

Call Sign: WL7BHL
Joel D Elrod
Glennallen AK 99588

Call Sign: KL1DA
Richard F Lampe
Glennallen AK 99588

Call Sign: KL1EQ
Douglas L Ode
Glennallen AK 99588

Call Sign: KL7WX
Richard D Kenyon Sr

Glennallen AK 99588

Call Sign: KL7WZ
Bonnie L Kenyon
Glennallen AK 99588

Call Sign: WL7CCD
Kelly M Bay
Glennallen AK 99588

Call Sign: WL7CCE
Natalie Bay
Glennallen AK 99588

Call Sign: WL7CEU
Walter R Mueller
Glennallen AK 99588

Call Sign: WL7CEV
Ursel M Mueller
Glennallen AK 99588

FCC Amateur Radio Licenses in Gustavus

Call Sign: WL7ZC
William L Unkel
4 B River Bend Rd
Gustavus AK 99826

Call Sign: WL7BRR
Jacob G Musslewhite
Gustavus AK 99826

Call Sign: WL7CSI
Bruce R Shingledecker
Gustavus AK 99826

Call Sign: KL1HE
John F Fors
Gustavus AK 99826

Call Sign: WL7CSJ
Charles L Schroth
Gustavus AK 998260300

Call Sign: KL7XK
Michael S Pedersen
Box 420
Gustavus AK 99826

FCC Amateur Radio Licenses in Haines

Call Sign: WL7CNR
Richard B Boyce
Box 84
Haines AK 99827

Call Sign: KL7BP
Leonard V Banaszak
HC 60 Box 2631
Haines AK 99827

Call Sign: AL7CI
Robert P Fitzpatrick
HC 60 Box 2634
Haines AK 998279702

Call Sign: KL1UQ
Vernon Allen
153 First St
Haines AK 99827

Call Sign: NL7RD
George Meacock Jr
Piedad Rd Box 568
Haines AK 99827

Call Sign: KL7YXF
Lynn C Hyder
41 Skyline Dr
Haines AK 99827

Call Sign: WA7YXF
Lynn C Hyder
41 Skyline Dr
Haines AK 99827

Call Sign: KE7RCT
Austin R Anderson
38 Sunshine St
Haines AK 99827

Call Sign: KL3FL
Roger L Maynard
112 Union St
Haines AK 99827

Call Sign: KL7HI
Roger L Maynard
112 Union St
Haines AK 99827

Call Sign: KL7RN
Barbara C Maynard
112 Union St
Haines AK 99827

Call Sign: KA7HHF
Barbara C Maynard
112 Union St
Haines AK 99827

Call Sign: KA7HOX
Roger L Maynard
428 Young Rd
Haines AK 99927

Call Sign: KL0MV
Dirk L Hinman
Haines AK 99827

Call Sign: KL7CQF
Harold E Hopper
Haines AK 99827

Call Sign: N7INQ
Tamsen L Cassidy
Haines AK 99827

Call Sign: N7NNK
Nancy M Seright
Haines AK 99827

Call Sign: N7VWB
Kenneth R Seright
Haines AK 99827

Call Sign: WL7CFI
Scott A Hamilton
Haines AK 99827

Call Sign: WL7CNS
Barbara E Woods
Haines AK 99827

Call Sign: WL7CNT
Richard S Woods
Haines AK 99827

Call Sign: WL7CNX
Mark A Van Horne
Haines AK 99827

Call Sign: KL7IR
Martin A Cordes
Haines AK 99827

Call Sign: WL7BMJ
Donna L Truax
Haines AK 99827

Call Sign: WL7LO
Larry S Baker
Haines AK 99827

Call Sign: WL7ALW
James A Wilson
Box 745
Haines AK 99827

FCC Amateur Radio Licenses
in Healy

Call Sign: KC0VDN
Peter W Ganzlin
Healy AK 99743

Call Sign: KL7DE
Peter W Ganzlin
Healy AK 99743

Call Sign: AL7QJ
Robert F Begnoche
Healy AK 99743

Call Sign: KL0AX
Charles B Burnell
Healy AK 99743

Call Sign: WL7KR
Lisa D Hamel
Healy AK 99743

Call Sign: WL7VZ
Willie J Schutt
Healy AK 99743

Call Sign: KL1DU
Bonni Burnell
Healy AK 99743

Call Sign: KL1HP
Steven E Barb
Healy AK 99743

Call Sign: AL3V
Daniel J Hoffman
Healy AK 997430286

Call Sign: KL1IE
Daniel J Hoffman
Healy AK 997430286

Call Sign: KL8DX

Phillip L Sauvey
Healy AK 997430497

Call Sign: KL8SU
Suann N Sauvey
Healy AK 997430497

Call Sign: WL7BM
Kerry L Mac Lachlan
Healy AK 99743

Call Sign: WL7KE
Kevin M Hamel
Box 82
Healy AK 99743

Call Sign: KL2PQ
William J Nemec II
HC-1 Box 5001
Healy AK 99743

Call Sign: KL2PR
Linda J Nemec
HC-1 Box 5001
Healy AK 99743

FCC Amateur Radio Licenses
in Holy Cross

Call Sign: AL3K
Victor Ladeira
Holy Cross AK 99602

Call Sign: KB2FWF
Victor Ladeira
Holy Cross AK 99602

FCC Amateur Radio Licenses
in Homer

Call Sign: NP4FU
Joni M Cody
35460 Aurora Cir
Homer AK 99603

Call Sign: WL7CJW
Mervin B Cody
35460 Aurora Cir
Homer AK 99603

Call Sign: AL7RR
William G Bradshaw
60816 Bear Creek Dr
Homer AK 99603

Call Sign: N7JOL
Charles E Stock
67800 Bluff Rd
Homer AK 996033713

Call Sign: KL1RV
Gregg L Browngoetz
4049 Calhoun St
Homer AK 99603

Call Sign: KC8WWS
Jason J Sodergren
1660 Eagle View Dr
Homer AK 99603

Call Sign: KL3CW
Douglas A Stark
2073 Horizon Ct
Homer AK 99603

Call Sign: KL0RF
Sandra L Stark
2073 Horizon Ct
Homer AK 99603

Call Sign: NL7KZ
Jimmie W James
36745 James Rd
Homer AK 99603

Call Sign: WL7AKZ
Del L Thomas Mr
4201 Kachemak Way
Homer AK 99603

Call Sign: KL1YY
Marvin C Baur
4275 Kachemak Way
Homer AK 99603

Call Sign: KA7TDH
Marvin C Baur
4275 Kachemak Way
Homer AK 99603

Call Sign: KA7ZOZ
Sharon A Baur
4275 Kachemak Way
Homer AK 99603

Call Sign: KD7ERU
John M Scovell
4047 Main 105

Homer AK 99603

Call Sign: KL2NB
Wynona R Prouse
1295 Mission Rd
Homer AK 99603

Call Sign: W7PWA
Wynona R Prouse
1295 Mission Rd
Homer AK 99603

Call Sign: W0URD
Clarence F Jacobs
4208 North Main
Homer AK 99603

Call Sign: KL7BC
Dennis Johnson
53154 Peterson Bay Rem
Homer AK 99603

Call Sign: WL7BNR
Corinne Johnson
53154 Peterson Bay Rem
Homer AK 99603

Call Sign: WL7BCB
Gerald J Jones
704 Rangeview
Homer AK 99603

Call Sign: WL7FC
James P Cunningham
4734 Sabrina St
Homer AK 99603

Call Sign: WL7EH
Frank J Vondersaar
1740 Saltwater Dr
Homer AK 99603

Call Sign: WL7PM
Dean H Ravin
990 Sea Plane Ct
Homer AK 99603

Call Sign: K9ROO
David L Ross Jr
60825 St Olaf Ave B
Homer AK 99603

Call Sign: KL5AJK
Shanley E Kerls

40996 Woodman Ln
Homer AK 99603

Call Sign: KL1XA
Stephen C Drew
Homer AK 99603

Call Sign: KL2DV
John T Reich
Homer AK 99603

Call Sign: KL2FB
Harold C Smith
Homer AK 99603

Call Sign: KL2HD
Jeffrey C Williams
Homer AK 99603

Call Sign: KL2KM
Donald M Fell
Homer AK 99603

Call Sign: KL2LY
James J Lempe
Homer AK 99603

Call Sign: KL2MT
David L Ross Jr
Homer AK 99603

Call Sign: KL3DH
Karen J O'Block
Homer AK 99603

Call Sign: KD6NFV
Gartly N Curtis
Homer AK 99603

Call Sign: KF4JET
John J Martin
Homer AK 99603

Call Sign: KL0KH
William J Wiebe
Homer AK 99603

Call Sign: KL0SY
Susan Mc Ln
Homer AK 99603

Call Sign: N8JBO
James E Cook III
Homer AK 99603

Call Sign: NL7RR
Thomas F Mayhan
Homer AK 99603

Call Sign: NL7UU
Anne E Nixon
Homer AK 99603

Call Sign: WL7FQ
Donald D Deadrick
Homer AK 99603

Call Sign: AL7DB
David F Becker
Homer AK 996030109

Call Sign: KL7HSB
David F Becker
Homer AK 996030109

Call Sign: WD6EXD
Ernest R Sinclair
Homer AK 996030992

Call Sign: KL1UB
Jeanne S Deloach
Homer AK 996032278

Call Sign: KL1UC
Darren L Deloach
Homer AK 996032278

Call Sign: AL7I
Ben H Le Norman
Homer AK 99603

Call Sign: NL7ET
David D Coughenower
Homer AK 99603

Call Sign: NL7TX
Patricia K Pearson
Homer AK 99603

Call Sign: NL7WK
Thomas R Kerns
Homer AK 99603

Call Sign: NL7XF
Loren E Johnson Jr
Homer AK 99603

Call Sign: W7CLY

Enid M Jones
Homer AK 99603

Call Sign: WL7BTM
Scott R Grandmontagne
Homer AK 99603

Call Sign: WL7BY
Diane M Ford
Homer AK 99603

Call Sign: WL7CEQ
Aaron R Weisser
Homer AK 99603

Call Sign: KL7HKU
Kemp A Absher
Homer AK 99517

Call Sign: KA7ZSX
Dani Bettridge
Hoonah AK 99829

Call Sign: KC6WFM
Robert Jimenez
Hoonah AK 99829

Call Sign: N7YQS
Keith W Bettridge
Hoonah AK 99829

Call Sign: WL7BKS
Rosemary E Lebowitz
Hoonah AK 99829

Call Sign: WL7BKT
Gary J Lebowitz
Hoonah AK 99829

Call Sign: WL7AMR
David E Austin
Box 95
Hoonah AK 99829

Call Sign: KL1NC
George S Ballard
Hooper Bay AK 99604

Call Sign: N6CHV
Michael J Neverdosky
Houston AK 99694

Call Sign: KL0VO
Thomas F Baird
Houston AK 99694

Call Sign: WL7DL
Ben G Courtney Sr
Bear Paw Sbdv
Houston AK 99694

Call Sign: WL7CPX
Richard W Kotsch
HC-52 Box 8585
Indian AK 99540

Call Sign: KL2JG
Richard G Gillin
HC52 Box 8616
Indian AK 99540

Call Sign: KL2RG
Richard G Gillin
HC52 Box 8616
Indian AK 99540

Call Sign: KL1CI
Randall C Miller
Jber AK 99506

Call Sign: K1LKF
David E Tobias
604 4th St
Juneau AK 99801

Call Sign: KL3JU
Ayaire Cantil-Voorhees
504 5th St
Juneau AK 99801

Call Sign: WL7ZI
Peter J Klein
504 5th St Apt 4
Juneau AK 99801

Call Sign: KL0MX
Dan N Branch
119 7th St
Juneau AK 99801

Call Sign: KL0TL
Carl W Childers
213 7th St
Juneau AK 99801

Call Sign: KL7GPG
Juneau Amateur Radio Club
1117 A St
Juneau AK 99801

Call Sign: KB3INX
Gerald M Donohoe
17240 Andreanoff Dr
Juneau AK 99801

Call Sign: KL2ZW
Bradley V Peterson
1021 Arctic Cir
Juneau AK 99801

Call Sign: KL7JBC
Mary Claire Harris
115 Ash St
Juneau AK 99801

Call Sign: WL7ME
Donald L Kirstine
4119 Aspen Ave
Juneau AK 99801

Call Sign: KL1WM
Brent O Bartlett
8247 Aspen Ave
Juneau AK 99801

Call Sign: KL7GC
William W Rose
A-10 Aurora
Juneau AK 99803

Call Sign: WL7RE
Anselm C Staack
9330 Betty Ct

Juneau AK 99801

Call Sign: KL7FT
Michael L Murphy
4121 Birch Ln
Juneau AK 99801

Call Sign: KL1IY
Brian M Bezenek
8212 Birch Ln
Juneau AK 998018910

Call Sign: KL3HH
Carl J Uchytil
2921 Blueberry Hills Rd S
Juneau AK 99801

Call Sign: NL7LT
Richard Meeker
Box 021344
Juneau AK 99802

Call Sign: KA0SGK
Marjorie E Bryson
Box 022185
Juneau AK 99802

Call Sign: N7BMS
Craig Z Kenneck
Box 20867
Juneau AK 99802

Call Sign: KL7GT
Jon C Newstrom
Box 22596
Juneau AK 998022596

Call Sign: NL7VS
David E Bach
Box 32514
Juneau AK 99803

Call Sign: WL7BRD
Ke Mell
Box 3-2951
Juneau AK 99803

Call Sign: WL7RF
Alexis M Rippe
Box 33141
Juneau AK 99803

Call Sign: KL1WX
Stephen C Mattson

Box 33461
Juneau AK 99803

Call Sign: WL7UX
James C Tomlinson
Box 34784
Juneau AK 99801

Call Sign: AL7IQ
Robert H Martin
Douglas Harbor
Juneau AK 99802

Call Sign: KL0NW
William W Rose
PO Box 34242
Juneau AK 99803

Call Sign: KL7JVD
Jeffrey V Deaner
PO Box 34321
Juneau AK 998034321

Call Sign: N0JVD
Jeffrey V Deaner
PO Box 34321
Juneau AK 998034321

Call Sign: KL7HLP
Walter M Gregg
923 C St
Juneau AK 99801

Call Sign: WL7CJT
Rita E Thompson
8890 Cedar Ct
Juneau AK 99801

Call Sign: KE7WLL
Stephen C Free
4530 Chelsea Ct
Juneau AK 99801

Call Sign: KL3FR
Kathleen A Miller
20135 Cohen Dr
Juneau AK 99801

Call Sign: KE4GAJ
Richard J Angell
4467 Columbia Blvd
Juneau AK 99801

Call Sign: KL2ZY

Calvin F Zuelow
4485 Columbia Blvd
Juneau AK 99801

Call Sign: KL2ZZ
James F Zuelow Jr
4485 Columbia Blvd
Juneau AK 99801

Call Sign: NL7B
Ronald D Ward
10010 Crazy Horse Dr
Juneau AK 99801

Call Sign: WL7ZO
Sara L Gotschall
10010 Crazyhorse Dr
Juneau AK 99803

Call Sign: WL7KT
Larry G Gotschall
10010 Crazyhorse Dr
Juneau AK 99803

Call Sign: WL7CMR
Kyle M Brady
2201 Crowhill Dr Apt C13
Juneau AK 99824

Call Sign: N7JUX
Thomas J Matthews
2770 David St
Juneau AK 99801

Call Sign: NL7UD
Rolf W Numme
8402 Decoy Blvd
Juneau AK 99801

Call Sign: KL7R
Michael S Caughran
9018 Division St
Juneau AK 998014696

Call Sign: KL0EL
Erik H Pedersen
10410 Dock St
Juneau AK 99801

Call Sign: KL0BN
Karl Twelker
10430 Dock St
Juneau AK 99801

Call Sign: KL0EM
Janeann R Twelker
10430 Dock St
Juneau AK 99801

Call Sign: KL0FG
Evan Twelker
10430 Dock St
Juneau AK 99801

Call Sign: KL0FH
Eric Twelker
10430 Dock St
Juneau AK 99801

Call Sign: KL1EV
Keith L Bettridge
8486 Duran St
Juneau AK 99801

Call Sign: KL3LE
Steven E Otnes
8936 Duran St
Juneau AK 99801

Call Sign: AL7AE
Terence O Hoskinson
129 East 7th St
Juneau AK 99801

Call Sign: WA6AXO
Frederick A Hoskinson
129 East 7th St
Juneau AK 99801

Call Sign: KL3GC
Mikko R Wilson
607 East St
Juneau AK 99801

Call Sign: KL0EK
Sarah C Moore
607 East St
Juneau AK 99980

Call Sign: KL7IXO
Donald E Richter
9225 Emily Way
Juneau AK 99801

Call Sign: WL7XJ
Jufer M Librando
9227 Emily Way
Juneau AK 99801

Call Sign: KL1MV
John M Kinney
1751 Evergreen
Juneau AK 99801

Call Sign: KL1NW
Nina K Kinney
1751 Evergreen Ave
Juneau AK 99801

Call Sign: KL0GJ
Wesley R Brooks
1775 Evergreen Ave
Juneau AK 99801

Call Sign: KL1MB
Stephen F Byers
2008 Fairbanks St
Juneau AK 99801

Call Sign: WL7QN
Alexander E Hazelton
531 Fifth St
Juneau AK 99801

Call Sign: WL7CJ
Barbara T Greening
10497 Fox Farm Trail
Juneau AK 99801

Call Sign: KL0BP
Rhonda A Salerno
1180 Fritz Cove
Juneau AK 99801

Call Sign: KL2ZU
Donna R Leigh
123 Fritz Cove Rd
Juneau AK 99801

Call Sign: KL2ZV
Nathan C Leigh
123 Fritz Cove Rd
Juneau AK 99801

Call Sign: KL2ZT
Abram C Leigh
1223 Fritz Cove Rd
Juneau AK 99802

Call Sign: KL0PM
Lee W Buchhorn
1260 Fritz Cove Rd

Juneau AK 99801

Call Sign: WL7PW
John O Furuness
1285 Fritz Cove Rd
Juneau AK 99801

Call Sign: NL7XZ
Robert R Simpson
1310 Fritz Cove Rd
Juneau AK 99801

Call Sign: WL7QA
Marion E Simpson
1310 Fritz Cove Rd
Juneau AK 99801

Call Sign: KL7UY
Ken W Wallace
1640 Fritz Cove Rd
Juneau AK 99801

Call Sign: KL0ZM
William E Morris III
2290 Fritz Cove Rd
Juneau AK 99801

Call Sign: WL7ZD
Andrew M Spear
2765 Fritz Cove Rd
Juneau AK 99803

Call Sign: KL0BU
Frank C Arnold
2900 Fritz Cove Rd
Juneau AK 99801

Call Sign: KL0BV
Frances C Arnold
2900 Fritz Cove Rd
Juneau AK 99801

Call Sign: WL7CQH
Matt W Christian
223 Gastineau Ave
Juneau AK 99801

Call Sign: KL1AT
Brent L Fischer
9213 Gee St
Juneau AK 99801

Call Sign: KL1FB
Deborah S Penrose-Fischer

9213 Gee St
Juneau AK 99801

Call Sign: KL2UH
Ernst W Mueller
3990 Glacieer Hwy
Juneau AK 99801

Call Sign: KL1AC
Edward L Nygard
1652 Glacier Ave
Juneau AK 99801

Call Sign: KL3JO
Russell L Strandtmann
1401 Glacier Hwy
Juneau AK 99801

Call Sign: KL2QZ
Richard C Anderson
1670 Glacier Hwy
Juneau AK 99801

Call Sign: KL0ZK
Chad L Guertin
1670 Glacier Hwy
Juneau AK 99801

Call Sign: KL0ZL
Frank L Guertin Jr
1670 Glacier Hwy
Juneau AK 99801

Call Sign: KL0KZ
Samuel R Smith
3770 Glacier Hwy
Juneau AK 99801

Call Sign: AL7MC
Philip K Wells
8745 Glacier Hwy
Juneau AK 99801

Call Sign: KL1AB
Alan R Degener
17050 Glacier Hwy
Juneau AK 99801

Call Sign: KH6UY
Fred M Boehme
17525 Glacier Hwy
Juneau AK 99801

Call Sign: NH6WC

Joanne L Boehme
17525 Glacier Hwy
Juneau AK 998018330

Call Sign: KL2GX
Boyde J Fagan
9400 Glacier Hwy -2445
Juneau AK 99801

Call Sign: KL3KV
Thomas J Malsack
5875 Glacier Hwy 56
Juneau AK 99801

Call Sign: W1WWS
Jonathan W Smith
12175 Glacier Hwy Apt D3
Juneau AK 99801

Call Sign: KL1JK
Christopher J Custer
4850 Glacier Hwy B-3
Juneau AK 99801

Call Sign: WD6CET
Marc Finkelstein
12175 Glacier Hwy E405
Juneau AK 99801

Call Sign: KC9OLZ
Jarvis Schultz
4543 Glacier Spur Rd
Juneau AK 99801

Call Sign: KL7LW
Daniel L Haase
2941 Glacierwood Ct
Juneau AK 99801

Call Sign: WL7PL
Kenneth B Hydock
2956 Glacierwood Ct
Juneau AK 99801

Call Sign: KE7MJF
Alki Point Amateur Radio Club
3081 Glacierwood Dr
Juneau AK 99801

Call Sign: KL0QZ
Glenn C Sicks
3081 Glacierwood Dr
Juneau AK 99801

Call Sign: KH0NF
Scott A Miller
8302 Gladstone
Juneau AK 99801

Call Sign: WL7CWH
Alaska Wireless Society
8298 Gladstone St
Juneau AK 99801

Call Sign: KL3R
Alaska Wireless Society
8298 Gladstone St
Juneau AK 99801

Call Sign: K3QMR
Greenfield Amateur Radio Club
8298 Gladstone St
Juneau AK 99801

Call Sign: KH0NG
Katharine B Miller
8302 Gladstone St
Juneau AK 99801

Call Sign: KL2OQ
Anthony D Smith
6590 Glaicier Hwy 44
Juneau AK 99801

Call Sign: KL0AZ
Scott M Clark
116 Gold St
Juneau AK 998011209

Call Sign: NL7EE
Beverly R Skaggs
709 Gold St
Juneau AK 99801

Call Sign: KL0TN
Jonathan C Pollard
814 Goldbelt Ave
Juneau AK 99801

Call Sign: KL0XF
Susan R Pollard
814 Goldbelt St
Juneau AK 99801

Call Sign: KL3JJ
Barry M Bredehoft
3030 Hamilton St
Juneau AK 99801

Call Sign: KL1MC
Phillip L Mc Ree
1695 Harbor Way
Juneau AK 99801

Call Sign: WL7YH
Tom Wagner
417 Harris St
Juneau AK 99801

Call Sign: WL7BOS
Albertus Willemsen
423 Harris St
Juneau AK 99801

Call Sign: KF6CCO
Bryan R Turner
8616-A Hayes Way
Juneau AK 99801

Call Sign: KL0FJ
George F Jessup
9455 Herbert Place
Juneau AK 99801

Call Sign: KL7LO
David B Epstein
10705 Horizon Dr
Juneau AK 998017626

Call Sign: WL7YJ
Virginia P Palmer
1990 Hughes Way
Juneau AK 99801

Call Sign: WL7YK
Walter I Palmer
1990 Hughes Way
Juneau AK 99801

Call Sign: WL7BVB
Lucas B Mesdag
4937 Hummingbird Ln
Juneau AK 99801

Call Sign: KL2QH
Daniel M Babcock
9178 James Blvd
Juneau AK 99801

Call Sign: KL7JHU
David P Loomis
9205 James Blvd 202

Juneau AK 99801

Call Sign: N4SAM
Sam F Binkley III
8525 Jennifer Dr Apt 8
Juneau AK 99801

Call Sign: KL7SAM
Sam F Binkley III
8525 Jennifer Dr Apt 8
Juneau AK 99801

Call Sign: AL7V
Sam F Binkley III
8525 Jennifer Dr Apt 8
Juneau AK 99801

Call Sign: WL7FE
Marijo Binkley
8525 Jennifer Dr Apt 8
Juneau AK 99801

Call Sign: KL0CU
Jim Ruotsala
2723 John St
Juneau AK 99801

Call Sign: NL7EO
John A Leque
5895 Lemon St
Juneau AK 99803

Call Sign: KL0TK
John P Orbistondo
9855 Lone Wolf Dr
Juneau AK 99801

Call Sign: WL7BXX
Jennings A Hall Jr
9028 Long Run Dr
Juneau AK 99801

Call Sign: WL7AFT
Gary W Pond
9037 Lupine Ln
Juneau AK 99801

Call Sign: WL7BRE
Stephen A Scott
4361 Manor Ave
Juneau AK 99801

Call Sign: KL0WD
Nathaniel S Abbott

6738 Marguerite St
Juneau AK 99801

Call Sign: WL7BIJ
William H Leque
8613 Marilyn Ave
Juneau AK 99801

Call Sign: KL0EJ
Gerald W Buckley
245 Marine Way
Juneau AK 99801

Call Sign: KL1MA
John B Bishop
4229 Marion Dr
Juneau AK 99801

Call Sign: KL7GI
Dean K Williams
1401 Martin Rd
Juneau AK 99801

Call Sign: WL7PZ
Seth S Moody
3788 Mc Ginnis Dr
Juneau AK 99801

Call Sign: KL7JJB
Delores E O Mara
9570 Meadow Ln
Juneau AK 99801

Call Sign: AL7L
Patrick A Moore
9570 Meadow Ln
Juneau AK 99801

Call Sign: WL7CVK
National Weather Service -
Juneau Amateur Radio Club
8500 Menden Hall Loop Rd
Juneau AK 99801

Call Sign: WL7NWS
National Weather Service -
Juneau Amateur Radio Club
8500 Menden Hall Loop Rd
Juneau AK 998019218

Call Sign: KL2MV
Sean R Grant
3262 Mendenhall 2
Juneau AK 99801

Call Sign: AL7GM
Lowell S Barrick
9505 Mendenhall Loop Rd
Juneau AK 99801

Call Sign: KA6DBB
Paul F Merrill
10200 Mendenhall Loop Rd
""N""
Juneau AK 99803

Call Sign: WL7ZG
Byron F Morris
940 Mendenhall Penn Rd
Juneau AK 99801

Call Sign: KL7DFW
Louis S Bandirola
5992 Montgomery St
Juneau AK 99801

Call Sign: WL7BXW
Peter W Bonnell
9476 Moraine Way
Juneau AK 99801

Call Sign: NL7UC
Carol A Bruce
9500 Moraine Way
Juneau AK 99801

Call Sign: WL7BKA
David Bruce
9500 Moraine Way
Juneau AK 998018707

Call Sign: WL7CKN
Jack R Kreinheder
9850 Nine Mile Creek Rd
Juneau AK 99801

Call Sign: WL7ZE
Kristina R Kiernan
9080 Ninnis Dr
Juneau AK 99801

Call Sign: KL0BT
Stephen F Kunz
5125 North Douglas
Juneau AK 99801

Call Sign: WL7CJV
Douglas D Gardner

4280 North Douglas Hwy
Juneau AK 99801

Call Sign: WL7OK
Jerry W Mastin
7670 North Douglas Hwy
Juneau AK 99801

Call Sign: KL7KD
Anne C Fuller
7943 North Douglas Hwy
Juneau AK 99801

Call Sign: KL7KE
Michael F Sakarias
7943 North Douglas Hwy
Juneau AK 99801

Call Sign: WL7ZF
Gene Randall
11346 North Douglas Hwy
Juneau AK 99801

Call Sign: WL7CKJ
Stanley A Mc Alister
2209 North Jordan Av
Juneau AK 99801

Call Sign: AL7WN
Daniel J Squires
5993 North St
Juneau AK 99801

Call Sign: KD7WN
Daniel J Squires
5993 North St
Juneau AK 99801

Call Sign: KL7JAW
Harold R Hogberg
6001 North St
Juneau AK 99801

Call Sign: WL7RH
Misti L Hogberg
6001 North St
Juneau AK 99801

Call Sign: WL7UW
Perthena M Hogberg
6001 North St
Juneau AK 99801

Call Sign: WL7UV

Steven F Gebert
9357 Northland St
Juneau AK 99801

Call Sign: WL7CJQ
Diane L Aldrighette
9362 Northland St
Juneau AK 99801

Call Sign: KL7DAV
David R Palmer
3317 Park Place
Juneau AK 99801

Call Sign: WB7RRK
David R Palmer
3317 Park Place
Juneau AK 99801

Call Sign: KL2WT
Stephen R Eshnaur
9175 Parkwood Dr
Juneau AK 99801

Call Sign: KL0ZP
Michael A Richmond
2806 Peters Ln
Juneau AK 99801

Call Sign: WL7ZJ
Judith M Klein
1208 Pike Ct
Juneau AK 99801

Call Sign: KL2ZX
Jimmie L Rosenbruch
8144 Pinewood Dr
Juneau AK 99801

Call Sign: NL7UM
Robert D Carnes
3211 Pioneer Ave
Juneau AK 99801

Call Sign: NL7UZ
Matthew P Musslewhite
17585 Point Lena Loop Rd
Juneau AK 99801

Call Sign: KE4JFB
Julie F Briden
8236 Poplar Ave
Juneau AK 99801

Call Sign: N4DBX
Ken Briden
8236 Poplar Ave
Juneau AK 99801

Call Sign: KL7GP
Gary B Parker
4403 Portage Blvd
Juneau AK 99801

Call Sign: KB7UBH
Gary B Parker
4403 Portage Blvd
Juneau AK 99801

Call Sign: WL7CVN
Northern Se Ak Ares
4220 Ptarmigan St
Juneau AK 99801

Call Sign: KL0QP
Maria T Mattson
2216 Radcliffe Rd
Juneau AK 99801

Call Sign: WL7QE
Bob D Mattson
2216 Radcliffe Rd
Juneau AK 99801

Call Sign: KL7IYD
James H Cummins
8504 Rainbow Row
Juneau AK 99801

Call Sign: WL7BMW
William J Zentner II
19191 Randall Rd
Juneau AK 99801

Call Sign: AL7NR
Mark J Richardson
19296 Randall Rd
Juneau AK 99801

Call Sign: KL1EX
Jacob A Carpenter
2213 Raven Rd
Juneau AK 99801

Call Sign: WL7QD
Steve E Ignell
3466 Richard Dr
Juneau AK 99801

Call Sign: WL7BGI
David S Pierce
4018 Ridge Way
Juneau AK 99801

Call Sign: KL0BQ
Gregory W Lessmeier
4509 River Rd
Juneau AK 99801

Call Sign: KL0BR
Deborah L Lessmeier
4509 River Rd
Juneau AK 99801

Call Sign: W4TFS
Thomas F Sherwood
3865 Seaview Ave
Juneau AK 99801

Call Sign: WL7CMQ
James M Dillon
315 Seward St
Juneau AK 99801

Call Sign: NL7GQ
Robert M Fagen
9084 Sheiye Way
Juneau AK 99801

Call Sign: KB7FZY
Martha A De Freest
6716 Sherri St
Juneau AK 99801

Call Sign: KL3JM
Scott L Novak
10102 Silver St
Juneau AK 99801

Call Sign: KL1ZO
James Craig
2950 Simpson Ave
Juneau AK 99801

Call Sign: KL2GU
Lenka K Craigova
2950 Simpson Ave
Juneau AK 99801

Call Sign: KL7SAR
James T Craig
2950 Simpson Ave
Juneau AK 99801

Call Sign: KL7JC
James T Craig
2950 Simpson Ave
Juneau AK 99801

Call Sign: WL7CLZ
Paul J Wistrand
2958 Simpson Ave
Juneau AK 99801

Call Sign: KL1VN
Nicholas D Axmaker
1001 Ski St
Juneau AK 99801

Call Sign: WL7ZP
Robyn L Carlisle
230 South Franklin 501
Juneau AK 99801

Call Sign: KL3JL
John F Kimball
9000 Stephen Richard Dr Apt
107
Juneau AK 99801

Call Sign: AL7QB
John A Aldrighette
9621 Stikine St
Juneau AK 99801

Call Sign: KL7MK
Mark D Miles
5946 Sunset St
Juneau AK 99801

Call Sign: KL0UY
Mark D Miles
5946 Sunset St
Juneau AK 99801

Call Sign: KL2KP
Frederick C Funk
6017 Sunset St
Juneau AK 99801

Call Sign: WL7EY
Jesse J Armstrong
639 Sw 149th St
Juneau AK 99801

Call Sign: WL7VT

William L Diebels
8923 Tanis Dr
Juneau AK 99801

Call Sign: KL7JBM
Christine M Prussing
4655 Thane Rd
Juneau AK 99801

Call Sign: KL1UY
William C Heumann
6000 Thane Rd
Juneau AK 99801

Call Sign: WL7ZN
Ron C Hagerup
4895 Thanerd
Juneau AK 99801

Call Sign: KL7QJ
Mark W Kissel
8187 Threadneedle
Juneau AK 998019125

Call Sign: KL3JK
Blain A Garrett
8198 Threadneedle
Juneau AK 99801

Call Sign: AL7OF
Michael L Wittig
4479 Trafalgar
Juneau AK 99801

Call Sign: KL0SG
Kenneth S Willis
9345 Turn St
Juneau AK 99801

Call Sign: WL7YI
Richard A Svobodny
527 West 11th St
Juneau AK 99801

Call Sign: KL7FPA
Douglas L Gregg
615 West 12th St
Juneau AK 99801

Call Sign: WL7CSZ
Jacob R Cook
712 West 12th St
Juneau AK 99801

Call Sign: KL1EZ
Peter R Hettinger
9585 Whitewater Ct
Juneau AK 99801

Call Sign: KL7DB
Bruce R Morgan
617 Willoughby Ave 264
Juneau AK 99801

Call Sign: KL7PE
Kiernan K Holliday
617 Willoughby Ave 276
Juneau AK 99801

Call Sign: AL7NU
Richard L Shideler
617 Willoughby Ave Pmb 187
Juneau AK 99801

Call Sign: WL7CKQ
Shelly J Brady
3019 Wood Duck
Juneau AK 99801

Call Sign: WL7CMS
Charles R Brady
3019 Wood Duck
Juneau AK 99801

Call Sign: WL7CKO
Thomas D Kohler
8995 Yandukin Dr K
Juneau AK 998018086

Call Sign: KL2ZS
Joseph S Johnson
Juneau AK 99802

Call Sign: KL3FP
Rob W Cadmus
Juneau AK 99802

Call Sign: KL3FQ
Katharine S Glover
Juneau AK 99802

Call Sign: AL7KZ
Joseph P Rafferty
Juneau AK 99802

Call Sign: KC6TNI
Jeff M Coult
Juneau AK 99802

Call Sign: KC7MRO
Sarah M Gaul
Juneau AK 99802

Call Sign: KL0FI
William C Leighty
Juneau AK 99802

Call Sign: KL0SI
Jimmie G Clemmons
Juneau AK 99802

Call Sign: KL0TI
Theodore A Deats
Juneau AK 99802

Call Sign: KL7IKP
Barbara A Kelly
Juneau AK 99802

Call Sign: KL7PF
John T Moore
Juneau AK 99802

Call Sign: N7JIZ
Jeff S Jordan
Juneau AK 99802

Call Sign: NL7KT
Donald J Gotschall
Juneau AK 99802

Call Sign: NL7OC
Richard A Wood
Juneau AK 99802

Call Sign: WL7AN
Scott M Fairchild
Juneau AK 99802

Call Sign: WL7CQB
Diane J Kyser
Juneau AK 99802

Call Sign: WL7CSM
Leimomi Matunding
Juneau AK 99802

Call Sign: WL7RM
Kenneth A Airozo
Juneau AK 99802

Call Sign: WL7WB

Paulette Y Sill
Juneau AK 99802

Call Sign: KL0VV
Constncio P Bolima
Juneau AK 99802

Call Sign: KL0WE
Thomas A Rozek
Juneau AK 99802

Call Sign: KL0XE
Paul Hamby
Juneau AK 99802

Call Sign: KL1AS
John W Gregson
Juneau AK 99802

Call Sign: KL1EG
Gregory L Welpton
Juneau AK 99802

Call Sign: KL1EW
Shirley F Kohls
Juneau AK 99802

Call Sign: KL1KA
Jacquelyn L Smail
Juneau AK 99803

Call Sign: KL1MD
Joshua L Schrader
Juneau AK 99803

Call Sign: KL1NN
Sean P Caughran
Juneau AK 99803

Call Sign: KL2NM
Sarah M Bettridge
Juneau AK 99803

Call Sign: KL2OG
Michael R Branum
Juneau AK 99803

Call Sign: KL2ZO
Ashley Bruce
Juneau AK 99803

Call Sign: KL2ZR
Larry B Harris
Juneau AK 99803

Call Sign: KL3KW
Cyndi S Megli
Juneau AK 99803

Call Sign: KL3KY
Craig R Tiedemann
Juneau AK 99803

Call Sign: AA7DM
Sandra E Parkinson
Juneau AK 99803

Call Sign: KA4KSE
Martha J Feinberg
Juneau AK 99803

Call Sign: KL0BO
Benjamin C Tidswell
Juneau AK 99803

Call Sign: KL0RX
Christopher L Chiles
Juneau AK 99803

Call Sign: KL0RY
Leif Lie
Juneau AK 99803

Call Sign: KL0TJ
Richard S Wirtz
Juneau AK 99803

Call Sign: KL7GY
William E Burnett III III
Juneau AK 99803

Call Sign: KL7IPD
James S Webb
Juneau AK 99803

Call Sign: N7XTW
Rom L Folger
Juneau AK 99803

Call Sign: NL7ZV
Thomas R Gundelfinger
Juneau AK 99803

Call Sign: WL7CCA
Sean C Mc Dermott
Juneau AK 99803

Call Sign: WL7CJS

Kris B Hildre
Juneau AK 99803

Call Sign: WL7CNL
Robin F Lown
Juneau AK 99803

Call Sign: WL7CQD
Dorothy M Allen
Juneau AK 99803

Call Sign: WL7ZH
Lester G Leatherberry Jr
Juneau AK 99803

Call Sign: KD7IQF
Jean H Lambert
Juneau AK 99803

Call Sign: N6NIC
Nicholas A Adamson
Juneau AK 99803

Call Sign: KL0ZG
Belinda G Burch
Juneau AK 99803

Call Sign: KL0ZH
Kimberly B Custer
Juneau AK 99803

Call Sign: KL0ZI
Melanie A Fluharty
Juneau AK 99803

Call Sign: KL0ZJ
Harry L Fluharty
Juneau AK 99803

Call Sign: KL0ZO
Edward W Plumb
Juneau AK 99803

Call Sign: KL1ET
Diana E Leatherberry
Juneau AK 99803

Call Sign: KL1EU
Kenneth A Judson
Juneau AK 99803

Call Sign: KL1IM
James A Wycoff
Juneau AK 99803

Call Sign: WL7ZK
Thomas A Karpstein
Juneau AK 998020393

Call Sign: KL1FC
Douglas J Wessen
Juneau AK 998021282

Call Sign: NL7DT
Douglas H Alsip
Juneau AK 998022161

Call Sign: KL7WF
Steven D Hildebrand
Juneau AK 998032736

Call Sign: WL7BKB
Laurie A Fuglvog
Juneau AK 998032826

Call Sign: KC7HAI
Barbara V Anderson
Juneau AK 998033403

Call Sign: KL7IWC
Lawrence H Walter
Juneau AK 998033915

Call Sign: WL7CQA
Teresa C Walter
Juneau AK 998033915

Call Sign: AE6I
Joseph D Mastroianni
Juneau AK 998035171

Call Sign: KL3JN
Craig L Smith
Juneau AK 998035204

Call Sign: WL7BMX
Robert H Crabtree
Juneau AK 99801

Call Sign: KL7TV
Robert L Mell
Juneau AK 99802

Call Sign: NL7UG
Larry A Dawson
Juneau AK 99802

Call Sign: WL7BJV

Richard A Sill
Juneau AK 99802

Call Sign: WL7BRF
William E Fleek
Juneau AK 99802

Call Sign: WL7BXY
Dan S Alden
Juneau AK 99802

Call Sign: WL7HM
Tommy P Quieve Jr
Juneau AK 99802

Call Sign: WL7PX
Curtis I Harden
Juneau AK 99802

Call Sign: NL7LS
Thomas E Bruckman
Juneau AK 99803

Call Sign: NL7TN
George H Messerschmidt
Juneau AK 99803

Call Sign: WL7ADF
Tim Banaszak
Juneau AK 99803

Call Sign: WL7AK
Paul A Hunt
Juneau AK 99803

Call Sign: WL7BUM
Brian D Perkins
Juneau AK 99803

Call Sign: WL7CHC
Lynden H Cothary
Juneau AK 99803

Call Sign: WL7ET
Joanne R Richter
Juneau AK 99803

Call Sign: WL7GO
Leo M Bayeur
Juneau AK 99803

Call Sign: AL7AQ
Bruce E Gordon
Juneau AK 99850

Call Sign: WB6IIM
Jeffrey L Gnass
Juneau AK 998035415

FCC Amateur Radio Licenses in Kaktovik

Call Sign: KL0IZ
Fred N Tagarook
Kaktovik AK 99747

Call Sign: KL0JI
Vincent T Nageak Jr
Kaktovik AK 99747

Call Sign: NL7BE
Fenton O Rexford
Kaktovik AK 99747

FCC Amateur Radio Licenses in Kasaan

Call Sign: WL7BRM
Skip F Escoffon Jr
4th & Beach Front Rd
Kasaan AK 99924

FCC Amateur Radio Licenses in Kasilof

Call Sign: KL7HHE
J Cosmo Mercurio
26994 Johansen Dr
Kasilof AK 99610

Call Sign: WL7UR
Karen M Lawrence
47630 South View Ave
Kasilof AK 99610

Call Sign: NL7PW
Charles F Kuhlmann Jr
Mile 105 Sterling Hwy
Kasilof AK 996101151

Call Sign: KL1LR
Edward M Chesney
Kasilof AK 99610

Call Sign: KL2HB
Cynthia J Sadler
Kasilof AK 99610

Call Sign: KL3CZ
John A Bell
Kasilof AK 99610

Call Sign: AL7FD
Dennis L Timm
Kasilof AK 99610

Call Sign: KC7YZR
David E Padvorac
Kasilof AK 99610

Call Sign: KL0IC
Michael C La Cava
Kasilof AK 99610

Call Sign: KL7UR
Robert M Christl Sr
Kasilof AK 99610

Call Sign: N8HOJ
Melanie G Osterman
Kasilof AK 99610

Call Sign: WL7CMG
David A Silva
Kasilof AK 99610

Call Sign: WL7UQ
Gregory D Lawrence
Kasilof AK 99610

Call Sign: NL7HO
Tom M Warren
Box 15
Kasilof AK 99610

Call Sign: W7ZZL
Lennart B Wikstrom
Box 596
Kasilof AK 99610

Call Sign: WB7UZH
Cozene L Wikstrom
Box 596
Kasilof AK 99610

FCC Amateur Radio Licenses in Kenai

Call Sign: KL7VIC
Victor A Hett
1507 Barabara Dr
Kenai AK 99611

Call Sign: KL7EKN
Clarice Kipp
Box 308
Kenai AK 99611

Call Sign: NL7QR
Robert J Mulholland
Box 3267
Kenai AK 99611

Call Sign: WL7AYE
Connie M Eldredge
ST 1 Box 1063
Kenai AK 99611

Call Sign: WL7APE
Carol E Louthan
36705 Chinulna Dr
Kenai AK 996118721

Call Sign: W4BJR
Edward B East Sr
1002 Crow Ct
Kenai AK 99611

Call Sign: KL7EBE
Edward B East Jr
1002 Crow Ct PO Box 2797
Kenai AK 99611

Call Sign: N5UKX
Edward B East Jr
1002 Crow Ct PO Box 2797
Kenai AK 99611

Call Sign: KC5QPJ
Tim H Tolar
1201 Equinox Way
Kenai AK 996116628

Call Sign: KC5THY
Stacey E Tolar
1201 Equinox Way
Kenai AK 996116628

Call Sign: AL2B
Robert L Rowley
37270 Even Ln
Kenai AK 99611

Call Sign: N7BUO
Robert L Rowley
37270 Even Ln

Kenai AK 99611

Call Sign: AL7LY
Rex W Eagle
38340 Golden Eagle Ct
Kenai AK 99611

Call Sign: WL7YE
James C Baisden
1009 Inlet Woods Dr
Kenai AK 99611

Call Sign: KL1DL
Christopher D Lawrence
48135 Irrlyn Cir
Kenai AK 99611

Call Sign: KL7ISO
T J Hinkle
46745 Kenai Spur Hwy
Kenai AK 99611

Call Sign: KL7GNH
Barbara J Ruckman
1510 Kittiwake
Kenai AK 99611

Call Sign: KL2DO
Donald T Noble
52830 Lisburne Ave
Kenai AK 99611

Call Sign: KL2GQ
Martin E Kunz
52854 Lisburne Ave
Kenai AK 99611

Call Sign: KL9MEK
Martin E Kunz
52854 Lisburne Ave
Kenai AK 99611

Call Sign: AL7RC
James R Jenckes
616 Maple Dr
Kenai AK 99611

Call Sign: KL2DS
Paul J Davis Jr
49273 Mercedes Ct
Kenai AK 99611

Call Sign: KL7JD
Paul J Davis Jr

49273 Mercedes Ct
Kenai AK 99611

Call Sign: KL7CMN
Gerald R Brookman
715 Muir Ave
Kenai AK 996118816

Call Sign: KL0KA
William J Carsner
1320 Nighthawk Ln
Kenai AK 99611

Call Sign: KL2RU
Robert S Peterson
214 North Forest Dr
Kenai AK 99611

Call Sign: WL7CHB
Russell J Taylor
2745 Set Net Ct
Kenai AK 99611

Call Sign: KL2RV
James F Mccurdy
36805 Short Ln
Kenai AK 99611

Call Sign: KL7JHJ
Philip N Nash
110 South Willow 104
Kenai AK 99611

Call Sign: KL1NB
Lois M Nelson
209 Susieana Ln
Kenai AK 99611

Call Sign: W0OPT
William R Nelson
209 Susieana St
Kenai AK 996116875

Call Sign: KL7RHJ
William R Nelson
209 Susieana St
Kenai AK 996116875

Call Sign: KL2EM
Clyde R Kendall
36650 Virginia Dr
Kenai AK 99611

Call Sign: WL7CHF

Richard W Main
207 Walker Ln
Kenai AK 99611

Call Sign: WL7DB
David C Haring
1121 Walnut
Kenai AK 99611

Call Sign: KL1EA
Nathan J Wood
1121 Walnut
Kenai AK 99611

Call Sign: WL7O
David C Haring
1121 Walnut
Kenai AK 99611

Call Sign: KL2GP
Ruth A Haring
1121 Walnut St
Kenai AK 99611

Call Sign: KF7CXJ
Julie M Cruse
606 Westwood Cir
Kenai AK 99611

Call Sign: KL7JUL
Julie M Cruse
606 Westwood Cir
Kenai AK 99611

Call Sign: KL3CX
Phillip A North
3810 Wildrose Ave
Kenai AK 99611

Call Sign: KL7IFX
Leslie E Schneider
3820 Wildrose Ave
Kenai AK 99611

Call Sign: N7QAN
Kenneth R Dickinson
2707 Wildwood Dr 6
Kenai AK 99611

Call Sign: WL7COX
David A Darsey
1603 Woodside Ave
Kenai AK 99611

Call Sign: KL1ZQ
Craig V Phillips
Kenai AK 99611

Call Sign: KL2DQ
Jeanne E Spinney
Kenai AK 99611

Call Sign: KL2DR
Millard E Spinney Jr
Kenai AK 99611

Call Sign: KL2DT
Jane L Linderman
Kenai AK 99611

Call Sign: KL2LZ
Daniel L Greene
Kenai AK 99611

Call Sign: AL7IB
Thomas Moliere
Kenai AK 99611

Call Sign: AL7NJ
Bernhard Buettner
Kenai AK 99611

Call Sign: KA5HPO
Winston J Gillies III
Kenai AK 99611

Call Sign: KL0AT
Lawrence M Linderman
Kenai AK 99611

Call Sign: KL0DF
Joseph C Nightingale
Kenai AK 99611

Call Sign: KL0JY
Martin J Pettingill
Kenai AK 99611

Call Sign: KL7GSA
Pete O Hansen
Kenai AK 99611

Call Sign: KL7RA
Richard A Strand
Kenai AK 99611

Call Sign: N9IUY
Robert S Dillingham

Kenai AK 99611

Call Sign: WL7BUJ
Bernard J Doyle
Kenai AK 99611

Call Sign: WL7CSY
Curtis D Fisher
Kenai AK 99611

Call Sign: KL1BK
John S Bittle
Kenai AK 99611

Call Sign: WL7COY
Katherin J Robbins
Kenai AK 996111273

Call Sign: KL7EKO
Glenn J Kipp
Kenai AK 99611

Call Sign: NL7LM
Hallam N Fain
Kenai AK 99611

Call Sign: NL7VG
Rodney A Kaas
Kenai AK 99611

Call Sign: WL7AQY
Scott R Richmond
Kenai AK 99611

Call Sign: WL7BYC
James H Saling
Kenai AK 99611

Call Sign: AL4H
Simon Schelkshorn
Kenai AK 99611

FCC Amateur Radio Licenses in Ketchikan

Call Sign: KL7ST
Evard A Schlais
2314 1st Ave
Ketchikan AK 999015904

Call Sign: WL7AUV
Le Roy J Roth
2306 2nd Ave
Ketchikan AK 99901

Call Sign: AL3O
John H Bender
3316 Arnold Ave
Ketchikan AK 99901

Call Sign: AL2P
Michael V Sebring
212 Austin Apt 7
Ketchikan AK 99901

Call Sign: KL2ME
Ken G Koons
119 Austin St 1106
Ketchikan AK 99901

Call Sign: KL7GIH
Dwight C John
Box 7962
Ketchikan AK 99901

Call Sign: WL7BRN
Mae M Peterson
Box 8184
Ketchikan AK 99901

Call Sign: KL7IFP
John M Markle
Box 8743
Ketchikan AK 99901

Call Sign: WL7RN
Leslie W Brendible Jr
Box 9327
Ketchikan AK 99901

Call Sign: WL7LV
Gary A Treffry
Pob Ppv
Ketchikan AK 99950

Call Sign: KF5ETW
Shawn J Rickman
10555 Collins Ct
Ketchikan AK 99901

Call Sign: KL3DL
Shawn J Rickman
10555 Collins Ct
Ketchikan AK 99901

Call Sign: KE7DFO
Lou M Hu
4 Creek St

Ketchikan AK 99901

Call Sign: KL7GCN
Henry L Wise Sr
1913 Cub Ct
Ketchikan AK 99901

Call Sign: WL7AZO
Llewellyn M Williams III
3250 Denaili 38
Ketchikan AK 99901

Call Sign: KB9AXM
Devin S Fox
141 Dogwood Place S Apt B
Ketchikan AK 999015743

Call Sign: KL7UG
Steve D Hales
5984 Dotson Ln
Ketchikan AK 99901

Call Sign: KL7UH
Anita F Hales
5984 Dotson Ln
Ketchikan AK 99901

Call Sign: N7ZYS
Neil E Ensign
2034 First Ave
Ketchikan AK 99901

Call Sign: WB7FET
Geneal L Colby
94 Franklin St
Ketchikan AK 999017664

Call Sign: WL7AZM
Llewellyn M Williams Jr
755 Grant St
Ketchikan AK 99901

Call Sign: WL7SI
Archie G Diment
1004 Jackson
Ketchikan AK 99901

Call Sign: WA7VOT
Stewart R Emery
654 Lermo
Ketchikan AK 99901

Call Sign: WL7NP
Michael C Puckett

608 Lotus St
Ketchikan AK 99901

Call Sign: WL7CHW
Robert E Haldy
332 Madison St Upper
Ketchikan AK 99901

Call Sign: KA7SFJ
Robert S Phair
125 Main St 131
Ketchikan AK 99901

Call Sign: KL1A
Alaskan Dx Club
125 Main St 218
Ketchikan AK 99901

Call Sign: KL7HS
Arnt Sorset
1258 Millar St
Ketchikan AK 99901

Call Sign: KL7HKA
M June Zenge
525 Monroe St
Ketchikan AK 99901

Call Sign: KL2TK
Jess T Mickelson
708 North Pt Higgins Rd
Ketchikan AK 99928

Call Sign: WB7TLC
Jess T Mickelson
708 North Pt Higgins Rd
Ketchikan AK 99928

Call Sign: WL7CUG
James L Bruce
5324 North Tongass Ave
Ketchikan AK 99901

Call Sign: KF5CVM
John H Bender
5324 North Tongass Hwy
Ketchikan AK 99901

Call Sign: WL7IT
Dwight P Lindemann
5581 North Tongass Hwy
Ketchikan AK 99901

Call Sign: WL7CUH

Margeret L Hink
8983 North Tongass Hwy
Ketchikan AK 99901

Call Sign: NL7LL
Gary R Freitag
5786 Roosevelt Dr
Ketchikan AK 99901

Call Sign: KL7IHB
James J Daly
2051 Sealevel Dr 301
Ketchikan AK 99901

Call Sign: KF8PE
Jason W Evison
3225 South Tongass Hwy
Ketchikan AK 99901

Call Sign: KB7BZZ
Jeffrey W De Freest
4650 South Tongass Hwy
Ketchikan AK 99901

Call Sign: WL7CWJ
Last Frontier Contest Club
7866 South Tongass Hwy
Ketchikan AK 99901

Call Sign: KL8C
Last Frontier Contest Club
7866 South Tongass Hwy
Ketchikan AK 99901

Call Sign: AL7KH
Gene G Wyman
5854 South Tongrass Hwy
Ketchikan AK 99901

Call Sign: AL7MA
David D Christensen
105 Stedman
Ketchikan AK 99901

Call Sign: AL3E
Wekenborg L Richard
1010 Stedman St
Ketchikan AK 99901

Call Sign: KB1CUU
Nathan L Spencer
441 Thatcher Way Apt 3
Ketchikan AK 99901

Call Sign: KL1NI
Robert B Ball
4831 Tongass - Apt A3
Ketchikan AK 999019013

Call Sign: KB6UFB
Robert B Ball
4831 Tongass - Apt A3
Ketchikan AK 999019013

Call Sign: KL2OJ
Orville J Wiley Jr
2450 Tongass Ave
Ketchikan AK 99901

Call Sign: KH0RF
William L Vlasievsky
2450 Tongass Ave 333
Ketchikan AK 999015928

Call Sign: KL7BS
William L Vlasievsky
2450 Tongass Ave 333
Ketchikan AK 999015928

Call Sign: KH6IQX
David M Good
2450 Tongass Pmb 143
Ketchikan AK 99901

Call Sign: WL7CUO
Floyd O Minor
2417 Tongass Ste 111 227
Ketchikan AK 99901

Call Sign: KL0YC
Darlene O Minor
2417 Tongass Ste 111 227
Ketchikan AK 99901

Call Sign: KL7EQA
George D Hale
219 Tower Rd
Ketchikan AK 99901

Call Sign: WL7CWB
Dx Scavengers Radio Club
135 Tuttle Way
Ketchikan AK 99901

Call Sign: KL7FF
Dx Scavengers Radio Club
135 Tuttle Way
Ketchikan AK 99901

Call Sign: KL0RG
Kevin J O Connell
135 Tuttle Way
Ketchikan AK 99901

Call Sign: W7TFS
Brad L Cunningham
945 Venetia Way
Ketchikan AK 99901

Call Sign: KF6ILC
Brett W Hinkle
6572 Vista Dr South
Ketchikan AK 99901

Call Sign: KF6ILD
Marina R Hinkle
6572 Vista Dr South
Ketchikan AK 99901

Call Sign: KL1VO
Floyd O Mcclellan
16643 Waterfall Rd
Ketchikan AK 99901

Call Sign: KF6IOT
Floyd O Mcclellan
16643 Waterfall Rd
Ketchikan AK 99901

Call Sign: AL3C
Stephen J Aldrich Sr
Ketchikan AK 99901

Call Sign: KL3HM
John C Mccormick
Ketchikan AK 99901

Call Sign: KL3HN
Connor R Mccormick
Ketchikan AK 99901

Call Sign: AL7ES
Terence M Bills
Ketchikan AK 99901

Call Sign: KL0GL
Daniel G Walker
Ketchikan AK 99901

Call Sign: KL7CS
Michael J Sallee
Ketchikan AK 99901

Call Sign: KL7IFN
Raymond M Holt
Ketchikan AK 99901

Call Sign: KM6GE
John L Wray
Ketchikan AK 99901

Call Sign: N7VQP
Nicole A Bonham-Colby
Ketchikan AK 99901

Call Sign: NL7ZF
Robert A Haskell
Ketchikan AK 99901

Call Sign: WL7ANH
Robert L Brown
Ketchikan AK 99901

Call Sign: WL7CUI
Michael R L Kern
Ketchikan AK 99901

Call Sign: WL7XG
Richard R Watson
Ketchikan AK 99901

Call Sign: KL0XV
Stephen F Lowney
Ketchikan AK 99901

Call Sign: KD7QIM
Alan J Knettel
Ketchikan AK 999018304

Call Sign: AL7NW
Kay L Long
Ketchikan AK 99901

Call Sign: KL7NC
Robert J Kern
Ketchikan AK 99901

Call Sign: NL7ZQ
Timothy J Long
Ketchikan AK 99901

Call Sign: WL7AIA
Andral E Scrivens
Ketchikan AK 99901

Call Sign: WL7BQO

Stuart W Mattison
Ketchikan AK 99901

Call Sign: WL7BSX
Richard J Lowe
Ketchikan AK 99901

Call Sign: WL7BXQ
Bryn A Bitzer
Ketchikan AK 99901

Call Sign: WL7BXR
Elizabeth D Janin
Ketchikan AK 99901

Call Sign: WL7BXS
Sarah E Janin
Ketchikan AK 99901

Call Sign: WL7CGP
Lannea A Lee
Ketchikan AK 99901

Call Sign: WL7KN
Myron Chaitoff
Ketchikan AK 99901

Call Sign: N7VQQ
Kent L Colby
Ketchiken AK 999017664

FCC Amateur Radio Licenses in King Cove

Call Sign: KC8DXI
Jay S Guikema
1 Rams Loop
King Cove AK 99612

Call Sign: WL7COB
Mark M Lapinskas
King Cove AK 99612

Call Sign: WL7MR
Gregory G Moser
King Cove AK 99612

FCC Amateur Radio Licenses in King Salmon

Call Sign: KL3HL
Eric D Heffelfinger
King Salmon AK 99613

Call Sign: KB6FTN
Petar Orlich
King Salmon AK 99613

Call Sign: KL0NQ
Michael G Willmon
King Salmon AK 99613

FCC Amateur Radio Licenses in Kipnuk

Call Sign: WL7BSP
Kenneth W Eddy
Kipnuk AK 99614

FCC Amateur Radio Licenses in Kivalina

Call Sign: KL2UA
Thomas M Hanifan
Mcqueen School
Kivalina AK 99750

FCC Amateur Radio Licenses in Klawock

Call Sign: KA7TOM
Thomas L Harden
Lot 9 Clark Bay Subdivision
Hollis Ak
Klawock AK 99925

Call Sign: KF6GNM
Thomas L Harden
Lot 9 Clark Bay Subdivision
Hollis Ak
Klawock AK 99925

Call Sign: KB7YNO
Robert E Olmstead
6488 Klawock Hollis Hwy 407
Klawock AK 99925

Call Sign: KL3BV
Myron A Fribush
Klawock AK 99925

Call Sign: K6YLS
David L Hahnes
Klawock AK 99925

Call Sign: K6YLT
David E Hahnes
Klawock AK 99925

Call Sign: KC7PLQ
Maryanna A Murphy
Klawock AK 99925

Call Sign: KF6SHS
K Michelle Harden
Klawock AK 99925

Call Sign: WL7NX
James M Dessert
Klawock AK 99925

FCC Amateur Radio Licenses in Kodiak

Call Sign: N5QF
William V Stenberg
204C Albatross Ave
Kodiak AK 99615

Call Sign: KD5WCF
Parker S Stenberg
204C Albatross Ave
Kodiak AK 99615

Call Sign: KL2MI
Parker S Stenberg
204C Albatross Ave
Kodiak AK 99615

Call Sign: KD7IEO
Brian C Myers Jr
2201 A Barrett Cir
Kodiak AK 99615

Call Sign: N6SQR
Mark C Hickman
208B Beacon Ave
Kodiak AK 99615

Call Sign: NL7WC
Martin H Conley
720E South Alyeska Ave
Kodiak AK 99615

Call Sign: WL7RJ
Brian E Willis
202A Albatross Ave
Kodiak AK 99615

Call Sign: WL7RK
Dean E Willis
202A Albatross Ave

Kodiak AK 99615

Call Sign: WL7RL
Karen A Willis
202A Albatross Ave
Kodiak AK 99615

Call Sign: WP3AZ
Michael F Nasitka
1 Anton Larson Rd
Kodiak AK 99619

Call Sign: KL3GE
Jack G Brisbane
PO Box 8825 Antone Way
Kodiak AK 99615

Call Sign: AL7NZ
John D Durham
3275 Balika Ln
Kodiak AK 996158706

Call Sign: KL0KD
Jeffrey B Dorwart
759 Barometer Apt F
Kodiak AK 99615

Call Sign: AL7GC
Elmer D Crandall
515 Bonaparte Cir
Kodiak AK 99615

Call Sign: NL7QE
Joseph S Slusser
421 Curlew
Kodiak AK 99615

Call Sign: KL2EH
Craig L Eckert
1225 East Rezanof Dr
Kodiak ΛK 99615

Call Sign: KL2OL
Peter Irwin
4774 East Rezanof Dr
Kodiak AK 99615

Call Sign: KL0YL
Richard W Courtney II
3425 Harlequin Ct
Kodiak AK 995167067

Call Sign: KL0OL
Richard W Courtney II

3425 Harlequin Ct
Kodiak AK 996157067

Call Sign: KL2VX
Marlon D Rivera
811 Hemlock St
Kodiak AK 99615

Call Sign: NL7ER
John W Kimmel
2107 Island Cir
Kodiak AK 99615

Call Sign: WL7NV
Bill Guy
1211 Kouskog
Kodiak AK 99615

Call Sign: WL7BRL
Jerome P Alterman
773 F Lake Louise Dr
Kodiak AK 99615

Call Sign: WL7CQE
Darell L Blocker
1820 Larch St C4
Kodiak AK 99615

Call Sign: KA1NBL
Joseph B O'Gorman
1618 Lechner Way
Kodiak AK 99615

Call Sign: WL7NM
Tracy S Allen
207D Lighthouse Ave
Kodiak AK 99615

Call Sign: WL7VF
Robert J Roberts
721 Lower Mill Bay Rd
Kodiak AK 99615

Call Sign: KD7TMY
William W Smith
1622 Lynden Way
Kodiak AK 99615

Call Sign: KL7HIX
Andrew K Brumbaugh
1623 Mill Bay 6
Kodiak AK 99615

Call Sign: KD6AGT

Michael E Nielsen
1234 Mill Bay Rd
Kodiak AK 99615

Call Sign: WL7BZN
Mark I Miller
2610 Mill Bay Rd C4
Kodiak AK 99615

Call Sign: KL3HS
Matthew T Martens
1518 Mission Rd
Kodiak AK 99615

Call Sign: NL7ZX
Louise B Cusson
1820 Mission Rd
Kodiak AK 99615

Call Sign: KL3FC
Perry L Dehne
1833 Mission Rd
Kodiak AK 99615

Call Sign: KL7ALJ
Albert H Stewart
Box 341 1128 Mission Rd
Kodiak AK 99615

Call Sign: KL7JBV
Michael F Dolph
326 Plover Way
Kodiak AK 99615

Call Sign: WL7UH
Stanley P Reiff Sr
1944 Rezonof Dr E
Kodiak AK 99615

Call Sign: KL7PD
Christy L Moore
1312 Selief 25
Kodiak AK 99615

Call Sign: KL1JW
Kenneth D Cameron
354 Shahafka Cir
Kodiak AK 99615

Call Sign: NL7LQ
Joseph E Kelley
1618 Simeonoff
Kodiak AK 99615

Call Sign: WL7BYV
William C Pearce III
732 South Alyeska Apt C
Kodiak AK 99615

Call Sign: KL2LQ
Andrew R Clark
11371 South Russian Creek Rd
Apt A3
Kodiak AK 99615

Call Sign: KL7BDK
Wilton T White
221 Upper Millbay Rd
Kodiak AK 99615

Call Sign: NL7GF
Thomas A Durr
416 West Rezanof
Kodiak AK 99615

Call Sign: KL1AR
Stephen E Bodnar
Kodiak AK 99516

Call Sign: KL1KE
Gody D Zarate
Kodiak AK 99615

Call Sign: KL1LF
Milton E Bohac
Kodiak AK 99615

Call Sign: AL2C
Harald Raeker
Kodiak AK 99615

Call Sign: KL1RQ
Lothar Harry D Zarate
Kodiak AK 99615

Call Sign: KL1RR
David M Davis
Kodiak AK 99615

Call Sign: KL1VR
Joseph M Smith
Kodiak AK 99615

Call Sign: KE7KAT
James M Cook Sr
Kodiak AK 99615

Call Sign: KL2EJ

Brian D Butcher
Kodiak AK 99615

Call Sign: KL2IB
Raymond D Vining
Kodiak AK 99615

Call Sign: KL2LR
John A Parker
Kodiak AK 99615

Call Sign: KL2UU
Delores M Parker
Kodiak AK 99615

Call Sign: WL7CWZ
Kodiak Amateur Radio
Emergency Service
Kodiak AK 99615

Call Sign: KL3DI
Arthur T Taban Ud
Kodiak AK 99615

Call Sign: AL7LQ
Curtis D Law
Kodiak AK 99615

Call Sign: KL0PK
Jenny L Stevens
Kodiak AK 99615

Call Sign: KL0UI
Judy A Rogers
Kodiak AK 99615

Call Sign: KL7Z
Frederick Voge
Kodiak AK 99615

Call Sign: NH6XU
Douglas S Vander Leest
Kodiak AK 99615

Call Sign: WL7CMV
Jesse A Gifford
Kodiak AK 99615

Call Sign: WL7CO
Robert M Hatcher
Kodiak AK 99615

Call Sign: WL7EM
Charles A Mackey

Kodiak AK 99615

Call Sign: WL7WV
Dustin M Tallent
Kodiak AK 99615

Call Sign: KG6ALN
Gody D Zarate
Kodiak AK 99615

Call Sign: KL0XW
Paul K Van Dyke
Kodiak AK 99615

Call Sign: KL1BT
Douglas S Vander Leest
Kodiak AK 99615

Call Sign: WL7CMJ
James E Stamper
Kodiak AK 99619

Call Sign: WL7CRX
Justin P Matthews
Kodiak AK 99619

Call Sign: NL9WX
Richard W Courtney II
Kodiak AK 995168293

Call Sign: WL7AML
Joseph B Stevens
Kodiak AK 996150628

Call Sign: KL0PN
William D Beaty
Kodiak AK 996151082

Call Sign: NL9H
Richard W Courtney II
Kodiak AK 996158293

Call Sign: AL7FW
Steven H Kostlin
Kodiak AK 99615

Call Sign: KL7JBR
Kenneth J Gregg
Kodiak AK 99615

Call Sign: WL7AWH
William A Maloney
Kodiak AK 99615

Call Sign: WL7BB
Gordan C Mc Cormick
Kodiak AK 99615

Call Sign: WL7EL
Robin A Ochoa
Kodiak AK 99615

Call Sign: WL7BYM
Harold C Terry
Kodiak AK 99619

Call Sign: WL7SB
Daniel P Svetlak
Kodiak AK 99619

Call Sign: KL7CYL
Victor E Marconi
Box 101
Kodiak AK 99615

Call Sign: KL0WN
John W Pfeifer
Box 2210
Kodiak AK 99615

Call Sign: NL7PK
Matthew C Miller
Box 547
Kodiak AK 99615

Call Sign: KL1XB
Dawna J Eickhoff
PO Box 1185
Kodiak AK 99615

Call Sign: K0BHC
Bradley D Hedges
PO Box 4162
Kodiak AK 99615

Call Sign: KI6HGW
Michael R Chiesa
PO Box 459
Kodiak AK 99615

Call Sign: NL1D
Uscg Contest Group
US Coast Guard Air Station
Hanger2 Building 20
Kodiak AK 996190033

Call Sign: KL7HKX

Coast Guard Amateur Radio
Club
USCGSC
Kodiak AK 99619

Call Sign: AL7MP
Douglas K Foncree Jr
USCGSC
Kodiak AK 99619

FCC Amateur Radio Licenses in Kongiganak

Call Sign: KL2AT
Kristina L Stone-Otinel
Kongiganak AK 99545

FCC Amateur Radio Licenses in Kotzebue

Call Sign: KL7FAC
Rondal G Hogan
640 Wolverine Dr
Kotzebue AK 99752

Call Sign: KL2II
Norman P Westdahl
Kotzebue AK 99572

Call Sign: KL1UF
Kathleen M Douglass
Kotzebue AK 99752

Call Sign: KL3KD
Kathleen M Douglass
Kotzebue AK 99752

Call Sign: KG4HYP
Earl W Harding Jr
Kotzebue AK 99752

Call Sign: KL3DY
Ella R Derbyshire
Kotzebue AK 997520868

Call Sign: KB5WPI
Robert T Harris
Kotzebue AK 997520982

Call Sign: KL3BD
Bob D Douglass
Box 956
Kotzebue AK 99752

Call Sign: N7HER
Bob D Douglass
Box 956
Kotzebue AK 99752

Call Sign: WL7AZU
Robert J Hawk
Ge/Gs Cape Lisburne
Kotzebue AK 99752

Call Sign: WL7CUB
Red Dog Amateur Radio Club
Msc 280
Kotzebue AK 99752

FCC Amateur Radio Licenses in Lake Minchumina

Call Sign: KL7RD
Julie H Collins
Box 69 1 Mile Foraker River
Lake Minchumina AK 99757

Call Sign: KL7IS
Richard H Collins
102 Delphinium Way
Lake Minchumina AK 99757

Call Sign: NL7BR
Florence D Collins
1 Mi Furaker River
Lake Minchumina AK
997570069

Call Sign: W2KEY
Tonya M Schlentner
Lake Minchumina AK 99757

Call Sign: WL7BCZ
Carol G Schlentner
Lake Minchumina AK 99757

Call Sign: WL7MU
Jonathan A Blackburn
Box 34
Lake Minchumina AK 99757

FCC Amateur Radio Licenses in Manley Hot Springs

Call Sign: KL7RL
Arthur D Mortvedt
90 Polar Rd
Manley Hot Springs AK 99756

Call Sign: KL7JAH
Damaris C A Richmond
Mortvedt
90 Polar Rd Box 86
Manley Hot Springs AK 99756

Call Sign: KL1LZ
Harry E Henneman Jr
Manley Hot Springs AK 99756

Call Sign: KL7IF
Donna M Scott
Manley Hot Springs AK 99756

Call Sign: KL7KV
Darrell J Scott
Manley Hot Springs AK 99756

Call Sign: WL7BJL
Linda J Johnson
Dog Rd
Manley Hot Springs AK 99756

FCC Amateur Radio Licenses in Mc Kinley

Call Sign: NL7HJ
Kenneth F Karle
Box 181
Mc Kinley Park AK 99755

FCC Amateur Radio Licenses in Mc Grath

Call Sign: KL1YN
Raine D Malone
McGrath AK 99627

FCC Amateur Radio Licenses in Metakatla

Call Sign: WL7ADS
Paul D Askren
Box 68 13th Ave
Metlakatla AK 99926

Call Sign: WL7OT
Carol J Hildebrand
Hillcrest
Metlakatla AK 99926

FCC Amateur Radio Licenses in Meyers Chuck

Call Sign: WL7BWW
Patricia A Chapman
Box 9
Meyers Chuck AK 99903

FCC Amateur Radio Licenses in Moose Pass

Call Sign: WL7XV
Rebekah L Banse
48178 Seward Hwy
Moose Pass AK 99631

Call Sign: KL0TA
Joseph Silva
Moose Pass AK 99631

FCC Amateur Radio Licenses in Naknek

Call Sign: KL7GSC
Stanley F Chmiel
Naknek AK 99633

Call Sign: N7PHB
Richard D Pearson
Naknek AK 996330567

Call Sign: KD0IXU
Benjamin S Dahl
Alaska Peninsula Hwy Mile 2
Naknek AK 99633

Call Sign: KL3IM
Benjamin S Dahl
Alaska Peninsula Hwy Mile 2
Naknek AK 99633

Call Sign: KL7TY
Sam Egli
Box 188
Naknek AK 99633

Call Sign: KC5KDA
Jeremy M Crowell
PO Box 507
Naknek AK 99633

FCC Amateur Radio Licenses in Nenana

Call Sign: WL7BDO
Carl R Horn
707 Market St
Nenana AK 997600069

Call Sign: KL1RC
Jay Bean
28865 Parks Hwy
Nenana AK 99760

Call Sign: KL1CA
Aaron R Burmeister
14223 Wilderness Dr
Nenana AK 99760

Call Sign: KL1NQ
Tim R Horn
Nenana AK 99760

Call Sign: KL1ON
Richard H Baumfalk
Nenana AK 99760

Call Sign: KL1PP
Mel W Harvey
Nenana AK 99760

Call Sign: KL1PQ
Grady L Baumfalk
Nenana AK 99760

Call Sign: KL1QG
Ronnie C Peebles
Nenana AK 99760

Call Sign: KL1VC
Miles W Martin III
Nenana AK 99760

Call Sign: KL1VD
Miles W Martin 3
Nenana AK 99760

Call Sign: KL1VE
Miles W Martin III
Nenana AK 99760

Call Sign: KL1VF
Miles W Martin 3
Nenana AK 99760

Call Sign: KL1VG
Miles W Martin III

Nenana AK 99760

Call Sign: KL1WB
Wesley L Alexander
Nenana AK 99760

Call Sign: KL1XY
Brian E Blair
Nenana AK 99760

Call Sign: KL1XZ
Elliot J Blair
Nenana AK 99760

Call Sign: KL1YA
Gabriella A Blair
Nenana AK 99760

Call Sign: KL1YB
Laurie A Blair
Nenana AK 99760

Call Sign: KL1YC
Adam K White
Nenana AK 99760

Call Sign: KL1YD
Darcia M Grace
Nenana AK 99760

Call Sign: KL1YE
Ruth M Grace
Nenana AK 99760

Call Sign: KL0AY
Sandra L Akers
Nenana AK 99760

Call Sign: KL0PG
Glyn V Carson
Nenana AK 99760

Call Sign: KL0SE
Robert D Ketzler
Nenana AK 99760

Call Sign: KW1W
Jason P Mayrand
Nenana AK 99760

Call Sign: WL7BLW
Dwight W Hales
Nenana AK 99760

Call Sign: WL7CMF
Kari L Ketzler
Nenana AK 99760

Call Sign: WL7CNA
Kelvin G Schubert
Nenana AK 99760

Call Sign: WL7CSC
Carolyn L Farr
Nenana AK 99760

Call Sign: WL7RT
Nancy L Rawliuk
Nenana AK 99760

Call Sign: WL7TM
Henry R Ketzler
Nenana AK 99760

Call Sign: WL7TT
Teresa G Mayrand
Nenana AK 99760

Call Sign: WL7WT
Ruth M Coy
Nenana AK 99760

Call Sign: AB2JQ
Joseph D Grimes
Nenana AK 99760

Call Sign: KL0YS
Michael N Almendarez Jr
Nenana AK 99760

Call Sign: NL7VT
Robert A Rawliuk
Box 317
Nenana AK 99760

Call Sign: WL7VX
Larry E Coy
Box 515
Nenana AK 99760

Call Sign: WL7CLO
David R Akers
Box 528
Nenana AK 99760

Call Sign: WL7TH
Arthur C Hanks
Box 93

Nenana AK 99760

Call Sign: KL1OX
Rowland G Powers
HC 33 Box 31180
Nenana AK 99760

Call Sign: AL7QH
Cecil F Gates
HC 66 Box 28850
Nenana AK 99760

Call Sign: KL1PO
Robert J Bean
HC 66 Box 28855
Nenana AK 99760

Call Sign: KL7FNL
Robert W Mitchell Jr
HC66 Box 30050
Nenana AK 99760

Call Sign: KL7FNM
Elaine J Mitchell
HC66 Box 30050
Nenana AK 99760

FCC Amateur Radio Licenses in New Stuyahok

Call Sign: W7QB
Terry R Roelfsema
New Stuyahok AK 99636

FCC Amateur Radio Licenses in Nikiski

Call Sign: KL7IQQ
Lawrence E Nudson
52420 Teal St
Nikiski AK 996358055

Call Sign: WL7AEG
Annette L Nudson
52420 Teal St
Nikiski AK 996358055

Call Sign: KL1RZ
Edward L Ness
Nikiski AK 99635

Call Sign: KL7UW
Edward R Cole Jr
Nikiski AK 99635

Call Sign: AL7EB
Edward R Cole Jr
Nikiski AK 99635

Call Sign: AL7LW
Lawrence R Plessinger
Nikiski AK 99635

Call Sign: AL7LX
Brenda L Plessinger
Nikiski AK 99635

Call Sign: KL0IO
Jeffrey L Plessinger
Nikiski AK 99635

Call Sign: KL7IZH
Stephen L Tanner
Nikiski AK 99635

Call Sign: KL7JHP
George K Leighton
Nikiski AK 99635

Call Sign: WL7H
David W Eldredge
Nikiski AK 99635

Call Sign: WL7WZ
Bernard W Whitehead
Nikiski AK 99635

Call Sign: K7CUT
James E Davidson
Nikiski AK 99635

Call Sign: KL7MR
Mike W Romine
Nikiski AK 99635

Call Sign: WL7BP
Jerry L Sandidge
Nikiski AK 99635

Call Sign: WL7BXO
Anna L Ritter
Nikiski AK 99635

Call Sign: WL7XA
Sharon M Gaines
Box 8103
Nikiski AK 99635

FCC Amateur Radio Licenses in Nikolaesvk

Call Sign: KD0NSG
Glenn A Pearston
Nikolaesvk AK 99556

Call Sign: KA1LZN
Robert E La Vigueur
Box 5056
Nikolaeusk AK 99556

FCC Amateur Radio Licenses in Ninilchik

Call Sign: KC4FFY
Heinz A Giese
15620 Kingsley Rd
Ninilchik AK 99639

Call Sign: KK6LL
Joel T Hilbrink
Ninilchik AK 99639

Call Sign: KL7IQ
Clifford D Mattingley
Ninilchik AK 996390287

Call Sign: NL7AI
Lynn M Mattingley
Ninilchik AK 996390287

FCC Amateur Radio Licenses in Nome

Call Sign: KL0FM
Wesley S Perkins
1105 East 5th Ave
Nome AK 99762

Call Sign: KL0EH
John J Mikulski
103 East First St Box 2094
Nome AK 99762

Call Sign: KL0HV
Matthew B Johnson
301 Fore And Aft Dr
Nome AK 99762

Call Sign: KL1JA
Dennis D Hammond
609 Steadman
Nome AK 99762

Call Sign: KB9PFL
Elizabeth A Recchia
304 West 1st Ave
Nome AK 99762

Call Sign: KG4WAH
Julie A Taylor
Nome AK 99762

Call Sign: KL1LX
Cyril E Lyon
Nome AK 99762

Call Sign: KL1OC
James M Saghafi
Nome AK 99762

Call Sign: KL1OD
Neil D Peterson
Nome AK 99762

Call Sign: KL1OE
John D Weidler
Nome AK 99762

Call Sign: KL1TW
Garrett S Glodek
Nome AK 99762

Call Sign: KL1WQ
Edward T Stang
Nome AK 99762

Call Sign: KL1WR
Ronald S Davena
Nome AK 99762

Call Sign: KL1YH
Earl W Wellen
Nome AK 99762

Call Sign: KL1YI
Charlene A Keehn
Nome AK 99762

Call Sign: KL1YJ
Kenneth S Shapiro
Nome AK 99762

Call Sign: KL1ZE
Robert S Piscoya
Nome AK 99762

Call Sign: KL1ZH
Anna R Dummer
Nome AK 99762

Call Sign: KL1ZI
William T Merchant
Nome AK 99762

Call Sign: KL1ZJ
Benjamin N Koelsch
Nome AK 99762

Call Sign: KL1ZS
Debbie J Merchant
Nome AK 99762

Call Sign: KL1ZU
Paula L Johanson
Nome AK 99762

Call Sign: KL1ZZ
Ruth A Piscoya
Nome AK 99762

Call Sign: KL2AA
Hunter C Bellamy
Nome AK 99762

Call Sign: KL2AC
Jerome L West
Nome AK 99762

Call Sign: KL2AF
Jeremy B Perkins
Nome AK 99762

Call Sign: KL2AG
Donald K Handeland
Nome AK 99762

Call Sign: KL2AH
Jerry L Dickson
Nome AK 99762

Call Sign: KL2AI
Mary I Ruud
Nome AK 99762

Call Sign: KL2AQ
Jasen S Perkins
Nome AK 99762

Call Sign: KL2AR
Zachary A Nashalook

Nome AK 99762

Call Sign: KL2AS
Irene R Merchant
Nome AK 99762

Call Sign: KL2CB
Mark C Steiger
Nome AK 99762

Call Sign: KL2CS
Lauren E Steiger
Nome AK 99762

Call Sign: KL2CT
Autumn L Falls
Nome AK 99762

Call Sign: KL2CU
Linda M Steiger
Nome AK 99762

Call Sign: KL2DF
Anthony C Parsons
Nome AK 99762

Call Sign: KL2DG
James T Sherman
Nome AK 99762

Call Sign: KL2DH
Adam E Martinson
Nome AK 99762

Call Sign: KL2DK
Myra L Murphy
Nome AK 99762

Call Sign: KL2DW
Amy J Flaherty
Nome AK 99762

Call Sign: KL2DX
Joe W Adkins Jr
Nome AK 99762

Call Sign: KL2EP
Angela S Marble
Nome AK 99762

Call Sign: KL2HG
Samuel D Schmidt
Nome AK 99762

Call Sign: KL2JB
Scot F Henderson
Nome AK 99762

Call Sign: KL2JK
Charles L Tobin
Nome AK 99762

Call Sign: KL2JL
Nicholai K Olson
Nome AK 99762

Call Sign: KL2JM
David W Olson
Nome AK 99762

Call Sign: KL2JO
Glen A Pardy
Nome AK 99762

Call Sign: KL2JQ
Toby M Schield Mr
Nome AK 99762

Call Sign: KL2JR
Roger E Thompson
Nome AK 99762

Call Sign: KL2JT
Russell J Rowe
Nome AK 99762

Call Sign: KL2JU
Sandra L Morgan
Nome AK 99762

Call Sign: KL2JV
Benjamin S Rowe
Nome AK 99762

Call Sign: KL6TS
Toby M Schield Mr
Nome AK 99762

Call Sign: WL7CWO
Ragchew Amateur Magic Inc
Nome AK 99762

Call Sign: KL2KD
Simon N Kinneen
Nome AK 99762

Call Sign: KL2KE
Fen T Kinneen

Nome AK 99762

Call Sign: KL2KF
Darrin L Otton
Nome AK 99762

Call Sign: KL2KQ
Erica J Wieler
Nome AK 99762

Call Sign: KL2KR
Iris J Wieler
Nome AK 99762

Call Sign: KL2KS
Matthew S Culley
Nome AK 99762

Call Sign: KL2KT
Richard A Anderson
Nome AK 99762

Call Sign: KL2KU
George R Bard
Nome AK 99762

Call Sign: KL2KV
Loki G Tobin
Nome AK 99762

Call Sign: KL2KW
Casey D Perkins
Nome AK 99762

Call Sign: KL2LS
Dana L Handeland
Nome AK 99762

Call Sign: KL2LW
Benjamin D Head
Nome AK 99762

Call Sign: KL2LX
Darcee A Perkins
Nome AK 99762

Call Sign: KL2MW
Jarvis J Miller
Nome AK 99762

Call Sign: KL2MX
Yvonne P Martinson
Nome AK 99762

Call Sign: KL2QI
Paul B Fox
Nome AK 99762

Call Sign: KL2QJ
Stephanie M Johnson
Nome AK 99762

Call Sign: KL2TY
Ralph Olanna Jr
Nome AK 99762

Call Sign: WL7MR
Martin K Ruud
Nome AK 99762

Call Sign: KL7RAM
Ragchew Amateur Magic Inc
Nome AK 99762

Call Sign: KL2ZF
Donnell E Erickson
Nome AK 99762

Call Sign: KL3GA
David J Rutter
Nome AK 99762

Call Sign: KL3GD
Mark T Cardinal
Nome AK 99762

Call Sign: KL3HO
Jack J Gadamus
Nome AK 99762

Call Sign: KL3IU
James T Abbott
Nome AK 99762

Call Sign: KL3IV
Elizabeth M Korenek-Johnson
Nome AK 99762

Call Sign: KL3IW
Terry R Taylor
Nome AK 99762

Call Sign: KL3LY
Mark W Whitcher
Nome AK 99762

Call Sign: KL3MA
Jacob P Carl

Nome AK 99762

Call Sign: AL7RJ
Scott R Webber
Nome AK 99762

Call Sign: KB0CIQ
Phillip D Schobert
Nome AK 99762

Call Sign: KD7DSE
Billie Coyle
Nome AK 99762

Call Sign: KD7DSG
Adam C Reddaway
Nome AK 99762

Call Sign: KL0BY
Geoffrey A Hubert
Nome AK 99762

Call Sign: KL0BZ
Garry W Curtiss
Nome AK 99762

Call Sign: KL0CR
Colby E Carter
Nome AK 99762

Call Sign: KL0DL
Howard W Appel
Nome AK 99762

Call Sign: KL0EF
Warren R Little
Nome AK 99762

Call Sign: KL0FN
Douglas H Johnson
Nome AK 99762

Call Sign: KL0FO
Mark W Kelso
Nome AK 99762

Call Sign: KL0FP
Carl E Emmons
Nome AK 99762

Call Sign: KL0FR
Nathan T Barron
Nome AK 99762

Call Sign: KL0GK
Mary A Carter
Nome AK 99762

Call Sign: KL0HH
Douglas A Doyle
Nome AK 99762

Call Sign: KL0HI
Claudia S Doyle
Nome AK 99762

Call Sign: KL0HJ
Daniel J Stang
Nome AK 99762

Call Sign: KL0HQ
Paul A Thompson
Nome AK 99762

Call Sign: KL0HR
Terrie A F Perkins
Nome AK 99762

Call Sign: KL0HS
Michael G Murphy
Nome AK 99762

Call Sign: KL0ID
Paul L Rauch
Nome AK 99762

Call Sign: KL0IE
Margaret R Gandia
Nome AK 99762

Call Sign: KL0IG
Christine A C Perkins
Nome AK 99762

Call Sign: KL0IH
John G Osborn
Nome AK 99762

Call Sign: KL0II
Vaughn K Munn
Nome AK 99762

Call Sign: KL0IJ
Constance D Madden
Nome AK 99762

Call Sign: KL0IK
N Todd Lovell

Nome AK 99762

Call Sign: KL0IN
Steffen Andersen
Nome AK 99762

Call Sign: KL0JQ
Louis C Stang
Nome AK 99762

Call Sign: KL0JR
Gary A Samuelson
Nome AK 99762

Call Sign: KL0JS
Randy M Oles
Nome AK 99762

Call Sign: KL0JT
Ginny L Emmons
Nome AK 99762

Call Sign: KL0JV
Dennis L Barron
Nome AK 99762

Call Sign: KL0JX
Richard N Wolf
Nome AK 99762

Call Sign: KL0JZ
Mark Hunt
Nome AK 99762

Call Sign: KL0LK
Annette E West
Nome AK 99762

Call Sign: KL0LL
James R Stimpfle
Nome AK 99762

Call Sign: KL0MY
Maggie M Thrasher
Nome AK 99762

Call Sign: KL0MZ
Douglas E Martinson
Nome AK 99762

Call Sign: KL0NK
Kathi A Tweet
Nome AK 99762

Call Sign: KL0OF
Sasha L Tweet
Nome AK 99762

Call Sign: KL0OR
Mackenzie L Oles
Nome AK 99762

Call Sign: KL0OS
Gary M Garner
Nome AK 99762

Call Sign: KL0OT
Bruce C Tungwenuk
Nome AK 99762

Call Sign: KL0OU
Roy C Ashenfelter
Nome AK 99762

Call Sign: KL0OV
Arne M Handeland
Nome AK 99762

Call Sign: KL0OX
Annie H Stang
Nome AK 99762

Call Sign: KL0RC
Charles M Coyle
Nome AK 99762

Call Sign: KL0RD
Lisa M Coyle
Nome AK 99762

Call Sign: KL0TC
Stanley L Morgan
Nome AK 99762

Call Sign: KL0TG
Wilson S Bourdon
Nome AK 99762

Call Sign: KL3NP
Nathan E Perkins
Nome AK 99762

Call Sign: WL7CRU
Frank W Carruthers
Nome AK 99762

Call Sign: WL7CSG
Victor M Hubert

Nome AK 99762

Call Sign: WL7FZ
Martin K Ruud
Nome AK 99762

Call Sign: KL0UK
Michael H Nurse
Nome AK 99762

Call Sign: KL0VI
Thomas S Sparks
Nome AK 99762

Call Sign: KL0VQ
Michael J Warren
Nome AK 99762

Call Sign: KL0VR
Karin M Lacanne
Nome AK 99762

Call Sign: KL0WB
Charles F Lean
Nome AK 99762

Call Sign: KL0WC
Lynette C Schmidt
Nome AK 99762

Call Sign: KL0WR
Michael A Dunham
Nome AK 99762

Call Sign: KL0WT
Victoria I Pasquantonio
Nome AK 99762

Call Sign: KL0YA
Eleanor R Oakes
Nome AK 99762

Call Sign: KL0YB
Eric A Tweet
Nome AK 99762

Call Sign: KL1CB
Charles A Painter
Nome AK 99762

Call Sign: KL1CC
Keith L Andrews
Nome AK 99762

Call Sign: KL1CD
Vicky R Lovell
Nome AK 99762

Call Sign: KL1CE
Jerry A Steiger
Nome AK 99762

Call Sign: KL1CG
Christian T Blount
Nome AK 99762

Call Sign: KL1CV
Roy G Johnston
Nome AK 99762

Call Sign: KL1CW
Benjamin M Lewis
Nome AK 99762

Call Sign: KL1CX
George M Fullwood
Nome AK 99762

Call Sign: KL1CY
Stephen L Willson
Nome AK 99762

Call Sign: KL1GG
Beverly J Hampton
Nome AK 99762

Call Sign: KL1IP
Margaret E Stang
Nome AK 99762

Call Sign: KL1IQ
Robert D Nelson
Nome AK 99762

Call Sign: KL1IR
Derrick J Leedy
Nome AK 99762

Call Sign: KL1ZT
John K Handeland
Nome AK 997620295

Call Sign: KL0PH
Laura L Samuelson
Nome AK 997620300

Call Sign: AG4WR
Robert E Taylor

Nome AK 997620335

Call Sign: KL1YL
Michael J Thomas
Nome AK 997620474

Call Sign: KL0TH
Randy W Pomeranz
Nome AK 997620509

Call Sign: KL1UE
Gabriel L Muktoyuk Sr
Nome AK 997620602

Call Sign: KL1UG
Steven C Eckroate Sr
Nome AK 997620663

Call Sign: KL2MO
Dudley J Homelvig
Nome AK 997620951

Call Sign: AL7X
Ramon F Gandia
Nome AK 997620970

Call Sign: KL0OE
James D West Jr
Nome AK 997620970

Call Sign: KL0HW
Patrick L Hahn
Nome AK 997620982

Call Sign: KL2GZ
Evan E Raber
Nome AK 997621165

Call Sign: KL0QB
Earl Merchant III
Nome AK 997621321

Call Sign: KL0NA
Kimberly S Carter
Nome AK 997621517

Call Sign: KL0LM
Earle J Martinson
Nome AK 997621605

Call Sign: KL2JN
Susan A Steinacher
Nome AK 997621609

Call Sign: KL0QU
Kevin M Glynn
Nome AK 997621847

Call Sign: KL2MN
Shanna M Moeder
Nome AK 997621853

Call Sign: KL0OH
Edna D Ruud
Nome AK 997621963

Call Sign: KL1YS
Carl O Merchant
Nome AK 997622037

Call Sign: KL0QE
Kevin G Walker
Nome AK 997622078

Call Sign: KL0EI
Bruce H Tweet
Box 1126
Nome AK 99762

Call Sign: KL2JP
Jay H Wieler
Box 27
Nome AK 99762

Call Sign: KL2JS
John C Johnson
Box 277
Nome AK 99762

**FCC Amateur Radio Licenses
in North Pole**

Call Sign: WL7CDD
Curtis E Johnson
863B Stol Dr
North Pole AK 99705

Call Sign: KF6YBT
Gary W Hunt
1103 Airline Dr
North Pole AK 99705

Call Sign: NL7SC
Ronald W Bennett
1265 Airline Dr
North Pole AK 99705

Call Sign: WL7ARP

Claud R Magar Jr
1805 Alder Ave
North Pole AK 997055422

Call Sign: KL2LK
Anthony L Zenrick
2995 Amanda Loop
North Pole AK 99705

Call Sign: NL7ZE
John W Fountain
1852 Badger Rd
North Pole AK 99705

Call Sign: NL7MV
Patrick A Weis
2009 Badger Rd
North Pole AK 99705

Call Sign: WL7BLI
Thomas M Carpender
401 Beaver Blvd
North Pole AK 99705

Call Sign: WA5MWI
Jerry B Harwood
357 Blanket Blvd
North Pole AK 99705

Call Sign: W5MWI
Jerry B Harwood
357 Blanket Blvd
North Pole AK 99705

Call Sign: KL0ZE
Casey A Moore
2597 Boulder Ave
North Pole AK 99705

Call Sign: KL7HF
Lorrie M Moore
2597 Boulder Ave
North Pole AK 997055554

Call Sign: KL0RM
Lorrie M Moore
2597 Boulder Ave
North Pole AK 997055554

Call Sign: KL0TX
Jerry D Moore
2597 Boulder Ave
North Pole AK 997055554

Call Sign: KL0AM
Robbie L Parker
1455 Brock Rd
North Pole AK 99705

Call Sign: WL7LE
Albert D Sevy
3156 Brookview Ln
North Pole AK 99705

Call Sign: KL0FW
Ivan B Gallagher
575 Canoro Rd
North Pole AK 99705

Call Sign: KL1SY
Jeff Muehlbauer
1127 Cassier St
North Pole AK 99705

Call Sign: KL1SZ
Debbie C Muehlbauer
1127 Cassier St
North Pole AK 99705

Call Sign: KL7II
James A Strickland
2922 Cecile St
North Pole AK 99705

Call Sign: KC5PNW
Theodore E Howk
1165 Chiming Bells Ct
North Pole AK 997055868

Call Sign: KC5SAB
Becky L Howk
1165 Chiming Bells Ct
North Pole AK 997055868

Call Sign: KL0RT
Catherine A Cory
1761 Christine Dr
North Pole AK 99705

Call Sign: KE4TUU
Simon V Howell
1910 Christine Dr
North Pole AK 99705

Call Sign: KE4ZVE
Lorri A Howell
1910 Christine Dr
North Pole AK 99705

Call Sign: KL3AB
Clayton L Cranor
2876 Cir Loop Rd
North Pole AK 99705

Call Sign: NL7KR
Linda K Wheeler
4830 Cul De Sac Ct
North Pole AK 99705

Call Sign: KL7IKG
Borealis Amateur Radio Club
4830 Culde Sac Ct
North Pole AK 99705

Call Sign: WL7BSA
Stephen B Melton
2485 Dawson Rd
North Pole AK 99705

Call Sign: KL0DC
John G Krieg
3641 Dubia Rd
North Pole AK 99705

Call Sign: KL1JQ
Nathan A Dobberpuhl
3466 Durham Cir
North Pole AK 997056470

Call Sign: KL1PI
Rochelle A Dobberpuhl
3466 Durham Cr
North Pole AK 99705

Call Sign: KL1UV
Joseph E Sipes
3459 Durhamm Cir
North Pole AK 99705

Call Sign: NL7OR
Frank P Bodiker Sr
231 East 7th Ave
North Pole AK 99705

Call Sign: KB6HJB
Christopher M Hampton
2396 Eire Rd
North Pole AK 99705

Call Sign: WL7CQN
Michael J Sampson
1193 England Cir

North Pole AK 99705

Call Sign: KL3DT
Aaron V Vanderweele
654 Feliz St
North Pole AK 99705

Call Sign: WL7CMK
Patrick F Atwood
3361 Fernwood Ave
North Pole AK 99705

Call Sign: WL7CRI
Walter D Lunsford
2515 Gordon Rd
North Pole AK 99705

Call Sign: KL1WY
Amy L Nusunginya
820 Hickman
North Pole AK 99705

Call Sign: KL1LN
Chad Nusunginya Sr
820 Hickman Ave
North Pole AK 99705

Call Sign: AL2D
Chad Nusunginya Sr
820 Hickman Ave
North Pole AK 99705

Call Sign: KL2LJ
Nelowa V Nusunginya
820 Hickman Ave
North Pole AK 99705

Call Sign: KL1JL
Amanda L Williams
3508 Kaltag Dr
North Pole AK 99705

Call Sign: KE4JVW
Gary J Vanderveer
3508 Kaltag Dr
North Pole AK 99705

Call Sign: WL7CHZ
Lynn D Vanderveer
3508 Kaltag Dr
North Pole AK 99705

Call Sign: N5XJE
Johnny L Watts

1521 Katy Jill Ct
North Pole AK 99702

Call Sign: KL1TG
Stacey Jividen
1521 Katy Jill Ct
North Pole AK 99705

Call Sign: KL1CH
Lamkje H Ellsworth
665 Keeling Rd
North Pole AK 99705

Call Sign: KL1AX
Michael E Ellsworth
665 Keeling Rd
North Pole AK 99705

Call Sign: N6TZY
Heidi S Morgan
3800 Kensington Ave
North Pole AK 99705

Call Sign: KL1PJ
Kevin C Tennant
3121 Kris Kringle Dr
North Pole AK 99705

Call Sign: KL1WZ
Aaron M File
3150 Kris Kringle Dr
North Pole AK 99705

Call Sign: WL7FO
Tracy K Saltmarsh
3800 Lakewood Loop
North Pole AK 99705

Call Sign: KL2KI
Anthony T Mustered
1289 Lakloey Dr
North Pole AK 99705

Call Sign: AL7KC
William M Sambuco Jr
771 Landing Rd
North Pole AK 99705

Call Sign: WL7UI
Scott A Traylor
3077 Larkspur Ct
North Pole AK 99705

Call Sign: KL0DQ

William G Tapscott
4288 Lauesen
North Pole AK 99705

Call Sign: KL7RO
Fred E Austin III
3191 Laurance Rd
North Pole AK 99705

Call Sign: KL7VY
Margery S Austin
3191 Laurance Rd
North Pole AK 99705

Call Sign: WL7BZC
John K Brauchle
2583 Lisa Ann
North Pole AK 99705

Call Sign: KL3DZ
Roy A Lashley
2545 Lisa Ann Dr
North Pole AK 99705

Call Sign: KL1UA
Nowell V Grothe
2538 Lisa Ann Dr Apt 1
North Pole AK 99705

Call Sign: KE4LJD
Clinton D Rowlett
3821 Lismore Cir
North Pole AK 99705

Call Sign: KL2NR
Frank J Lovett
3325 Magneto Ct
North Pole AK 99705

Call Sign: KC2KMU
Joshua Tokita
876 Mattie St
North Pole AK 99705

Call Sign: KL7PJ
Patrick J Gargan
2301 Moonlight Dr
North Pole AK 99705

Call Sign: KF6MOU
Patrick J Gargan
2301 Moonlight Dr
North Pole AK 99705

Call Sign: KD7TIE
Katy V Hardman
1334 Morning Glory Loop
North Pole AK 99705

Call Sign: KL0MJ
Gary E Wengert
3678 Navaho Ct
North Pole AK 99705

Call Sign: KL1SV
Jamey Wicklund
2745 Newby Rd
North Pole AK 99705

Call Sign: KL1SX
Gerald L Wicklund
2745 Newby Rd
North Pole AK 997056602

Call Sign: KL1W
Gerald L Wicklund
2745 Newby Rd
North Pole AK 997056602

Call Sign: KL1AJ
Scott A Mcdonnell
2649 Newby Rd 1
North Pole AK 99705

Call Sign: AL1M
Scott A Mcdonnell
2649 Newby Rd 1
North Pole AK 99705

Call Sign: KL3DS
Robert M Leal
2566 Noatak Dr
North Pole AK 99705

Call Sign: KL0QF
Robert J Flavell
1024 Nordale Rd
North Pole AK 99705

Call Sign: WL7TV
Sterling W Muth
912 North Stol Dr
North Pole AK 99705

Call Sign: WL7CPO
Lwell F Meister
2469 Old Richardson Hwy
North Pole AK 99705

Call Sign: KB0AOS
Thomas J Bialkowski
3383 Osage St
North Pole AK 99705

Call Sign: N0HXK
Tampa J Bialkowski
3383 Osage St
North Pole AK 99705

Call Sign: KL1LV
John G Froehlich
3418 Osage St
North Pole AK 99705

Call Sign: WL7PK
David S Castor
1184 Paige Ave
North Pole AK 99705

Call Sign: WL7X
Kenneth D Thompson
1743 Parham Mc Cormick Rd
North Pole AK 99705

Call Sign: KL2DB
Jason C Mellinger
2193 Peede Rd
North Pole AK 99705

Call Sign: WL7CIJ
Sarah J Kuenzli
2025 Persinger
North Pole AK 99705

Call Sign: WL7CIK
Ab J Kuenzli
2025 Persinger
North Pole AK 99705

Call Sign: WL7UC
Robert W Tinsley
2761 Pky 1
North Pole AK 99705

Call Sign: KL1WJ
Rodney B Rutherford
3414 Plack Rd
North Pole AK 99705

Call Sign: WL7UX
Daniel R Rivera Jr
3800 Plack Rd

North Pole AK 997056278

Call Sign: N0FGH
Daniel R Rivera Jr
3800 Plack Rd
North Pole AK 997056278

Call Sign: NL7DW
Helen E Connor
3803 Plack Rd
North Pole AK 99705

Call Sign: WL7TB
Steve R Connor
3803 Plack Rd
North Pole AK 99705

Call Sign: NL7PI
Kathryn A Tuharsky
1710 Pool St
North Pole AK 99705

Call Sign: NL7YC
Charles H Jordan
2400 Poppy Dr
North Pole AK 99705

Call Sign: KL2RD
Michael E Perry
1233 Rangeview Rd
North Pole AK 99705

Call Sign: AL7F
Michael E Perry
1233 Rangeview Rd
North Pole AK 99705

Call Sign: AL7NM
Arthur N Flavell
1452 Redmond Ave
North Pole AK 99705

Call Sign: KL0WF
Carolyn W Flavell
1452 Redmond Ave
North Pole AK 99705

Call Sign: WL7CVS
Nenana Amateur Radio Club
679 Ridge Loop
North Pole AK 99705

Call Sign: WL7TY
Nenana Amateur Radio Club

679 Ridge Loop
North Pole AK 99705

Call Sign: NL7V
Paul R Young Sr
679 Ridge Loop
North Pole AK 99705

Call Sign: WL7LC
Dianne Y Young
679 Ridge Loop
North Pole AK 99705

Call Sign: WL7UG
Steven M Morrow
679 Ridge Loop
North Pole AK 99705

Call Sign: WL7CIU
Edgar L Enochs
3499 Rosehip Dr
North Pole AK 99705

Call Sign: AL7RY
Scott W Leonard
2455 Schutzen St
North Pole AK 99705

Call Sign: KJ5TU
Scott W Leonard
2455 Schutzen St
North Pole AK 99705

Call Sign: NL7M
Charles R Carr
3336 Sharon Rd
North Pole AK 99705

Call Sign: AB3HR
Donald B Mentch
2363 Shelia Way
North Pole AK 99705

Call Sign: KL0OP
Jerrolynne J Ely
1004 Sirlin Dr
North Pole AK 997055714

Call Sign: WL7CW
Charles L Beaudreault
109 South Santa Claus Ln Apt 1
North Pole AK 99705

Call Sign: WL7CIG

Laurie A Muth
912 Stol Dr
North Pole AK 99705

Call Sign: WL7CR
Vicki M Johnson
863B Stol Dr
North Pole AK 99705

Call Sign: WL7CIW
Rodney T Dimon
1915 Tunnels Rd
North Pole AK 99705

Call Sign: WL7CIX
Catherine H Dimon
1915 Tunnels Rd
North Pole AK 99705

Call Sign: WL7UD
James P Van Nort
709 Wanda Dr
North Pole AK 99705

Call Sign: KL3JS
Misty R Provost
507 West 6th Ave
North Pole AK 99705

Call Sign: WL7JV
Lyle E Allison
283 West 7th Ave
North Pole AK 99705

Call Sign: KL2LT
Harry F Cook
3400 White Spruce St
North Pole AK 99705

Call Sign: WB1GZL
Harry F Cook
3400 White Spruce St
North Pole AK 99705

Call Sign: KL1TC
Clarence N Gortmaker
North Pole AK 99705

Call Sign: AC0CW
Raymond J Davis
North Pole AK 99705

Call Sign: WL7MH
Victor M Hubert Mr

North Pole AK 99705

Call Sign: KC9VB
Virgil W Hoppe
North Pole AK 99705

Call Sign: WL7CWY
Hutchison Amateur Radio
Experimenters Society
North Pole AK 99705

Call Sign: KL7EX
Hutchison Amateur Radio
Experimenters Society
North Pole AK 99705

Call Sign: KL3IZ
Alec P Bennett
North Pole AK 99705

Call Sign: KL7VB
Virgil W Hoppe
North Pole AK 99705

Call Sign: K4TQI
James A Goforth
North Pole AK 99705

Call Sign: KL0CE
Homer L Rothenhoffer Jr
North Pole AK 99705

Call Sign: KL0CF
D Marie O Neil
North Pole AK 99705

Call Sign: KL0DE
Duane I Beland
North Pole AK 99705

Call Sign: KL0GU
Suzanna Rothenhoffer
North Pole AK 99705

Call Sign: KL0HK
Terry A Rush
North Pole AK 99705

Call Sign: KL7AJ
Eric P Nichols
North Pole AK 99705

Call Sign: N5LSC
Laurence C Dunn

North Pole AK 99705

Call Sign: N5LXX
Larry W Hoevelman
North Pole AK 99705

Call Sign: NL7HH
Don W Churchill
North Pole AK 99705

Call Sign: NL7QM
Peter L Bean
North Pole AK 99705

Call Sign: NL7ZT
Georganna Churchill
North Pole AK 99705

Call Sign: WL7AI
Joel A Ballek
North Pole AK 99705

Call Sign: WL7BRW
Greg E Brownwood
North Pole AK 99705

Call Sign: WL7CID
Timothy L Ristow
North Pole AK 99705

Call Sign: WL7CIY
Eric M Cosmutto
North Pole AK 99705

Call Sign: WL7CNI
Darrell R Needham
North Pole AK 99705

Call Sign: WL7GF
Shana K Clay
North Pole AK 99705

Call Sign: WL7TC
James A Corbin Sr
North Pole AK 99705

Call Sign: WL7TZ
Preston M Roberts
North Pole AK 99705

Call Sign: NL7DS
Durell Smith
North Pole AK 99705

Call Sign: KL1AH
Christie B Ward
North Pole AK 99705

Call Sign: KL1AZ
John S Slater
North Pole AK 99705

Call Sign: KL1GL
Stan J Grzeskowiak
North Pole AK 99705

Call Sign: KL1GM
Tim D Grzeskowiak
North Pole AK 99705

Call Sign: KC7IUV
Brian J Korycinski
North Pole AK 997050937

Call Sign: WL7BR
Joseph P Belegrin III
North Pole AK 997051174

Call Sign: WL7CTU
Dorothy M Belegrin
North Pole AK 997051174

Call Sign: KL5X
Thomas Hoedjes
North Pole AK 997051274

Call Sign: AL0L
Thomas Hoedjes
North Pole AK 997051274

Call Sign: KL0KX
Carola Hoedjes
North Pole AK 997051274

Call Sign: WL7CVI
Cg Cw Operators Assoc
North Pole AK 997053689

Call Sign: WL7CE
John A Poirrier
North Pole AK 997056539

Call Sign: KL0MF
John H Reid II
North Pole AK 997056803

Call Sign: AL7OH
Patrick M Bookey Sr

North Pole AK 99705

Call Sign: AL7P
James E Dawson
North Pole AK 99705

Call Sign: KL7AC
Andre M Clay
North Pole AK 99705

Call Sign: NL7EK
Richard Shenberger
North Pole AK 99705

Call Sign: NL7QQ
Lewis W Myers
North Pole AK 99705

Call Sign: WL7BQT
Calvin N Hartman
North Pole AK 99705

Call Sign: WL7BRA
James A Rowland Jr
North Pole AK 99705

Call Sign: WL7IR
Kenneth R Brune
North Pole AK 99705

Call Sign: WL7LS
Joanne Sipes
North Pole AK 99705

Call Sign: WL7NK
David E Nichols
North Pole AK 99705

Call Sign: WL7QG
Kent M Herman
North Pole AK 99705

Call Sign: WL7BRX
Arthur A Ford
Box 55305
North Pole AK 99705

Call Sign: KL7RN
Dale B Mc Kiernan
Box 55452
North Pole AK 99705

Call Sign: WL7FN
Joe E Sipes

Po 55776
North Pole AK 99705

Call Sign: KB0UVK
Scott E Lanis
PO Box 56055
North Pole AK 99705

Call Sign: KD5UYL
Kirk F Bricker
PO Box 56709
North Pole AK 99737

Call Sign: AL1U
Kazuhiko Kuroi
North Pole AK 99705

Call Sign: AL3T
Steffen Pelinski
North Pole AK 99705

Call Sign: WL7LP
Russell Ely
1004 Sirlin Dr
North Pole AK 99705

FCC Amateur Radio Licenses in Northway

Call Sign: KL0HB
Rosemarie Maher
Northway AK 99764

Call Sign: KL7ORT
Terry J Maher
Northway AK 99764

FCC Amateur Radio Licenses in Nuiqsut

Call Sign: KL0JG
Herman A Oyagak
Nuiqsut AK 99789

Call Sign: KL0JH
Eli Nukapigak
Nuiqsut AK 99789

FCC Amateur Radio Licenses in Nulato

Call Sign: KL2PT
Henry V Madros
Nulato AK 99765

FCC Amateur Radio Licenses in Old Harbor

Call Sign: WL7BAC
Edward Pestrikoff Sr
Box 93
Old Harbor AK 99643

FCC Amateur Radio Licenses in Ouzinkie

Call Sign: KL1SJ
George A Hartman Sr
Ouzinkie AK 99644

FCC Amateur Radio Licenses in Palmer

Call Sign: KL0OG
Leslie W Brown
690A East Primrose Cir
Palmer AK 99645

Call Sign: KL2OE
Clark S Garlock
505 A North Old Glenn Hwy
Palmer AK 99645

Call Sign: KL7CK
Clark S Garlock
505 A North Old Glenn Hwy
Palmer AK 99645

Call Sign: KL2HZ
David C Eastman Jr
901A North Richmond Ln
Palmer AK 99645

Call Sign: KF6MFK
David C Eastman Jr
901A North Richmond Ln
Palmer AK 99645

Call Sign: KB9TBK
Richard H Pitts
6081 Anjanette Dr
Palmer AK 99645

Call Sign: KB9TNU
James M Pitts
6081 Anjanette Dr
Palmer AK 99645

Call Sign: KE7IVY
Craig A Garrett
8500 Bemis Rd
Palmer AK 99645

Call Sign: KL7COX
Russell W Arnold
108 Campbell Ct
Palmer AK 996456501

Call Sign: KC6FRJ
Brian K Brandon
9551 Chanlyut Cir
Palmer AK 99645

Call Sign: AL3W
John P Lowrey
585 Coville Ln
Palmer AK 99645

Call Sign: WL7CI
John P Lowrey
585 Coville Ln
Palmer AK 99645

Call Sign: AL2Q
John P Lowrey
585 Coville Ln
Palmer AK 99645

Call Sign: WL7XK
Kenneth P Allen
636 East Auklet Ave
Palmer AK 99645

Call Sign: AL0E
Wayne D Mears
9400 East Bernard Ct
Palmer AK 99645

Call Sign: KL0HX
Sharon R Mears
9400 East Bernard Ct
Palmer AK 99645

Call Sign: KL2SN
Evan S Rockwell
20115 East Birch Hill Dr
Palmer AK 99645

Call Sign: KL2IE
Shawn J Connelly
11427 East Cienna Ave
Palmer AK 99645

Call Sign: KL7FLZ
Jack W Jordan
15200 East Clark Wolverine Rd
Palmer AK 99645

Call Sign: AD5PT
Michael P Fannin
7400 East Denelle St
Palmer AK 99645

Call Sign: KL3HK
Donna C Fannin
7400 East Denelle St
Palmer AK 99645

Call Sign: KL3HZ
Robert L Fannin
7400 East Denelle St
Palmer AK 99645

Call Sign: AL1AK
Michael P Fannin
7400 East Denelle St
Palmer AK 99645

Call Sign: KL1UW
Patrick N Warber
424 East Dogwood Ave Apt C6
Palmer AK 99645

Call Sign: KB7BUX
Robert T Ekelmann
5376 East Edgerton Parks Rd
Palmer AK 99645

Call Sign: KL3LZ
William P Raymond Jr
659 East Eklutna
Palmer AK 99645

Call Sign: NL7YE
Merlin W Harlamert Jr
11155 East Equestrian St
Palmer AK 99645

Call Sign: WL7KG
Robert L Stasco
408 East Fireweed Ave
Palmer AK 99645

Call Sign: W2LUV
Jaime P Mencias
432 East Fireweed Ave

Palmer AK 99645

Call Sign: KL7SM
Steven R Mullin
1140 East Hidden Ranch Cir
Palmer AK 99645

Call Sign: AL7FX
Steven J Banse
25836 East Justin Rd
Palmer AK 99645

Call Sign: N7FXX
Claude T Adams Jr
17253 East Lake George Dr
Palmer AK 99645

Call Sign: KL1PX
Matt F Gebhardt
8911 East Lexington St
Palmer AK 99645

Call Sign: KL7TV
Matt F Gebhardt
8911 East Lexington St
Palmer AK 99645

Call Sign: KL3BX
Jon H Devendinger
18153 East Maud Rd
Palmer AK 99645

Call Sign: KL3BF
Ashley M Bennett
17190 East Melin Rd
Palmer AK 99645

Call Sign: KL7AM
Allen P Martin
17975 East Plumley Rd
Palmer AK 99645

Call Sign: W7APM
Allen P Martin
17975 East Plumley Rd
Palmer AK 99645

Call Sign: KL3DV
David D Blehm
8613 East Prospect Hill Cir
Palmer AK 99645

Call Sign: KL3GQ
Bryant T Robbins

20179 East Reich Ct
Palmer AK 99645

Call Sign: KL7CW
Frederick L Dwight
15641 East Rodeo Dr
Palmer AK 99645

Call Sign: KL7GHB
Guy H Greene Jr
11658 East Soapstone Rd
Palmer AK 996453799

Call Sign: WL7QJ
Birdie L Gehring
10225 East Strand Dr
Palmer AK 99645

Call Sign: NL7W
Steven J Gehring
10225 East Strand Dr
Palmer AK 996458975

Call Sign: NL7QP
Robert E Elyard
16448 East Vera Way
Palmer AK 99645

Call Sign: KL0NH
Doris P Hendrickson
13301 East Verda Dr
Palmer AK 99645

Call Sign: KL0XP
Garth M Massay
12120 East Woodstock Dr
Palmer AK 99645

Call Sign: KL3FF
Guner Wilson
1930 Glenn Hwy
Palmer AK 99645

Call Sign: KL7LT
Robert J Burek
531 Jepson Ct
Palmer AK 99645

Call Sign: WB7CIV
Steve M Adair
2125 Kentucky Derby Dr
Palmer AK 996451223

Call Sign: WL7CLS

Roland Erbey
230 Lloyd St
Palmer AK 99645

Call Sign: KL1TO
Finn O Rye
321 Lloyd St
Palmer AK 99645

Call Sign: KL7PG
Harold W Hitchen
537 North Alaska St
Palmer AK 996456035

Call Sign: KL7DJE
Nathan O Smith
450 North Bailey St
Palmer AK 99645

Call Sign: AL1H
Maxwell D Thomas
516 North Bailey St
Palmer AK 99645

Call Sign: KL7XN
Henery R Roesing
2075 North Belmont Ave
Palmer AK 99645

Call Sign: AL7QW
John G Kolehmainen
1251 North Calero Dr
Palmer AK 99645

Call Sign: KL7DY
Richard C Plack
8600 North Dalton Cir
Palmer AK 996451213

Call Sign: KD7KON
William H West
3794 North Diana Ave
Palmer AK 99645

Call Sign: KL8RV
Lawrence R Lewis
4788 North Doty Cir
Palmer AK 99645

Call Sign: KL7IPJ
Milton H Souter Jr
3260 North Dove Ln
Palmer AK 99645

Call Sign: KL3FM
Brian E Winnestaffer
10175 North Glenn Hwy
Palmer AK 99645

Call Sign: KL7DO
David P Oradei
7298 North Highlander Loop
Palmer AK 996450819

Call Sign: KB6DKJ
Lawrence R Lewis
2208 North Kelso Ln
Palmer AK 99645

Call Sign: WV7E
John E Collins
1775 North Kendy Cir
Palmer AK 99645

Call Sign: KL3DK
John G Montgomery
1420 North Landmark Dr
Palmer AK 99645

Call Sign: KL0GH
Aaron H Harrop
175 North Lauren Ln
Palmer AK 99654

Call Sign: KL2EI
David L Stricklan
2291 North Manhattan Way
Palmer AK 99645

Call Sign: NL7OL
Eric S Sanford
4300 North Oakwood Dr
Palmer AK 996459622

Call Sign: NL7PG
Ruth E Sanford
4300 North Oakwood Dr
Palmer AK 996459622

Call Sign: KD6JZJ
James S Goodman
250 North Oscar
Palmer AK 99645

Call Sign: KL3KE
Ronnie I Loughran
240 North Oscar St
Palmer AK 99645

Call Sign: KL3LT
Victoria D Loughran
240 North Oscar St
Palmer AK 99645

Call Sign: KL2GA
Kelsey M Kelley
8901 North Palmer Fishhook Rd
Palmer AK 99645

Call Sign: KL2ED
Judith A Keech
8901 North Palmer Fishhook Rd
Palmer AK 99645

Call Sign: WL7CSE
Gary D Clark
9461 North Pine Dr
Palmer AK 99645

Call Sign: KB7YEC
William D Kreiss
5720 Old Glenn
Palmer AK 99645

Call Sign: WL7CM
Rose L Anderson
3440 Seagull Dr
Palmer AK 99645

Call Sign: AL7PR
Lyle S Anderson
3440 Seagull Dr
Palmer AK 996459106

Call Sign: WL7JU
Vernon A Henricksen
427 South Bailey
Palmer AK 99645

Call Sign: KL3KK
Guinevere Allen
5105 South Bodenburg Spur
Palmer AK 99645

Call Sign: WL7AWJ
Glenn C Hitchen
4100 South Caudill Rd
Palmer AK 996458507

Call Sign: NL7IN
Michael J Curley
1322 South Chugach St

Palmer AK 99645

Call Sign: KL2RY
Clint H Thomas
1150 South Colony Way 3
Palmer AK 99645

Call Sign: KL3DX
George E Sahlstrom
126-1050 South Colony Way
Ste 3
Palmer AK 99645

Call Sign: KL2LN
Ellen W Johnson
1150 South Colony Way Ste 3
228
Palmer AK 99645

Call Sign: KL2MP
James F Johnson
1150 South Colony Way Ste 3
228
Palmer AK 99645

Call Sign: KL3CM
John J Gentry
1150 South Colony Way Ste 3
Pmb 166
Palmer AK 99645

Call Sign: KL2YF
Samuel Castro Espinoza
1150 South Colony Wy Ste 3
Pmb 175
Palmer AK 99645

Call Sign: KL0KQ
M Brian Mc Elroy I
3755 South Cottonwood St A
Palmer AK 99645

Call Sign: AL1X
George S Blackett
1183 South Frontier Dr
Palmer AK 99645

Call Sign: KL1MG
Grainger H Blackett
1183 South Frontier Dr
Palmer AK 99645

Call Sign: KL7VX
George S Blackett

1183 South Frontier Dr
Palmer AK 99645

Call Sign: KI7PZ
George S Blackett
1183 South Frontier Dr
Palmer AK 996451509

Call Sign: KL1QF
Hunter C Blackett
1183 South Frontier Dr
Palmer AK 996459365

Call Sign: KL1QB
Richard A Moore
615 South Gulkana St
Palmer AK 996456677

Call Sign: W9CNS
Robert F Montella
1740 South Heirloom Cir
Palmer AK 99645

Call Sign: KL2QV
Mark W Lehman
905 South Iris Dr
Palmer AK 99645

Call Sign: AL1EN
Mark W Lehman
905 South Iris Dr
Palmer AK 99645

Call Sign: KL2TP
Michael P Kennedy
4900 South Old Glenn Hwy 3
Palmer AK 99645

Call Sign: N9RNL
R James Wardman
1765 South Ragosa Cir
Palmer AK 996456786

Call Sign: NL7RT
Del A Sandvik
3315 South Sandvik Cir
Palmer AK 99645

Call Sign: KL1DH
Stephen J Bliss
465 South Timberwood Cir
Palmer AK 99645

Call Sign: WL7WW

Alan A Barnsley
3955 South Tustin
Palmer AK 99645

Call Sign: KL1RK
Jesse L Jones
1326 South Vermillon Dr
Palmer AK 99645

Call Sign: KL0QQ
Thomas E Stuart
725 South Violet Cir
Palmer AK 996459351

Call Sign: AL7HN
Jack D Easley
1300 South Williwaw Dr
Palmer AK 996457023

Call Sign: KL2OO
Paul W Carter
1435 South Williwaw Dr
Palmer AK 99645

Call Sign: KL1TN
David J Gehring
10225 Strand Dr
Palmer AK 99645

Call Sign: KL1QP
Maynard G Perkins Jr
9331 Tern Dr
Palmer AK 99645

Call Sign: KD7APU
Brian K Player
1205 West Granville
Palmer AK 99645

Call Sign: AL7TC
Terry W Clark
Palmer AK 99645

Call Sign: KL1KB
Jackie S Sanders
Palmer AK 99645

Call Sign: KL1KX
Renee A Havey
Palmer AK 99645

Call Sign: KL1SB
Emanuel Hignutt Jr
Palmer AK 99645

Call Sign: KL1VV
Stephanie L Miner
Palmer AK 99645

Call Sign: AL4A
Kerry D Garrison
Palmer AK 99645

Call Sign: KL1XO
Kevin D Baum
Palmer AK 99645

Call Sign: KL1XS
Rich R Olsen
Palmer AK 99645

Call Sign: KL1ZV
Richard D Bohman
Palmer AK 99645

Call Sign: AL3F
John M Stroup
Palmer AK 99645

Call Sign: KL2SR
John E Richtarcsik
Palmer AK 99645

Call Sign: KL3BL
Sean M Grande
Palmer AK 99645

Call Sign: KL3CA
Michael C Coons
Palmer AK 99645

Call Sign: KL3CJ
James T York
Palmer AK 99645

Call Sign: KL3FW
Jerilyn L Burtch
Palmer AK 99645

Call Sign: AL4C
John W Spencer
Palmer AK 99645

Call Sign: AL7K
Alexander H Hills
Palmer AK 99645

Call Sign: AL7LA

John R Mears
Palmer AK 99645

Call Sign: K4SBI
John E Beasley
Palmer AK 99645

Call Sign: KB3CVM
Renee A Havey
Palmer AK 99645

Call Sign: KL0CS
Christine M Nelson
Palmer AK 99645

Call Sign: KL0DY
Richard C Plack
Palmer AK 99645

Call Sign: KL0FD
Patrick M Kammermeyer
Palmer AK 99645

Call Sign: KL0LH
Joel A Miner
Palmer AK 99645

Call Sign: KL0PI
Theron L Bair
Palmer AK 99645

Call Sign: KL0RZ
Kerry D Garrison
Palmer AK 99645

Call Sign: KL7IKF
Helmut Kostlin
Palmer AK 99645

Call Sign: KL7UPS
Karl A Wurlitzer
Palmer AK 99645

Call Sign: N0WIX
Russel D Miner
Palmer AK 99645

Call Sign: NL7E
Melvin T Jennings
Palmer AK 99645

Call Sign: NL7SK
Timothy H Comfort
Palmer AK 99645

Call Sign: WL7ACI
Thomas W Bowers
Palmer AK 99645

Call Sign: WL7CLX
Daniel L Horvath
Palmer AK 99645

Call Sign: WL7CSP
Kenneth A Neslund
Palmer AK 99645

Call Sign: WL7KQ
Kelly J Sherman-Hall
Palmer AK 99645

Call Sign: WL7YD
Lila D Gill
Palmer AK 99645

Call Sign: KL0WA
Earl Merchant Jr
Palmer AK 99645

Call Sign: KL1FL
Neal E Miner
Palmer AK 99645

Call Sign: KL1HO
Michael C Sanders
Palmer AK 99645

Call Sign: KL1HZ
Melissa S Sanders
Palmer AK 99645

Call Sign: WL7BXM
Julie L Deiser
Palmer AK 996450221

Call Sign: WL7PB
James A Harpster
Palmer AK 996452846

Call Sign: KL7Y
Seth M Gasper Scavette
Palmer AK 996453837

Call Sign: K1YS
Seth M Gasper Scavette
Palmer AK 996453837

Call Sign: KL0QM

Melody M Stokes
Palmer AK 996454580

Call Sign: KL1PZ
Stephanie L Bass
Palmer AK 996454666

Call Sign: AL7EH
William R Redding
Palmer AK 99645

Call Sign: KL7AE
Gary A Miner
Palmer AK 99645

Call Sign: KL7AT
Teriann P Miner
Palmer AK 99645

Call Sign: KL7DTK
John G Sindorf
Palmer AK 99645

Call Sign: KL7IQG
Milner L Maynard
Palmer AK 99645

Call Sign: KL7QOW
Michael V Dillon
Palmer AK 99645

Call Sign: NL7XD
Frederick M Goodwin
Palmer AK 99645

Call Sign: WL7AWK
Charles H Reynolds
Palmer AK 99645

Call Sign: WL7BVA
Sandra A Dillon
Palmer AK 99645

Call Sign: WL7BVM
David I Tokich
Palmer AK 99645

Call Sign: WL7CGW
John L Maketa
Palmer AK 99645

Call Sign: WL7CHD
Robert A Cottrell
Palmer AK 99645

Call Sign: WL7MT
Joyce R Sherman
Palmer AK 99645

Call Sign: WL7GN
Susanne M Goodwin
Box 1265
Palmer AK 99645

Call Sign: WL7FD
Adam D Aposik
Box 2966
Palmer AK 99645

Call Sign: WL7AIL
Peter B Neuburg
Box 318
Palmer AK 99645

Call Sign: KL7DOB
Frank E Knapp
Box 78
Palmer AK 99645

Call Sign: WL7GD
Jay N Dearborn
HC 01 6124
Palmer AK 99645

Call Sign: WL7CLR
Barry C Dearborn
HC 01 Box 6123
Palmer AK 99645

Call Sign: KL7FB
Christopher C Hazlitt
HC 01 Box 6185 A10
Palmer AK 99645

Call Sign: KL7GBI
Christopher G Fowler
HC 02 Box 7304
Palmer AK 996459704

Call Sign: KL7CSR
Lyla U Inman
HC 02 Box 7630
Palmer AK 99645

Call Sign: WL7CLB
Peter E Oliva II
HC 03 Box 8364
Palmer AK 99645

Call Sign: WL7CLC
Daniel C Oliva
HC 03 Box 8364
Palmer AK 99645

Call Sign: WL7CML
Hans D Stricker
HC 03 Box 8364X
Palmer AK 99645

Call Sign: NL7JB
Brian J Anderson
HC 03 Box 8392
Palmer AK 99645

Call Sign: KL7OJ
Larry De Vilbiss
HC 04 Box 9302
Palmer AK 996459504

Call Sign: WL7YB
David H Hendrickson
HC 05 Box 9986
Palmer AK 99645

Call Sign: KL0DH
Patricia S Fisher
HC 2 Box 7691 20
Palmer AK 99645

Call Sign: KB1AWK
Christopher W Kirchhof
HC 2 Box 7726
Palmer AK 99645

Call Sign: KL1NG
Dennis J Dunn
HC 5 Box 6757D
Palmer AK 99645

Call Sign: KL1QA
Marion J Dunn
HC 5 Box 6757D
Palmer AK 996459611

Call Sign: KL1PW
Lori A Restad
HC 5 Box 6761F
Palmer AK 99645

Call Sign: WL7BYF
Kathi S Baldwin
HC01 Box 6105B

Palmer AK 99645

Call Sign: KL1LE
Karen M Eshbaugh
HC04 Box 9023 ~G
Palmer AK 99645

Call Sign: KL1NM
Joe Velasquez
HC04 Box 9162
Palmer AK 99645

Call Sign: WL7BYE
Michael M Pease
HC04 Box 9357
Palmer AK 99645

Call Sign: KF4NBS
Robert K Hewitt
PO Box 3226
Palmer AK 99645

FCC Amateur Radio Licenses in Pedro Bay

Call Sign: KL7DD
Usaral Vets Arc
1.5 Mi West Of Po
Pedro Bay AK 99647

Call Sign: AL7DX
Ronald N Aaberg
Pedro Bay AK 99647

FCC Amateur Radio Licenses in Pelican

Call Sign: WL7BDN
Michael E Ferguson
Box 32 Salmon Way
Pelican AK 99832

Call Sign: WL7BRK
Wally A Warm
Pelican AK 998320078

Call Sign: KL1EY
Eli J Derenoff
Pelican AK 998320764

FCC Amateur Radio Licenses in Petersburg

Call Sign: WA7RRH

David L Hurrelbrink
5644376N/13245604W
Petersburg AK 99833

Call Sign: AL0K
Zachary A Canright
507 Haugen
Petersburg AK 99833

Call Sign: KL7BCS
Harold M Jenny
16 North 12th St Apt 708
Petersburg AK 99833

Call Sign: KL1KH
John K Pickens
Petersburg AK 99833

Call Sign: KL1NP
Mark W Tuccillo
Petersburg AK 99833

Call Sign: KL1PR
Joe N Teter
Petersburg AK 99833

Call Sign: KL1RE
William N Davidson
Petersburg AK 99833

Call Sign: KL1WC
Carl G Forgey
Petersburg AK 99833

Call Sign: KC7DRZ
Jonathan T Kludt Painter
Petersburg AK 99833

Call Sign: KL7FFP
Harvey C Gilliland
Petersburg AK 99833

Call Sign: NL7TQ
Bernard M Engebretson
Petersburg AK 99833

Call Sign: WL7CJA
William C Gilliland
Petersburg AK 99833

Call Sign: KL1DI
Gerald S Laubhan
Petersburg AK 99833

Call Sign: KL7DYS
Edwin O Fuglvog
Petersburg AK 99833

Call Sign: KL7JCP
Michael P Leonard
Petersburg AK 99833

Call Sign: KL7KG
Keith H Gerlach
Petersburg AK 99833

Call Sign: NL7JA
Bruce L Morrison
Petersburg AK 99833

Call Sign: W6SJJ
Edward F Shilling
Petersburg AK 99833

Call Sign: WL7ALG
Mildred H Fuglvog
Petersburg AK 99833

Call Sign: WL7BLC
Myrna E Morrison
Petersburg AK 99833

Call Sign: WL7CFT
Arne J Fuglvog
Petersburg AK 99833

Call Sign: WL7CFZ
Edward E Sarff
Petersburg AK 99833

Call Sign: WL7EW
Sally A Guiney
Petersburg AK 99833

Call Sign: WL7EX
Caroline F Engebretson
Petersburg AK 99833

Call Sign: WL7FV
Roland L Gohmert
Petersburg AK 99833

Call Sign: WL7FW
Anthony P Moran
Petersburg AK 99833

Call Sign: WL7FY
Aaron A Mearig

Petersburg AK 99833

Call Sign: WL7GC
Karen A Lawrence Gohmert
Petersburg AK 99833

Call Sign: WL7LW
Thomas H Laurent Jr
Petersburg AK 99833

Call Sign: WL7EV
Esther V Livingston
Box 1041
Petersburg AK 99833

Call Sign: WL7EU
Miriam M Mearig
Box 990
Petersburg AK 99833

FCC Amateur Radio Licenses in Point Baker

Call Sign: WL7BFO
Terry Kline
Point Baker AK 99927

Call Sign: KL2GT
Joseph R Caughey
General Delivery
Point Baker AK 99927

FCC Amateur Radio Licenses in Point Lay

Call Sign: KL0JD
Julius M Rexford
Point Lay AK 99759

Call Sign: KL0JE
Danny Pikok Jr
Point Lay AK 99759

Call Sign: WL7BVL
James M Dutton
Box 106
Point Lay AK 99759

FCC Amateur Radio Licenses in Port Alexander

Call Sign: WL7BRO
Peter O Kimzey
Port Alexander AK 99836

FCC Amateur Radio Licenses in Port Alsworth

Call Sign: KL1LQ
Lyle D Wilder
3323 Dry Creek
Port Alsworth AK 99653

FCC Amateur Radio Licenses in Port Baker

Call Sign: WL7CDL
Rochelle L Rollenhagen
Port Baker AK 99927

FCC Amateur Radio Licenses in Port Lions

Call Sign: WL7ANL
Janet R Thomsen
Box 155
Port Lions AK 99550

Call Sign: WL7ANM
Stanley J Thomsen
Box 55
Port Lions AK 99550

FCC Amateur Radio Licenses in Prudhoe Bay

Call Sign: KL1QX
Scott M Crafton
C/O Aes 624 Kuparuk Base
Camp Pouch 340014
Prudhoe Bay AK 99734

Call Sign: AC5ZY
Edwin M Higginbotham III
Oliktok Radar Station Pouch 34 0099
Prudhoe Bay AK 99734

Call Sign: KE6CHV
Candida A Szabo
Pouch 340121
Prudhoe Bay AK 99734

FCC Amateur Radio Licenses in Quinhagak

Call Sign: KL2PA

Michael P Michael
Quinhagak AK 99655

FCC Amateur Radio Licenses in Russian Mission

Call Sign: NL7TE
David C Penz
Russian Mission AK 99657

FCC Amateur Radio Licenses in Saint Marys

Call Sign: KL7EPN
Francis X Nawn
Saint Marys AK 99658

FCC Amateur Radio Licenses in Salcha

Call Sign: WL7BZJ
Kim A Whitson
6782 Old Richardson Hwy
Salcha AK 99714

Call Sign: WL7CLL
Roderick L Beaman
5731 Old Valdez Trail
Salcha AK 99714

Call Sign: WL7CLM
Elsie S Beaman
5731 Old Valdez Trail
Salcha AK 99714

Call Sign: KL7DUY
Wilbur P Green
6831 Orchid Dr
Salcha AK 997140101

Call Sign: KL2ON
James M Leflore
6530 Richardson Hwy
Salcha AK 99714

Call Sign: WL7NW
Steven B Gulmon
8830 Richardson Hwy
Salcha AK 99714

Call Sign: KC7UZY
Brent T Greenwood
8841 Richardson Hwy
Salcha AK 99714

Call Sign: KC7WOA
Shiloh E Greenwood
8841 Richardson Hwy
Salcha AK 99714

Call Sign: KL7IOT
John H Betters
6375 River Running Rd
Salcha AK 99714

Call Sign: KL7IWR
Yvonne L Betters
6375 River Running Rd
Salcha AK 99714

Call Sign: NL7AL
Rodger W Rinker
6390 River Running Rd
Salcha AK 99714

Call Sign: NL7AY
William Crandall
Salcha AK 99714

Call Sign: WL7CKZ
James Batcheller
Salcha AK 99714

Call Sign: WL7IIP
Thomas A Griffith
Salcha AK 99714

Call Sign: KL0NL
Richard N Johnson
Salcha AK 997140014

Call Sign: NL7XI
Thomas A Stewart Sr
Box 140094
Salcha AK 99714

Call Sign: NL7ZU
Alma E Widdis
Box 50
Salcha AK 99714

FCC Amateur Radio Licenses in Sand Point

Call Sign: KL3IG
Nathaniel S Julian
9 Red Cove Rd
Sand Point AK 99661

FCC Amateur Radio Licenses in Savoonga

Call Sign: WL7COG
Andrew H Davis
RR 2 Box 184
Savoonga AK 99769

FCC Amateur Radio Licenses in Seldovia

Call Sign: KL7FFH
Charles H Gillick
310 Main
Seldovia AK 99663

Call Sign: WB7FFH
Charles H Gillick
310 Main
Seldovia AK 99663

FCC Amateur Radio Licenses in Seward

Call Sign: KL1VY
Mark P Ernst
27243M Seward Hwy
Seward AK 99664

Call Sign: KL1WN
Jakob M Ernst
27243M Seward Hwy
Seward AK 99664

Call Sign: WL7CFL
Harold T Wright
2513 Birch St
Seward AK 99664

Call Sign: KI8JT
Brian D Sarka
1921 Dora Way
Seward AK 996649998

Call Sign: KL7EIE
Patrick M Marrs
204 Nash Rd
Seward AK 99664

Call Sign: WL7BNP
Matthew E Jones
14550 Rainforest Cir
Seward AK 99664

Call Sign: KL1RJ
Bill Stevens
Seward AK 99664

Call Sign: KE5CVD
Kathleen E Martin
Seward AK 99664

Call Sign: KL1SL
Kathleen E Martin
Seward AK 99664

Call Sign: KL1UD
John C Williamson
Seward AK 99664

Call Sign: KL2RC
David L Christensen
Seward AK 99664

Call Sign: KL3KR
Paul C Rupple
Seward AK 99664

Call Sign: KD5GAL
Kathleen E Martin
Seward AK 99664

Call Sign: KF6RPC
Cindi B Eberle
Seward AK 99664

Call Sign: KF6THP
Darrel E Harpham
Seward AK 99664

Call Sign: KL0GD
Terry E Doane
Seward AK 99664

Call Sign: KL7EU
Marshall G Ronne Jr
Seward AK 99664

Call Sign: KL7FJ
Michael L Brittain
Seward AK 99664

Call Sign: N8EX
Jeffrey S Wolf
Seward AK 99664

Call Sign: NL7DP

Sue A Mc Clure
Seward AK 99664

Call Sign: NP4EC
Paul D Belcher
Seward AK 99664

Call Sign: WL7ARE
Frances S Harmon
Seward AK 99664

Call Sign: WL7ARJ
Linda E Sewall
Seward AK 99664

Call Sign: WL7BKF
Karl H Rosenkranz
Seward AK 99664

Call Sign: WL7BLH
James A Weaverling
Seward AK 99664

Call Sign: WL7CJG
Patrick A Brown
Seward AK 99664

Call Sign: WL7CNG
Jeffrey A Sheehan
Seward AK 99664

Call Sign: KL1AM
Brett J Marquis
Seward AK 99664

Call Sign: KL1EM
Milo R Jaynes
Seward AK 99664

Call Sign: NL7IX
Clinton D Steele Jr
Seward AK 996643106

Call Sign: KL7EW
Richard Goshorn
Seward AK 996643745

Call Sign: WL7GA
Patricia A Phelps
Seward AK 99664

Call Sign: KL7FLO
Brent L Whitmore
Box 1046

Seward AK 996641046

Call Sign: WL7CNF
Austin L Meyer
Box 745
Seward AK 99664

FCC Amateur Radio Licenses in Shageluk

Call Sign: WL7JF
Timothy G Stathis
1111 River-View Rd
Shageluk AK 99665

FCC Amateur Radio Licenses in Sitka

Call Sign: KL7BUS
Walter A Dangel
1324 Cannon Island Dr
Sitka AK 99835

Call Sign: KL7BYA
Margaret L Dangel
1324 Cannon Island Dr
Sitka AK 99835

Call Sign: KL7FFR
Sitka Amateur Radio Club
1324 Cannon Island Dr
Sitka AK 99835

Call Sign: KL7DL
David A Lewis
1326 Cannon Island Dr
Sitka AK 99835

Call Sign: WL7DRA
David R Arnold
2000 Cascade Creek Rd
Sitka AK 99835

Call Sign: WL7CKU
David J Krause
Box 1065 C9 Crescent Harbor
Sitka AK 99835

Call Sign: NL7CB
Arthur J Atkinson
111 Darrin Dr
Sitka AK 99835

Call Sign: KL1SA

Roger J Golub
1502 Davidoff St
Sitka AK 99835

Call Sign: KB0PLS
Roger J Golub
1502 Davidoff St
Sitka AK 99835

Call Sign: KB7KKH
Joe S Hubbard
1104 Edgecumbe Dr
Sitka AK 99835

Call Sign: WD0CZV
David R Stevenson
1613 Halibut Point Rd
Sitka AK 99835

Call Sign: WL7XE
N Parker Jones
1724 Halibut Point Rd
Sitka AK 998359601

Call Sign: KF6AWG
Todd D Dokey
3315 Halibut Point Rd
Sitka AK 99835

Call Sign: KB7DEL
Henry S Louie
1212 Halibut Point Rd - Unit A
Sitka AK 99835

Call Sign: KL2GF
Benjamin F Smith
2039 Halibut Point Rd 15
Sitka AK 99835

Call Sign: KD9TK
Allen A Bell Jr
2002 Halibut Point Rd Apt A
Sitka AK 998350502

Call Sign: WL7CGJ
Jack E Hughes
485 Katlian St
Sitka AK 99835

Call Sign: WL7BKI
Kathleen M Warm
507 Katlian St
Sitka AK 99835

Call Sign: KB6HVZ
Larry A Edgerton
617 Katlian St Unit A-3
Sitka AK 99835

Call Sign: WL7CLE
Patrick S Pennoyer
400 Lake St
Sitka AK 99835

Call Sign: KA0ZXX
Margaret J Andrews
207 Lakeview Dr
Sitka AK 99835

Call Sign: WL7BXK
Joseph W Adams II
6 B Lifesaver Dr
Sitka AK 99835

Call Sign: NL7WX
Frances E G Hallgren
403 Lincoln St
Sitka AK 99835

Call Sign: NL7XW
Leo F Golden
224 Marine St
Sitka AK 99835

Call Sign: NL7GJ
Walter Moy
301 Marine St
Sitka AK 99835

Call Sign: KL7FNH
Lawrence W Downie Sr
503 Marine St
Sitka AK 99835

Call Sign: KK7I
Richard D Smith
616 Monastery St
Sitka AK 99835

Call Sign: WL7CLV
Joshua I Corduan
712 Monastery St
Sitka AK 99835

Call Sign: WL7CMM
Daniel P Corduan
712 Monastery St
Sitka AK 99835

Call Sign: KL7FCV
Melvin H Holmgren
236 Observatory St
Sitka AK 99835

Call Sign: KL1DD
Steven P Johnson
100 Peace Ln
Sitka AK 998359793

Call Sign: WL7CLU
Garth M Kanen
802 Pherson St
Sitka AK 99835

Call Sign: WL7CMN
Evelyn L Kanen
802 Pherson St
Sitka AK 99835

Call Sign: K4MDB
Mark D Branson
825 Pherson St
Sitka AK 99835

Call Sign: KL2UF
Benjamin C Downing
2012 Sawmill Rd
Sitka AK 99835

Call Sign: KL7MS
Gary L Downie Sr
108 A Shuler Dr
Sitka AK 99835

Call Sign: WL7CGE
William F Peters
714 Sirstad St
Sitka AK 99835

Call Sign: KL7ETZ
David A Lewis
309 Wachusetts
Sitka AK 99835

Call Sign: AL7RS
Daniel J Kowell
Sitka AK 99835

Call Sign: KA7OIB
Orval S Weckel III
Sitka AK 99835

Call Sign: KA7OON
Darlene Dehlin
Sitka AK 99835

Call Sign: KB7GEE
Barry W Mc Elhose
Sitka AK 99835

Call Sign: KB8LJT
Lynn E Gras
Sitka AK 99835

Call Sign: KL0BH
Howard T Pendell
Sitka AK 99835

Call Sign: KL0UH
Michael O Rogers
Sitka AK 99835

Call Sign: KL7FBU
Paul G Arvin
Sitka AK 99835

Call Sign: N3NCS
Daniel J Kowell
Sitka AK 99835

Call Sign: KL0XS
Thomas R Calhoun
Sitka AK 99835

Call Sign: K8TVO
John D Mc Millen Jr
Sitka AK 998351393

Call Sign: NL7BY
Michael B Sullivan
Sitka AK 998352396

Call Sign: AL7KX
William L Mc Vey
Sitka AK 99835

Call Sign: KL7BLZ
Fermin Gutierrez
Sitka AK 99835

Call Sign: KL7FSO
Rubye A Rottluff
Sitka AK 99835

Call Sign: KL7SC
Salvatore J Cucchiari

Sitka AK 99835

Call Sign: N7COP
Robert W Cowell
Sitka AK 99835

Call Sign: WL7BXB
Christopher G Grau
Sitka AK 99835

Call Sign: KL1ZM
John W Totten
Box 6009
Sitka AK 99835

Call Sign: WL7BZF
Jan W Payne
General Delivery
Sitka AK 99835

Call Sign: WL7BUY
Rene A Reuben
Rowan Bay
Sitka AK 99835

Call Sign: W1LYD
Brian M Lafont
Box 217 Cor Of 12th & State St
Skagway AK 998400217

Call Sign: N1HUT
Brian M Lafont
Box 217 Cor Of 12th & State St
Skagway AK 998400217

Call Sign: KL7TRB
Todd R Brown
Skagway AK 99840

Call Sign: KL1YM
John G Briner
Skagway AK 99840

Call Sign: KE4MQD
Todd R Brown
Skagway AK 99840

Call Sign: KL7DX
Robert L Rapuzzi
Skagway AK 99840

Call Sign: KL2CF
Daniel J Downing Jr
Box 1036
Skagway AK 99840

Call Sign: KL0PR
Joyce A Logan
100 Happiness Ln
Skwentna AK 99667

Call Sign: KL0PS
John A Logan
100 Happiness Ln
Skwentna AK 99667

Call Sign: NL7BW
Larry C Asplund
Towhead Lake
Skwentna AK 99667

Call Sign: NL7BZ
Beth L Asplund
Towhead Lake
Skwentna AK 99667

Call Sign: WA0PMR
Steven T Schmit
Skwentna AK 99667

Call Sign: KL7EKF
Myles C Yerkes III
Box 36
Skwentna AK 99667

Call Sign: KL1RM
Kent N Aslett
44470-B Sports Lake Rd
Soldotna AK 99669

Call Sign: KL2IP
Stephen F Stringham
39200 Alma Ave
Soldotna AK 99669

Call Sign: KL2IQ
Jacqueline W Stringham
39200 Alma Ave
Soldotna AK 99669

Call Sign: WL7DH
Mark S Pearson
338 Banner Ln
Soldotna AK 99669

Call Sign: WA7B
Max D Carpenter
375 Beluga
Soldotna AK 99669

Call Sign: AL7R
Brent E Burnett
169 Brentwood St
Soldotna AK 99669

Call Sign: WL7PD
Van E Wilson
127 Briarcliff Ct
Soldotna AK 99669

Call Sign: KL7HQK
Matthew W Dammeyer
32800 Brown's Lake Rd
Soldotna AK 99669

Call Sign: KL1NA
Michael Z Dunn
48330 Center Ave
Soldotna AK 99669

Call Sign: WL7XL
D Roger Liebner
207 Corral Ave
Soldotna AK 99669

Call Sign: WL7NR
William R Thomas
36630 Edgington Rd
Soldotna AK 99669

Call Sign: KL7RSG
Ralph S Sterling
355 Fairway Dr
Soldotna AK 996694015

Call Sign: KL2UC
Shawn G Symington
36765 Frazier Rd
Soldotna AK 99669

Call Sign: WA7UTE
John Junkert Jr
48486 Garden Ave

Soldotna AK 99669

Call Sign: AL7KW
Jim S Campbell
48145 Igloo Ave
Soldotna AK 99669

Call Sign: WL7JP
Stanley J Gerlitz
48236 Igloo Ave
Soldotna AK 99669

Call Sign: KL0YK
Mack D Wade
48175 Independence Ave
Soldotna AK 99669

Call Sign: KL1ME
Caleb H Martin
47885 Kaye Way
Soldotna AK 99669

Call Sign: KL1OI
Everett E Martin
47885 Kaye Way
Soldotna AK 99669

Call Sign: AL7KY
William C Johnson
35555 Kenai Spur Hwy
Soldotna AK 99669

Call Sign: WL7IA
Donald K Gill Jr
35555 Kenai Spur Hwy
Soldotna AK 99669

Call Sign: KL3HR
Brayden T Storms
33555 Kenai Spur Hwy 430
Soldotna AK 99669

Call Sign: KL2MB
Daniel J Bevington
35555 Kenai Spur Hwy Pmb
391
Soldotna AK 99669

Call Sign: WL7M
John W Pfeifer
529 Knoll Cir
Soldotna AK 99669

Call Sign: KL2AO

Donald C Merry
37295 Lancashire Ln
Soldotna AK 99669

Call Sign: KL2IO
Martha L Merry
37295 Lancashire Ln
Soldotna AK 99669

Call Sign: NL7BP
Robert P Tachick Jr
37395 Lancashire Ln
Soldotna AK 99669

Call Sign: KL2TQ
Stephen D Mcmaster
49840 Leisure Lake Dr
Soldotna AK 99669

Call Sign: AL7BU
Hans R Amundsen
135 Little Ave
Soldotna AK 99669

Call Sign: KL7GRM
David A Tremper
48257 Magic Dragon Ln
Soldotna AK 99669

Call Sign: WL7CGF
Patricia K Ham
48257 Magic Dragon Ln
Soldotna AK 99669

Call Sign: KL7WK
Robert W Holifield
228 Marydale Dr
Soldotna AK 99669

Call Sign: KL0IB
Larry W Lawrence
167 North Birch Ln 27
Soldotna AK 99669

Call Sign: WL7CSW
Larry R Geordan
167 North Birch St 30
Soldotna AK 99669

Call Sign: KL7AN
George A Van Lone
303 North Fireweed St
Soldotna AK 99669

Call Sign: KL7J
Les N Buchholz
48450 Prairie Ave
Soldotna AK 996699482

Call Sign: NL7CE
Kevin J Austin
35315 Rockwood Rd
Soldotna AK 99669

Call Sign: AL7OT
Hazel C Schofield
35765 Ryan Ln
Soldotna AK 99669

Call Sign: WL7JX
William P Schofield
35765 Ryan Ln
Soldotna AK 99669

Call Sign: W9JMC
James M Cook Sr
33385 Scotch Run Dr
Soldotna AK 99669

Call Sign: WB9VOY
Robert L Patterson
131 Shady Ln C1
Soldotna AK 99669

Call Sign: KL3CV
Tim M Smith
39920 Shishmaref Dr
Soldotna AK 99669

Call Sign: KL3HQ
Gregory J Mangione
48995 Sirocco Dr
Soldotna AK 99669

Call Sign: KC5KIG
Gregory J Mangione
48995 Sirocco Dr
Soldotna AK 99669

Call Sign: KL7OZ
Daniel L Quick
33335 Skyline Dr
Soldotna AK 996699752

Call Sign: WL7CSX
Gary A Eisert
35555 Spur Hwy 350
Soldotna AK 99669

Soldotna AK 99669

Call Sign: KL0SW
Frank W Henrikson
35555 Spur Hwy 445
Soldotna AK 99669

Call Sign: KI6KSZ
Paul H Smith
35555 Spur Hwy Pmb 456
Soldotna AK 99669

Call Sign: KB1CRT
Trevor C Davis
35876 Teresa Way
Soldotna AK 99669

Call Sign: WL7COI
Brenda B Wise
46050 Toros Ct
Soldotna AK 99669

Call Sign: KL0AJ
Robynn K Gille
173 Trumpeter Ave
Soldotna AK 99669

Call Sign: KL7GIC
Barbara J Gille
173 Trumpeter Ave
Soldotna AK 99669

Call Sign: KL7GIC
Robert M Gille
173 Trumpeter Ave
Soldotna AK 99669

Call Sign: KL3IN
Michael L Huckabay
367 West Arlington
Soldotna AK 99669

Call Sign: WA6RBV
Joy M Wilborg
323 West Arlington Ave
Soldotna AK 99669

Call Sign: KL7HHF
James K Pearson
354 West Beluga
Soldotna AK 99669

Call Sign: KL2RT
Donna L Kralick
378 West Beluga

Call Sign: KL7FG
Larry N Halvarson
346 West Beluga Ave
Soldotna AK 99669

Call Sign: NL7OK
Barbara J Halvarson
346 West Beluga Ave
Soldotna AK 99669

Call Sign: WL7WX
Daughn R Carpenter
375 West Beluga Ave
Soldotna AK 99669

Call Sign: KC8KVG
Cassandra J Winslow
35214 West Brook Dr
Soldotna AK 99669

Call Sign: KC8KVH
Richard W Winslow
35214 West Brook Dr
Soldotna AK 99669

Call Sign: KL7BY
Daniel A Hill
330 West Corral Ave
Soldotna AK 99669

Call Sign: KL7IGZ
John L Miller
309 West Rockwell Ave
Soldotna AK 996697312

Call Sign: KL1QZ
Jeshua L Jefferson
29665 Wilson St
Soldotna AK 99669

Call Sign: KL3KN
Andrew I Jefferson
29665 Wilson St
Soldotna AK 99669

Call Sign: KL1NJ
James D Robb
Soldotna AK 99669

Call Sign: KL1PS
Ben L Widman
Soldotna AK 99669

Call Sign: KL1PT
Glynn B Brown
Soldotna AK 99669

Call Sign: KL1XX
Joshua J Rhoten
Soldotna AK 99669

Call Sign: KI4RMY
John Siceloff
Soldotna AK 99669

Call Sign: KL2DU
Alisa Siceloff
Soldotna AK 99669

Call Sign: KL2FW
Patrick T Mccabe
Soldotna AK 99669

Call Sign: KL7BH
Patrick T Mccabe
Soldotna AK 99669

Call Sign: KL2KO
Larry D Davis
Soldotna AK 99669

Call Sign: KL2RS
Shirley A Junkert
Soldotna AK 99669

Call Sign: KL2SAJ
Shirley A Junkert
Soldotna AK 99669

Call Sign: KL2UL
Andrew W Paxson
Soldotna AK 99669

Call Sign: AL7AC
Wilbur A Darsey
Soldotna AK 99669

Call Sign: AL7HA
Jimmy E Thompson
Soldotna AK 99669

Call Sign: AL7PC
John Mc Donald III
Soldotna AK 99669

Call Sign: KA1SJX

Erin Lawton
Soldotna AK 99669

Call Sign: KB7IQJ
Shaya N L Straw
Soldotna AK 99669

Call Sign: KB8VUX
David M Standerfer
Soldotna AK 99669

Call Sign: KE4PO
James B Heinicke
Soldotna AK 99669

Call Sign: KF4PLR
Randal L Brown
Soldotna AK 99669

Call Sign: KL0DM
Donna G Van Lone
Soldotna AK 99669

Call Sign: KL7JDR
Bruce W Mills
Soldotna AK 99669

Call Sign: KL7JFY
Kenneth H Smith
Soldotna AK 99669

Call Sign: KL7RJ
Barbara L Darsey
Soldotna AK 99669

Call Sign: WL7BHH
Melanie J Scritchfield
Soldotna AK 99669

Call Sign: WL7CMH
Ben W Ratky
Soldotna AK 99669

Call Sign: WL7CRM
Ronald D Susser
Soldotna AK 99669

Call Sign: WL7SJ
Terry M Shedd
Soldotna AK 99669

Call Sign: WL7UP
Charles W Bishop
Soldotna AK 99669

Call Sign: WL7XF
Robert M Widman
Soldotna AK 99669

Call Sign: KL7PB
Charles R Armstrong
Soldotna AK 996691837

Call Sign: KL0SX
Judith C Newman Reese
Soldotna AK 996694058

Call Sign: NL7FR
Keith A Hewitt Jr
Soldotna AK 996694338

Call Sign: AL7OJ
Michael A Endsley
Soldotna AK 99669

Call Sign: NL7VC
Matt A Buchholz
Soldotna AK 99669

Call Sign: NL7VW
Jan B Brophy
Soldotna AK 99669

Call Sign: WL7ACJ
Fred T Bowers
Soldotna AK 99669

Call Sign: WL7FB
Marvin D Baker
Soldotna AK 99669

Call Sign: WL7IK
Doug A Anderson
Soldotna AK 99669

Call Sign: WL7JN
Marilynn B Endsley
Soldotna AK 99669

Call Sign: WL7NN
George A Van Lone
Soldotna AK 99669

Call Sign: WL7BLD
Leonard J Olson
Box 1056
Soldotna AK 99669

Call Sign: KL7GMW
Charles E Crapuchettes
Box 109
Soldotna AK 99669

Call Sign: KL7EAN
Alvin L Hershberger
Box 280
Soldotna AK 99669

Call Sign: KL7EJM
Zilla M Maile
Box 467
Soldotna AK 99669

Call Sign: NL7OJ
Russell W Mc Nutt
HC 1 Box 1240
Soldotna AK 99669

Call Sign: WL7JO
Jesse L Evans
HC 3 Box 5550 Echo Lake Rd
Soldotna AK 99669

Call Sign: KL7HPY
Robert D Reece
HC1 Box 1420
Soldotna AK 99669

Call Sign: NE7T
Charles R Armstrong
PO Box 1837
Soldotna AK 996691837

Call Sign: AL7LE
Moose Horn Amateur Radio
Club
Soldotna AK 99669

**FCC Amateur Radio Licenses
in Stebbins**

Call Sign: KB5EON
Barbara G Dunn
Teacherage 4 Plex Apt 2
Stebbins AK 996710049

**FCC Amateur Radio Licenses
in Sterling**

Call Sign: AL7PK
Dennis H Powell
37998 Greatland St

Sterling AK 99672

Call Sign: KL1BL
Larry R Adams
39665 Moose Range Dr
Sterling AK 99672

Call Sign: KL1RG
Jeff L Worner
32697 Sterling Hwy
Sterling AK 99672

Call Sign: KL0VG
Kathy C Cullings
30096 Wildlife Ave
Sterling AK 99672

Call Sign: AL7P
Clifford D Cullings
30096 Wildlife Ave
Sterling AK 99672

Call Sign: KL2DP
Leland R West
Sterling AK 99672

Call Sign: AL7D
David E Arnold
Sterling AK 99672

Call Sign: AL7GG
Charles H Lockner
Sterling AK 99672

Call Sign: AL7PZ
John P Nussbaum
Sterling AK 99672

Call Sign: KE6MVN
Terry A Buffo Sr
Sterling AK 99672

Call Sign: KL7DJO
Rodney W Shamburger
Sterling AK 99672

Call Sign: KL7ZG
Linda K Sorrick
Sterling AK 99672

Call Sign: NL7SM
Donna L West
Sterling AK 99672

Call Sign: WL7BNJ
Arlene G Jasky
Sterling AK 99672

Call Sign: WL7BQM
Michael D West
Sterling AK 99672

Call Sign: WL7BTQ
Robert W Patterson Jr
Sterling AK 99672

Call Sign: WL7COH
Harald Wopperer
Sterling AK 99672

Call Sign: WL7CTL
Raymond D Wall
Sterling AK 99672

Call Sign: WL7XU
Chris D Titus
Sterling AK 99672

Call Sign: KL2JW
Edward G Von Breyman
Sterling AK 996721120

Call Sign: AL7NL
Peter H Graeter
Sterling AK 99672

Call Sign: KL7NN
Harold E Caligan
Sterling AK 99672

Call Sign: WL7ACQ
Leslie G Augustson
Sterling AK 99672

Call Sign: WL7BDK
Eric W Zuber
Sterling AK 99672

Call Sign: WL7CAB
Gary J Titus
Sterling AK 99672

Call Sign: KL7XJ
Dale L Hershberger
Box 616
Sterling AK 99672

Call Sign: WL7NF

Donald M Fanning
PO Box 462
Sterling AK 99672

FCC Amateur Radio Licenses in Sutton

Call Sign: KL3KJ
Danny J Allen
66333 South Keith Rd
Sutton AK 99674

Call Sign: KL3KL
Gary C Wolske
35089 West Glenn Hwy
Sutton AK 99674

Call Sign: KL2PM
Richard D Brenden
31076 West Lee Cir
Sutton AK 99674

Call Sign: KL7ZF
David G Vancleve
Sutton AK 99674

FCC Amateur Radio Licenses in Talkeetna

Call Sign: KB7WAS
Ronald A Quilliam
HC 89 Box 8103
Talkeetna AK 99676

Call Sign: WL7KD
Bruce M Hamler
61 Talkeetna Spur Rd
Talkeetna AK 99676

Call Sign: KF7CBI
Felicia T Toth
Talkeetna AK 99654

Call Sign: KL3FS
Felicia T Toth
Talkeetna AK 99654

Call Sign: KL1XT
Eleanor J Loveroff
Talkeetna AK 99676

Call Sign: AL7RX
Harry A Searles
Talkeetna AK 99676

Call Sign: KL2CJ
Timothy S Morgan
Talkeetna AK 99676

Call Sign: KL2HQ
Sally A Noe
Talkeetna AK 99676

Call Sign: KL2HR
Marion L Cook
Talkeetna AK 99676

Call Sign: KL2JI
Billy J Peck
Talkeetna AK 99676

Call Sign: KL2QY
Tamara D Hamler
Talkeetna AK 99676

Call Sign: KL3CQ
Carol A Lincoln
Talkeetna AK 99676

Call Sign: KC7LGM
Kurt E Jansson
Talkeetna AK 99676

Call Sign: KL7IPN
Edna P Norris
Talkeetna AK 99676

Call Sign: WL7BQC
Stanley S Parrott
Talkeetna AK 99676

Call Sign: NL7XN
Francis L Twigg
Box 266
Talkeetna AK 99676

Call Sign: WL7DJ
Constance M Twigg
Box 266
Talkeetna AK 99676

Call Sign: KL7HRY
Fred B Arvidson
Tract C Katie Lake
Talkeetna AK 99676

FCC Amateur Radio Licenses in Tanana

Call Sign: NL7OZ
Karen L Williams
Tanana AK 99777

Call Sign: NL7BQ
David H Williams
Faa Unit 100
Tanana AK 99777

FCC Amateur Radio Licenses in Teller

Call Sign: KL1EB
Kenneth A Hughes III
Teller AK 99778

Call Sign: NL7RZ
W Patrick Crawford
Teller AK 99778

FCC Amateur Radio Licenses in Tenakee Springs

Call Sign: WB7TYK
Alan K Hunter
642 Tenakee Ave
Tenakee Springs AK 99841

Call Sign: KL2PU
Rudolf T Debus
Tenakee Springs AK 99841

Call Sign: KL7IHR
Darrel L Sonnenberg
General Delivery
Tetlin AK 99779

Call Sign: KD5DWV
Dan B Justice
1212 Shoreline Dr
Thorne Bay AK 99919

Call Sign: KL7FHN
Ralph E Marsh
Thorne Bay AK 99919

Call Sign: KL7FJW
Betty C Marsh
Thorne Bay AK 99919

Call Sign: WL7COV
Angela Schermerhorn
Thorne Bay AK 99950

FCC Amateur Radio Licenses in Tok

Call Sign: NL7AT
Louis Peterson
1 Chisana Airport
Tok AK 99780

Call Sign: KC0ATI
Louis M Kendall
Midnight Sun & Willow Way
Tok AK 99780

Call Sign: KL7JN
James R Cliver Jr
1 Mile Mckenzie Tr
Tok AK 99780

Call Sign: KL1IX
Douglas N Harmon
Tok AK 99780

Call Sign: KL1OR
Noah C Williams
Tok AK 99780

Call Sign: KL1OS
Sky B Williams
Tok AK 99780

Call Sign: KL2EE
Noelle N Helmer
Tok AK 99780

Call Sign: KL2EF
Susann C Helmer
Tok AK 99780

Call Sign: KL2FQ
Barbara A Cliver
Tok AK 99780

Call Sign: KL2TF
Judd L Rutledge
Tok AK 99780

Call Sign: AL7MW
Zachary D Knaebel
Tok AK 99780

Call Sign: AL7NA
Mark E Helmer
Tok AK 99780

Call Sign: KL0FT
Lowell Mcginnis
Tok AK 99780

Call Sign: KL2NH
William J Broome
Tok AK 997800802

Call Sign: KL2NO
William J Broome
Tok AK 997800802

Call Sign: KG4NIY
William J Broome
Tok AK 997800802

Call Sign: WL7BUX
Jeff L Worner
Tok AK 997800807

Call Sign: WL7CLJ
Linda S Mc Ginnis
Tok AK 997800944

Call Sign: KL7AQ
Guy A Matthews
Tok AK 99780

Call Sign: NL7TA
Myron C Severson
Tok AK 99780

Call Sign: NL7WE
Randal K Barnhart
Tok AK 99780

Call Sign: WL7BYR
Ron L Lawson
Tok AK 99780

Call Sign: WL7BYS
James T Donnelly
Box 112
Tok AK 99780

Call Sign: AL7BV
Michael C Buck
Box 444
Tok AK 99780

Call Sign: WL7BYT
Christopher J Button
Box 656

Tok AK 99780

Call Sign: WL7ALH
Robert N Couch
East Chena Way
Tok AK 99780

Call Sign: K1MVV
John P Sanders
HC63 Box 1221
Tok AK 99780

FCC Amateur Radio Licenses in Trapper Creek

Call Sign: N1IFR
Edward R Grube III
Trapper Creek AK 99683

Call Sign: KL2ER
Gary L Baker
Trapper Creek AK 99683

Call Sign: KL2HT
Katrina D Deyoung
Trapper Creek AK 99683

Call Sign: KL2IA
Juliah L Deloach
Trapper Creek AK 99683

Call Sign: AL7IK
Joseph J May
Trapper Creek AK 99683

Call Sign: AL7IO
Sandra May
Trapper Creek AK 99683

Call Sign: AL7MR
Charles L Elliott III
Trapper Creek AK 99683

Call Sign: KL7DS
Patricia A Danly
Trapper Creek AK 99683

Call Sign: KL7IKR
William R Hall
Trapper Creek AK 99683

Call Sign: KL7IRA
Johnny R Moore
Trapper Creek AK 99683

Call Sign: N7HQK
Ray D Congdon
Trapper Creek AK 99683

Call Sign: NL7KU
Catherine M Kershner
Trapper Creek AK 99683

Call Sign: NL7NA
James R Kershner
Trapper Creek AK 99683

Call Sign: NL7YK
Vilma M Anderson
Trapper Creek AK 99683

Call Sign: WL7XB
Robert H Anderson
Trapper Creek AK 99683

Call Sign: KL0VH
Janice R Elliott
Trapper Creek AK 99683

Call Sign: KL0WX
Sylvan H Morgan Jr
Trapper Creek AK 99683

Call Sign: KL1AU
Nancy V Morgan
Trapper Creek AK 99683

Call Sign: KL7BW
George P Menard Jr
Trapper Creek AK 99683

Call Sign: WL7BQR
Zona G Devon
Trapper Creek AK 99683

Call Sign: WL7CCW
Andrew L Kershner
Trapper Creek AK 99683

Call Sign: WL7CEZ
Lynn I Moore
Trapper Creek AK 99683

Call Sign: WL7DK
Davin J Anderson
Trapper Creek AK 99683

Call Sign: WL7CNK

Rodney N Marsh
Box 13037
Trapper Creek AK 99683

Call Sign: KL7NG
Betty I Menard
Box 13168
Trapper Creek AK 99683

Call Sign: WL7KH
Nancy J Richar
Box 13191
Trapper Creek AK 99683

Call Sign: WL7BQJ
William H Devon
Box 13209
Trapper Creek AK 99683

Call Sign: NL7OX
Richard C Leo
Box 13-227
Trapper Creek AK 99683

Call Sign: AL7ME
S Douglas Hartman
Box 13327
Trapper Creek AK 99683

Call Sign: KB7RXZ
Bruce R Johnson
Mp 24
Trapper Creek AK 99683

FCC Amateur Radio Licenses in Tununak

Call Sign: KL7GHK
Henry G Hargreaves
Box 113
Tununak AK 99681

FCC Amateur Radio Licenses in Two Rivers

Call Sign: AL7RN
John M Piehl
15450 Chena Hot Springs Rd
Two Rivers AK 997160133

Call Sign: KL0NN
Marty A Meierotto
Two Rivers AK 99716

Call Sign: KL1WI
Weiyuan Wang
Two Rivers AK 99716

Call Sign: KL2FT
Edwina R Haase
Two Rivers AK 99716

Call Sign: KL2FY
Kim Nielsen
Two Rivers AK 99716

Call Sign: KL7VH
Edwina R Haase
Two Rivers AK 99716

Call Sign: KL0MS
Marty A Meierotto
Two Rivers AK 99716

Call Sign: KL7VI
Kathleen M Swenson
Two Rivers AK 99716

Call Sign: AL7ID
John D Antonuk
Two Rivers AK 997160220

FCC Amateur Radio Licenses in Unalaska

Call Sign: WB1CAC
Scott C Darsney
Unalaska AK 99685

FCC Amateur Radio Licenses in Valdez

Call Sign: WL7CG
Alan J Sorum
5485 Chalet Dr
Valdez AK 99686

Call Sign: NL7R
Denis M Allen
406 Derk Way
Valdez AK 996863610

Call Sign: KL2FF
Scott A Randall
3265 Eagle Ave
Valdez AK 99686

Call Sign: KL1V

Kent D Reinke
3251 Falcon
Valdez AK 99686

Call Sign: WL7BTA
James A Whalen
Box 1569 3430 Falcon
Valdez AK 99686

Call Sign: KG6AWU
John W Pace III
610 Fiddlehead Ln
Valdez AK 99686

Call Sign: KL1NY
Steven C Peterson
810 Pacific Ave
Valdez AK 99686

Call Sign: KL7GQ
Roy H Hansen
614 Pacific St
Valdez AK 99686

Call Sign: KL1BS
Robert G Rountree
404 West Oumalik
Valdez AK 996863690

Call Sign: KL1JU
Larry F Mc Intosh
Valdez AK 99686

Call Sign: WL7CVV
Valdez Amateur Radio
Emergency Service
Valdez AK 99686

Call Sign: KL1NX
Lisa A West
Valdez AK 99686

Call Sign: KL1QU
Brad K Arvidson
Valdez AK 99686

Call Sign: KL1QV
Gail R Colby
Valdez AK 99686

Call Sign: KL1SM
Dennis L Murphy
Valdez AK 99686

Call Sign: KL1ZW
Jeff M Moustafa
Valdez AK 99686

Call Sign: KL1ZX
Barbara A Moustafa
Valdez AK 99686

Call Sign: KL1ZY
Sarah L Rountree
Valdez AK 99686

Call Sign: K7DOE
Barbara A Ensminger
Valdez AK 99686

Call Sign: KL2FE
Christopher J Walker
Valdez AK 99686

Call Sign: AL2Z
Peter A Marsh
Valdez AK 99686

Call Sign: KL2FG
Bryan W Vincent
Valdez AK 99686

Call Sign: KL2GK
Thierry P Otmezguine
Valdez AK 99686

Call Sign: KL2GL
Amelle A Otmezguine
Valdez AK 99686

Call Sign: KL2NA
Gina M Rountree
Valdez AK 99686

Call Sign: AL3Y
Ronald B Lawrence
Valdez AK 99686

Call Sign: KL0PZ
Doreen E Ferguson
Valdez AK 99686

Call Sign: N1LTE
David L Trombley Jr
Valdez AK 99686

Call Sign: NL7CA
L R Lick

Valdez AK 99686

Call Sign: WL7AZP
Lynn M Bellezza
Valdez AK 99686

Call Sign: WL7CHV
Sean V Thurston
Valdez AK 99686

Call Sign: WL7CJO
Ernst K Hug
Valdez AK 99686

Call Sign: KG6DBF
David R Curtis
Valdez AK 99686

Call Sign: KL0YZ
Dona A Kubina
Valdez AK 99686

Call Sign: KL0ZA
Eugene G Kubina Mr
Valdez AK 99686

Call Sign: KL1DR
Lydia R Rountree
Valdez AK 99686

Call Sign: KL1GI
Martha D Peterson
Valdez AK 99686

Call Sign: KL1GJ
Robert G Burks
Valdez AK 99686

Call Sign: KL1GK
Donald W Young
Valdez AK 99686

Call Sign: KL1IN
Miles D France
Valdez AK 99686

Call Sign: KL1IO
James R Gifford
Valdez AK 99686

Call Sign: KL0PJ
James M Mcintyre
Valdez AK 996860824

Call Sign: KL1QS
Nikki Newcome
Valdez AK 996860853

Call Sign: WL7CUQ
Patrick C Johnson
Valdez AK 996863206

Call Sign: WL7BH
Katherine B Walters
Valdez AK 99686

Call Sign: WL7BJR
Larry F Mc Intosh
Valdez AK 99686

Call Sign: KL7IVE
Jimmy P Littrell
Allied Trailer Ct
Valdez AK 99686

Call Sign: WL7LT
Rodney W Mitchell
Box 2142
Valdez AK 99686

Call Sign: NL7BO
Joel A Kopp
Box 2449
Valdez AK 99686

FCC Amateur Radio Licenses in Wainwright

Call Sign: KL0IY
Terry L Tagarook
Wainwright AK 99782

Call Sign: KL0JF
George Patkotak
Wainwright AK 99782

FCC Amateur Radio Licenses in Ward Cove

Call Sign: KL7DJD
Daniel J Downing Jr
Ward Cove AK 99928

Call Sign: WL7N
Mark A Perez
Ward Cove AK 99928

Call Sign: AL7QU

Robert A Olsen
Ward Cove AK 99928

Call Sign: KB7BNG
Angela I Crump
Ward Cove AK 99928

Call Sign: WL7CRO
Brian A Crump
Ward Cove AK 99928

Call Sign: KM7N
Mark A Perez
Ward Cove AK 99928

Call Sign: KL7GOH
Robert M Massenburg
Ward Cove AK 99928

FCC Amateur Radio Licenses in Wasilla

Call Sign: KL1MR
Jeremiah M Stewart
801 Agate Ln
Wasilla AK 99654

Call Sign: KL7GHQ
Merrill D Whybark
1120 Balboa Dr
Wasilla AK 99654

Call Sign: KL7CB
Christine D Betts
3090 Bald Eagle Dr
Wasilla AK 99654

Call Sign: KL7LB
Leonard E Betts
3090 Bald Eagle Dr
Wasilla AK 99654

Call Sign: NL7MY
Christine D Betts
3090 Bald Eagle Dr
Wasilla AK 99654

Call Sign: NL7NF
Leonard E Betts
3090 Bald Eagle Dr
Wasilla AK 99654

Call Sign: KL2TR
Carl A Hereford

3401 Banner Wy
Wasilla AK 99654

Call Sign: KL7JDG
Jack A Diebag
800 Blind Nick Dr 4
Wasilla AK 99687

Call Sign: WL7CVT
Warrior Amateur Radio Club
701 Bogard Rd
Wasilla AK 99654

Call Sign: KL7WHS
Warrior Amateur Radio Club
701 Bogard Rd
Wasilla AK 99654

Call Sign: KL1JD
Daniel A Kelly Jr
581 Briar Dr
Wasilla AK 99654

Call Sign: KL0UO
Jake O Warner
4000 Bull Moose Dr
Wasilla AK 99654

Call Sign: N0UVS
Victor H Rosenberg
825 Bunker Hill St
Wasilla AK 99687

Call Sign: KL7IZ
Gary L King
4161 Carefree Dr
Wasilla AK 99654

Call Sign: NW7F
Alexander S Ludlum
560 Carpenter Cr
Wasilla AK 99654

Call Sign: AL2I
David R Mcgraw
1500 Catalina Dr
Wasilla AK 99654

Call Sign: KL1TX
Kayla C Mcgraw
1500 Catalina Dr
Wasilla AK 99654

Call Sign: KL2DZ

Mary R Lavarnway
1620 Catalina Dr
Wasilla AK 996546021

Call Sign: NL7BJ
Mary R Lavarnway
1620 Catalina Dr
Wasilla AK 996546021

Call Sign: KL7E
John P Lavarnway
1620 Catalina Dr
Wasilla AK 996546021

Call Sign: KL2DZ
Mary R Lavarnway
1620 Catalina Dr
Wasilla AK 996546021

Call Sign: NL7BK
John P Lavarnway
1620 Catalina Dr
Wasilla AK 996546021

Call Sign: KL7NV
John R Cuzzocreo Jr
1701 Catalina Dr
Wasilla AK 99654

Call Sign: KE5CWN
Leonard E Collins
1201 Century Cir   D3
Wasilla AK 99654

Call Sign: KL7CWN
Leonard E Collins Mr
1201 Century Cir   D3
Wasilla AK 99654

Call Sign: KL1DC
Steven G Washam
1001 Colonial Dr
Wasilla AK 99654

Call Sign: KL1FK
Daniel J Waller
1051 Colonial Dr
Wasilla AK 99654

Call Sign: KL2DN
Jonathan A Zylstra
3225 Cottle Loop Apt 10
Wasilla AK 99654

Call Sign: KL7HRX
Lee O Seagondollar
1840 Cottonwood Loop
Wasilla AK 996544269

Call Sign: KL2SB
Tyler B Sutcliffe
2055 Cranberry Ct
Wasilla AK 99654

Call Sign: KL3AI
Shane E Laboucane
951 Creekside Dr 1
Wasilla AK 99654

Call Sign: KL1LD
Michael R Lutes
225 Crestwood
Wasilla AK 99654

Call Sign: KL1QC
Alroy I Robinson
101 Crestwood Ave
Wasilla AK 996545531

Call Sign: KL7GLM
Florence R Hicks
535 Crestwood Ave
Wasilla AK 99654

Call Sign: KL1MT
Eric Z Wieliczkiewicz
2155 Debra Cir
Wasilla AK 99654

Call Sign: KL1XJ
Eldon D Jenkins
1055 Dellwood Apt 2
Wasilla AK 99654

Call Sign: KL1YP
Ivan V Frohne
4461 Doubletree Rd
Wasilla AK 99654

Call Sign: KL3AK
Brandon N Lazar
3710 Dumbarton Ct
Wasilla AK 99654

Call Sign: KL3BK
Robert G Gordon
4815 East Alder Dr
Wasilla AK 99654

Call Sign: KL0OJ
Wesley A Schlueter
5901 East Beaver
Wasilla AK 99654

Call Sign: KL7Q
Roger G Brown
4590 East Birch Dr
Wasilla AK 99654

Call Sign: NL7FP
Roger G Brown
4590 East Birch Dr
Wasilla AK 99654

Call Sign: KC7IKE
Joseph M Johnson
1980 East Black Bear Dr
Wasilla AK 99654

Call Sign: KC7IKF
Lucinda A Johnson
1980 East Black Bear Dr
Wasilla AK 99654

Call Sign: KL2QG
Ian C Pierce
7141 East Breezewood Rd
Wasilla AK 99654

Call Sign: KI6WSJ
Yvonne A Newcomb
851 East Fairview Loop
Wasilla AK 99654

Call Sign: KL2QS
David R Newcomb
851 East Fairview Loop Rd
Wasilla AK 99654

Call Sign: KL3DE
William A Poole
1380 East Fairview Meadows
Ave
Wasilla AK 99654

Call Sign: AL9A
Gary R Senesac
6432 East Finger Lake So View
Dr
Wasilla AK 99654

Call Sign: KC9UM

Gary R Senesac
6432 East Finger Lake So View
Dr
Wasilla AK 99654

Call Sign: KL3AY
Michael V Wilson
5645 East Fir Rd
Wasilla AK 99654

Call Sign: KL2IF
Zachary T Keller
4501 East Foxtrot Ave
Wasilla AK 99654

Call Sign: N7QLM
Eldon L Lacy
103 East Frank Smith Way Apt
107
Wasilla AK 99654

Call Sign: KL1X
Laurence J Howell
5699 East Frost Cir
Wasilla AK 99654

Call Sign: KL7UK
Laurence J Howell
5699 East Frost Cir
Wasilla AK 99654

Call Sign: KL2CK
Robert C Diaz
1000 East Mcadoo Way
Wasilla AK 99654

Call Sign: KL2CI
David J Allison Sr
1830 East Parks Hwy A113
Pmb 236
Wasilla AK 99654

Call Sign: KL3HI
Kristie A Harper
1830 East Parks Hwy A113 694
Wasilla AK 99654

Call Sign: KL3LI
Cindilee M Dupuis
1830 East Parks Hwy A113 Pmb
344
Wasilla AK 99654

Call Sign: KL3LJ

Jean L Dupuis Jr
1830 East Parks Hwy A113 Pmb 344
Wasilla AK 99654

Call Sign: KL2TA
Christine J Lloyd
1830 East Parks Hwy A113 Pmb 350
Wasilla AK 99654

Call Sign: KD6RSU
Jo Ellen D Nuttall
1830 East Parks Hwy A113 Pmb 390
Wasilla AK 99654

Call Sign: KL2YM
Jeffrey Eastgate
1830 East Parks Hwy A113 Pmb 629
Wasilla AK 99654

Call Sign: KL0AL
Martin L Baston
1830 East Parks Hwy A113 Pmb 653
Wasilla AK 99654

Call Sign: WL7CPB
Nicholas M Derenoff
5200 East Pine St
Wasilla AK 99654

Call Sign: KD5NAH
Marshall P Watson II
1560 East Pintail Dr
Wasilla AK 99654

Call Sign: KL7FP
Harold R Hartman
4335 East Serendipity Loop
Wasilla AK 99654

Call Sign: KL3LN
Cody L Musgrave
4355 East Serendipty Loop
Wasilla AK 99654

Call Sign: KL7DT
Dale O Turner
500 East Silver Fox Ln
Wasilla AK 99654

Call Sign: WS6Z
Dale O Turner
500 East Silver Fox Ln
Wasilla AK 99654

Call Sign: WL7BD
Danny R O Barr
760 East Susitna Dr
Wasilla AK 996543922

Call Sign: WL7IN
Gretchen I O Barr
760 East Susitna Dr
Wasilla AK 996543922

Call Sign: NH7UO
Joshua W Buckwalter
3100 East Tamarak Ave
Wasilla AK 99654

Call Sign: KL7NCO
Joshua W Buckwalter
3100 East Tamarak Ave
Wasilla AK 99654

Call Sign: KL7EG
Francine A Strother
5935 East Tex-Al Dr
Wasilla AK 99654

Call Sign: KL7GS
George C Strother
5935 East Tex-Al Dr
Wasilla AK 99654

Call Sign: N7VYQ
Bruce A Flint
1730 East Valley Loop Extension
Wasilla AK 99687

Call Sign: KL1II
Pat R Brooker
3544 East Wanamingo Dr
Wasilla AK 99654

Call Sign: KL1XL
Betty A Carrington
600 Edlund Rd
Wasilla AK 99654

Call Sign: KL1XM
John M Carrington
600 Edlund Rd

Wasilla AK 99654

Call Sign: KL7WE
Peter J La Plante
101 E Frank Smith Way Apt 103
Wasilla AK 99654

Call Sign: KE4WJP
George P De Loach
475 Fallen Leaf Cir
Wasilla AK 996547989

Call Sign: KL1HY
Theodore L Walden
3874 Grey Wolf Dr
Wasilla AK 99654

Call Sign: KL1QE
Kenneth D Horn
2061 Gwene Ln
Wasilla AK 996543115

Call Sign: KL1VJ
Carmel N Sergio
575 Hallea Ln
Wasilla AK 99654

Call Sign: KL2YQ
Deanna B Davis
4411 Hamilton Ct
Wasilla AK 99654

Call Sign: KL1MM
Christi D Gibson
126 Haworth Cir
Wasilla AK 99654

Call Sign: KL0WQ
Harlan N Endreson
1031 Hay St
Wasilla AK 99654

Call Sign: WL7COP
Michele M Olson
1501 Hay St
Wasilla AK 99654

Call Sign: AL2K
Robert B Molloy
1370 Ivy Cir
Wasilla AK 99654

Call Sign: WL7SH

Robert B Molloy
1370 Ivy Cir
Wasilla AK 99654

Call Sign: KL7IOZ
Violet E Redington
Mi 13 1/2 Knik Rd
Wasilla AK 99687

Call Sign: KL1ZA
James E Bond
7790 Leisure Cir
Wasilla AK 99623

Call Sign: KC8MUV
Alma Repeater Club
7790 Leisure Cir
Wasilla ak 99623

Call Sign: NL7SA
Milo M Rousculp
1530 Morrie Cir
Wasilla AK 99654

Call Sign: KL7HJ
James R Bruton
1000 Mulchatna Dr
Wasilla AK 99654

Call Sign: KG6HCY
James R Bruton
1000 Mulchatna Dr
Wasilla AK 99654

Call Sign: AA0NN
John R Wolfe
4023 North Alderney Cir
Wasilla AK 99654

Call Sign: KL7FBI
Shemya Afb Amateur Radio
Club
4023 North Alderney Cir
Wasilla AK 99654

Call Sign: KL2NS
Steven J Katkus
1881 North Ashford Blvd Unit
A
Wasilla AK 996545320

Call Sign: KL1ZL
Brigida L Mertin
3001 North Banner Way

Wasilla AK 99654

Call Sign: KL0YM
Kathy Matlock
3150 North Bear St
Wasilla AK 99654

Call Sign: KL0GG
Jimmy C Matlock
3150 North Bear St
Wasilla AK 996544646

Call Sign: KL7QC
Dwight D Clift
1245 North Brass Ring Dr
Wasilla AK 99654

Call Sign: KL2KC
Richard K Vogt
1351 North Cache Dr
Wasilla AK 99654

Call Sign: KL2OK
Doris W Vogt
1351 North Cache Dr
Wasilla AK 99654

Call Sign: KL0VT
Ronald K Phillips
1901 North Cottonwood Loop
Wasilla AK 99659

Call Sign: KL1FH
Donald E Warble
1129 North Elkhorn Dr
Wasilla AK 996546392

Call Sign: KL7OT
Lydia A Clay
889 North Elkhorn Dr 221
Wasilla AK 99654

Call Sign: WL7CJB
Timothy S Veenstra
4338 North Gunflint Trail
Wasilla AK 99654

Call Sign: KL2CL
Dennis E Brodigan
3302 North Inspiration Loop
Wasilla AK 99654

Call Sign: KL7P
David C Haring

1201 North Jack Nicklaus Dr
Wasilla AK 99654

Call Sign: KL3JE
Jacob A Bettridge
2861 North Jasper Dr
Wasilla AK 99654

Call Sign: AL4K
Keith W Bettridge
2861 North Jasper Dr
Wasilla AK 99654

Call Sign: AL4D
Dani Bettridge
2861 North Jasper Dr
Wasilla AK 99654

Call Sign: KL3AT
Douglas A Stroble
1601 North Kerry Ln
Wasilla AK 99654

Call Sign: KL7YB
Sherman W Bear
2849 North Kyle Cir
Wasilla AK 99654

Call Sign: K3JMI
Sherman W Bear
2849 North Kyle Cir
Wasilla AK 99687

Call Sign: WL7CPR
Anita C Cagle
3060 North Lazy 8 Ct Ste 2
Wasilla AK 99654

Call Sign: KD5EVE
William O Kraus IV
3060 North Lazy Eight Ct 2-363
Wasilla AK 99654

Call Sign: KL2OB
Cindy I Welbourne
3060 North Lazy-Eight Ct 2
Pmb 186
Wasilla AK 99654

Call Sign: KL7EFL
Edmund F Leavitt
1240 North Rainbow Park Dr
Wasilla AK 996549242

Call Sign: KL0SM
Anthony R Morrison
2530 North Rosebud Cir
Wasilla AK 99654

Call Sign: N8JKB
Cynthia A Gastrich
4359 North Rover Ridge Cir
Wasilla AK 996549340

Call Sign: WJ8M
Tom F Gastrich
4359 North Rover Ridge Cir
Wasilla AK 996549340

Call Sign: KL0CW
Clyde H Raymer Jr
2273 North Saddle Horse Dr
Wasilla AK 99645

Call Sign: KL3LV
Gary W Hale
351 North Southway
Wasilla AK 99654

Call Sign: KL7GH
Gary W Hale
351 North Southway
Wasilla AK 99654

Call Sign: WL7KK
David L Summersill
1150 North Star
Wasilla AK 99654

Call Sign: KL7UV
Gilbert L Gavitt
3601 North Travelair Dr
Wasilla AK 99654

Call Sign: KL7HRN
Edward B Luteran
5731 North Wildwood Dr
Wasilla AK 99654

Call Sign: KL3BA
Donald G Gates
2341 North Willow Dr
Wasilla AK 99654

Call Sign: WL4JC
Donald G Gates
2341 North Willow Dr
Wasilla AK 99654

Call Sign: KL2OP
James J Nagl
1100 Northstar Cir
Wasilla AK 99654

Call Sign: NL7WT
Marna A Martin
2150 Patsy St
Wasilla AK 99654

Call Sign: WL7BAT
Ralph R Wesser Jr
521 Pioneer Dr
Wasilla AK 99654

Call Sign: WL7BAU
Wendy A Wesser
521 Pioneer Dr
Wasilla AK 99654

Call Sign: KL0FZ
Rodney L Reese
1655 Pioneer Peak
Wasilla AK 99654

Call Sign: AL7F
Richard E Lilly
1308 Pioneer Peak Dr
Wasilla AK 99654

Call Sign: KL1IL
Ray A Hollenbeck
1457 Pioneer Peak Dr
Wasilla AK 99654

Call Sign: WL7SP
Daniel S Cloud
2800 Quartz Cir
Wasilla AK 99654

Call Sign: KL3EA
Oliver Straten
1400 Regine Ave
Wasilla AK 99654

Call Sign: KL3EB
Frank Sihler
1400 Regine Ave
Wasilla AK 99654

Call Sign: N0GDR
Frances A Widner
3830 Ruth Dr

Wasilla AK 99654

Call Sign: N0GDU
Craig E Widner
3830 Ruth Dr
Wasilla AK 99654

Call Sign: N0GLI
Ronda J Widner
3830 Ruth Dr
Wasilla AK 99654

Call Sign: N0GDT
S Gene Widner
3830 Ruth Dr
Wasilla AK 996547537

Call Sign: KL1QD
Jeff B Schmidt
550 Sarahs Way
Wasilla AK 99654

Call Sign: KL2AD
Jeffrey V Collins
1050 Serrano Dr
Wasilla AK 99654

Call Sign: KL7CEV
William F Dewey
6151 Shalestone Loop
Wasilla AK 99629

Call Sign: KL2MF
Edward D Van Krevelen
2969 South Aimees Cir
Wasilla AK 99654

Call Sign: KE4DGR
Bernie F Jarriel Jr
2813 South Avalon Cir Unit 1
Wasilla AK 99654

Call Sign: KL1BR
Glenn A Hansen
3075 South Caskill Cir
Wasilla AK 99654

Call Sign: KL3AO
Eric J Reeves
890 South Century Dr
Wasilla AK 99654

Call Sign: KL2OR
Jennifer M Watson

2865 South Donovan Dr
Wasilla AK 99654

Call Sign: KL3IX
Christopher P Nugent
4051 South Eagle Bay Dr
Wasilla AK 99623

Call Sign: KL7BK
Michael A Romanello
8237 South Foxworth Dr
Wasilla AK 99654

Call Sign: WL7CWI
Alaska D-Star Group
8237 South Foxworth Dr
Wasilla AK 99654

Call Sign: KL2GN
Timothy O Dey
375 South Jerome Dr
Wasilla AK 99654

Call Sign: KL7TZ
Marien A Rutigliano
8265 South Knik Goose Bat Rd
Wasilla AK 99623

Call Sign: KL7KZ
Alaska Aprs Group
8265 South Knik Goose Bay Rd
Wasilla AK 99623

Call Sign: NL7TZ
Thomas J Rutigliano
8265 South Knik Goose Bay Rd
Wasilla AK 99623

Call Sign: KL2VW
Matthew C Swalling
7969 South Lahti Cir
Wasilla AK 99654

Call Sign: KL1XQ
Timothy W Flannery
1839 South Lodge Dr
Wasilla AK 99654

Call Sign: KL1XR
Lori D Flannery
1839 South Lodge Dr
Wasilla AK 99654

Call Sign: KL1YR

Ronald E Godden
660 South Maney Dr
Wasilla AK 99654

Call Sign: KL2AE
E Ellen Godden
660 South Maney Dr
Wasilla AK 99654

Call Sign: AL2V
Ronald E Godden
660 South Maney Dr
Wasilla AK 99654

Call Sign: AJ4ZI
William J Taccarino
5101 South Outrigger Dr
Wasilla AK 996874697

Call Sign: WL7COD
Adam R Hanshew
2960 South Rapid Creek St
Wasilla AK 99654

Call Sign: KL7FLR
Paul E Fillmore Jr
660 South Rosemary Place
Wasilla AK 99654

Call Sign: KL3AW
Dustin G Tolsrup
4935 South Sailors Loop
Wasilla AK 99654

Call Sign: KL0WW
Teresa M Nunes
991 South Vine
Wasilla AK 99654

Call Sign: KL7AP
Young Ladies Radio League Of
Alaska
991 South Vine Rd
Wasilla AK 99654

Call Sign: KL1VI
Gabrielle J Frank
911 Susitna Dr
Wasilla AK 99654

Call Sign: WL7CGD
Barry W Paige
2029 Sweetie Pie
Wasilla AK 99654

Call Sign: KL7ILA
George M Eppler
3401 Tamarak Ave
Wasilla AK 99654

Call Sign: KL7IRE
Rosana L Eppler
3401 Tamarak Ave
Wasilla AK 99654

Call Sign: AL7HP
Richard A Gallear
3281 Tungsten Dr
Wasilla AK 99654

Call Sign: AL7QX
Thomas S Teallow
3730 Valley View
Wasilla AK 996874064

Call Sign: WL7BXF
John D Ward
2450 Wards Rd
Wasilla AK 99687

Call Sign: KL7UT
Ray D Congdon
3641 West Carl Dr
Wasilla AK 99654

Call Sign: KC4ZUQ
Norman O Thompson Jr
1885 West Church Ridge Dr
Wasilla AK 99654

Call Sign: KL7GLH
Doris A Hagedorn
535 West Crestwood Ave
Wasilla AK 99654

Call Sign: KL2VJ
Bryen K Bartgis
2884 West Discovery Loop
Wasilla AK 99654

Call Sign: KL7JHY
John C Morrone
9290 West Easy St
Wasilla AK 996549206

Call Sign: KL1AE
Scott A Stewart
5251 West Greensward Dr

Wasilla AK 99654

Call Sign: KL7TB
Thomas F Baird
14804 West Heath Dr
Wasilla AK 99654

Call Sign: NL7VZ
Donald P Hepler
10105 West Herkimer Dr
Wasilla AK 99654

Call Sign: KL3KA
Linda S Mcdougall
2860 West Lee Trevino Av
Wasilla AK 99623

Call Sign: WA0NJZ
Donald R Helling
4484 West Museum Dr
Wasilla AK 99654

Call Sign: KL3DB
Patrick Brown
693 West Nelson Ave
Wasilla AK 99654

Call Sign: KL1WW
William R Borden
643 West Nelson Ave - 201
Wasilla AK 99654

Call Sign: KL2TD
David E Taylor
7362 West Parks Hwy 384
Wasilla AK 99654

Call Sign: KL1MS
George D Morse
7362 West Parks Hwy 189
Wasilla AK 99654

Call Sign: KL7HK
Terry A Homan
7362 West Parks Hwy 230
Wasilla AK 996549132

Call Sign: WL7VM
Steven J Cooper
7362 West Parks Hwy 240
Wasilla AK 99654

Call Sign: WL7VA
Gene F Birky

7362 West Parks Hwy 400
Wasilla AK 99654

Call Sign: KL3AA
Dustin J Pianalto
7362 West Parks Hwy 731
Wasilla AK 99654

Call Sign: KL2MG
Wanda J Jennings
7362 West Parks Hwy 781
Wasilla AK 99654

Call Sign: KL3II
Matthew T Schumacher
7362 West Parks Hwy Box 526
Wasilla AK 99654

Call Sign: KL0WN
Jay I Jennings
7362 West Parks Hwy Pmb 781
Wasilla AK 99654

Call Sign: KL7JGU
Jay I Jennings
7362 West Parks Hwy Pmb 781
Wasilla AK 99654

Call Sign: KL7DUA
James Matuszewski
4100 West Peterson Bay Ct
Wasilla AK 99654

Call Sign: W0PPJ
James Matuszewski
4100 West Peterson Bay Ct
Wasilla AK 99654

Call Sign: KL3HX
Gregory S Box
401 West Ponderosa Loop
Wasilla AK 99654

Call Sign: AB7XO
Shawna E Ellisor
5069 West Reliance Rd
Wasilla AK 99654

Call Sign: KL1TP
Zabrina M Russell
580 West Scheelite
Wasilla AK 99684

Call Sign: N9XPN

Kerry M Hagerty
7877 West Tia Terrace Dr
Wasilla AK 99687

Call Sign: KC5DJA
Leonard S Simons Jr
4385 West Trisa Way
Wasilla AK 99623

Call Sign: KB7FXJ
Arthur C Peterson
668 West Winter Ave
Wasilla AK 99654

Call Sign: KB7FXK
Joyce L Peterson
668 West Winter Ave
Wasilla AK 99654

Call Sign: KL2BS
Marlene Cameron
567 Westcove Dr
Wasilla AK 99654

Call Sign: KL2CA
James N Lewis
567 Westcove Dr
Wasilla AK 99654

Call Sign: KL7RU
Marlene Lewis
567 Westcove Dr
Wasilla AK 99654

Call Sign: KL7TU
James N Lewis
567 Westcove Dr
Wasilla AK 99654

Call Sign: KL0GE
Ralph L Van Allen
2400 Whispering Woods Dr
Wasilla AK 99654

Call Sign: KL2OD
Maurice D Hendrickson
3950 Wickersham Way
Wasilla AK 99654

Call Sign: KL7OD
Maurice D Hendrickson
3950 Wickersham Way
Wasilla AK 99654

Call Sign: KL5A
Chris F Brosh
4400 Wickersham Way
Wasilla AK 99654

Call Sign: WL7PV
Chris F Brosh
4400 Wickersham Way
Wasilla AK 99654

Call Sign: KB8VYJ
Gregg L Browngoetz
1135 Winter Ave
Wasilla AK 99654

Call Sign: KL1WH
Robert A Morgan
Wasilla AK 99629

Call Sign: KL7FZ
Stephen E Tolley
Wasilla AK 99629

Call Sign: AL7NX
Harvel H Young
Wasilla AK 99645

Call Sign: KL1IZ
Chris C Schmidt
Wasilla AK 99687

Call Sign: KL1JV
William Wh Hobart J
Wasilla AK 99687

Call Sign: KL1KJ
Robert E Birnel
Wasilla AK 99687

Call Sign: KL1LB
Rod Ewing Jr
Wasilla AK 99687

Call Sign: KL1MH
Trevor W Thomas
Wasilla AK 99687

Call Sign: KL1MI
William C Casler
Wasilla AK 99687

Call Sign: KL7MSC
Matsu College Amateur Radio
Club

Wasilla AK 99687

Call Sign: KB1KYH
John Grube
Wasilla AK 99687

Call Sign: KL1RN
Tim J Slauson
Wasilla AK 99687

Call Sign: KL7JV
William J Hobart
Wasilla AK 99687

Call Sign: AL7RW
Kendell D Meek
Wasilla AK 99687

Call Sign: KL1VH
Tucker W Minnick
Wasilla AK 99687

Call Sign: KL1VQ
Robert I Lewellen
Wasilla AK 99687

Call Sign: KL1WK
Brendon J Bruns
Wasilla AK 99687

Call Sign: KL1ZK
R'Nita L Rogers
Wasilla AK 99687

Call Sign: KL7WOW
R'Nita L Rogers
Wasilla AK 99687

Call Sign: KD7SIX
Heidiann E Gaffney
Wasilla AK 99687

Call Sign: KL7SIX
Ronald G Gaffney
Wasilla AK 99687

Call Sign: KL2BZ
Kathleen M Kenville
Wasilla AK 99687

Call Sign: KL2CG
Margaret J Meek
Wasilla AK 99687

Call Sign: KL2CH
Edward E Peck
Wasilla AK 99687

Call Sign: WL7Y
Kendell D Meek
Wasilla AK 99687

Call Sign: KL2FA
Carol G Bush
Wasilla AK 99687

Call Sign: KL2HF
Kenneth L Hudson
Wasilla AK 99687

Call Sign: KL2IZ
Randy Nabb
Wasilla AK 99687

Call Sign: KL2KG
Edward R Grube III
Wasilla AK 99687

Call Sign: KL2NF
William L Miller
Wasilla AK 99687

Call Sign: KL2NK
Tena C Lewellen
Wasilla AK 99687

Call Sign: KL2QF
Kelsey R Trimmer
Wasilla AK 99687

Call Sign: KL7KRT
Kelsey R Trimmer
Wasilla AK 99687

Call Sign: KL2QQ
Kenneth K Dabney
Wasilla AK 99687

Call Sign: K4DRC
James F Hruby
Wasilla AK 99687

Call Sign: KL2SV
Edward O Gurtler Jr
Wasilla AK 99687

Call Sign: KL2UI
Gregory A Jetter Jr

Wasilla AK 99687

Call Sign: KL7KKD
Kenneth K Dabney
Wasilla AK 99687

Call Sign: KL3AL
Conrad L Mccloakey
Wasilla AK 99687

Call Sign: KL3AQ
Daniel L Schwartz
Wasilla AK 99687

Call Sign: KL3DA
Travis J Rider
Wasilla AK 99687

Call Sign: KL3DQ
Aurora L Rogers
Wasilla AK 99687

Call Sign: KL3EO
John C James
Wasilla AK 99687

Call Sign: KL3IT
Takeshi J Morgan
Wasilla AK 99687

Call Sign: KL3JT
Patrick W Mckibbon
Wasilla AK 99687

Call Sign: KL3LC
Matthew L Underbakke
Wasilla AK 99687

Call Sign: AL7QV
John W Shrader
Wasilla AK 99687

Call Sign: KC5YIB
Joshua D Morris
Wasilla AK 99687

Call Sign: KD6XR
Ronald L Viets
Wasilla AK 99687

Call Sign: KE6IPM
Thomas M Gillett
Wasilla AK 99687

Call Sign: KE7EG
Kendell D Meek
Wasilla AK 99687

Call Sign: KL0CO
Jerry L Hudspeth
Wasilla AK 99687

Call Sign: KL0FE
Andrew J Bunker
Wasilla AK 99687

Call Sign: KL0GF
Charles E Spencer
Wasilla AK 99687

Call Sign: KL0HY
Jessica A Reilly
Wasilla AK 99687

Call Sign: KL0KU
Randol C Bruns
Wasilla AK 99687

Call Sign: KL0NB
Dolores L Waffen
Wasilla AK 99687

Call Sign: KL7HIW
Gilbert L Brewington
Wasilla AK 99687

Call Sign: KL7JFT
Donald E Bush Jr
Wasilla AK 99687

Call Sign: KL7JFU
Matanuska Amateur Radio Assn
Wasilla AK 99687

Call Sign: NL7MZ
Katrina L Reyes
Wasilla AK 99687

Call Sign: NL7PZ
Martin J Nance
Wasilla AK 99687

Call Sign: NL7QB
Jo L Simmons
Wasilla AK 99687

Call Sign: W7SOV
Peter J La Plante

Wasilla AK 99687

Call Sign: WA5ZKN
Rickey D Simmons
Wasilla AK 99687

Call Sign: WL7AIY
Gary J Kuehn
Wasilla AK 99687

Call Sign: WL7CNW
Matsu College Amateur Radio
Club
Wasilla AK 99687

Call Sign: WL7CPM
Greg T Beach
Wasilla AK 99687

Call Sign: WL7CRP
Fred S Greene
Wasilla AK 99687

Call Sign: WL7CSF
Rob A Apel
Wasilla AK 99687

Call Sign: WL7FG
Kathy L Greene
Wasilla AK 99687

Call Sign: WL7RC
Gregory J Pepperd
Wasilla AK 99687

Call Sign: KL0VS
Mark H Jenks
Wasilla AK 99687

Call Sign: KL0ZT
Christine Lloyd
Wasilla AK 99687

Call Sign: KL1CZ
Robert M Jones
Wasilla AK 99687

Call Sign: KL1FF
Randall W Westbrook
Wasilla AK 99687

Call Sign: KL1HJ
Thomas S Westall
Wasilla AK 99687

Call Sign: KL1HK
James D Nehl
Wasilla AK 99687

Call Sign: KE7VZ
Harry A Searles
Wasilla AK 99687

Call Sign: KL1IH
John D Norris
Wasilla AK 99687

Call Sign: KL1IJ
John T Phillips
Wasilla AK 99687

Call Sign: KL0NS
Terry C Boyle
Wasilla AK 996870311

Call Sign: KL2QE
Glenn S Lowrey
Wasilla AK 996870629

Call Sign: KL3KT
Eric T Olson
Wasilla AK 996870837

Call Sign: KI0HM
Gregory J Larson
Wasilla AK 996871022

Call Sign: KL0SP
Paul B Shawler
Wasilla AK 996871172

Call Sign: KL7BT
Arnold C Perry
Wasilla AK 996871643

Call Sign: KL2QD
James F Hruby
Wasilla AK 996871662

Call Sign: KL2QT
Carolyn M Hruby
Wasilla AK 996871662

Call Sign: WL7CWW
Paradise Radio Club
Wasilla AK 996871662

Call Sign: KL7PRC

Paradise Radio Club
Wasilla AK 996871662

Call Sign: KB7WWU
Dale C Isakson
Wasilla AK 996871944

Call Sign: WL7BZ
Kevin S Early
Wasilla AK 996872185

Call Sign: KL0TS
Douglas W Duncan
Wasilla AK 996873812

Call Sign: KL7GO
Gretchen I O Barr
Wasilla AK 996873981

Call Sign: KL7DR
Danny R O Barr
Wasilla AK 996873981

Call Sign: KL2YN
Darrell M Moseley
Wasilla AK 996874006

Call Sign: WA7MDS
Darrell M Moseley
Wasilla AK 996874006

Call Sign: KL2CM
Sharon H Groomer
Wasilla AK 996874045

Call Sign: KL7HHO
Wayne O Groomer
Wasilla AK 996874045

Call Sign: NL7PR
Aryn L Hegg
Wasilla AK 996874391

Call Sign: NL7PS
Peter M Hegg
Wasilla AK 996874391

Call Sign: KL7KH
James E Tozer
Wasilla AK 996874442

Call Sign: KL3DN
Steve R Campbell
Wasilla AK 996874493

Call Sign: NL7BD
Timothy J Baughman
Wasilla AK 996874593

Call Sign: KL1MU
Gabriel W Sharrow
Wasilla AK 996874596

Call Sign: KL2YO
Jonathan A Moseley
Wasilla AK 996874606

Call Sign: KL7IE
John J Rogers
Wasilla AK 996876269

Call Sign: KL7VE
Ken L Slauson
Wasilla AK 996877193

Call Sign: KL1RP
Patrick L Slauson
Wasilla AK 996877193

Call Sign: KL7VF
Denise Slauson
Wasilla AK 996877193

Call Sign: WB7SFO
Ken L Slauson
Wasilla AK 996877193

Call Sign: KL1OB
Frank R Keirn
Wasilla AK 996877945

Call Sign: AL7EE
Laurence B Craig Jr
Wasilla AK 99687

Call Sign: AL7MV
James Godwin Sr
Wasilla AK 99687

Call Sign: KB5LNU
Roy D Thorp
Wasilla AK 99687

Call Sign: KL7AF
Tony P Smaker Jr
Wasilla AK 99687

Call Sign: KL7AVS

Merritt W Tegeler
Wasilla AK 99687

Call Sign: KL7EKI
Logan G Groomer
Wasilla AK 99687

Call Sign: KL7MD
D Jasper Heath
Wasilla AK 99687

Call Sign: NL7CW
Edward D Fitzgibbon
Wasilla AK 99687

Call Sign: NL7WR
Melody D Cooper
Wasilla AK 99687

Call Sign: NL7WY
Brett A Cooper
Wasilla AK 99687

Call Sign: WL7BU
Glenn W Stinson
Wasilla AK 99687

Call Sign: WL7KF
Diane L Forster
Wasilla AK 99687

Call Sign: AL7OC
Pierre A Loncle
Wasilla AK 996870742

Call Sign: KL7DV
George C Strother
Wasilla AK 996871870

Call Sign: KL7ERV
Robert E Christensen
Box 871075
Wasilla AK 99687

Call Sign: WL7CFW
Lorraine T Perry
Box 871643
Wasilla AK 99687

Call Sign: KL7Y
Daniel K Robbins
Box 873271
Wasilla AK 99687

Call Sign: WL7CFX
Walter L Harris
Box 873395
Wasilla AK 99687

Call Sign: KL7KY
Kevin G Forster
Box 877326
Wasilla AK 99687

Call Sign: NL7Z
Kevin G Forster
Box 877326
Wasilla AK 99687

Call Sign: NL7ZO
Peter Elstub
Box 877628
Wasilla AK 99687

Call Sign: KL1CO
Marien A Rutigliano
HC 30 Box 5388
Wasilla AK 99654

Call Sign: KL0LC
Lisa M Phillips
HC 31 Box 5132
Wasilla AK 99654

Call Sign: WL7RD
Wayne Di Sarro
HC 31 Box 5215G
Wasilla AK 99654

Call Sign: WL7BE
Robert R Gabel
HC 31 Box 5247 A8
Wasilla AK 99654

Call Sign: KL2FX
Daniel C Green
HC 31 Box 5263 B
Wasilla AK 99654

Call Sign: AL7MS
Margaret E Brockman
HC 32 Box 3123
Wasilla AK 99687

Call Sign: KL0PT
Russel J Megargle
HC 32 Box 3131
Wasilla AK 996549734

Call Sign: NL7HD
Patrick W Martin
HC 32 Box 6517
Wasilla AK 99645

Call Sign: NL7HE
Kathy J Martin
HC 32 Box 6517
Wasilla AK 99654

Call Sign: KD7PXM
Kenneth W Fisher
HC 32 Box 6551S
Wasilla AK 996549718

Call Sign: WL7MB
John B Pinckley
HC 33 2941D
Wasilla AK 99687

Call Sign: WL7BTU
Douglas C Sanderlin
HC 33 Box 2905A
Wasilla AK 99687

Call Sign: WL7BTX
Diane L Sanderlin
HC 33 Box 2905A
Wasilla AK 99687

Call Sign: WL7BWJ
Carol A Hepler
HC 34 Box 2195
Wasilla AK 99654

Call Sign: WL7BWV
David R Hepler
HC 34 Box 2195
Wasilla AK 99654

Call Sign: WL7CVY
Alaska Aprs Group
HC 35 Box 5388
Wasilla AK 99654

Call Sign: KL1PE
Robert L Ray
HC 35 Box 5538-A
Wasilla AK 99654

Call Sign: KA6UGT
Robert L Ray
HC 35 Box 5538-A

Wasilla AK 99654

Call Sign: KC7MFV
Amanda R Isakson
HC 36 Box 2949
Wasilla AK 99654

Call Sign: WL7IH
Ronald Briggs
HC30 5421E
Wasilla AK 99654

Call Sign: KL1MN
Brian T Wilson
HC30 Box 5355L
Wasilla AK 99654

Call Sign: KL1IK
James A Davis
HC32 Box 6650F
Wasilla AK 99654

Call Sign: KL1LS
Donnita R Burks
HC33 Box 2885-I
Wasilla AK 99654

Call Sign: N1CNN
Robert D Coviello
HC33 Sr2906
Wasilla AK 99687

Call Sign: KL1XP
Jason R Bradford
HC34 Box 2045
Wasilla AK 99654

Call Sign: KL7VW
Willis R Patterson
HC34 Box 2137
Wasilla AK 99687

Call Sign: KD7IRP
George J Hill Jr
PO Box 877647
Wasilla AK 99687

Call Sign: KL1ID
Bernhard M Baur
Wasilla AK 99515

**FCC Amateur Radio Licenses
in White Mountain**

Call Sign: KL2EQ
Shane E Bergamaschi
White Mountain AK 99784

Call Sign: KL0CQ
Thomas L Gray
White Mountain AK 99784

Call Sign: KL0HT
Eric E Morris
White Mountain AK 99784

Call Sign: KL1FO
Jason D Currier
White Mountain AK 99784

Call Sign: KL1FP
Gar F Powell
White Mountain AK 99784

Call Sign: KL1FQ
Shawn E Bergamaschi
White Mountain AK 99784

Call Sign: KL1FR
Amy Titus
White Mountain AK 99784

Call Sign: KL1FS
Steven E Titus
White Mountain AK 99784

Call Sign: KL1FV
Louise C Simon
White Mountain AK 99784

Call Sign: KL1FW
Billy Simon
White Mountain AK 99784

Call Sign: KL1FX
Leslie R Richards
White Mountain AK 99784

Call Sign: KL1FY
Jared B Buffas
White Mountain AK 99784

Call Sign: KL1FZ
Cody W Amaktoolik
White Mountain AK 99784

Call Sign: KL1GA
Jack J Adams

White Mountain AK 99784

Call Sign: KL1GB
Patrick Lincoln
White Mountain AK 99784

Call Sign: KL1GC
Christopher J Brown
White Mountain AK 99784

Call Sign: KL1GD
Jeenean L Ferkinhoff
White Mountain AK 99784

Call Sign: KL1GE
Jack G Adams
White Mountain AK 99784

Call Sign: KL1GF
Jenna R Fagundes
White Mountain AK 99784

Call Sign: KL7BJV
Alfred Apodruk
White Mountain AK 99784

**FCC Amateur Radio Licenses
in Whittier**

Call Sign: KB7PHT
Kristoffer P Kerce
Phase 2 Block 12 Lot 3 Salmon
Run Rd
Whittier AK 99693

Call Sign: NI7X
Richard G Cushing
Whittier AK 99693

Call Sign: KL1MX
Kristoffer P Kerce
Whittier AK 996930790

**FCC Amateur Radio Licenses
in Willow**

Call Sign: WL7CKV
Johnny W Holland
Gen Del Mile 385 Hatcher Pass
Rd
Willow AK 99688

Call Sign: N7QOV
William J Grimes

16655 Hidden Hills Rd
Willow AK 99688

Call Sign: KL7MT
Marvin E Trimmer
9893 North Kime Ln
Willow AK 996880361

Call Sign: AL7H
Gale T Pearce
50147 South Caswell Creek Dr
Willow AK 99688

Call Sign: K4RND
Zack W Lee
24945 West Long Lake Rd
Willow AK 996880281

Call Sign: KL2EC
Mark K Allan
Willow AK 99688

Call Sign: KL2EO
Eugene L Latendresse
Willow AK 99688

Call Sign: KL2HU
Mary L Frahm
Willow AK 99688

Call Sign: KL2HY
Pamela A Warren
Willow AK 99688

Call Sign: KL2LP
Robert J Sexton
Willow AK 99688

Call Sign: KL2PN
Norman S Wakeman Sr
Willow AK 99688

Call Sign: KL2PO
Shirley E Wakeman
Willow AK 99688

Call Sign: KL2PP
Nancy R Binder
Willow AK 99688

Call Sign: WL7CWU
Susitna Wireless Amateur
Group
Willow AK 99688

Call Sign: KL7XX
Susitna Wireless Amateur
Group
Willow AK 99688

Call Sign: KL2QW
James A Courtney Sr
Willow AK 99688

Call Sign: KL2QX
Alexander J Courtney
Willow AK 99688

Call Sign: KL7TT
Alexander J Courtney
Willow AK 99688

Call Sign: KL2RP
Laurie B Courtney
Willow AK 99688

Call Sign: KL7VV
James A Courtney Sr
Willow AK 99688

Call Sign: KL7QQ
Laurie B Courtney
Willow AK 99688

Call Sign: AL3P
Justin M Frahm
Willow AK 99688

Call Sign: KL2ZN
Dana L Hills
Willow AK 99688

Call Sign: KL3CH
Doyle E Holmes
Willow AK 99688

Call Sign: KL3CR
Andrew J Giddens
Willow AK 99688

Call Sign: KL3IA
James G Kincheloe Jr
Willow AK 99688

Call Sign: KL3IP
Christopher E Carlson
Willow AK 99688

Call Sign: KL3JF
Marvin J Peterson
Willow AK 99688

Call Sign: KL4PP
Marvin J Peterson
Willow AK 99688

Call Sign: KK7KY
Russell E Sherfick
Willow AK 99688

Call Sign: KK7LM
Deborah S Sherfick
Willow AK 99688

Call Sign: KL0LG
Charles D Moore
Willow AK 99688

Call Sign: KL7HFY
Wayne B Hanson
Willow AK 99688

Call Sign: N7MVR
Paul D Charron
Willow AK 99688

Call Sign: N7YIS
Sharon D Lind-Charron
Willow AK 99688

Call Sign: WL7CKX
Patrick M Jehlen
Willow AK 99688

Call Sign: AA6CW
James A Courtney
Willow AK 996880130

Call Sign: AL7OY
Marvin E Trimmer
Willow AK 996880361

Call Sign: AL7OZ
Jackie F Trimmer
Willow AK 996880361

Call Sign: KL7ES
Paul J Williams
Willow AK 996880750

Call Sign: KC2BYX
Paul J Williams

Willow AK 996880750

Call Sign: AL7MD
Michael S Jackson
Willow AK 99688

Call Sign: WL7CN
Earle E Bu Bar
Box 225
Willow AK 99688

Call Sign: KL7FBR
Frank O Hillier
Box 538
Willow AK 99688

Call Sign: KL7LA
Rosemary K Hanrath
HC 89 Box 484
Willow AK 996889705

Call Sign: KL2HS
Kenneth D Christianson
HC 89 Box 52
Willow AK 99688

Call Sign: KL2IK
Ray T Medbery
HC 89 Box 5602
Willow AK 99688

Call Sign: KL2IL
Joan F Medbery
HC 89 Box 5602
Willow AK 99688

Call Sign: KL2TE
Charlotte Rose
HC 89 Box 69
Willow AK 99688

Call Sign: KL3IO
Scott P Whitlock
HC 89 Box 81
Willow AK 99688

Call Sign: KL7JKW
Delbert E Hanrath
HC89 Box 484
Willow AK 99688

Call Sign: KL3KC
Andrew T Rose
HC89 Box 6

Willow AK 99688

Call Sign: KL3KB
Jennifer L Dewitt
HC89 Box 69
Willow AK 99688

Call Sign: KL3KG
John E Tilton
HC89 Box 69
Willow AK 99688

Call Sign: KL7JJ
Jackie F Trimmer
Kime Ln Dr
Willow AK 99688

FCC Amateur Radio Licenses in Wrangell

Call Sign: KL7BCD
James R Silverthorn
241 Berger St
Wrangell AK 99929

Call Sign: KL7JIO
Joanne Silverthorn
241 Berger St
Wrangell AK 99929

Call Sign: K0JIO
Joanne Silverthorn
241 Berger St
Wrangell AK 99929

Call Sign: WL7ACR
Fred P Thruston
1034 Case Ave
Wrangell AK 999290964

Call Sign: KL7HMG
Phoebe J Kvale
42 Mi Zimovia Hwy 125 Ft N
Wrangell AK 99929

Call Sign: KL7GOG
Jack C Kvale
42 Mi Zimovia Hwy S 125 Ft N
Wrangell AK 99929

Call Sign: WL7QT
John E Eilertsen
13 Mile Zimovia Hwy
Wrangell AK 99929

Call Sign: WL7DA
Jeremy M Maxand
633 Reid St
Wrangell AK 99929

Call Sign: KC6WCL
Jack M Schirmer
8.5 Zimovia Hwy
Wrangell AK 99929

Call Sign: AL3I
Joan M Martin
Wrangell AK 99929

Call Sign: KL3DJ
Benjamin O Mccandless
Wrangell AK 99929

Call Sign: KL0AU
Sylvia Ettefagh
Wrangell AK 99929

Call Sign: W7CFA
Benn A Griffin
Wrangell AK 99929

Call Sign: WL7COW
Margaret R Byford
Wrangell AK 99929

Call Sign: WL7CUD
Dukies Island Amateur Radio
Club
Wrangell AK 99929

Call Sign: WL7KO
Tom A Leslie
Wrangell AK 99929

Call Sign: WL7SD
James L Branham
Wrangell AK 99929

Call Sign: WL7WE
Jacqueline L Eilertsen
Wrangell AK 99929

Call Sign: KL1OV
Douglas J Allison
Wrangell AK 999291644

Call Sign: KL0QY
Douglas J Allison

Wrangell AK 999291644

Call Sign: WL7CH
Burrell C Byford
Wrangell AK 99929

Call Sign: WL7LR
Douglas B Smith
Wrangell AK 99929

Call Sign: WL7CB
Joel H Hanson
Box 1783
Wrangell AK 99929

Call Sign: KL7CYB
Donald K Schirmer
Box 773
Wrangell AK 99929

Call Sign: WL7CBJ
Robert H Reif Jr
Burnett Inlet
Wrangell AK 99929

FCC Amateur Radio Licenses in Wrangell Island

Call Sign: NL7QT
Donald I Roher Jr
Eastern Passage
Wrangell Island AK 99929

Call Sign: KL0VW
Bonnie J Roher
Eastern Passage
Wrangell Island AK 99929

FCC Amateur Radio Licenses in Yakutat

Call Sign: WL7BT
Joseph L Story
Yakutat AK 99689

www.ingramcontent.com/pod-product-compliance
Lightning Source LLC
Chambersburg PA
CBHW082132290526
45794CB00008B/3001